Saucerful of Secrets
The Pink Floyd Odyssey

D1375228

Also by Nicholas Schaffner

NON-FICTION
The Beatles Forever
The Boys From Liverpool
505 Rock 'n' Roll Questions (with Elizabeth Schaffner)
The British Invasion
John Lennon – In My Life (with Pete Shotton)

POETRY
The Fool's Journey (The Tarot in Verse)

RECORD ALBUM
Magical Kingdoms

Saucerful of Secrets
The Pink Floyd Odyssey

Nicholas Schaffner

SIDGWICK & JACKSON
LONDON

First published in Great Britain in 1991 by
Sidgwick & Jackson Limited
This trade paperback first published in 1992 by
Sidgwick & Jackson Limited,
a division of Pan Macmillan Limited,
Cavaye Place, London SW10 9PG

9 8 7 6 5 4 3 2

ISBN 0 283 06127 8

Typeset by Florencetype Ltd, Kewstoke, Avon
Printed and bound in Great Britain by
Mackays of Chatham PLC, Chatham, Kent

Contents

Preface and Acknowledgments   vii

Prologue: Wish You Were Here   1

Part One: A Smile from the Veil

 1   Set the Controls for the Heart of the Sun   9
 2   Embryo   19
 3   Learning to Fly   32
 4   Let There Be More Light   45
 5   Have a Cigar   54
 6   Games for May   61
 7   Interstellar Overdrive   76
 8   Paranoid Eyes   88
 9   The Thin ice   97
10   Shine On You Crazy Diamond   107

Part Two: Heroes for Ghosts

11   Burning Bridges   121
12   Yet Another Movie   133
13   The Amazing Pudding   140
14   Return of the Son of Nothing   150
15   Eclipse   159
16   Comfortably Numb   172
17   The Hero's Return   184
18   Pigs on the Wing   194
19   Another Brick in the Wall Part 1   206
20   Another Brick in the Wall Parts 2 & 3   223
21   Terminal Frost   237

Part Three: Cold Comfort for Change

22   Apples and Oranges   247
23   One of These Days   262
24   Us and Them   273

Epilogue: Wish You Were Here   287

Discography   295

Sources   301

For Richard Barone:
friend, fan, musician, and star

Preface and
Acknowledgments

I have always considered myself Pink Floyd's original American fan.
That distinction, I should quickly add, was conferred quite by chance.
During the late summer of 1967, my mother, on a visit to her native
London, happened to tell her trendy hairdresser about her young son's
obsession with English pop groups like the Beatles, the Rolling
Stones, the Kinks, and the Who. 'Then you simply *must* get him the
Pink Floyd,' she was advised. And so she did, bless her – returning to
New York with a copy of the *Piper at the Gates of Dawn* LP, which had
yet to be released in the United States.

The beguiling melodies, imaginative lyrics, and distinctly English
flavour made *Piper* one of my favourite albums of that 'Summer of
Love'. Barely in my teens, however, I had yet to recognise every facet
of its brilliance – let alone perceive that the psychological instability
of the Floyd's original mastermind, Syd Barrett, was even then jeo-
pardising his band's very existence. When I snapped up the second
Floyd LP on my own London visit during the summer of '68, I did
notice that only one song was credited to Barrett. In *A Saucerful of
Secrets'* new Roger Waters compositions, Syd's delirious fantasy
seemed to have given way to a remote and atmospheric futurism, but I
liked it nearly as much.

I saw the Floyd perform in 1970, with David Gilmour firmly
established in Syd's place, at a college gymnasium a few blocks from
my Manhattan childhood home. Over the following decade, as Pink
Floyd evolved from a psychedelic cult group to one of the world's most
popular and influential bands, I managed to attend many of their
milestone concerts: the free Hyde Park preview of *Atom Heart Mother*
in 1970; the Radio City Music Hall launching of *Dark Side of the Moon*
in 1973; the *Wish You Were Here* and *Animals* tours of 1975 and 1977;
The Wall at Earl's Court in 1980.

And yet, unlike my other lifelong musical heroes – such as those Beatles and Stones – the peculiarly anonymous Pink Floyd had little public identity outside their albums and stage performances. The personalities in the group, and much of its background and history, remained largely mysterious. This book represents, in part, my own attempt to penetrate that veil and discover *who* – as well as what – was behind the Pink Floyd legend.

Though this is by no means an officially authorised biography, I had the good fortune to travel with and interview the latterday Pink Floyd line-up on the 1988 American leg of their world tour which I covered for *Musician*. (Long-time Floyd manager Steve O'Rourke told me that I was the first writer ever accorded such total access.) For so freely sharing their time and their insights with me that weekend, I would like to thank David Gilmour, Nick Mason, and Richard Wright – and their musical accomplices John Carin, Scott Page, Guy Pratt, Tim Renwick, and Gary Wallis (not to forget back-up singers Rachel Fury, Durga McBroom, and Margaret Taylor and lighting designer Marc Brickman). I would also like to extend special thanks to tour manager Jane Sen, Mary Ellen Cataneo of CBS, and Scott Isler of *Musician*, for arranging this unique opportunity and experience for me.

The two key players in the Pink Floyd odyssey whom I did not personally interview are Barrett and Roger Waters. In the case of Syd, I felt it would be wrong for me to attempt any intrusion into his reclusive post-Pink existence – which was nonetheless described to me in detail by certain people who knew (and know) him well.

I did, however, try repeatedly to elicit Roger's participation. At one point he seemed interested, going so far as to telephone me at my London hotel; unfortunately, I was out at the time, visiting his old friend Ron Gessin. Though Ron, Nick Griffiths and Timothy White were among those who spoke highly of Roger, the longtime Floyd leader drew less favourable comment from many of my other contacts (not least his three ex-partners), and – as I once told him by letter – I was anxious to produce as fair and balanced an account as possible. In the end, the most I ever got out of him was a brief handwritten note:

Dear Nicholas Schaffner
Good luck with the book! Don't let your anxiety to produce a balanced account spoil your summer!
       Best wishes
        Roger Waters

Roger's voice, opinions, and recollections are nonetheless heard throughout this book. I have drawn upon dozens of interviews that he has given over the past twenty-five years, along with literally hundreds of articles and reviews relating to him and the rest of Pink Floyd, published in the likes of – to name but a few – *Melody Maker*, *New Musical Express*, *Sounds*, and *Q* (in Britain); and *Billboard*, *Rolling Stone*, *Musician*, *The Trouser Press*, *Spin*, *Penthouse*, and *The New York Times* (in the U.S.A.). Perhaps the two most useful archival interviews were a 1973 Roger Waters–Nick Mason marathon in Britain's short-lived *ZigZag* magazine; and Capital Radio's seven-part 'Pink Floyd Story', broadcast in late 1976 and early 1977.

During the course of my research on both sides of the Atlantic, I also taped extensive interviews with (Barry) Miles and original Floyd manager Peter Jenner (both of whom were exceptionally helpful, reviewing parts of my manuscript and, in the case of Miles, providing research materials and taped interviews of his own); and John Hopkins, Chet Helms, David Medalla, Pete Brown, June Bolan, Peter and Susie Wynne Willson, Clive Welham, Ron Geesin, Mick Rock, Storm Thorgerson, and Nick Griffiths. I also spoke, more briefly and in some instances by telephone, with Sumi Jenner, Chris Charlesworth, Jonathon Green, Robyn Hitchcock, Jonathan Park, David Fricke, Karl Dallas, and Lee Wood (who also kindly took time off his busy schedule to show me round his – and Barrett, Waters, and Gilmour's – native Cambridge); as well as with several further sources who asked to remain anonymous. Last but by no means least, Timothy White took the trouble to set forth for me in writing his provocative views on many Floyd-related issues.

The co-operation of several of the above was freely and generously rendered despite their having themselves published books on the Floyd or related topics – all of which provided valuable sources for my own research and writing. (Throughout this book, incidentally, I have generally used the present tense [e.g., 'says', 'recalls'] for quotes derived from my own interviews, and the past tense ['said', 'remembered'] for those drawn from other sources. The origins of the latter, when not identified in the text, may be found in the appendix 'Source for Quotes'.) Miles is the author of the 'fan's bible' *Pink Floyd; A Visual Documentary* (London: Omnibus Press, 1980), and Karl Dallas of the thoughtful study *Bricks in the Wall* (London: Baton Press, 1987). Jonathon Green is the compiler and editor of the definitive oral history of London's 1960s counterculture, *Days in the Life: Voices from the English Underground 1961–1971* (London: Heinemann, 1988); I am especially grateful to him for providing me with unedited transcripts of Floyd-related interviews. Storm Thorgerson is the author of *Walk Away Renee* (Limpsfield, Surrey, U.K.: Paper Tiger, 1978), chronicling his classic rock 'n' roll artwork with Hipgnosis. Yet another helpful fellow Floyd author was Berlin's Andreas Kraska (*Pink Floyd: The Records* [Berlin: Buchverlag Michael Schwinn, 1988]).

One whom I did not track down was the very first – Rick Sanders, author of the nonetheless excellent paperback *Pink Floyd* (London: Futura Press, 1975). Also of interest were the published memoirs of Clive Davis (*Clive* [New York: William Morrow, 1974]), Gerald Scarfe (*Scarfe by Scarfe* [London: Hamish Hamilton, 1986]), and Bob Geldof (*Is That It?* [London: Sidgwick and Jackson, 1986]); Ray Coleman's biography *Clapton!* (New York: Warner Books, 1985); Derek Taylor's 'Anniversary Celebration of 1967,' *It Was Twenty Years Ago Today* (New York: Fireside, 1987); Mick Gold's *Rock on the Road* (London: Futura, 1976); Frederic Dannen's *Hit Men* (New York: Times Books, 1990); and the late Malcolm Jones's privately printed account *Syd Barrett: The Making of 'The Madcap Laughs'* Middlesex, U.K.: Orange Sunshine Pill Press, 1986).

But the most helpful resource of all was the definitive Pink Floyd and Roger Waters fan magazine *The Amazing Pudding* – whose editors Andy Mabbett and Bruno McDonald provided further assistance in the form of rare Floyd clippings, interviews and recordings (and, thanks to Bruno's lovely parents, Madeleine and Douglass, several hot meals). Inquiries may be directed to Andy Mabbett, *The Amazing Pudding*, 61 Meynell House, Browns Green, Birmingham B20 1BE, England.

Thanks also to Glenn Povey of the 1980s Floyd fanzine *Brain Damage*, and to John Steele of the 1970s Syd Barrett Appreciation Society; to Jean Yuscavage for transcribing many of my interviews; to my perceptive editor, Michael Pietsch, and my agent (and brother), Tim Schaffner, who between them sparked this project; and to Rosemary Bailey; P.J. Dempsey; Patrick Dillon; Barrie Duryea; Mark Marone; Lee Minoff; Rob Norris; Parke Puterbaugh; Louise Rush and Alan Bamberger; Nicholas Scarim; Virginia L. Smyers; and Sue Weiner. And to the late Brant Mewborn, whose rock 'n' roll spirit will shine forever in the hearts of his many friends.

Prologue

Wish You Were Here

The final weeks of 1967, rock and roll's most magical year, caught Britain's most promising new band on the horns of an excruciating dilemma. The Pink Floyd epitomized, more than any other new act, the emerging revolution in young attitudes, fashion and music that had already transformed the look, sound, and message of the Beatles, the Rolling Stones, and other established pop idols. As 'the movement's house orchestra', in bassist Roger Waters's phrase, the Pink Floyd were already renowned for their futuristic multi-media concert happenings – for Britain's first psychedelic liquid light show, and a pioneering quadrophonic PA system that enabled the Floyd to ravish an audience from all directions with their trademark flights of free-form electronic noise.

During much of the Summer of Love, their second single, 'See Emily Play', had ridden the British charts in the company of those other Flower Power anthems, 'A Whiter Shade of Pale' by Procol Harum and the Beatles' 'All You Need is Love'. The first Pink Floyd album, *The Piper at the Gates of Dawn* – recorded in the same Abbey Road building and at virtually the same time as the Beatles' *Sergeant Pepper's Lonely Hearts Club Band* – entranced listeners with its innovative blend of lyrical fantasy, melodic pop inventiveness, spaced-out improvisation, and surreal sound effects. Some even said that *Piper* picked up where *Pepper* left off: the ultimate tribute, in those days.

But for Waters, drummer Nick Mason and keyboards player Richard Wright, all former architecture students, any aura of promise and triumph surrounding the group had been all but nullified by the problem of Syd. The band's songwriter and artistic catalyst, as well as only member endowed with unalloyed pop star charisma, guitarist Syd Barrett had provided the Pink Floyd with its voice, its identity, even its mysterious name.

Onstage, when the players weren't altogether obscured by visual projections and flashing multicoloured lights, Barrett would dominate the line-up with the intensity of his presence, shrouded in a cape,

1

ominously flailing his arms between transports of interstellar feedback while the spotlight cast his enlarged shadow onto the screen behind. On record, the words and music evoked a magical world – peopled by futuristic space travellers, transvestites, and the gnomes and unicorns of English fairytale lore – that was distinctively Barrett's own. 'The imagination that he had . . .' Rick Wright marvels a generation later. 'He was brilliant.'

The Pink Floyd without Syd seemed unthinkable. Yet, the way Syd was going, the prospect of the band continuing with him was becoming inconceivable. Sometimes Barrett was so remote as to be almost invisible; other times he was simply impossible.

In London's 'underground' and pop music circles, tales of Syd's erratic behaviour were already legion. The Pink Floyd had been invited to make three consecutive appearances on *Top of the Pops* promoting 'See Emily Play'. For their first performance, Barrett and his fellow band members were duly arrayed in satins and velvets from the exclusive pop-star boutiques that then lined the King's Road. The next time Syd retained his Summer of Love finery – yet looked as if he had slept in it over the past week. Then, for the third show, he arrived at the TV studio resplendent in a trendy new costume – but clutching a pile of smelly old rags into which he changed just before the Floyd's appearance. Syd later allowed that since the Beatles no longer claimed to peddle their hits on the tacky *Top of the Pops*, he didn't see why the Pink Floyd should either.

Friends and associates variously attributed Barrett's decline to some long-dormant mental dislocation: to the pressures of terrestrial celebrity on a highly strung 21-year-old visionary artist; and to a steady diet of LSD and other such brain-frying substances. Whatever the cause, everyone could agree the situation was going from mad to worse.

In the autumn of 1967, the group's first American tour had ended after only eight days – during which the singer kept his lips firmly sealed when the Floyd were supposed to mime 'Emily' on Dick Clark's *American Bandstand* TV programme, and then on *The Pat Boone Show* mutely rewarded the host's ingratiating questions with a catatonic stare. By the time the Floyd toured Britain in November as a supporting act for Jimi Hendrix, Barrett's mirrored Telecaster was often left to dangle unplayed throughout their set.

On one date while Syd lingered before the dressing room mirror, primping up a luxuriant Afro modelled after the American guitar hero's – '*the obligatory Hendrix perm*', as Roger Waters would call it twelve years later in *The Wall* – his exasperated colleagues finally hit the stage without him. This apparently prodded Barrett to take decisive measures: impulsively crushing the contents of a jar of his beloved Mandrax tablets, he ground the fragments into his hair along with a full tube of Brylcream. Syd then joined the group on stage, where the heat of the spotlights soon turned his unique beauty treatment into a dribbling mess that left him looking, in the eyes of their dumbstruck lighting director, 'like a guttered candle'. It could hardly be said of the other Floyds that they didn't miss a beat – especially since the only note to emanate from Syd's guitar all night was an endlessly repeated middle-C.

The rest of the band decided that they had to augment the line-up with another singer/guitarist to pick up the slack Syd so often left. The blond sometime male model David Gilmour seemed the perfect choice: he was as steady and easygoing as Barrett was not, and had known and worked with him even longer than the rest of the band had. Growing up with Syd in Cambridge, Dave had taught him Stones licks before the pair developed the guitar style each in turn would make famous. In the likely event that Barrett might not be all there during a gig, Gilmour could flawlessly recreate all his parts and few would be the wiser.

For a while, the other Floyds discerned a possible solution to their dilemma in the precedent set by the Beach Boys, whose similarly mercurial songwriter and resident genius, Brian Wilson, was left at home to compose new material in his sandpit when the band went off on tour. But Barrett's new songs were taking a decidedly non-commercial turn. His harrowing self-portraits, 'Vegetable Man' and 'Scream Thy Last Scream', hardly seemed calculated to boost the Floyd's popular appeal. And 'Have You Got It Yet?' appeared to acquire a completely new melody and chord progression each time Syd rehearsed it with his colleagues. Calling the piece 'a real act of mad genius', Roger Waters later remembered: 'I stood there for an hour while he was singing . . . trying to explain that he was changing it all the time so I couldn't follow it. He'd sing, '*Have you got it yet?*' and I'd sing, '*No, no!*'[1]

Roger, for one, was out of all patience with Syd. Perceiving his own cherished dreams of fame and acclaim fast slipping down the tubes, he increasingly responded to Barrett's transgressions with a withering antagonism that he was to rue profoundly in the years to come.

One afternoon in February 1968, Waters, at the wheel of the band's old Bentley-Rolls, was collecting the band members before driving down to the next gig on the south coast. On such occasions Barrett, living in suburban Richmond, was always the last to be collected. 'Shall we pick Syd up?' said one of the group. 'Oh, no, let's not,' groaned another. And in that moment, everyone suddenly understood that they much preferred simply to manage without him as best they could.

There had been many gigs in recent months when Barrett had been in no shape to perform, but that night in Southampton marked the first time that Waters, Mason, Wright and Gilmour had themselves made the decision to appear onstage without him. Henceforth, there was to be no looking back: when they returned to EMI's Abbey Road studio to record their second album, a bemused Syd was sometimes left holding his guitar in the reception area while the others put down tracks for A *Saucerful of Secrets*.

Soon thereafter – on April 6, 1968 – it was officially confirmed that Syd Barrett was no longer a member of the Pink Floyd. As far as the London pop music media – and even the group's own managers – were concerned, that newsflash spelled the end of the Floyd. Syd, after all, *was* Pink.

Barrett himself never did accept the notion that the Pink Floyd were anything other than *his* group. He continued to turn up unannounced for subsequent Floyd shows at 'alternative' London clubs like Middle Earth, planting himself at the front of the audience and levelling an unblinking stare at Dave Gilmour throughout the admittedly shambolic performances. 'It was a paranoid experience,' said Gilmour. 'It took me a long time to feel a part of the band.'[2]

Twenty years later, Pink Floyd – as they have long been called, the 'the' having followed Syd into oblivion – are still filling vast arenas and stadiums the world over. On the band's first major tour in a decade, 1987's *Delicate Sound of Thunder* tour, the throngs continued for nearly three hours to greet every familiar lick with a response so ecstatic that the musicians onstage were often hard put to hear themselves play. The setting for this 'comeback' could hardly have been more different from the underground London clubs of a generation earlier; yet, once again, someone was missing.

The conspicuous absentee on this tour was Roger Waters, who had gradually assumed artistic command after Barrett's departure and who was accorded much of the credit for the Floyd's eventual ascendancy, against all odds, to the pinnacle of worldwide commercial success and popular acclaim. Nick Mason and Rick Wright were still in the picture, but this time round the lodestar of Pink Floyd was none other than David Gilmour – the man originally recruited as Syd Barrett's stand-in.

The circumstances surrounding the iron-willed Waters's exit had, of course, borne little resemblance to Barrett's. Fed up with the group and its image, Roger had simply proclaimed Pink Floyd defunct, confidently expecting his disgruntled colleagues to disperse accordingly. When they failed to do so he threatened the remaining Floyds not with blank stares but with vitriolic public denunciations and a battery of lawsuits. Once again, however, the pop pundits had dismissed the reconstituted Floyd in advance as a hopeless enterprise, a sham, even a betrayal. And once again, Pink Floyd proved them – if only from the perspective of the record industry and the paying consumer – spectacularly wrong.

Much had changed in the intervening twenty years. The makeshift, freewheeling qualities of the Floyd's sixties performances have evolved into a highly-orchestrated multi-media extravaganza engaging 100 additional musicians, technicians, and assistants, along with enough equipment to fill over fifty trucks. 'Mr Screen', Pink Floyd's giant eye into another universe remains the show's centrepiece, but has swelled to thirty-two feet in diameter, and is now ringed with computer-controlled Vari-Lites. The feedback-charged improvisation of yore has long since given way to a minutely choreographed operation in which every note must be synchronized to the mindbending film animations, and laserbeam pyrotechnics. Such legendary totems as the forty-foot flying pig are displayed, and an airplane crashes into the stage in flames. Nothing can be left to chance.

Barrett's influence, however, lingers on in such Floyd trademarks as the incorporation of sound effects into musical composition, and in the otherworldly timbre of much of the material: to the fans, Pink Floyd remains – as one popular T-shirt slogan would have it – FIRST IN SPACE. At the same time, Syd's own descent into madness has provided subject matter for the multimillion-selling concept albums *The Wall*, *Wish You Were Here*, and – most especially – *The Dark Side of the Moon*, whose unprecedented 700-week ride on the *Billboard* 200 listings make it the longest-charting album ever. These, of course, are the works on which Pink Floyd's renown primarily rests among their 1990s audiences, and it is these which continue to dominate the concert programme.

All the key elements of the fabled Pink Floyd sound – the trance-inducing bass/drum throb, the ethereal organ backdrop, the soaring slide-guitar figures, the airy vocal harmonies – are very much in evidence in the 1990s Pink Floyd. Their concerts feature a nonstop sequence of 'progressive' classics like 'One of These Days (I'm Going to Cut You Into Little Pieces)', 'Time', 'Us and Them', 'Welcome to the Machine', and 'Comfortably Numb', taking flight at a stately, almost glacial pace that bears little or no kinship to anything associated with the term rock and roll as originally conceived some thirty years earlier from the mating of white country with black blues. No major rock legend has ever flourished at such a far remove from the vaunted 'street' of which rock critics are so enamoured – which may be why the scribes have never given the Floyd much consideration or respect.

Notwithstanding the sniping of Waters and his partisans (who insist that it's his pig and airplane, not to mention his lyrics), the 1990 model Floyd certainly looks and sounds like the same saucerful of secrets whose credo was 'we've always thought there was more to playing rock and roll than playing "Johnny B. Goode" ' – and whose futuristic dirges foreshadowed Eurodisco, Synth Rock, and New Age music, and outsold and outpolled all other Anglo-American bands in such traditionally rock-resistant countries as Italy and France (where *Dark Side of the Moon* was the best-selling rock album ever). When the *Delicate Sound of Thunder* world tour was finally over, nearly two years after it began, Gilmour and company had grossed about $135 million, making this – from a financial standpoint, at the very least – the most successful musical roadshow of all time.*

Waters's spirit, like that of Barrett before him, was inescapable; yet it seems that the physical presence of neither is a prerequisite to the activation of the distinctive Floyd magic. After Syd fell by the wayside, the members of Pink Floyd cultivated an impassive onstage demeanour calculated to keep audiences entirely focused on the music and the state-of-the-art razzle-dazzle – and an almost wilful anonymity that enabled them to walk unrecognized through the crowds at their own concerts. For years (until the Waters-Gilmour schism made each camp want to tell its side of the story) the Floyd shunned interviews and ignored the media (another likely reason why the critics snubbed *them*). Through their determination to guard against the world's intrusions, the artists themselves did not intrude upon the fantasies of their fans. Even the covers of albums omitted the performers' faces in

---

* In *Forbes* magazine's 1989 chart of the world's highest-paid entertainers, Pink Floyd ranked seventh: ahead of all other rock groups – including the Rolling Stones, at No.

favour of surreal or bizarre images that have acquired an almost mythical resonance among Floyd aficionados: a cow in a pasture on *Atom Heart Heart Mother*; a Rock-biz mogul consumed by flames, genially shaking hands with his lookalike on *Wish You Were Here*; the aforementioned inflatable pig soaring over the chimneys of Battersea Power Station on *Animals*. Pink Floyd came to possess a life and mystique of its own that altogether transcended any of the band's individual components.

Yet despite all the band's high-tech overlay, the most poignant moment of the *Delicate Sound* tour came during one of the few acoustic ballads, when the special effects were briefly put on hold. Without any incitement from the stage, thousands of fans were moved to sing along with David Gilmour yet another lyric Waters is said to have written with Syd Barrett partly in mind – the one whose wrenching imagery culminates in the wistful refrain, '*How I wish, how I wish you were here . . .*'

8 – and behind only Michael Jackson, Steven Spielberg, Bill Cosby, Mike Tyson, Charles M. Schultz, and Eddie Murphy.

Part One

A SMILE FROM THE VEIL

Chapter 1

Set the Controls
for the Heart of the Sun

Once well underground, you know exactly where you are.
Nothing can happen to you, and nothing can get at you. You're
entirely your own master, and you don't have to consult anybody
or mind what they say. Things go on all the same overhead, and
you let 'em, and don't bother about 'em. When you want to, up
you go, and there the things are, waiting for you.
                                    – Mole in *The Wind in the Willows*,
                                              by Kenneth Grahame

In 1966 London was wide open. Following the grey decade of postwar
austerity, the economy was booming; Harold Wilson's ostensibly
progressive new Labour government was in power, and idealism and
optimism were rife.

The class system appeared to be loosening its grip on the British
psyche, as young working-class photographers, designers, playwrights
and pop stars set the new tone and style. Clothes and records were
comparatively cheap and their accessibility enabled working class
youth to turn fashion and music into vehicles for a self-expression that
was soon adopted even by the aristocracy. And among disparate
groups of musicians, poets, directors, painters, and political activists
across London something was stirring: 'the sixties' (as we now remember them) sprang into being.

By the spring of 1966, the British capital's vitality was such that a
Time cover story christened it 'Swinging London' – the city of the
decade as surely as Paris had been for the twenties, or Rome for the
fifties. 'As never before in modern times,' the magazine declared,
'London is switched on. Ancient elegance and a new opulence are all
tangled up in a dazzling blur of op and pop . . .'

Time's Anglophile editors were not the first American writers to discover the new London. In a day when intercontinental jet travel was still far from commonplace, Beat authors like Allen Ginsberg and William S. Burroughs made the city a virtual second home in the mid-sixties. Talented young expatriates ranging from Elektra Records' man-on-the-scene Joe Boyd to the electric guitar sorcerer Jimi Hendrix fuelled the transatlantic synergy.

The Philippines-born experimental artist, dancer and sixties-London scene-maker, David Medalla, remembers, 'American writers and artists had a very big impact. American painters of the postwar generation, abstract expressionists and especially the pop artists were often first exhibited in England before they were even accepted in New York. The early rock and roll stars who came here, like Gene Vincent and Eddie Cochran, had *such* an effect. The English were absolutely fertilized by all this, and with their wonderful craftsmanship they even improved on it. Where you had raw American rock and roll, by the time you got to England you had people like the Beatles experimenting and creating a synthesis. There was a kind of naiveté with the Beatles generation about the discovery of all these new things – new types of haircuts, new clothing.'

Nineteen sixty-six was the year the Beatles redefined pop music with *Revolver* – John Lennon and Paul McCartney (with a little help from George's sitar, string quartets, and tape loops) having in little over two years transmuted *yeah yeah yeah* and 'I Want to Hold Your Hand' into 'Eleanor Rigby' and *turn off your mind, relax, and float downstream*. The Rolling Stones were filling the airwaves with hard-edged psychodramas like 'Nineteenth Nervous Breakdown' and 'Paint It Black'. Pete Townshend was marketing The Who's heady mix of Mod fashions, power chords, feedback and anarchic theatrics – incorporating video and smokebombs – as 'Pop Art'. The Scottish folkie Donovan, a pallid Bob Dylan clone no more, had not only seen the Eastern light but turned simultaneously electric and 'mediaeval' en route to hitting the charts with 'Sunshine Superman' and 'Mellow Yellow', Ray Davies of the Kinks had become arguably the first rock star to sing and write in a strictly British accent about strictly British concerns with his highly literate trio of hits in 1966 – 'Dedicated Follower of Fashion', 'Sunny Afternoon', and 'Dead End Street'.

One of the things Davies, Townshend, Lennon, and the Stones' Keith Richards had in common was that they all had attended art school – the traditional English sanctuary for bright young misfits who couldn't cut it at the more rigorously academic institutions. The art schools had also come to represent, to many of their 100,000-plus students, a government-subsidized excuse to postpone contact with 'the real world' in favour of partying in an intellectually stimulating environment.

Unsurprisingly, the art schools had long provided a fertile breeding ground for such manifestations of bohemia as CND, drug experimentation, Beat literature – and, not least, jazz, blues, and rock and roll. Yet there was initially little overt 'Art' in the music of the pop groups that came out of art school. What there was was mostly implicit: a visual flair, a sense of style, and an ironic self-consciousness quite lacking in their American counterparts.

According to graphic designer Pearce Marchbank, Britain's 'whole sixties culture' could be traced back to the art schools – 'the laboratories that were making rock musicians and designers and painters . . . Art students had very open minds – we were interested in everything that was going on. The fact that we were technically being trained to design ceramic pots or books or theatre sets was irrelevant. You'd go to the canteen and you'd have a painter, a typographer, a film-maker, a graphic designer all at the same table, all talking, and you wouldn't get that anywhere else.'[1]

The impact of art school upon British rock was illustrated in the early 1970s, when the poet and performer Pete Brown made a record called *The Art School Dance Goes on for Ever* and sought to adorn its cover with sketches of famous musician friends and acquaintances who had been educated there. His list of names included Lennon (among the few whose approval was not forthcoming); an assortment of Yardbirds, Stones, and Who; Eric Clapton, Ginger Baker, and Jack Bruce (for whose short-lived powertrio, Cream, Brown supplied lyrics) – and one Syd Barrett.

Barrett differed from the others in that he was among the third generation of pop musicians: just young enough to have been drawn into rock and roll as much by the Beatles and the Stones as by first-generation stars like Buddy Holly or Elvis Presley. By the time this talented nineteen-year-old painter joined forces with Roger Waters, Rick Wright, and Nick Mason, the Byrds had already scored a worldwide number one with their electric pop rendering of Bob Dylan's visionary 'Mr Tambourine Man', and the Beatles were in the throes of creating *Rubber Soul*. A new sophistication and self-consciousness was already well established in 'beat music' by the time Syd got started; unlike previous art school rock and roll groups the band Syd made famous conceived their music as Art virtually from day one.

In America longhaired youths were dropping *en masse* out of 'plastic straight society'. Repelled by the Vietnam War and impelled by the drugs (ranging from the relatively innocuous marijuana to Dr Albert Hoffman's potent 1938 invention lysergic acid dyethylamide) that were then viewed as keys to consciousness-expansion rather than a ticket to oblivion, the so-called hippies and flower children coalesced in such oases as San Francisco's Haight-Ashbury district. These alternative communities found their voice in a host of defiantly anti-commercial bands who had also been weaned on the Beatles and Stones – the Grateful Dead, Jefferson Airplane, Moby Grape – and who almost invariably performed in tandem with a 'psychedelic' light show.

It was a while yet before any of this Acid Rock surfaced on records, and Londoners' familiarity with the counterculture percolating in San Francisco and New York was limited. Nonetheless, the American youth revolution struck a responsive chord among the vanguard of London's young musicians, writers, and artists, who were not long in fashioning a British equivalent.

Notting Hill became to London more or less what the Haight was to San Francisco, or the East Village to New York. Racially mixed, Notting Hill was then both a suitably low-rent neighbourhood and a mecca for black music and the cannabis trade. Yet few groups of drop-outs have ever been so well-bred and well-educated as the leading lights of its emerging alternative community. In the words of one of them, Cambridge graduate Peter Jenner, the grandson of a Labour Party Member of Parliament, 'We were all very successful in conventional terms, and found it lacking. We'd won in the lottery, and yet it seemed terribly unsatisfactory.'

Jenner, at least, was still respectably employed as a lecturer in economics and sociology at the London School of Economics. His early partner, the charismatic peace campaigner John Hopkins, also known as Hoppy, had also earned a degree at Cambridge only to abandon his career as a reactor physicist to work as a freelance photographer, while publishing a series of 'little' magazines on the side.

The butterflylike Hoppy's enthusiasm for jazz found an outlet in a stint at the London music weekly *Melody Maker*, but with the early 1960s British pop explosion, the paper's emphasis shifted, and the jazz musicians in front of his cameras made way for the Beatles and the Rolling Stones. These early encounters with the new rock royalty were, Hopkins says, 'good fun. I was much more interested in jazz, personally – but I started to learn about *that* sort of music.'

Hoppy's partner in short-lived publishing ventures like *Longhair Times* was the deceptively mild-mannered Barry Miles (who discarded his Christian name at an early age to distinguish himself from the three other Barrys in his painting class). Initially best known as Allen Ginsberg's leading British disciple and acolyte (he finally completed the poet's authorized biography in 1989), Miles was instrumental in organizing a seminal poetry reading at London's Royal Albert Hall in June 1965. Featuring American Beat poets like Gregory Corso and Lawrence Ferlinghetti – along with such British counterparts as Adrian Mitchell and Pete Brown – the event drew 6,000 indigenous hipsters out of the woodwork, culminated in Ginsberg's oracular recitation of his 'Tonight Let's All Make Love in London', and has since been cited as the first rumble of the British underground movement.

In early 1966, Miles co-founded the innovative and influential Indica bookshop and art gallery, which was financed by Peter Asher, the brother of Paul McCartney's then girlfriend Jane. Indica thus became the place (and Miles the person), to nourish the Beatles in their new incarnation of spiritual seekers and culture vultures; it is perhaps best remembered today as the site of John Lennon's first encounter with Yoko Ono. (The name was mischievously derived from the herb *cannabis indica*, without which . . .) Jane Asher, for her part, went on to marry Gerald Scarfe, who figures in our story much later as the illustrator of *The Wall*.

Jenner and Hoppy, meanwhile, banded together with what the latter describes as 'just a weird bunch of people' including authors John Mitchell and Felix de Mendelsohn, the poet Neil Oram, Elektra Records' Joe Boyd, and the Black Power activist Michael X – to launch the London Free School at Powis Terrace in Notting Hill. 'We were all graduates and things,' explains Jenner, 'but we realized that what they teach you at schools and universities is only a very selected part of the truth, and that there's a lot of other stuff you could do well to learn. That's what the London Free School was about – combined with a social-worky attitude about the gap between the educated elite and the uneducated ordinary people around in North Kensington. But it didn't last long. We spent a lot of time talking about what we were going to do, and we didn't get going until late spring – with a couple of sessions in some terribly seamy rooming house of Michael X's. Then we had to break for summer, because a lot of people were going away.' Though this Anti-university remained less a concrete reality than a galvanizing concept, Jenner remembers it as 'possibly the first public manifestation of the underground in England'.

13

With its founders united as much as anything in their Beat-like zeal for jazz, one of the Free School's immediate byproducts was a visionary record company called DNA. Jenner, Hoppy, and de Mendelsohn planned thereby to harness Joe Boyd's Elektra connections, to distribute the work of musicians too progressive to land a contract with the stuffy major labels.

The sole album thus spawned was *AMMusic* by the innovative free-form jazz band AMM, noted for their white lab coats, lighting effects adapted from experimental theatre, and hand-crafted instruments of their own devising. Among these was a foot pedal attached to a radio; when this was activated during their performances, the AMMusicians would adapt their improvisations to whichever pop hit happened to be riding the airwaves at the time. Their LP consisted of just two tracks, one on each side, titled with evocative surrealism 'Later During a Flaming Riviera Sunset' and 'After Rapidly Circling the Plaza'. While never amounting to much in commercial terms, AMM exerted a profound influence on at least one band that would.

'Alternative London' gathered steam with a series of Sunday afternoon happenings at the Marquee Club, the celebrated Soho venue whence several generations of musicians (including the Rolling Stones, the Yardbirds, and the Who just a few years earlier) launched their legends. 'Spontaneous Underground' – constituting in roughly equal measure jam session, costume party, and anarchic free-for all – offered a British variation on the American Be-in. The promoter, Steve Stollman, was a New Yorker whose brother ran the avant-garde U.S. record label ESP which had recently augmented its experimental-jazz roster with the more or less rock-oriented group the Fugs.

Miles remembers Stollman as 'filled with brilliant ideas for putting on things. He had all that New York energy and chutzpah which English people totally lack.' The invite to his inaugural Marquee happening, in February 1966, read: 'Who will be there? Poets, pop singers, hoods, Americans, homosexuals (because they make up 10 per cent of the population), twenty clowns, jazz musicians, one murderer, sculptors, politicians, and some girls who defy description . . .'

Though a rock band or two might be included in the afternoon's entertainment, no one act could expect to be the sole focus of attention. Eight-millimetre films flickered on the wall throughout the performances, and little distinction was made between player and audience. The latter were encouraged to dress as outrageously as possible, and to contribute to the general mayhem with such 'found' instruments as toilet plungers, cardboard tubes, and even transistor radios.

'The great thing was that Stollman didn't advertise any acts: he didn't promise anything at all,' says Miles. 'You had to pay money to get in, but there was nothing necessarily there. You had to make your own entertainment.

'All these poets would appear, and I remember a girl having a haircut on stage once. Ginger Johnson's African drummers came one day – about a dozen of them playing enormous African drums. Donovan was there, completely out of his brain on acid with Cleopatra-painted eyes – and six sitar players. I asked him about it later, and he didn't remember it at all.'

Spontaneous Underground was promoted strictly through word of mouth, and cryptic invitations on the order of:

TRIP   bring furniture toy prop paper rug
       paint balloon jumble costume mask
       robot candle incense ladder wheel
       light self all others march 13th 5 pm

marquee club 90 wardour street w1
5/–

Though their own presence was not advertised, such is the sole surviving record of the Spontaneous Underground debut of a group of four students, identified by the inscription on the bassist's amplifier as the Pink Floyd Sound.

John Hopkins, as was his wont, was there. 'There weren't many people, maybe forty or fifty,' he recalls. 'The band was not playing music, they were playing *sounds*. Waves and walls of sounds, quite unlike anything anybody in rock and roll had played before. It was like people in serious, non-popular music experimenting wildly with sound. John Cage had done stuff like that. And suddenly here were these young students, and they were playing the most crazy stuff. It blew a lot of people's minds. It was exciting.'

During the spring of 1966, the Pink Floyd Sound became a regular feature of Spontaneous Underground, and the buzz gradually spread among Hoppy's arty friends, including Miles. 'They were the first people I'd ever heard,' he says, 'who were combining some kind of intellectual experimentation with rock and roll, which I'd always

15

loved. 'Cause the stuff you grow up with is always there – you know the words to all the songs, no matter how cruddy they are.

'All through the late fifties I was a rock and roller, a vague teddy boy type. Then I became very involved with jazz, and there was a period of about four years when I didn't know what the hell was going on with rock and roll. I was an art college product, into American abstract impressionism and the Beat Generation. I'd met the Beatles at Allen Ginsberg's birthday party, but wasn't involved in their music yet. The Floyd synthesis, or so it seemed to me, was really quite remarkable.'

The proprietor of the fabled Indica bookshop was sufficiently impressed to give the Floyd their first press coverage – in, of all places, New York, where the new underground paper the *East Village Other* had asked him to write a column on Britain's alternative arts scene. 'Initially,' Miles notes, 'I never saw the Floyd as individuals. I saw them as part of an avant-garde movement that was happening in London at the time.'

Peter Jenner, however, did not initially make it a top priority to check out any rock and roll band, – 'experimental' or otherwise. 'As a middle-class intellectual snob, I had a jazz background,' he explains. 'In that era, you weren't allowed to get off on pop music; it wasn't really on. Even young people were supposed to be into classical music – that was "proper music". If you were a bit wacky, you'd get into Chicago blues. I was into electric blues, things like Bo Diddley and Muddy Waters, but not played by white boys in London – that wasn't the real thing. Even though I'd hung out with Eric Clapton – but then he felt the same way as well.'

By early 1966 Jenner's aversion to rock had been somewhat tempered: 'With Bob Dylan and the Byrds, you began to realize that pop music had something more interesting to say than "*itsy-bitsy-yellow-polka-dot-bikini*".' It had, moreover, dawned on 'the business beatnik' (as friends called him) that under the terms of his fledgling avant-jazz label's contract with Elektra, 'we'd have to sell millions of albums to make any money. I'm not talking about getting rich, I'm talking about making anything at all. We couldn't even pay off the recording costs out of our 2 per cent royalty. I concluded we needed a pop group – because I thought pop groups made money.'

One Sunday in May 1966, Jenner was overwhelmed by the 'crucifyingly boring chore' of correcting year-end examination papers. A generation earlier, a similarly bored professor, J.R.R. Tolkien, had found relief by scribbling on an empty page of one of his students' papers, '*In a hole in the ground there lived a hobbit,*' thereby sparking the mythical saga of Middle-earth that was to become a virtual Bible for Britain's emerging underground. Peter Jenner, in his turn, pushed the exams aside to drop by the Marquee Club, where he 'discovered' that subculture's definitive band.

As far as many of the Spontaneous Undergrounders were concerned, the chief attraction that afternoon was one of the first of the great pink jellies that were to become an obligatory feature of alternative-London happenings (the jelly babies with which Beatlemaniacs once pelted the Fab Four having given way, in the march of pop history, to giant jellies).

Several daring young hipsters doffed their King's Road finery to writhe and squirm in the pink ooze to the music of the appropriately named Pink Floyd Sound.

More impressed by the band than the jelly, Jenner found himself wondering whether this might be the pop group of his fantasies, the act that could put DNA Records on the map and in the black. 'They were avant-garde, they were good,' says Jenner. 'My ears were tweaked because, during very straightforward blues songs or "Louie Louie" they would go off into these psychedelic interludes.

'I have this recollection of walking round the stage the first time I saw them at the Marquee, trying to work out where the noise was coming from, who was playing it. Normally you'd have the bass, *bomp, bomp, bomp*; the piano, *clink, clink, clink*, and *clang, clang, clang*, that's the guitar. But during the solo instrumental bits, I couldn't work out whether it was the guitar or the keyboards. It fascinated and intrigued me. It wasn't neat and tidy like most pop music, which I'd found quite boring: *My baby loves me, yeah, yeah, yeah*, with the same chords going round and round.

'I was able to relate to them in my uptight upper-middle-class way; I could see that what they were doing was interesting.'

Jenner subsequently tracked down the bassist and drummer at their flat in Highgate in north London. In a 1973 interview, Roger Waters recalled Jenner proclaiming, ' "You lads could be bigger than the Beatles" – and we sort of looked at him and replied in a dubious tone, "Yes well, we'll see you when we get back from our hols," because we were all shooting off for some sun on the Continent.'[2]

During this encounter, the would-be-music mogul also learned that the Pink Floyd Sound was thinking of breaking up, due to a dearth of gigs, the strain of finding new work, and Roger and Nick's commitment to their architectural studies at the Regent Street Polytechnic. The singer/guitarist Syd Barrett, moreover – the one Jenner thought had star quality – was still more interested in his painting than in the band.

Chapter 2

Embryo

It was in London, home-town of Nick Mason and Rick Wright, that the Floyd coalesced and made its mark. However, the band's three successive helmsmen, Barrett, Waters and Gilmour, were all natives of Cambridge.

Dominated since the thirteenth century by the university – whose colleges own most of the town's property, and whose students, staff, and other employees comprise about a fifth of its 100,000 inhabitants – Cambridge is exceptional in its affluence and sophistication. It is also an unusually well-preserved and beautiful place. By almost every outward measure of what is called 'quality of life', Cambridge represents the very best that England has to offer.

The heart of the town – by the River Cam that gave it its name – is a maze of narrow winding streets, lined with ancient inns and churches. These gradually give way to tidy red-brick suburbs such as Cherry Hinton, known for its annual folk-music festival, where Syd Barrett was brought up, and to the village of Grantchester, which David Gilmour once called home, with its cosy Tudor cottages and its Meadows, which Roger Waters was to celebrate in a lyric.

Yet further afield are the Fens that prior to their draining some 300 years ago were an impassable marshland haunted, according to legend, by web-fingered mutants given to grunting uncouth phrases like *umma-gumma*. The contemporary traveller is more likely to encounter cows, in idyllic settings reminiscent of the cover of the Pink Floyd LP *Atom Heart Mother* – or (with a little flexing of the imagination), that black and green scarecrow standing in a field of barley that Syd evoked on their first album.

Both Peter Jenner and John Hopkins went to Cambridge, but the gap between 'town' (local residents) and 'gown' (students) ruled out much likelihood of contact with their future musical standard-bearers. Unlike some other British rock luminaries, however, the leading lights of Pink Floyd never could (nor did) pretend to be 'working-class heroes'. Their backgrounds were strictly white collar, their parents middle-class. Doug Gilmour was a professor of genetics and his wife Sylvia a schoolteacher turned film editor. Max Barrett was a police pathologist also known as one of Britain's leading authorities on infant mortality. Mary Waters was a teacher active in local politics; her husband had also been a teacher, specializing in religious and physical education.

Eric Fletcher Waters, however, was dead long before the band was even thought of – gunned down in 1943 in Italy. Waters senior was only thirty when he died, on 9 September 1943. Along with 40,000 other British soldiers he was killed in a reckless British campaign to capture the bridgehead of Anzio from the Nazis, only a few months after his third child had been born. One need look no further for the original source of the chip on the shoulder that marked George Roger Waters throughout his years with the Floyd – to say nothing of the militant anti-militarism that increasingly featured in his song lyrics. In Waters's own terminology, the absence of his father amounted to the first – and the worst – brick in his wall.

'I'd wager that there isn't a day that goes by,' stresses former *Rolling Stone* editor Timothy White, 'when Roger Waters doesn't consciously *and* unconsciously mourn and miss the father he never knew – or hate the hierarchy of circumstances that robbed him of a [by all accounts loving] parent.'

Anyone familiar with the album and film of *The Wall* will recognize certain details drawn from Roger's actual childhood: stumbling upon his father's uniform and a scroll of condolence from King George VI, in one of his mother's drawers; rescuing a dying animal, only to be made to toss it in the rubbish by the aforementioned no-nonsense dominatrix; getting packed off to a grammar school staffed largely by Dickensian sadists bent on purging their hapless little victims of any remaining spark of creativity or individuality. 'It was terrible . . .' Waters recalled in 1979. 'Never encouraging them to do things, not really trying to interest them in anything, just trying to keep them quiet and still and crush them into the right shape so that they would go on to university and DO WELL.'[1]

All further bricks in the wall, but animated in Roger's magnum opus by a certain amount of caricature. *Some* of his teachers were 'very nice guys', he admitted; and his mum did give him a 'reasonable' view of the world and what it was like – or as reasonable as she could'. Mary Waters may have overcompensated for the absence of the father, but was at heart only trying to do the right thing by the youngest of her three boys. She was and is a person of strong convictions (including political ones, of a strongly leftist stripe): like mother, like son.

As a young teenager, Roger's favourite pursuits included playing with toy guns (and shooting real ones) and staying awake at night with his wireless tuned to American Forces Network or Radio Luxembourg (a memory that he was to draw upon thirty years later with his solo album *Radio K.A.O.S.*). 'In a solitary way, the radio station was the first thing I established a kind of relationship with, outside of my family or school,' he reminisced in 1987. 'You can grow with it, go with it, or go away with it, so it's an easy medium in that sense. It's not bombarding you or forcing you into corners, and yet you're getting other people's ideas through it, more so than with television. There's no image on the radio. Radio is much easier to concentrate on. You can't watch TV in the dark because it makes it light.'[2]

The first albums Waters bought were by blues legends like Leadbelly, Billie Holiday, and Bessie Smith. From there he progressed to more contemporary blues and jazz – 'everything but rock and roll'. Significantly, he never collected 45s.

His Cambridge peers remember him in those days as quick-witted and outwardly self-confident to the point of superciliousness. By his own account, he did have 'a fantastic time' at the relatively progressive Cambridge County High School for Boys, even if (in the words of his final report), 'Waters never fulfilled his considerable potential.'

He was less enchanted by his weekend apprenticeship as a naval cadet, despite attaining the rank of Leading Seaman. In one prophetic incident, his young subordinates, riled by Roger's overbearing manner, rose up and taught him a physical lesson. Waters subsequently decided military regimentation was not for him, summarily turned in his uniform, and was slapped with a dishonourable discharge. He became instead the chairman of the Campaign for Nuclear Disarmament's local youth chapter.

Also attending Cambridge County High School for Boys were several colleagues-to-be. One of Roger's classmates was Storm Thorgerson, son of Mary Waters's closest friend, and future mastermind of the Floyd's classic album covers. Two classes below them was Syd Barrett, with whom Storm became increasingly friendly, and two below *him* the latterday second Floyd guitarist Tim Renwick, who cherishes memories of Syd's stint as his Boy Scout patrol leader, hard as it may be to picture that fabled prophet of psychedelia from the dark side of the moon in a boy scout uniform.

21

Roger Keith Barrett, born on 6 January 1946, actually enjoyed a perfectly normal childhood. He was brought up in a large house on Hill Road, the nicest street in Cherry Hinton, by warm and loving parents. Popular at school, his youthful passions ranged from camping and sports to drama and painting, at which he particularly excelled. His father, Max, was a classical music buff around whose prized grand piano young Roger Barrett (or 'Syd', as he came to be nicknamed) and his two brothers and two sisters would regularly be drawn into musical family get-togethers. Max also encouraged his youngest son's interest in music with the gift of a banjo and then, at the boy's insistence, a guitar.

When Syd was fourteen, however, the idyllic picture shattered with Dr Barrett's sudden death. Storm Thorgerson proposes this trauma as the first 'catalyst' in his friend's eventual dementia. It was, in Waters-speak, the first brick in Syd's wall.

No such tragedy scarred the childhood of Storm's lifelong 'best mate' David Gilmour, who was born exactly two months after Syd, on 6 March 1946. In marked contrast to Roger Waters, the athletic young Dave was brought up by permissive, easygoing parents characterized by one Cambridge friend as 'fairly Bohemian, pretty trendy for that time'.

The only future Floyd, apart from Syd, to display much interest in music prior to his late teens, Dave counted as one of his treasured possessions a 78 of Bill Haley's 'Rock Around the Clock' (until the Gilmours' au pair girl sat on it!) and found his life's calling at the age of thirteen when he inherited a cheap Spanish guitar from a neighbour. To this day, Gilmour acknowledges a great debt to the American activist folkie Pete Seeger – 'one of my all-time favourite people' – whose popular book-and-record instructional sets enabled him to come to grips with his new instrument.

By 1962, Cambridge, like most British cities, was enlivened by a thriving music scene, with well over a hundred local bands springing up on both sides of the town-and-gown divide. Among the lesser of these was Geoff Mott and the Mottoes, whose line-up encompassed Syd Barrett on a proudly acquired electric guitar for which he had himself constructed a small amp; another guitarist named Nobby Clarke; bassist Tony Santi; and drummer Clive Welham, together with the singer and frontman whose full surname was Motlow. Partly to help Syd get his mind off his father's death, the ever-indulgent Mrs Barrett encouraged her son's band to rehearse and perform in the spacious front room of the home that her reduced circumstances had obliged her to turn into a boarding house. The Mottoes' repertoire consisted of copies of current British hit parade fodder by the likes of Cliff Richard's Shadows, with an occasional stab at Chuck Berry.

Clive Welham describes these Sunday afternoon bashes as 'a great time, marvellous salad days', albeit 'quite basic and naive. We were just keen on actually creating music, the novelty in making a few guitar chords with a crude drum session behind them.' A frequent visitor to their gigs was Barrett's older school chum Roger Waters, who would roar into Hill Road on his beloved old AJS motorbike, but had yet to evince great interest in playing music himself.

Like all Syd's Cambridge friends, Clive Welham detected few signs of incipient musical genius – or mental instability. Welham regarded Barrett first and foremost as 'an excellent painter, a much more talented painter than a musician. To be honest, Syd was a very rookie guitarist. Even when the Floyd became famous, his real skill was his innovations rather than his musical ability.

'I would not have thought of him at all as being potentially mentally ill. I just found him a very up and easy guy. Very laid back, very nice sense of humour in a Milliganesque sort of way – a bit Goonish.' (The Goon Show was a popular cultish British radio programme starring Spike Milligan and Peter Sellers).

The Mottoes' modest career culminated in a Saturday night hop at a local school, and a Campaign for Nuclear Disarmament (CND) benefit performance at Union Cellars in the centre of the town. Welham graduated to a semi-professional band called the Ramblers; and Geoff Motlow went on to sing in the Boston Crabs, who made a single, 'Down in Mexico' and were the first of the Cambridge groups to land a recording contract (with EMI's Columbia label, later the home of the Floyd). Following a brief stint on bass in another local band called the Hollering Blues, Syd Barrett was left to regale friends at parties solo with the songs of Lennon and McCartney and whimsical ditties like 'The Effervescing Elephant' that were his own first attempts at songwriting.

'He used to entertain us very much by singing and playing,' says Storm Thorgerson, 'and he was the first person who really got into the Beatles. He was talented to a degree, but it was quite a talented group anyway; writers, musicians, and artists, and people of the theatre, have come out of this particular peer group. So Syd was Syd, and although each of us was special, there was nothing to indicate the future.

'Those years when you are sixteen, seventeen, are jolly exciting, and he was just part of that excitement. We'd have picnics, go on the river, to parties, go driving, smoke dope together, laugh and play music. There were some fringe members who were pretty loony, even then, but Syd was not one of them. He was one of the guys.'

Another of 'the guys' was David Gilmour, who had dabbled with a band of his own called the Newcomers. He and Syd grew close after both left their respective schools to go to Cambridge's College of Arts and Technology. 'He was in the art department,' recalls Gilmour, 'and I was doing modern languages. He and I, and quite a lot of other people who were interested in music, would hang out in the art school every lunchtime and play songs, with guitars and harmonicas.'

The songs played at such gatherings were increasingly by *British* artists, the Beatles and their successors having given schoolboys like Syd and Dave a somewhat more plausible role model than Chuck Berry or even the Beach Boys, along with a pride in their own country's pop music that would have seemed inconceivable only a year or two earlier. When the Rolling Stones erupted into prominence, Gilmour – who was much the more fluent guitarist – helped a besotted Barrett work out Keith Richards's licks: the pair also experimented together with slide guitar and echo boxes (not to mention hashish). But until the Floyd's brief incarnation as a five-piece in early 1968, their musical partnership extended only to a handful of acoustic sessions at a Cambridge pub called the Mill, and duetting for spare change on the streets of southern France, where the two schoolchums learned about the pros and cons of hitchhiking.

In 1963, Gilmour sat in with ex-Motto drummer Clive Welham in his new band, the Ramblers. David, Clive, and rhythm guitarist John Gordon decided to reconstitute that band as Jokers Wild. Completing the new line-up were Mottoes bassist Tony Santi, and the versatile John Altham, who alternated between guitar, keyboards, and saxophone.

Because all five Jokers also saw themselves as singers, their initial stock-in-trade was vocal harmonies – and the songs of the Beach Boys and the Four Seasons. Gilmour was often the featured vocalist, even as he rendered the instrumental solos with his beloved little Hofner Club 60 guitar. His signature tune was Wilson Pickett's 'In the Midnight Hour'.

'Dave was always one to have his say about things, but always in a nice enough way,' says Welham. 'But it was run on a democratic basis. It was one of the most well-organized bands that I've ever worked

24

with, even at an older age. There was a level of maturity there when it came to dealing with musical matters. Everyone seemed to know what they were doing.'

The drummer recalls that Gilmour's greatest musical asset, even then, was 'his sense of feel and timing. What he does in a number is 99 per cent of the time *right*, and I used to love his guitar playing for that. Short riffs or whatever – whether he's playing a raunchy up-tempo number or something mellow and laid-back it was always perfect for what needed to be there. That's some intuition.'

Dr Gilmour, meanwhile, had moved to Manhattan in the 'brain drain': Britain's top scientists and scholars were able to command vastly higher salaries in America than at home. ('Roger,' Dave once quipped, 'lost his father in the war; I lost mine in Greenwich Village.')[3] Always encouraged to be independent by his parents, Dave was left to fend for himself in a small flat in Mill Road, at the heart of Cambridge. 'He was pretty hard up in those days,' says Welham. 'Just a pair of jeans and a donkey jacket, that was about it.'

Gilmour himself recalls nights of playing U.S. military bases with Jokers Wild and collapsing into bed at 4 a.m. only to arise three hours later to tackle odd jobs. Among these, the most lucrative standby for a tall, blond and handsome youth like Dave proved to be posing as a male model. All of which helped instill in the outwardly easygoing guitarist his underlying grit, and a single-minded determination to succeed on his own terms that was to resurface during the Floydian civil wars a generation later.

In 1964 and 1965, his top priority was to put Jokers Wild on the map of a British pop scene whose rewards seemed virtually limitless in the wake of the Beatles and Stones. After establishing themselves in Cambridge with a Wednesday night residency at the Victoria Ballroom, Jokers Wild served as an opening act at local gigs by the Animals and Zoot Money. Soon they were regularly steering their Ford transit van towards London, with Gilmour more often than not taking the wheel both figuratively and literally. At one of their club dates he even caught the eye of Brian Epstein; the Beatles' manager's infatuation, however, had more to do with Dave's good looks than with the Jokers' music, and nothing in the end came of it.

They also recorded a self-produced record in London, containing five songs on one LP side, with the other left blank. About a hundred copies were privately pressed and sold to friends back home. Twenty years later, one would be sold on the record collectors' market for £400. That Jokers Wild never had a distinctive original vision was intimated by a track line-up consisting mostly of covers of covers: Chuck Berry's 'Beautiful Delilah' and Frankie Lymon's 'Why Do Fools Fall in Love' by way of the Kinks and Beach Boys versions, plus Manfred Mann's arrangement of the R & B tune 'Don't You Ask Me' (with Gilmour aping the Manfred's Paul Jones on harmonica). Also included were the Four Seasons' evergreens 'Sherry' and 'Big Girls Don't Cry'.

The record nonetheless gave Jokers Wild an entrée with the oddball young producer Jonathan King, who was well-connected to Decca Records and had enjoyed a hit of his own with 'Everyone's Gone to The Moon'. At London's Regent Sound studios, King taped the Jokers' proposed Decca debut: Sam and Dave's 'You Don't Know What I Know', coupled with Otis Redding's 'That's How Strong My Love Is'. Before it could be issued, however, the ultimate nightmare for an English R & B cover band came to pass: Britain's influential pirate radio stations discovered the Sam and Dave original, spurring its release as a single. Jokers Wild's version of 'You Don't Know What I Know' was pronounced dead even before arrival – and with it slipped away the one 'lucky break' that the fates were ever to grant the Jokers.

Were it not for that sad little comedy of errors, the plot of this book might have unfolded somewhat differently. Over twenty years later, Gilmour expressed to Welham his conviction that, all else being equal, he might have achieved with Jokers Wild a success comparable to that which he has in fact enjoyed with Pink Floyd. But, Dave hastened to add, 'It would have been a very different band . . .'

While Gilmour and Jokers Wild remained based in Cambridge – 'local heroes' to young admirers like Tim Renwick – Waters and Barrett moved to London to pursue their destinies as, respectively, an architect and a painter. At Regent Street Polytechnic, Waters – having acquired a guitar after becoming a Rolling Stones fan – fell in with fellow architecture students Rick Wright and Nick Mason, who shared a flat in Highgate and wanted to form a band.

Born in London on 28 July 1945, Richard William Wright (son of Bridie and Cedric) had arrived at Regent Street Poly by way of the Haberdashers prep school, where he had been at a loss for a career to pursue. 'So,' Rick recalls, 'the careers master said, "Why don't you try architecture?" Amazingly, they accepted me – thank God, because that's where I met Nick, and Roger. But I didn't want to be an architect. I wanted to be a musician. Jazz was my main love then. The only time I've ever queued for tickets was for Duke Ellington, when I was seventeen.'

While all the Floyds were well-off by the standard of aspiring 1960s rock and rollers, Nicholas Berkeley Mason was rich. Born in Birmingham on 27 January 1945 – and, like Rick Wright, an only son in a family of girls – he was brought up by Bill and Sally Mason in a large house on Downshire Hill, one of the most exclusive streets in Hampstead. Bill Mason had achieved some renown as Britain's leading motor-sport documentary film-maker, and was himself an amateur racing-car driver and an avid collector of vintage cars – two passions that Nick, who began accompanying his dad to Vintage Sports Car Club events at a very early age, would develop in his turn. The Masons' driveway was often rendered impassable by all their flashy sports cars, including the Lotus Elan and Aston Martin that Nick himself already owned around the time he linked up with Wright and Waters. The young Mason had attended Frensham Heights boarding school in Surrey, where he is still remembered as a world-class mischief-maker.

Yet this seemingly spoilt brat took his architectural studies far more seriously than Wright or even Waters, who riled lecturers with his impertinence in questioning their teaching methods. Further disillusioned by the perception that Britain's architectural establishment was motivated by economic rather than aesthetic considerations, Roger took to squandering his grants on musical equipment.

Sigma 6 was the name of the first band featuring Waters, Wright, and Mason, on, respectively, lead guitar, rhythm guitar, and drums, none of which they particularly knew how to play. Roger had taken all of two lessons at London's Spanish Guitar Centre before his aversion to practising scales won out. The line-up also boasted Clive Metcalf on bass, Juliette Gale (with whom Wright was soon sharing a flat) and Keith Noble on vocals – and a manager named Ken Chapman who printed up cards proclaiming 'Sigma 6 available for clubs and parties.' Chapman also lumbered the band with his own material, characterized by Waters as '"*Have you seen a morning rose?*" to the tune of a Tchaikovsky prelude or something.'[4] Yet they played along because their would-be Svengali knew the producer Gerry Bron, who would one day work with Uriah Heep and the Bonzo Dog Doo Dah Band, but who passed up on Sigma 6.

After parting company with Chapman, Sigma 6 underwent a dizzying succession of name changes: from the T-Set and the Megadeaths to the Architectural Abdabs – or Screaming Abdabs – or just plain

Abdabs. It was in the latter guise that they landed their first press clipping, in *The Regent Street Poly Magazine*, which touted the Abdabs as 'an up-and-coming pop group [who] hope to establish themselves playing Rhythm and Blues.' Waters was quoted expounding on the latter's appeal: 'It's easier to express yourself rhythmically in Blues-style. It doesn't need practice. Just basic understanding.'[5]

By this time, Waters had moved into Mason's Highgate flat, whose owner happened to be Mike Leonard, a Hornsey art college lecturer with a pioneering interest in combining music with coloured lights. Given the tendency of students from Cambridge to seek one another out in the big city, it was hardly surprising that two guitar-toting acquaintances from back home should also wind up crashing there and playing in Roger's band. One was Bob Close, a fellow student at the Regent Street Poly, and an accomplished jazz guitarist who had cut his teeth in a group called Blues Anonymous. The other was Syd Barrett, who had a scholarship at Camberwell Art School.

'With the advent of Bob Close,' Waters recalled, 'we actually had someone who could play an instrument. It was really then that we did the shuffle job of who played what. I was demoted from lead guitar to rhythm guitar and finally bass. There was always this frightful fear that I could land up as the drummer.'[6]

Juliette left the band and eventually became Mrs Richard Wright: Metcalf and Noble disappeared from the picture. Rick, meanwhile, switched his allegiance from guitar to keyboards (he also played cello, but rarely in public), began listening to contemporary electronic composers like Karlheinz Stockhausen and flunked out of Regent Street Poly to enrol briefly at the London College of Music.

When Syd joined up, he very quickly clashed with the incorrigibly square Close, who failed to share the experimentally-minded art student's fascination with the possibilities of guitar feedback and echo boxes, let alone his burgeoning interest in Eastern mysticism, supernaturalism, ESP, and LSD. Bob bailed out leaving Syd, almost by default, fronting the group.

Shortly thereafter, Barrett found more permanent lodgings at 2 Earlham Street, near Covent Garden, which several young Cambridge acquaintances had already made their home. These included Susie Gawler-Wright, whose live-in boyfriend (and future husband) Peter Wynne Willson, a lighting technician at the New Theatre, was to become one of Syd's closest friends and artistic partners. The family backgrounds of both Susie and Peter could hardly have been more socially respectable; Wynne Willson's great-uncle, for instance, was the Bishop of Bath and Wells.

Respectable, however, was hardly the word for the clandestine publishing business that flourished on the ground floor under the auspices of another flatmate. A French Army deserter, Jean-Simon had found his metier reprinting X-rated Olympia Press 'classics' complete with his own graphic illustrations. The naughtiness at 2 Earlham Street was not to end there. Long after Barrett and Wynne Willson had departed, along with their distinctive brand of countercultural hijinks, their home became a whorehouse.

Alongside the likes of Jean-Simon, Syd initially came across as a relatively unassuming character who could often be found sitting in his room strumming an acoustic guitar. Susie remembers him then as a 'happy, balanced art student, who was quite sensitive and sweet, and thought he could write songs'.

Barrett was nonetheless profoundly troubled by an incident that Storm Thorgerson suggests may have been the second 'catalyst' for what was to come. Two years before the advent of the Maharishi in the Beatles story, many of Syd's Cambridge gang – most of whom had already taken LSD – became deeply involved with an Indian-based religious cult called Sant Mat, or the Path of the Masters. 'A lot of people tried to capture Syd and force him into their religion,' says Susie, who was herself one of its adherents.

Sant Mat's strictures included the avoidance of meat and alcohol, and the practice of meditation for two-and-a-half hours daily. 'The whole Oriental-guru-Eastern-bit,' as Thorgerson recalls it, 'was a concomitant of the acid generation. There were various things that happened on acid that seemed to make connections with an Oriental philosophy, even though the philosophy wasn't very well understood by Westerners. It certainly wasn't understood by us kids very well, but it seemed to have attractions.

'So Syd and I went to a hotel in the centre of London to meet the Master. I was more just curious, but Syd was seeking initiation to become, as it was called, a Sat Sanghi.' Unlike Cambridge friends Nigel Gordon and Susie Gawler-Wright, however, Barrett was rejected by the Maharaji Charan Singh Ji on the ground that he was a student who should focus instead on finishing his courses. This explanation was, Storm says, 'a euphemism' – but for what exactly, Syd never could quite understand. Though he seldom discussed it with his friends, they sensed that Barrett took the inscrutable guru's rejection very personally. Henceforth, he would feel obliged to seek his enlightenment elsewhere, notably through artistic expression, and through chemicals.

The fervour with which Syd subsequently stretched his psyche towards the breaking point recalls the famous credo set forth in France a century earlier by the similarly youthful Arthur Rimbaud: 'A Poet makes himself a visionary through a long, boundless, and systematic disorganization of *all* the senses. All forms of love, of suffering, of madness . . . he exhausts within himself all poisons, and preserves their quintessences.' Barrett was to attain his own apotheosis of 'love, suffering, and madness' via the late-twentieth-century formula of sex, drugs and rock and roll.

The strange moniker that Syd bequeathed to his band was suggested, not by a drug vision, but by two obscure names in his record collection: Georgia bluesmen Pink Anderson (1900–1974) and Floyd 'Dipper Boy' Council (1911–1976). The Pink Floyd Sound's early choice of material, however, was less esoteric, consisting mainly of the Rolling Stones' Greatest Hits and chestnuts like 'Louie Louie' and 'Road Runner'. The one feature to set the group apart from ten thousand others playing the same numbers at parties and pubs across Britain was the instrumental breaks, pregnant with distortion, feedback, and possibilities, during which the guitarist (increasingly abetted by the Stockhausen-influenced keyboards player), would drive his stolid little R & B band into another realm entirely.

The Pink Floyd Sound was first billed as such at London's Countdown Club, in late 1965, a gig for which the four students received £15. During the next several months, Jokers Wild and the Floyd often opened shows for one another in their respective balliwicks of Cambridge and London. One memorable evening, David Gilmour and Syd Barrett – 'twin luminaries from a small town', as Thorgerson puts it – co-starred with their bands at a large party in Shelford, just outside Cambridge. The traditional 'cabaret slot – during which an acoustic act or a comedian would give the dancing crowds a respite from the amplified rock and roll – was filled by a struggling New York folkie named Paul Simon.

The photographer Mick Rock, then a first-year student at Cambridge, was brought by mutual friends to hear Syd's band play at the local art college. 'I didn't know what the hell I was going to see,' he recalls. 'That was one of those moments when you see something unprecedented, with completely new possibilities.' After the show, they all accompanied Barrett to his den in his mother's basement, and smoked a series of giant joints.

The Cambridge student scene was one of the hippest in the country: 'a little acid explosion right there', says Rock. 'That was a very special place at that point in time.' On his frequent visits to Cambridge, with and without the Floyd, Barrett became an especially revered figure in that crowd. Rock remembers Syd as *'particularly* hip. His mind was always busting out on new turf before anybody's else. I was at Cambridge studying French and German literature; that was where all my fantasies came from. Being on the Left Bank of Paris doing drugs and writing wild poetry – that seemed to me what life was about; it was not about having lots of money. I was steeped in all that kind of mythology about the poets and the painters and the artists. And Syd became that kind of mythological figure for me – the Divine Light.' Though Gilmour was also a fixture of that Cambridge subculture – and, says Rock, 'you couldn't meet a nicer person' – nobody viewed Jokers Wild in the same light as the Pink Floyd Sound. Dave's was 'not wild, avant-garde music to excite wild Cambridge undergraduates. It was what you'd want if you went to a dance.'

But it was during another out-of-London date, at Essex University in early 1966, that epiphany struck for the Pink Floyd Sound. 'We'd already become interested in mixed-media, as it were,' Waters recalled, 'and some bright spark down there had done a film . . . given this paraplegic a film camera and wheeled him round London filming his view. Now they shoved it up on a screen behind us as we played . . .'[7]

Chapter 3
Learning to Fly

Back in London from their 1966 summer breaks, Barrett, Waters, Mason, and Wright were ready to talk business with Peter Jenner and his longtime friend and prospective partner Andrew King. Having recently parted ways with British Airways' training and educational department, the unemployed King had ample time on his hands, along with a modest inheritance that he was not averse to investing in a promising new venture.

At first, according to Jenner, Roger Waters suspected that the two men might be drug dealers. Nonetheless, the four students clearly had little to lose from the overtures of the effervescent lecturer and his open-handed sidekick. Amateurs in every sense of the word, the embryonic Floyd had no manager or agent, minimal equipement in varying states of decreptitude, and a van about to give up the ghost. After they agreed to throw in their lot with Jenner and King, one of the latter's first acts was to buy them about £1000-worth of new instruments and amplifiers. (These were almost immediately stolen, obliging the musicians to acquire yet another set of gear on an installment plan.) Jenner, for his part, turned Syd Barrett on to such AMM performance techniques as rolling ballbearings down guitar strings, and suggested that the Pink Floyd rid their name of the superfluous 'Sound'.

The original plan to turn the Floyd into a flagship for Jenner's DNA Records was quickly forgotten, after Roger insisted that what the group really needed was a full-time manager: a role that Peter and Andrew, shrugging off their sceptical friends' persistent choruses of a 'Pink *What?*' enthusiastically agreed to share. The relationship was eventually cemented with a six-way partnership called Blackhill Enterprises (named after a little farmhouse owned by Jenner and King). For a pop-music manager to give an artist an equal stake in a business venture, rather than simply skim 20 or 25 per cent off their gross income, was unprecedented. But the Floyd's new patrons, true to their psychedelic ideals, were determined, in the words of Peter

Jenner, 'to be alternative, all working together, and everything was going to be democratic and groovy.'[1]

On the Free School front, meanwhile, Jenner and the other usual suspects continued to spin their fanciful schemes. In August, spurred by a neighbourhood dispute over whether 'public property' should be fenced off from 'the people', they helped Michael X and a redoubtable wheelchair-bound housewife named Rhonnie Laslett mobilize the local West Indian community to launch the first Notting Hill Carnival (or Fayre, as it was initially called), for which Jenner served as treasurer. Though their glorified street party-cum-demonstration met with token resistance from the police (who went so far as to arrest a pantomime horse and a man in a gorilla suit), the Carnival has since been enshrined as a popular annual institution. It remains the Free School's most enduring legacy – with the possible exception of Pink Floyd.

The Floyd were tapped shortly thereafter for a Free School benefit at All Saints Church in Notting Hill's Powis Square, whose liberal vicar encouraged the use of his church hall for everything from community councils to black theatre groups. The Sound and Light Workshop, says John Hopkins, 'was a way to recoup some debts and have a good time'. Successful on both counts, it proved far more popular than anyone had anticipated and became a regular Friday evening event, even as the Free School itself fell by the wayside. The shows were advertised mostly by word of mouth and mimeographed handbills such as this:

Announcing:
POP DANCE featuring London's farthest-out group
**************THE PINK FLOYD*******************

in
INTERSTELLAR OVERDRIVE
STONED ALONE
ASTRONOMY DOMINI
(an astral chant)
& other numbers from
their space-age book

also:

33

************LIGHT PROJECTION SLIDES***********
****************LIQUID MOVIES******************

The Time: 8–11 pm
The Day: Friday 14 October
The Place: All Saints Hall, Powis Gardens, W.11
The Reason: Good Times

Another LONDON FREE SCHOOL Production

Rick Wright has described such early Floyd performances as 'purely experimental for us and a time of learning and finding out exactly what we were trying to do. Each night was a complete buzz because we did totally new things and none of us knew how the others would react to it.'[2] The mixed-media poet Pete Brown says All Saints Hall was also routinely rocked by 'incredible mad jam sessions', one of which 'ended up with Alexis Korner, Arthur Brown, Mick Farren, Nick Mason and me all singing "Lucille". Which was really frightening to a lot of people – including us!'

Miles nonetheless recalls that after a typical Sound and Light Workshop the Floyd 'took questions from the audience, while earnest young avant-gardists like myself asked about multi-media experiments and all the rest of it. It was an "educational event", very serious.'

An American couple, Joel and Tony Brown – friends of LSD guru Timothy Leary, no less – showed up at the first All Saints show with a slide projector, and proceeded to cast weird images onto the Floyd in time with their music. Though their slides were a far cry from the phantasmagoric swirl of the Haight-Ashbury light shows, the innovation had a galvanizing effect on both the band and its audience, and on Peter Jenner, who lost no time in constructing a rudimentary 'psychedelic' lighting system with the help of his wife Sumi and Andrew King.

Their handiwork consisted of bits of coloured perspex affixed to closed-beam spotlights, which they mounted upon boards and fitted with manually operated domestic light switches. Further refinements were subsequently added by the Floyd's first lighting director, Joe Gannon, a seventeen-year-old whiz kid with connections at Hornsey College of Art's lighting workshop, and Syd Barrett's housemates Peter Wynne Willson and Susie Gawler-Wright.

34

At a time when bands invariably relied upon a venue's house lights, Wynne Willson took to salvaging equipment discarded by the West End theatre where he worked, and renovating it for the Floyd's gigs. Then Gannon obtained spotlights that he played with a little keyboard instrument Wynne Willson created, and some little 500-watt, 1000-watt projectors. They also developed the liquid slides that became a trademark of the underground London era.

'Peter got into slapping Doctor Martin's inks on slides – very bright colours,' explains Susie. 'We'd drop in different chemicals; it was very messy and very good fun. We'd get a blowtorch to heat it and a hairdryer to cool it. I used to watch the bubbles moving and thought it was really wonderful.'

'We thought we were doing what they were doing in New York and California,' says Jenner. 'But in fact very few of us had been to America; people didn't just hop on planes then. Import records were expensive and hard to find, and there was no rock press really, so the information was incredibly filtered and vague. There were just sort of rumours about things like the Velvet Underground and the Jefferson Airplane.'

John Hopkins's girlfriend at the time who had scored her fifteen minutes of fame as the female 'filling' of the interracial sex sandwich in Andy Warhol's ultra-underground film *Couch*. She had recently returned from New York with particularly tantalizing tales of the Exploding Plastic Inevitable – the multi-media performances at the Dom that featured the Velvet Underground – and a tape of Lou Reed's songs. (The Velvets had yet to release their first album.)

'When I got the Floyd,' recalls Jenner, 'I thought I ought to become a "rock manager". I heard about the Velvet Underground at a party, then we heard their demos – "*kiss the boot of shiny leather*" and all that stuff. I thought, "They're good, I should manage them." I phoned up John Cale saying, "Hello, I'm Peter Jenner, I think I should manage you." '

The Velvets' electric viola player broke the news to him that the band's career was already being supervised by Mr Warhol. Jenner and his comrades had to content themselves with duplicating what they *imagined* the Exploding Plastic Inevitable – or the Haight-Ashbury's Avalon and Fillmore ballrooms – must be like.

'We didn't really know what was going on there,' says Jenner. 'And so we created *our* version of the underground. When I did come over, I discovered how totally different it was. On the original Pink Floyd lighting rig Andrew and myself had built, because of the low-powered lights we set them up so they'd throw a huge shadow. It was all very unlike the stunning high-tech flash of the Fillmore. But in a way, the Floyd's was more imaginative.' Another key difference was that the Airplane and the Dead never had their *own* lights shows: in San Francisco, independent outfits like the Joshua Light Show were hired by the venues rather than the bands. From the start, the Floyd's lights were far more closely integrated with the music.

Jenner says he experienced a strong sense of *déja vu* over twenty years later, when he accompanied his current client Billy Bragg on a ground-breaking concert tour of the USSR and developed a keen interest in Soviet rock. 'They have such a filtered awareness of Western music that there's some awfully interesting stuff going on that's gone a bit wrong. From those few hints, it's gone off into its own world. Consequently, it's developed its own life and character. That thing in the Soviet Union of not really knowing what's going on in Britain, but wanting to do it – they make their *own* scene. That's what happened in England in the 1960s.'

In staffing their budding enterprise, the Blackhill boys could hardly have looked any closer to home. Sharing Peter and Sumi Jenner's house on Edbrooke Road were a jeweller, Mick Milligan, and his girlfriend June Child, along with the Jenners' dozen-odd cats, most of them black and named Squeaky. The flat upstairs was occupied by a young Mod refugee from the provinces, John Marsh (and at one point, ironically, by Mike Ratledge of the Floyd's rival underground band the Soft Machine). As was then the fashion, this motley crew pursued a communal low-overhead lifestyle, sometimes subsisting on discarded fruit and vegetables retrieved from Portobello Road after the street market closed.

The energetic and efficient June Child – better known as June Bolan after her subsequent marriage to the pop legend Marc Bolan – became Blackhill's secretary and general factotum almost by default. 'I wasn't working at the time,' she recalls, 'so I was in the house all day, in my room in the basement. Peter was teaching at LSE then, and I'm not quite sure what Andrew was doing. But the phone kept ringing, and I kept answering it, and it would be message after message about the Floyd. And I just suddenly said to Peter and Andrew one day, "This is silly. Can't you pay me?" I got something like three pounds eight and six a week, really minimal. But it was cash in hand.' Jenner also stopped charging her rent.

36

In time June's duties came to encompass everything from driving the Floyd's van to collecting their fees and distributing their wages. John Marsh, meanwhile, became increasingly involved with the Floyd as an unpaid lighting assistant, until he was fired from his job at Dillon's bookshop for taking one too many days off, and was put on the Blackhill payroll.

After Joe Gannon split for the West Coast,* the main responsibility for designing and building the 'blob show' fell to the handy and inventive Peter Wynne Willson, who in the meantime had been supplementing his regular income with the sale of self-designed psychedelic goggles. Characterized in early press write-ups as the fifth Floyd, Wynne Willson was also designated 'road manager', his lack of a driving licence notwithstanding. As lighting director, he was actually awarded a percentage of the Floyd's earnings, an arrangement that was to be the source of some friction when these became more substantial.

Susie Gawler-Wright, who came to be known in underground circles as 'the psychedelic debutante', helped her boyfriend operate the Floyd light show. 'Susie was lovely,' says June Bolan. 'Thin as a stick, with perfect straight teeth and the most magical smile, always going "Wow!" like one did in those days.'

Syd Barrett was now sharing the top floor of Peter and Susie's house with his lookalike girlfriend, a stylish model named Lindsay Korner. Good-natured, and comparatively low-key, Lindsay was to remain devoted to Syd through all the ups and downs of his Floyd years.

The two couples enjoyed a relaxed, bohemian existence, sleeping all morning, lingering for hours at the Pollo Bar in Old Compton Street over sandwiches, and often playing the Oriental board game Go well into the night. Then Barrett's fascination with Go gave way to an obsession with the I Ching, which became the basis for a new song called 'Chapter 24'. '*Change returns success . . . Action brings good fortune . . .*'

Now that the Pink Floyd were taking flight, Syd had abandoned his canvasses to create 'music in colours' instead, writing songs with a flair and dedication that astonished even his closest associates. His typically 'underground' enthusiasms and influences – Chinese oracles and childhood fairy stories; pulp sci-fi and J.R.R. Tolkien's tales of

---

* Twenty years later Gannon would reappear behind the lighting console of Alice Cooper's comeback tour.

Middle-earth; English folk ballads, Chicago blues, avant-garde electronics, and Donovan, the Beatles, and the Rolling Stones – all mingled in the cauldron of his subconscious to re-emerge in a voice, sound, and style that was uniquely Syd.

'In the early days,' says Wynne Willson, 'much more time would be spent writing numbers than performing. He would be working on stuff, building towards a performance, rather than writing for a record. Writing the lyrics for a number, he would compose the basics of it, and then would be endlessly playing around with how he was going to take his improvisation during the gig. Those were halcyon days, everything was very pleasant then. It was going exactly the way Syd wanted it to. He would have endless time to write and play.

'I can remember him sitting around and playing with lyrics, and copious quantities of grass and hash would be smoked. It was all very mellow, and later became far too pressured and plastic.'

'Syd was very special, extraordinarily so,' says June Bolan. 'He wrote wonderful songs; the lyrics were unbelievable. In the early days, when he was together, he was like a blinkered horse. He'd sit for hours and play wonderful guitar, and write, and *do* – and that's all he did. He thrived on it.

'He was very, very much the creator of the group in those days. When he would sit at home and write a song, he'd think of what the drummer ought to play, how the bass line should be. He played very good rhythm as well as lead, and he'd know what he wanted to hear. He'd go into rehearsals and say to Nick, "this is what I want you to play" . . . and that's how it would come out.'

Sumi Jenner, for one, never found Syd a very communicative person; 'He just expressed himself through his music.' Her husband, who through the years has made the acquaintance of his share of artistic prodigies, remembers Barrett as 'the most creative person I've ever known. It was extraordinary – in those few months at Earlham Street he wrote nearly all his songs for the Floyd and the solo albums. It was all very casual, done off the top of the head. No tortured genius sweating through his pain, as far as I could see. When people just write without any inhibitions, they write so much better than when they start getting concerned that they're great writers.'

Peter Jenner's own most tangible contribution to this output, however inadvertent, may be found in the power-chord leitmotiv of 'Interstellar Overdrive', the long instrumental freak-out that became a highlight of all Syd's performances with the Floyd. It all began with Jenner's attempt to serenade Barrett with the guitar hook from Love's version of Burt Bacharach's 'My Little Red Book'. 'I'm not the world's greatest singer; in fact I've got a terrible sense of pitch,' says Jenner. 'He played back a riff on his guitar, said, "It goes like this?" And of course it was quite different, because my humming was so bad!'

By October 1966, the Floyd were in a position to meet the challenge posed by *Melody Maker*'s Allan Jones (their first champion in the London music press), who wrote: '"Psychedelic" versions of "Louie Louie" won't come off, but if they can incorporate their electronic prowess with some melodic and lyrical songs – getting away from dated R & B things – they could well score in the near future.' With the infusion of such Barrett originals as 'Astronomy Dominé', 'The Gnome', 'Matilda Mother', and the pot-smoking paean 'Let's Roll Another One', Chuck Berry and Bo Diddley were banished forever from the Pink Floyd repertoire.

The overnight flowering of Barrett's creativity was soon evinced onstage. There Syd emulated Pete Townsend in handling both lead and rhythm guitar duties – sometimes simultaneously. His innovations ranged from playing slide guitar with his cherished Zippo cigarette lighter to unleashing special effects through a Binson echo unit.

During the course of the shows' centrepieces – thirty to forty-five minute free-form disarrangements of 'Interstellar Overdrive' and 'Astronomy Dominé' – Barrett would transform himself into a whirling dervish; unleashing salvos of electric feedback, the guitarist would wave his arms in the air as the coloured spotlights cast his looming shadow on to the screen behind. Syd's Floyd, Miles observed, 'would take musical innovation further out than it had ever been before, walking out on incredibly dangerous limbs and dancing along crumbling precipices, saved sometimes only by the confidence beamed at them from the audience sitting a matter of inches away at their feet.

'Ultimately, having explored to their satisfaction, Nick would begin the drum roll that led to final run through of the theme and everyone could breathe again.'[3] 'He took you into a whole other world,' recalls Sumi Jenner. 'Syd on stage was just mesmerizing. The others always seemed to be struggling to keep up with him.'

He looked great, too. Among the first in his crowd to discover London's legendary psychedelic boutique Granny Takes a Trip, Barrett made himself a showcase for what June Bolan calls his 'wonderful dress sense. He was like a clothes horse, anything he put on looked ace. He'd wear satin blouses and bits and bobs, scarves and all those things. He also was the most beautiful member of the band physically. An Adonis-looking genius.'

Sumi remembers Barrett constantly altering his physical appearance; 'At one point he and Lindsay wore the same clothes and hairstyle – and you really couldn't tell them apart.' In light of all this dazzling flair, Peter Jenner was hardly alone in his conviction that of the four Floyds Barrett was 'far and away the most important' – indeed, that 'it was *his* band'.

Nick Mason, by contrast, often gave the impression that he was more or less along for the ride. (Even if he did maintain the definitive Pink Floyd scrapbook.) A supremely affable and amusing personality in later years, the 'playboy drummer' nevertheless rubbed a few of the Floyd's early associates the wrong way; one remembers him as 'arrogant, snobbish, and bitchy. He was probably insecure because he was supposed to be an ace drummer for an ace band – and he knew he wasn't. He seems to have softened up over the years, become much nicer.' Peter Jenner, on the other hand, always regarded Nick as the least neurotic of all the Floyds, and the easiest to work with.

Rick Wright's good nature, at least, appears to have been evident to everyone right from the start – as was his inherent vulnerability. One friend from the early Floyd days remembers him as 'gentle and sweet', yet 'willowy and shaky' – and highly dependent on his 'much more solid and grounded' wife, Juliette. Though initially twitted by his colleagues for always seeming to play the same lick no matter what the song – Rick's Turkish Delight, they called it – Wright was Barrett's closest partner in the Floyd both socially and musically. Onstage, Miles wrote, 'Rick would maintain a spectral presence, hanging ghost-like chords up to wave gently in the background.'[4]

'In the early days,' says Jenner, 'Rick used to tune everybody's guitars. Syd couldn't be bothered – wasn't terribly good at it, but could if he had to – and Roger was tone-deaf, didn't have a clue.

'I never rated Roger's bass-playing – no wonder he didn't like me. I never got over the fact that Roger was tone-deaf, and couldn't tune his bass. He wasn't an instinctive musician like Syd.'

Nonetheless, at least one key associate, Joe Boyd, recognized Waters's driving bass style, with its trademark octave swoops, as a major component of the Pink Floyd sound. Equally important to the Floyd's early success, the bassist was himself driven; it was he who assumed the responsibility of organizing the group's activities, and of serving as their articulate press spokesman. The fact that Waters was slightly older than the others – and, at six-foot-one, somewhat taller – also contributed to his aura of authority within the Floyd. Jenner does credit Roger for being 'incredibly hard-working and committed' and, without question, 'the strongest personality in the band.'

The Free School's next major spinoff was the first British underground newspaper, *International Times*, known as *IT*. Seeking to create a mass-circulation 'international culture magazine' comparable to New York's *Village Voice* or *East Village Other*, Miles and John Hopkins joined forces with (among others) the dynamic expatriate American Jim Haynes. The founder of Edinburgh's innovative Paperback Bookshop and Traverse Theatre – and, later on, London's Arts Lab, which in turn was to put Covent Garden back on the map – Haynes boasted such influential friends as George Orwell's widow Sonia (who donated the paper's first typewriter) and entrepreneur Victor Herbert (who lent £400). For office space, Miles provided the basement of Indica bookshop. The name *IT* materialized in response to the oft-asked question 'What should we call *it?*' – and was almost instantly determined to be an acronym for *International Times*.

Hoppy and Miles resolved to inaugurate their fortnightly publication with an epochal benefit happening to feature, it now went without saying, the Pink Floyd. For the site of their 'All Night Rave', they settled upon north London's grime-encrusted century-old Roundhouse, whose original incarnation as an engine shed was still betrayed by the railway lines on the floor. The facility had subsequently been appropriated by Gilbey's Gin Company, which built additional storage space for its vats of gin in the form of a balcony precariously supported by wooden pillars.

In 1966, Hopkins recalls, 'The Roundhouse was a cold, dusty, empty gin warehouse that nobody was using for anything, and seemed to be a suitable place to have the launch party for *IT*. Arnold Wesker had had his eye on it for years. He had an organization intended to bring culture to the masses through the trade unions, very traditional socialism. He'd acquired this building somehow, but hadn't got it set up.'

The difference between an Old Left do-gooder like Wesker and Hoppy's new breed of psychedelic impresario was that while the playwright patiently awaited the accumulation of half a million pounds in grants and contributions before doing up the Roundhouse, the boys from *IT* simply asked him for the keys, promised not to make a mess, and proceeded to do their thing. 'A lot of things happened in those days,' says Hopkins, 'because people didn't know that what they were trying to do was impossible. And it worked – whereas if you had analyzed it in any rational way, we would never have started the newspaper, I would never have started the UFO club. It was good not to know that what you were trying to do was impossible. That's why those days were so exciting.'

On the night of 15 October, Hoppy, Miles and company effectively launched not only *IT* and the Roundhouse – which became an established London venue for both musical and theatrical events – but also the Pink Floyd. 'That,' says Miles, 'was the first big concert they ever did. We paid them £15, which was more than the Soft Machine got – because the Pink Floyd had a light show and the Soft Machine didn't.'

Advertised as a 'Pop Op Costume Masque Drag Ball', the event attracted the cream of London's fashion, art, and pop-music worlds, dazzlingly arrayed in caftans, floral pyjamas, and antique military regalia. Paul McCartney and Marianne Faithfull were there, dressed, respectively, as a white-robed Arab and a partially disrobed nun. So was director Michaelangelo Antonioni, in town for the filming of his Swinging London saga *Blow Up*, with a scantily clad Monica Vitti in tow.

'We were all so cool,' says Miles, 'and pretended not to notice them.' Upon arrival, each ticket-holder was ceremoniously presented with a sugar cube, albeit one that, unlike so many then in circulation, lacked any active ingredient. Much of the audience, however, proceeded on the premise that their cubes *were* spiked.

'It was a nightmare, really,' Miles recalls. 'There were two toilets, for over two thousand people, which flooded out immediately. The staircase leading up to the actual Roundhouse from the street was so narrow you could only go up or down; there wasn't even room for two people to pass. It was a real fire trap.' After customers finally gained admittance, moreover, they had to contend with the absence of heating on a chilly autumn night, though Hoppy says that 'with two thousand people there the warehouse really warmed up'.

'We didn't know what the fuck we were doing,' Miles admits. 'We were just stupid kids. The police were hovering around but *they* couldn't get up the stairs either. At two in the morning there was still this queue right down the street. Finally people managed to break down the back door and come in. Alexander Trocchi, the writer and famous junkie, got in that way with a whole bunch of his friends.' The Pink Floyd's careening van, meanwhile, had accidentally toppled the happening's freshly minted six-foot jelly.

42

Despite these mishaps, the All-Night Rave succeeded famously in gathering under one roof for the first time all the scattered tribes of the emerging London underground. As the future science-fiction novelist Chris Rowley (then an *IT* office boy) was to recall, the Roundhouse saw them 'rubbing up against each other, sharing joints, talking frantically about . . . electrifying the clouds [with] messages of love and peace . . . When had there been such vast quantities of raw optimism among any group? Perhaps not since 1914 when the lads went off to die.'[5]

And the Floyd rose to the ecstatic occasion with their most power-ful performance to date. Their light show – projected from a hand-some old wagon left behind by Gilbey's Gin – was especially striking in the enveloping darkness of its barely wired surroundings. According to *IT*'s own report, the Floyd 'did weird things to the feel of the event with their scary feedback sounds, slide projections playing on their skin (drops of paint ran riot on the slides to produce outer space-prehistoric textures) . . . spotlights flashing in time with the drums.'[6] In keeping with the evening's total unpredictability, the concert came to an abrupt and dramatic end when the Roundhouse's meagre power supply finally blew out during 'Interstellar Overdrive'.

The event inspired press coverage as far afield as California. The *San Francisco Examiner* account by Miles's grumpy guest Kenneth Rexroth, however, did little to advance either of the featured groups' careers, insofar as it suggested that the promised musical entertain-ment had failed to materialize amid all the chaos and squalor:

> The bands didn't show, so there was a large pick-up band of assorted instruments on a small central platform. Sometimes they were making rhythmic sounds, sometimes not . . .
> I felt exactly like I was on the *Titanic*. Far be it for me to holler copper, but I was dumbfounded that the London police and fire authorities permitted even a dozen people to congregate in such a trap . . .[7]

That the Soft Machine or the Pink Floyd might be actually playing *music* apparently never occurred to the venerable American poet.

'The music,' Miles readily confesses, 'was very experimental, be-cause nobody had suggested otherwise. The Soft Machine had contact mikes on a motorcycle that a guy called Dennis, who never showed up on the records but was in the line-up at that point, did creative things with. Then when the Floyd played, he took girls for motorcycle rides around the outside of the Roundhouse.'

The Floyd did garner a mention in *The Sunday Times*, their first in an established British newspaper:

At the launching of the new magazine *IT* the other night a pop group called the Pink Floyd played throbbing music while a series of bizarre coloured shapes flashed on a huge screen behind them. Someone had made a mountain of jelly which people ate at midnight and another person had parked his motorbike in the middle of the room. All apparently very psychedelic.

The piece concluded with remarks by Roger Waters: 'Our music may give you the screaming horrors or throw you into screaming ecstasy. Mostly it's the latter. We find our audiences stop dancing now. We tend to get them standing there totally grooved with their mouths open.'[8]

Chapter 4
Let There be More Light

In the wake of the *International Times* launch, the Pink Floyd's regular All Saints engagements – which Blackhill had taken to advertising under Dr Leary's slogan 'Turn On. Tune In. Drop Out' – became so in vogue that the little church hall could no longer safely accommodate all those who showed up. On 3 December the Floyd graced a second Roundhouse benefit, promoting majority rule in Zimbabwe, dubbed 'Psychodelphia versus Ian Smith.' ('Bring your own happenings and ecstatogenic substances,' the poster advised. 'Drag optional.') Nine days later – in conjunction with an Oxfam benefit called 'You're Joking?' – they gave their first performance at the still larger (and far more prestigious) Royal Albert Hall. The Floyd's tightening schedule then called for a return to the Roundhouse to ring in the year 1967, as part of a 'Giant Freak-out All Night Rave', where their third-billed *son et lumiere* would upstage not only the Move (who ritualistically destroyed three televisions and a car) but even the Who (who took their own turn at blowing the power). In short, the Pink Floyd were *happening* every bit as quickly as their managers had naively expected all along.

IT, meanwhile, was losing money at an alarming clip. To attract record company advertising, the paper allocated much of its copy to interviews with sympathetic pop stars, notably the Beatles, who in turn appreciated the opportunity, seldom afforded by the fan mags or established music rags, to ramble on at length about drugs, politics, and God (and say 'fuck' as often as they liked). Miles had become particularly friendly with Paul McCartney, who was even known to drop by his flat and help stitch together the paper. 'But we couldn't live entirely on the advertising,' says Miles, 'because there was such a time lag with the money. And we didn't have a distributor; we were only selling through street vendors; and the few shops that had agreed to take it, we'd mail it to them. Our cash flow was disastrous.'

John Hopkins recalls that it was Joe Boyd – 'a pretty smart cookie' – who dreamed up a way not only to bail out *IT* with an ongoing source of 'instant cash', but also to accommodate the overflow crowds at All Saints Church Hall: all they had to do was move the Sound and Light Workshop to a larger space – preferably 'downtown'. Accordingly, Hoppy and Boyd scoured the West End until they found a seedy old dance hall in the basement of 31 Tottenham Court Road, called the Blarney Club, whose kindly Irish owner was willing to rent it out on Friday evenings for fifteen pounds a pop.

'We decided to run two evenings on successive Fridays,' says Hopkins, 'one before Christmas and one after Christmas. We said, "If it works, it works; if it doesn't, it's just two gigs." And we found some people to make some psychedelic posters, and we hired the Floyd, and lots of people came. The next time, even more people came.'

Joe Boyd, who was falling from favour with his Elektra Records superiors, thereby found himself a new vocation as the fledgling club's musical director. For its opening night, 23 December 1966, it was advertised on Michael English's poster as 'Night Tripper' – the name superimposed in spidery script over a photo of Pete Townshend's lovely fiancée Karen. A week later, the club became UFO (pronounced '*you*-foe').

'It was what we thought a San Francisco psychedelic night club must be like,' says Miles, 'though none of us had ever been to one, and had no idea really. We showed Marilyn Monroe movies, Kenneth Anger's films, William Burroughs's *Cut-Ups* – all of which in those days were regarded as very interesting and experimental. You could get fruit juice and sandwiches, but no alcohol – which, looking back, seems extraordinary. Then there was a special room where Caroline Coon would talk people down from bad trips. There were little head shops, and Granny Takes a Trip had a stand where you could order your next psychedelic suit. There was an underground press booth with free literature. And it seemed like the Floyd were always playing there, and that the club existed for years, even though it really wasn't around all that long.'

When UFO did fold, the same Miles reminisced in *IT*:

It was a club in the sense that most people knew each other, met there to do their business, arrange their week's appointments, dinners and lunches, and hatch out issues of *IT*, plans for Arts Lab, SOMA [a legalize-pot lobby], and various schemes for turning the

Thames yellow and removing the fences in Notting Hill. The activity and energy was thicker than the incense.[1]

In emulation of the 24-hour city of New York, what's more, the club stayed open all night – almost unheard of in London where even the public transport stopped running at midnight. In the final hours before the first trains started up again at dawn, however, the zonked-out flower children would be strewn like vegetables across the polished ballroom floor.

'It was the right place at the right time,' says Hopkins. 'And because nobody had ever seen anything like it before, it got to be very popular.' Especially after journalists like *Melody Maker*'s Chris Welch spread the word to the multitudes:

Today in London the Bell People already have their own head-quarters, and UFO (it stands for Unidentified Flying Object or Underground Freak Out) is believed to be Britain's first psychedelic club. Happy young people waving sticks of incense danced Greek-like dances, waving frond-like hands with bells jingling, neck scarves fluttering and strange hats abounding.

There were pretty slides casting beams of light over the jolly throng who stood or squatted in communion, digging the light show or listening to Love being relayed at sensible non-discotheque volume. There were frequent announcements warning patrons to be cool and that the fuzz might pay a call. In fact two young constables did pop in and seemed wholly satisfied that all was well, and in fact all *was* well. The light shows were 'wild', the music 'weird', but – all was well.[2]

'We just did what we wanted,' Hoppy allows. 'We didn't play records very loud like in other clubs. There were five-minute gaps when we changed the records, and people could say hello and talk to each other – which made a very nice atmosphere. It was very free and easy.'

So free and easy that at an early Floyd gig one freak, as Pete Brown tells it, 'leapt right out of his clothes, and rushed up the stairs and down the street, past the Tottenham Court Road police station. It was a warm evening and the police were standing outside taking some fresh air. And suddenly this person whizzes by them with no clothes on – which in 1966 was unbelievable! So they all chased him down the street.'

'It was *such* a cool place,' says Miles, 'that people like the Beatles and the Who and Jimi Hendrix could come down and wander around and nobody would rush up for an autograph. It was *the* hippest rock club in town, no doubt about it. Where the most interesting music could be heard, and where bands like the Floyd could play really long, extended versions of their songs.' Peter Jenner once even spotted Roy Orbison in the audience.

This 'trippy adventure playground', as Paul McCartney called it, became to the Pink Floyd – the featured attraction on its first four Friday nights – what Liverpool's Cavern Club had been to the Beatles. It was at UFO, says Hopkins, that 'the Floyd became everybody's favourite band in the underground culture, followed closely by the Soft Machine. They were like the Beatles and the Stones of alternative music.'

Joe Boyd later made equal use of such talents as Tomorrow (featuring future Barrett sideman Twink and Yes guitarist Steve Howe) and the Crazy World of Arthur Brown; and it was at UFO that Procol Harum played live for the second time ever on the day 'A Whiter Shade of Pale' was released, and returned a week later when the song was already number two. There was also an ever-revolving cast of poets, mimes and jugglers, along with conceptual theatre and free-form dance troupes like David Medalla's Exploding Galaxy. But it was the Floyd who were always considered the house band.

The dank, elongated cellar's woefully low ceiling and cramped stage were less than ideal in terms of both lighting and acoustics; the 120-decible reading of a Floyd UFO gig caused no less an authority than the chairman of the Royal Institute for the Deaf to warn that, 'It would certainly affect the hearing if this level of noise was heard regularly.' Nevertheless, says Peter Wynne Willson, 'UFO was where we all developed our ideas – the group musically, and me designing the lighting – because it was such a responsive situation. We used to put lighting all over the club. Russell Page and I would do one area, and Mark Boyle, who was extremely tasteful and artistic in his lighting, would do another.'

UFO's in-house lighting maestro, Boyle had been honing his craft since 1963 in the context of Jim Haynes's brand of avant-garde theatre; unlike Wynne Willson, he shrewdly furthered his own reputation and career by marketing his pyrotechnics as Art. (Not that he

48

was beyond such stunts as making bubbles rise out of the musicians'
flies.) Another corner of the club was illuminated by Jack Braceland,
who also ran one of Britain's leading nudist colonies.

Wynne Willson's own innovations included 'a group of four lights
for each member of the band. I made a thing that went round the
corner of Rick's organ to get his head and shoulders. There was one in
front of the drums, one each in front of Syd and Roger. Apart from
illuminating them, they would cast shadows up on the screen behind.
Where you've got a shadow of one spot, if you've got another playing
on the screen, then you'd get a coloured shadow. So you'd get these
coloured shadows of the band dancing on the screen – that was always
great. Especially because you had instant control of it, so you could
react to the music very nicely.

'We developed some really ludicrous polaroid effects, with a polar-
izer and analyzer in the projector, stretching polythene or latex
rubber. Tearing polythene in a particular way gave wonderful perspec-
tives running to infinity in gorgeous spectral colours. I used to put
endless receipts in to June for condoms, because they're very high
quality latex, which gave the very best effects in polaroid.'

One evening when the Floyd's van was stopped for a minor traffic
offence, the last thing the police expected to see was John Marsh with
an LP cover in his lap applying scissors to a heap of condoms. 'That's
just our roadie,' Wynne Willson demurred. 'He's cutting up johnnies,
but he's crazy.'[3]

Quite apart from all the aesthetic considerations, the light show
had a profound and permanent impact upon the Floyd's relationship
with their audience. Because the individual performers tended to
recede into (and be obscured by) the overall presentation, they were
as rarely recognized off-stage as on and thus were able to cultivate the
anonymity that was to remain a Floyd hallmark even after the group
had become world famous.

Like a smile from a veil, however, one individual presence did make
itself known amid the paisley swirl. 'Syd was recognized,' says Peter
Jenner. 'He was marked out almost instantly as a star. Everyone was in
love with him.'

It was at UFO that Pete Brown 'first saw Barrett doing "the act".
With the leaping around and the madness, and the kind of improvisation he was doing, my impression was that he was *inspired*. He would
constantly manage to get past his limitations and into areas that were
very, very interesting. Which none of the others could do. Quite
frankly, the rest of them were not even competent. Syd's songs were so

magical and ground-breaking. The whole thing was animated by those songs and his personality.

'Syd Barrett worked incredibly hard on stage. It might be overly poetic, but you could almost say that he appeared to exist and live in those light shows – a creature of the imagination. His movements were orchestrated to fit in with the lights, and he appeared to be a natural extension – the human element – to those melting images.'

'It was at UFO that everything started to gel', says Wynne Willson. 'There's no doubt that the music they played at UFO was the best they ever did. It's a shame there were no live recordings made there. Syd's improvisations would go on for extended periods, but would be absolutely immaculate.

'The music was wonderful and the audience rapport was total. UFO was an exceptional experience; everyone was rooting for the same direction and the same goals.'

Nick Mason, however, remembers the Floyd's UFO performances in a slightly more ambivalent light. 'It was almost a sort of punk thing – very free. It's funny when you're improvising and you're not particularly technically able; it's one thing if you're Charlie Parker, it's another thing if you're us. The ratio of good stuff to bad is not that great.

'In the very early Pink Floyd days in the clubs like UFO, there were people definitely prepared to go on the basis – perhaps because of the state they were in – that we were being great 80 per cent of the time rather than 20 per cent. But there was a hell of a lot of rubbish being played in order to get a few good ideas out.'

The discrepancy between those recollections of the UFO gigs ('They *were* great 80 per cent of the time,' insists Peter Jenner) may conceivably be traced back to the diverging attitudes and lifestyles within the Floyd camp at the time. Syd Barrett and Peter Wynne Willson *believed* in the miraculous new age arising all around them. Roger Waters and Nick Mason were content merely to provide the musical soundtrack, even as they increasingly set their sights on a broader-based pop success for the band, not that Barrett wasn't also initially attracted to the glamour of stardom.

As early as January 1967, Mason readily admitted that the psychedelic movement had 'taken place around us – not within us'.[4] Much as these words may also have applied to Waters, Barrett – whom Jenner has described as 'true Flower Power' – could hardly have been more unequivocal in his embrace of both the underground's ideals and its

50

excesses. One close associate from the period goes so far as to state that Waters and Mason actually 'represented exactly what Syd was rejecting. Even though they were now playing in a rock band, they were very pleased with themselves for having been architecture students, and for having followed that whole nice upper-middle-class script.'

By the beginning of 1967, LSD had come to rival cannabis as Barrett's drug of choice at Earlham Street. 'Syd was the only one of the group,' says Wynne Willson, 'who was part of the – these words sound absurdly pretentious now – consciousness-expanding experimental movement. Which isn't to say we didn't take acid for fun, but we were anticipating some *progress.*'

At first, the acid seemed to raise Barrett to even greater heights of inspiration and creativity. There were a few dodgy moments, such as when Lindsay faded into invisibility and Syd floated downstairs to collapse in Susie's arms in the hallway outside the loo. Or when the police arrived in search of a sometime tenant with a heroin habit and a criminal record: and Barrett – in an era when 'the fuzz' created instant paranoia even if a 'freak' *wasn't* tripping – appeared to lose all powers' of motion or speech as he fixed the men in blue with (in Susie's phrase) 'huge horror eyes'. Fortunately on this occasion another charming lady friend of Syd's named Carrie Anne stepped in to distract the police with small talk and tea.

In his self-published memoir *Rehearsal for the Year 2000: The Rebirth of Albion Free State*, their friend Alan Beam vividly describes a couple of the 'good trips' at Earlham Street. While Syd plays slide-guitar at ear-splitting levels, Peter solemnly intones Timothy Leary's Psychedelic Prayers and Susie (who had recently starred *au naturel* and daubed with bodypaint on the cover of *IT*) circulates postcard reproductions of William Blake's paintings. Everyone ends up clambering precariously up and down ladders to emblazon the walls with day-glo designs.

Though Susie calls this picture somewhat exaggerated and romanticized, Beam still fondly remembers No. 2 Earlham Street as 'my temple, my Mecca. I was eighteen, at Oxford, and pretty straight. Peter and Susie had been 'training' me for LSD with big joints. One day Syd put two drops of acid on my tongue and we all trooped off to the Albert Hall to listen to Handel's *Messiah*. After that, things were never the same.'

'We sat through *The Messiah* totally plastered out of our brains,' confirms Wynne Willson. 'I can't speak for anyone else's mental

51

experience, but *The Messiah* on acid was quite the most extraordinary thing I'd encountered.'

In January 1967, underground London finally came face to face with a high-level ambassador from its faraway sister wonderland of Haight-Ashbury. Chet Helms – the Avalon Ballroom's Texas-born acid-evangelist impresario – had crossed the Atlantic with visions of opening an English Avalon, to surpass his rival promoter Bill Graham's plan to establish a Fillmore East in New York. 'I had hair to my waist and a beard to my navel,' remembers Helms, 'and as the first principal player from the Haight-Ashbury that anybody there had ever met, I was immensely well received.'

After several days spent investigating the club potential of some catacomb-like World War II bomb shelters, Helms suddenly 'realized this was idiocy – that there was no way I was going to run a club 8,000 miles away from my home base. So I could relax and have a nice vacation.'

Shown the town by Miles and Hoppy, the legendary San Franciscan was uniquely equipped to compare the alternative London scene with its ostensible model. 'In the Haight-Ashbury at the time, we were all real *streety* people who had sort of come up the ranks,' says Helms. 'In England I was very impressed with the Indica Bookshop, which was so professional and so scholarly – yet was the centre of this whole orbit of underground London activity.

'UFO was pretty parallel to what was happening in the Haight – in the sense that your traditional rock and roll was run by a pretty hoody kind of criminal element, while the young rebellious politicos such as Hoppy and myself were creating their own alternative venue. The Pink Floyd were pretty much the house band, the way Big Brother and the Holding Company were for me. I remember feeling that our music was much more musical, probably because it had its roots in American R & B. They were more influenced by the avant-garde classical composers like Stockhausen. My experience of the Floyd was that it was atonal and amelodic – in large part, walls of sound and feedback-based space music. What was unique about them was they worked invariably with the light show; they were the only band in England at that time where that was part of the act.

'By '67, the light shows in San Francisco were pretty developed. It was pretty raw and undeveloped in England, though UFO was the best of what was there. It was fairly static compared to the sort of liquid projection stuff we were doing – depended more on traditional stage craft, coloured lights, gels over spotlights, that sort of thing.

'The only individual in the band I was aware of was Syd Barrett, though I didn't become as close to him as to, say, Miles or Hoppy. He seemed like a very bright, driven, improvisatory kind of guy, doing the same kind of thing I was.

'At least from my outside perception, there seemed to be little distinction between UFO and the Pink Floyd and *IT* magazine, for that matter. It was all the same circle of people who hung out together and smoked dope together.'

A journalist named Ann Sharply – who seemed 'very understanding and sympathetic for someone over thirty' – latched onto Helms early in his stay, proposing to write an underground London travelogue as seen through the eyes of the visiting American hippie, 'I really opened up to her, and because of who I was people were willing to take us into virtually any scene over there – and did.' Together they observed such events as an *IT*-sponsored Roundhouse fundraiser called Uncommon Market, featuring a record-setting 56-gallon jelly, which ended up splattered all over the customers 'because they were throwing it in a giant jello free-for-all'. Attending this bash, 'stoned out of their minds on acid', were two of the Beatles.

Helms recalls that Miss Sharpley's piece 'came out right before I left, with the double-banner headline LOST PSYCHEDELIC WEEKEND. She condensed three weeks of events into one weekend, which was a total distortion of the truth, and she slaughtered and decimated everyone but me in the article. She was fairly kind to me, but at the end she quoted me as essentially saying, "You think *this* is wild, you should see the way we do it back home!" I was trying to tell her that back home it wasn't as contrived; the happenings and stuff were a little more kind of natural.

'Anyway, I felt betrayed and horribly embarrassed for all the people I'd taken Ann Sharpley around to visit. Then UPI picked up on it, and misinterpreted the whole article to suggest I'd *promoted* all these events in England. So by the time the story was carried in the U.S. papers it had become "young, long-haired American promoter goes to England, knocks England off its ass, and returns triumphant!"'

Chapter 5

Have a Cigar

On 1 February 1967, the Pink Floyd at last officially 'went professional', shelving their academic careers to focus full-time on the band. 'Mind you,' bantered Nick Mason – who still thought he might return to college the following year – 'the best chance for an architect to find clients is in show business. I'm always on the lookout for someone who has half a million pounds to spare, and wants me to design him a house.'

The Floyd's number one priority was to put out a record. The original assumption had been that Joe Boyd would get the group a deal at Elektra, whose longtime folk/blues emphasis was altered with the signings of Love and the Doors in America. Boyd thought he had a mandate 'to come up with equivalents in England'.

He had already bought Elektra the Incredible String Band, which started out as a fairly traditional folk act. A subsequent dose of acid-fuelled fantasy and mysticism had transformed the Scottish duo into the underground icons of *The 5000 Spirits or the Layers of the Onion*. But Boyd – who became their manager as well as producer – proved mistaken in the assumption that his American boss Jac Holzman would welcome similarly progressive Brits like the Pink Floyd.

'He got more and more alarmed,' Boyd recalled, 'at my spending my time promoting groups instead of promoting Tom Paxton. He didn't want them. So virtually a year after I arrived at Elektra in London, Holzman and I had one of those "You can't fire me – I quit" conversations.'[1]

In the meantime, a hoary EMI executive named Beecher Stevens, having heard 'a lot of fuss about their music and lights and so on', had sniffed around All Saints Church, accompanied by his A & R man Norman Smith. Also an aspiring producer, Smith was best-known as a longtime engineer for the Beatles – whom Stevens, during his previous job at Decca, had deemed (to his subsequent regret and embarrassment) undeserving of a recording contract.

Now Stevens rated the Floyd 'weird but good', yet was given pause when 'one of the boys, and some of the people around them, seemed a bit strange'.[2] Whereupon Joe Boyd, operating as a free agent, persuaded Polydor Records to take on the band for an advance of about £1500, and founded his own Witchseason Productions in anticipation of the Floyd's imminent recording career.

Fate, however, intervened in the guise of a hungry pop-music broker named Bryan Morrison and his partner Tony Howard, in need of a hot new act for their faltering agency. Reduced to providing talent for the likes of the Architectural Association's Christmas dance, Morrison and Howard perked up when the college students spoke in glowing terms about the Pink Floyd (of which the pair had never heard) and refused to settle for anything but. Howard lost little time in tracking down the mysterious group and signing them up to the Bryan Morrison Agency for the customary 10 per cent of concert receipts.

Because the flashy and fast-talking 'Morrie' – who also managed the fading Pretty Things at the time – was the first seasoned Music Biz type to appear in their charmed circle, Peter Jenner and Andrew King eagerly sought his advice. He convinced them that they would be better off with a powerful giant like EMI than with Polydor, and that EMI would cough up a far larger advance than its small competitor if the Floyd could prove their worth with an independently recorded master that might be released as their debut single.

Accordingly, Joe Boyd steered the Floyd into Chelsea's Sound Techniques Studios to record 'Arnold Layne' – a catchy Barrett-penned fable about a kleptomaniac transvestite, which in the UFO musical director's sympathetic hands wound up sounding both bizarre *and* commercial. These late January sessions also yielded an early version of 'Interstellar Overdrive', and a proposed B-side hastily rewritten as 'Candy and a Currant Bun' after someone from the BBC took exception to the original title 'Let's Roll Another One'.

EMI's top brass were suitably impressed, and upped the ante to a then-considerable £5000. The Floyd and their managers were particularly pleased with the offer because, unusually for the time, it emphasized albums rather than singles. EMI's generosity, however, was contingent upon the band making yet another compromise, and agreeing henceforth to work exclusively with a staff producer at EMI's own Abbey Road studios.

This was par for the course with major record companies in those days: in light of the Floyd's association with certain dubious elements, moreover, Mr Stevens was determined that a sober-minded citizen –

specifically, Norman Smith – 'keep a firm hand on the sessions'. Thus was Joe Boyd rather unceremoniously dumped before the fruit of his labours – for which, to his further chagrin, he didn't receive a penny – had even hit the stands.

Upon its release on EMI's Columbia label on 11 March, the creepy yet seductive 'Arnold' drew both controversy and acclaim. *Melody Maker* hailed it as 'an amusing and colourful story about a guy who got himself put inside whilst learning of the birds and the bees . . . without a doubt, a very good disc. The Pink Floyd represent a new form of music to the English pop scene so let's hope the English are broadminded enough to accept it with open arms.'[3]

Oddly enough, those who weren't (and didn't) included the popular and supposedly hipper-than-thou pirate station, Radio London, which slapped the 'smutty' platter with a ban. 'If we can't write and sing songs about various forms of human predicament,' responded Roger Waters, 'then we might as well not be in the business.' Rick Wright suggested that 'the record was banned, not because of the lyrics – because there's nothing there you can really object to – but because they're against us as a group and against what we stand for.' The song's 21-year-old author, for his part, said, 'Arnold Layne just happens to dig dressing up in women's clothing; a lot of people do, so let's face up to reality!'[4]

That was no mere hyperbole on Barrett's part. The peculiarly English fascination with cross-dressing, stoked both by the culture's sexual repressiveness and its relish for eccentricity, was manifested in at least two of the era's top groups. The Rolling Stones had recently minced in full drag on the cover of their single 'Have You Seen Your Mother Baby Standing in the Shadow?' and three years after 'Arnold Layne', the similarly inclined 'Lola' would give the Kinks one of their biggest-ever hits.

According to Waters, 'Arnold Layne' and his 'strange hobby' were actually inspired by a real-life episode from Roger and Syd's Cambridge youth; after both their widowed mothers took in lodgers from a nearby women's college, the neighbourhood was scandalized by the continuing disappearance of bras and underwear from the ladies' washing lines. Syd's tightly plotted reconstruction adds a fictitious twist that even a Society for the Suppression of Vice could endorse: The protagonist (*'a nasty sort of person'*) is cast behind bars, and the song ends with the words, chorused in tones of ominous finality, *'Arnold Layne, don't do it again!'*

A little controversy, of course, has never harmed sales; the music and production, moreover, did not stint on good old-fashioned pop hooks. A decade later, Nick Mason said 'Arnold Layne' was expressly devised to establish the Floyd as 'a hit parade band . . . We were interested in the business of being in rock and roll and being a pop group: SUCCESSFUL – MONEY – CARS – that sort of thing. Good living. I mean, that's the reason most people get involved in rock music, because they want that sort of success. If you don't, you get involved in something else.'[5]

Making good on his promise of 'one hundred per cent promotion', Beecher Stevens and his colleagues Ron White and Roy Featherstone introduced the Pink Floyd to the overground media at an April Fool's Day reception at EMI House in Manchester Square. In a press release, the record company characterized its latest signing as 'musical spokesmen for a new movement which involves experimentation in all the arts' with the reassuring disclaimer that 'the Pink Floyd does not know what people mean by psychedelic pop and are not trying to create hallucinatory effects on their audiences'. (To which John Hopkins retorted in *IT*: 'Actually I think I *prefer* it when the Floyd give me hallucinations.')

'Arnold Layne' did crack the British Top Twenty – just – which was actually a better showing than all but two of the Floyd's singles were to achieve throughout the rest of the band's illustrious career. Yet the record rose far higher in the hearts and heads of underground London, and by dint of endless playings became a virtual anthem at clubs like UFO.

'"Arnold Layne" was probably the first ever pop hit,' declares Pete Brown, 'that dealt in an English accent with English cultural obsessions and English fetishes. There had never been anything quite like it; everyone had been behaving like Americans. Previous to that, I was completely blues. That was just when I started writing for Cream, so it came at a very good time for me. Things like "White Room" wouldn't have happened without Syd.'

The Floyd, as it happens, were similarly affected by Brown's colleagues Eric Clapton, Jack Bruce, and Ginger Baker. 'It was very clearly Cream,' says Nick Mason, 'who were the one band that made me really think, "*that's* what I want to do." The idea that you could have a band that actually was based on music, that sort of power music – rather than a band that was based on whether they looked lovable and had nice Beatle jackets. Although even the Stones were very glamorous, in their own way, Cream was a whole new approach to what was possible. That, for me, was a real turning point.'

Roger Waters also listed Cream (along with the Who, Buffalo Springfield, the Band, and, of course, the Rolling Stones) as one of the five bands he liked to fantasize having played in, had he not been a Floyd, 'Because they had been such a turn-on when I saw them as a kid: the curtains parted and there was a big bank of Marshall gear and it was an all-enveloping, loud, powerful bluesy experience.'[6]

The Pink Floyd were now well on their way; not only did they have a record out, their music was even featured in a movie. Peter Whitehead's trendy documentary *Tonite Let's All Make Love in London* included truncated snippets of 'Interstellar Overdrive' – one performed on-camera by the Floyd, and another used as background music for Allen Ginsberg's recitation of the poem from which the director took his film title.

The EMI advance, meanwhile, enabled Blackhill to acquire proper office space in a shopfront below Andrew King's flat in Alexander Street, after nearly a year of Peter Jenner always having his sitting room full of the band's equipment. By this time, the young lecturer had also finally agreed to take a 'leave of absence' from the London School of Economics, where Jenner's rapport with student revolutionaries had not endeared him to his senior colleagues.

Were it not for the tireless efforts and unwavering devotion of Jenner and King, many of the group's early associates agree, the Pink Floyd might never have taken off as they did. Yet Roger Waters was already betraying a certain impatience with the duo – especially with the more nervous and intense King. This was dramatized that spring, on the Floyd's first European tour, when Andrew managed to drop the contents of his pocket into a Copenhagen drain while fumbling for his keys, and Roger turned on him, sneering 'We can't have a manager who throws our money down the drain, now, can we?'

In the wake of 'Arnold Layne', Blackhill and the Floyd nonetheless acquired their first Rolls. No matter that the limousine was neither new nor, strictly speaking, a Rolls *Royce*: it was, June Bolan says, 'a conglomerate – half a Rolls Royce and half a Bentley. But you couldn't see where the joins were. It was very beautiful, and incredibly grand for the time.'

With additional purchases in the way of musical and lighting equipment, the £5000 advance was soon but a pleasant memory. Even so, the incurably optimistic Peter Jenner, who had adopted as his company's slogan STRAIGHT TO HEAVEN IN '67, was sure there would be plenty more just over the horizon.

The first Pink Floyd record hit just when alternative London was at its zenith. There was a real sense of community, and of expectation. The wider British music scene was feeling the heat of first albums by Cream and the Jimi Hendrix Experience, and the Beatles had just made the new psychic wavelength their own with the astonishing double-headed single 'Penny Lane' and 'Strawberry Fields Forever' – a milestone on the way to *Sergeant Pepper*. Yet the subculture (*Tonite Let's All Make Love in London* notwithstanding) hadn't yet become overly commercialized, and the authorities were only beginning to strike back.

'It was a very brief but rather beautiful moment a bit overtaken by events,' reminisces artist and dancer David Medalla. 'London was a cosmopolitan town in the true sense. Working-class, middle-class, aristocratic people came from all over England and got to meet people of different backgrounds. You could just crash anywhere, there was always food, and buses were cheap. If you needed a bit of money you'd set up a stall in Portobello Road. It was much easier to survive then than now; things have become more ordered, more organized. And there was this kind of continuous euphoria.

'The sexual experimentation was very interesting. Most of the people came from rather restricted backgrounds. Gays found that they were gay, or bisexual. By then antibiotics and contraceptives had settled into the normal routine of things, and the idea of getting married to have sex was transcended.

'There was also a group of rich people like Tara Brown and Robert Fraser, who were prepared to spend their money on the arts. They not only gave lovely parties, but helped create the idea that there was almost total freedom. I suppose that was really an illusion, that the freedom only existed for the few who wanted to be free.

'There were bookshops like Indica, where you could attend poetry readings and events, and meet actual writers like Allen Ginsberg. There was the whole discovery of the East; the Hare Krishna chanters hadn't become the joke they've become since.

'We used to gang together to start something like the London Film Co-op, because nobody had enough money to buy an editing machine. Now young film-makers can make films in their own homes; they don't have to meet anyone else. Young musicians have sixteen-track taperecorders at home, with drum machines and everything. They don't have to have a concert outside, they can press their own records. The same with visual artists and writers. It's liberating in one sense, but it's also alienating. The social aspect is totally gone; you don't have the feedback.

'Also the young generation was not so blasé then about technology. You'd see that with the Pink Floyd and their music; they'd experiment with new types of sound, with video. There was a real belief that these things could liberate the consciousness of people.

'On the whole, what we accomplished in the sixties was more positive than, say, in the seventies – which was more a cry of pain that's much more *serious*. But I prefer an ecstatic orgasm to a lot of angst.'

Chapter 6

Games for May

Many of the 'underground' luminaries interviewed for this book readily confess that their memories of the year 1967 are peculiarly . . . well, *blurred*. When it comes to the '14-Hour Technicolour Dream' at the Alexandra Palace on 29 April – the event which, as much as any, launched alternative London into the public domain – one is confronted with reminiscences of particularly marvellous diversity. A clue may be gleaned from Peter Jenner's estimate that 'at least half of the audience were doing acid' – along with a similar quota of performers, and even esteemed managers such as himself.

The grandiose notion of an all-night event in that Victorian exhibition hall had been conceived by – who else? – Miles, Jim Haynes, and John Hopkins (to whom Miles awards '99 per cent of the credit' for making it happen). The ostensible purpose this time was to raise desperately needed cash for *International Times* in the aftermath of a banana republic-style police raid. On 9 March the multi-coloured journal's subscription lists, unsold issues, uncashed cheques, and even the staff's personal address books (not to mention the contents of the ashtrays) had all been impounded, only to be returned without apology three months later, after the authorities could find no legal pretext for pressing charges.

In the meantime, the staff defiantly organized the Technicolour Dream, and continued to publish. The very next issue of *IT* contained editor Tom McGrath's ringing declaration of underground principles, which concluded with the words:

> The new movement is slowly, carelessly, constructing an alternative society. It is international, interracial, equisexual, with ease. It operates on different conceptions of time and space. The world of the future may have no clocks.

The Pink Floyd, despite having only one single out, were given the singular honour of closing the 41-act benefit. Chart-topping fellow

61

travellers like John Lennon and Paul McCartney, for their part, covered some of the initial costs. 'They were sort of putting back what they'd taken out,' says Hopkins. 'Not that they'd taken anything out of *us*, but everybody helped in some way.' Michael McInnerney, meanwhile, provided distinctive rainbow posters, and Michael X and his Black Power brigade the security. In the hours before the show, Miles wrote, 'Rockets burst over London in an underground bat-signal of a special event.' And, he continued, 'ten thousand people came, an army in tatty old lace and velvet, beads and bells, stoned out of their minds.'[1]

'It was a really freaky evening,' says David Medalla, whose Exploding Galaxy was one of the opening attractions. 'It began way before the fourteen hours because we were all congregating at Alexandra Palace. Hundreds of people, I don't know where they came from. It showed that the underground was a real underground, because we had no publicity.

'When I arrived there, Mike McInnerney said, "We've got to really programme this because the BBC are filming the whole thing and are out to show a lot of irresponsible hippies taking drugs and practising free love." So there was a bit of tension and inhibition. I had to put on a pair of underpants, cause they said they're not going to film you if you take off all your clothes. At that time I was quite good-looking, and I like dancing naked with body painting and things like that.

'Yoko Ono was going to do an event that she'd done for the "Destruction in Art" symposium, where she gives a pair of scissors to the audience, who cut away her kimono. I said to her husband Tony Cox, "I don't think this is the right place to do it with 10,000 screaming people, because somebody might just stab Yoko." She became absolutely paranoid – and ended up substituting a more suitable concept-piece.'

Ambling through the crowd, a sheepskin-swathed John Lennon, yet to displace Tony as the recipient of Yoko's affections, peered at the proceedings through granny glasses and his own lysergic daze. Sideshows included stalls selling incense and hippie crafts, and a fibreglass igloo where banana-peel joints were freely distributed in keeping with Donovan's dictum on 'Mellow Yellow' ("*electrical bana-na's gonna be a sudden craze*"). And at the very centre of the vast indoor fairground, laughing flower children could reclaim their lost innocence upon a helter skelter slide.

The music emanated from two stages, one at each end of the Palace – at times simultaneously – as enormous lighting towers projected films upon the bedsheet-draped walls. Never mind that these makeshift screens tended to billow in the breeze, making the cinematic action difficult to follow, or that the power was insufficient to provide the amount of juice to which most of the show's acid rockers were accustomed. Few of the bands – let alone 'fringe' types like Medalla, Yoko Ono, and future Floyd collaborator Ron Geesin – had ever been provided with a platform on this scale; and anyway, the sense of event was paramount.

Not that everyone was entranced. David Jenkins (now features editor of *Tatler*) has called it 'a bizarrely yawn-making event', noting that 'the full horror of how boring it was' struck around midnight with the realization that London's public transport had shut down, and that he and his fellow sceptics were trapped in the Technicolour Dream until dawn.[2]

David Medalla, however, insists (the ban on nudity notwithstanding), 'I'm not just being nostalgic when I say the event was a moment of total freedom.' And though it signally failed in its objective to raise funds for the embattled *IT* – thanks to the demands of some performers, a shady promoter or two, and his own cavalier attitude towards money – John Hopkins still maintains that the Technicolour Dream was 'really amazing by anybody's standards. All the musicians were really great.'

These included such UFO regulars as Tomorrow, Alex Harvey, the Soft Machine, and an Arthur Brown garbed in helmet, visor, and a saffron robe, who appeared to set himself afire at the climax of his performance. Miles's own account of the event ends on this lyrical note:

> Then there was a movement through the crowd and everyone turned to look at the huge east windows. They were glowing with the first faint approaches of dawn. At this magic moment of frozen time the Pink Floyd came on.
>
> Their music was eerie, solemn, and calming. After a whole night of frolicking and festivities and acid came the celebration of the dawn . . . Syd's eyes blazed as his notes soared up into the strengthening light. As the dawn was reflected in his famous mirror-disc Telecaster . . .[3]

It hardly seemed to matter that the Floyd themselves – who had rushed back from Europe for the occasion that very evening – were less than thrilled with their performance.

The Floyd's next major appearance, at Queen Elizabeth Hall on 12 May, was incontestably spectacular from the standpoint of almost everyone involved. Everyone, that is, but the posh South Bank venue's managers, who had little idea what they were letting themselves in for when they booked the multi-media performance billed as, 'GAMES FOR MAY: Space-age relaxation for the climax of spring – electronic compositions, colour and image projections, girls, and THE PINK FLOYD.'

'Andrew King was no idiot,' says Susie Wynne Willson. 'He was well into the idea of marketing it as an Art. He was thinking in terms of a high-profile kind of set-up. The newspapers started taking it seriously then, because it was the *South Bank* – unheard-of at the time for pop groups.' Equally unheard-of for a pop group (let alone one with so slim a discography), the Pink Floyd were to take the stage for the full two hours, without any warm-up act.

Games for May was presented by Christopher Hunt, a promoter whose speciality was classical chamber music. But the broadminded Hunt had four months earlier, at the urging of Sumi Jenner, who worked for him at the time, sponsored a multi-media event featuring the Floyd at London's Commonwealth Institute, and he liked what he saw and heard. It was Hunt who issued the tantalizing press release:

> The Floyd intend this concert to be a musical and visual exploration – not only for themselves, but for the audience too. New music has been written and will be given for the first time, including some specially prepared four-way stereo tapes. Visually, the lights men of the group have prepared an entirely bigger-than-ever-before show.

The 'four-way stereo' was both a true Floyd innovation, and one that the band would develop to stunning effect in the years to come. It had started out as an experiment at one of their first four-track Abbey Road recording sessions, when the boys got producer Norman Smith to add two extra speakers to the usual stereophonic pair. They were so pleased with the result that they adopted 'sound in the round' – 'Whereby,' explained Roger Waters, 'the sounds travel round the hall in a sort of circle, giving the audience an eerie effect of being absolutely surrounded by this music' – as an intrinsic part of the live Pink Floyd experience. The speakers at the back of the auditorium were largely used for the prerecorded sound effects (compiled mostly by Waters) – wind, waves, footsteps, birdsong, and the like – that the group was also beginning to incorporate into their performances.

At Queen Elizabeth Hall, the Floyd had yet to work out all the acoustic subtleties, and their rudimentary quad system had the desired effect only on a well-placed handful of ticket-holders. (It was also stolen after the show.) But there was plenty else to keep the audience enthralled, beginning with the artificial sunrise that Peter Wynne Willson cast in shades of deepest red upon the screen blanketing the back of the stage area. His liquid light show was augmented by 35 mm films and thousands of cascading soap bubbles. One of the roadies, decked out as an Admiral of the Fleet, showered daffodils upon the concertgoers, who were also treated to the sight of Roger Waters hurling potatoes at a huge gong, and the sound of Nick Mason carving up wood with an amplified saw.

'We just took a lot of props on stage with us and improvised . . . but we found this to be extremely difficult,' Mason subsequently admitted. 'I think it's important to know what you're going to do, to a certain extent anyway; we always like to be in control of the situation . . . But [Games for May] was the first of its kind and we, personally, learnt a lot from it.'[4]

In accordance with Jenner and King's Games plan, the event was widely covered by the 'better' papers, even getting a mention in the staid *Financial Times*:

The audience which filled the hall was beautiful, if strangely subdued, and to enjoy them was alone worth the price of a ticket. But when you add in the irrepressible Pink Floyd and a free authentic daffodil to take home, your cup of experience overflows.

International Times, meanwhile, hailed Games for May as 'a genuine twentieth-century chamber music concert', whose 'second half moved right into the hall and into the realm of . . . pure electronic music . . . It was good to see the strength of a hip show holding its own in such a museumlike and square environment.' A buoyant Syd Barrett declared (quite clairvoyantly insofar as the Floyd were concerned): 'In the future, groups are going to have to offer more than a pop show. They are going to have to offer a well-presented theatre show.'

The Queen Elizabeth Hall's management, however, was mortified by the rings that the bubbles had imprinted upon its leather seats, and by the daffodil petals that had been ground into its carpets, and banned the Pink Floyd from ever playing there again. 'It seems,' shrugged Roger, 'we contravened a regulation.'

The promised 'new material' at Queen Elizabeth Hall included a relatively infectious number called 'Games for May'. Though Norman Smith had already taped such tuneful Barrett compositions as 'The Gnome' and 'The Scarecrow' at Abbey Road, both he and the Floyd's managers instantly recognized the new ditty as the most suitable follow-up to 'Arnold Layne'. Syd then changed his title to 'See Emily Play'.

Barrett later put forth the story that 'Emily' had materialized whole clothed in a dream – à la Coleridge's 'Kubla Khan' – after he dozed off in the woods. Be that as it may, Pete Brown recalls that the lyric was directed at a flesh-and-blood Emily well-known to the UFO crowd – the 'psychedelic school girl' daughter of the aristocratic author Lord Kennet (aka Wayland Young of *Eros Denied* fame). And so Arnold the sex fetishist made way for Emily the flower child . . .

Notwithstanding Smith having handpicked the Floyd as the vehicle 'with which I could make my name as a producer' – much as his old boss George Martin had done with the Beatles – the prospect of coaxing saleable product out of these fabled undergrounders made 'Normal' (as the Fab Four had nicknamed him) by own account 'very nervous and apprehensive'.[5] So much so, in fact, that he resorted to moving the 'Emily' sessions on May 18 back to Sound Techniques Studios, where 'Arnold Layne' had been recorded, in a conscious effort to reconstruct Joe Boyd's magic formula on the new single.

Boyd, of course, found that bitterly ironic, but Peter Jenner has suggested that over the long haul, 'Joe might have let them become more indulgent, because he didn't have the age and experience at that time. There was enough madness flying around, and the sanity and the boringness of Norman helped insure that the Floyd made hits. Which was vital. If the Floyd hadn't had a hit they would never have got through the difficult times that they went into.'[6]

'See Emily Play' was, indeed, a hit, even if its candy-coated psyche-delic pop – and treacly lines like *'float on a river forever and ever'* – have not aged nearly so well as the more tart and cohesive 'Arnold Layne'. Radio London, as if atoning for its 'Arnold' gaffe, actually listed 'Emily' at number one almost instantly. And so the Pink Floyd, willy nilly, became pop stars.

There was, however, at least one bad omen. David Gilmour, briefly back from Europe to buy replacements for Joker's Wild stolen equipment, dropped by Sound Techniques to visit Syd during the 'Emily' sessions. He was thoroughly nonplussed when his old chum 'just looked straight through me, barely acknowledged that I was there. Very weird . . .'

'See Emily Play' was recorded midway through the sessions for the first Pink Floyd LP, which was completed in July 1968 and released in early August. Over twenty years and some dozen albums later, Rick Wright still cites it as one of his two or three favourite Floyd records. (As does David Gilmour, who wasn't even on it.) 'I love listening to it, just to listen to Syd's songs,' says Wright. 'It's sad in a way as well, because it reminds me of what might have been. I think he could have easily been one of the finest songwriters today.'

Barrett's photographer friend Mick Rock, on the other hand, now feels the album could only have been a one-off: 'What else could he have done after that? He'd already defined it all. There's nothing ever been done on God's earth like that – that's *Art*.'

The Piper at the Gates of Dawn – originally the title of the seventh chapter in Kenneth Grahame's children's classic *The Wind in the Willows* (a Barrett favourite) – was a remarkable achievement by any standard. It is also the work on which Syd's mythic reputation is almost entirely based and one that provided many of the blueprints for the albums that his colleagues were subsequently to make in his absence.

Piper does include one Roger Waters composition; less a song than a riff, the strident 'Take Up Thy Stethoscope and Walk' nonetheless demonstrates how far removed were the roots of his muse from Barrett's. The two instrumental space jams – 'Interstellar Overdrive' and 'Pow R Toch H' – are credited to the entire group, with the latter (if one looks beyond the primitive four-track recording techniques and the trebly tone of Syd's guitar) containing passages that could have fitted seamlessly into the Floyd's post-Barrett 1970s blockbusters. And throughout the album, much of the band's instrumental sound is defined by the 'Eastern' modal improvisations of Wright's reverb-drenched Farfisa organ.

Yet *Piper* was, as June Bolan says, 'very much Syd's baby – and such a wonderful baby.' Throughout the making of the album, according to Andrew King, Barrett 'was 100 per cent creative, and very hard on himself. He wouldn't do anything unless he thought he was doing it in an artistic way.' His distinctive flair extended even to the normally humdrum mixing process, when Syd 'would throw the levers on the boards up and down apparently at random, making pretty pictures with his hands.'[7] (The only *Piper* mix that the Floyd participated in and authorized, incidentally, was the mono version.)

Even when stripped of such gimmickry, Syd's playing is highly innovative and expressive, not to mention unpredictable. Melodic solos abruptly give way to harsh dissonance, and Dylanesque strumming to an almost jazzlike improvisation wherein key and time signatures are all but forgotten. Barrett was among the first rock guitarists to experiment with the wah-wah pedal and echo box, and – perhaps most remarkably – transformed the slide guitar (previously associated largely with the blues of the Mississippi Delta) into a fixture of the Floyd's thoroughly English dreamscapes.

But it is the songs themselves that truly shine. While easy to pigeonhole as stoned English whimsy – which many indeed are (e.g. *'sitting on a unicorn . . . swimming through the starlit sky . . . hey-ho! here we go, ever so high!'* from 'Flamingo') – they are also disarmingly ingenuous, infectiously melodic, and utterly original. Few other songwriters of that era, for instance, would have thought to frame their magical mystery tours in the context of a child imploring his mum to read another chapter of his bedtime fairytale, as Syd does on 'Mathilda Mother', in which a chorus of *'You only have to read the lines as scribbly black, and everything shines!'* will usher in a new verse sparkling with fantastic imagery of magic kings, tolling bells, and hordes of 'misty riders'. At the same time, *Piper* is refreshingly free of the usual rock and roll cliches relating to sex and love; indeed, Syd scarcely touches upon these topics at all.

Few successful sixties songsmiths, moreover, made less use than Barrett of traditional blues or pop formulae, and his song structures are often startlingly fragmented. Often, too, he would slyly undermine a lyric's ostensible message with musical effects suggesting something else entirely, as in 'Lucifer Sam', where menacing wah-wah and feedback give a spooky twist to an otherwise innocuous ode to a Siamese cat. Yet there is no shortage of 'hooks' in his compositions, even if these are apt to turn up in the most unexpected places.

Many of *Piper*'s selections were clearly shaped by editing (you can almost hear the scissors snip when the instrumental revery in 'Matilda Mother' metamorphoses into a concluding verse) – no mean achievement when dealing with Barrett. As Norman Smith has related, 'It was a pretty difficult job actually with Syd, because I think Syd used music . . . [as] a statement being made at a given time. That meant that if you came back five minutes later to do another take, you probably wouldn't get the same performance. You probably wouldn't get the same *tune*.'[8]

No editing, however, was required for the 'Interstellar Overdrive' track, which comprised two uninterrupted readings of the piece, one dubbed directly atop the other.

Yet unlike his later work, *Piper* captures Barrett in full command of his creative powers. Only the last song, 'Bike' seems to teeter on the edge of psychosis with its non sequiturs about a 'joke' of a cloak:

> *There's a tear up the front, it's red and black.*
> *I've had it for months.*

At the end, the listener is invited into Syd's 'other room' and all hell breaks loose. On one level, his collage – barrage! – of clockwork machinery also foreshadows the latter-day Floyd, specifically 'Time', but with the difference that here the sound effects bear no discernable relation to the rest of the song's content, and thus sound all the more diabolical and demented.

As much of *Piper* demonstrates, the Floyd got maximum mileage out of the limited studio facilities then available to them. 'Astronomy Dominé' (on which Peter Jenner can be heard reeling off the names of stars and galaxies through a megaphone) shows the band already using studio effects such as echo virtually as another instrument. Much of the credit in this regard is due Norman Smith – and, indirectly, George Martin and the Beatles, who were then concocting *Sergeant Pepper* at the same Abbey Road address, and for who Smith had engineered every album up to *Rubber Soul*. *Piper* abounds with studio wizardry borrowed from the Fab Four's bag of tricks, most notably the artificial double tracking of the vocals, which was applied to Barrett's even more liberally than it had been to Lennon's and McCartney's, and which contributed in no small measure to their otherworldly textures. Smith also coaxed the same distinctive thud from Nick Mason's snare drums that he and Martin had with Ringo Starr's, by the same distinctive method of covering them with tea towels.

The Smith and Abbey Road connections were but the first of many respects in which the two quartets' careers overlapped or paralleled one another. These ranged from numerous Beatles references within the Floyd's music to striking similarities in the circumstances whereby EMI's two bestselling groups broke up – even unto the domineering bass-player battling his three former colleagues in court. And, of course, *Piper* was to draw frequent comparison with *Pepper* in the wake of its release and ascendancy on the British LP charts, where it got to number six.

The two camps were formally introduced towards the end of April, when Miles was hanging out with Paul McCartney at Abbey Road during one of the final *Pepper* sessions. Told by an engineer that the Pink Floyd were working in the next studio, Miles mentioned it to Paul who proposed that they stop by to say hello. George Harrison and Ringo also tagged along.

'It was really extraordinary because the Floyd were so naive,' Miles recalls. 'They were saying, "Can you hear me?" because of the sound-proof glass, not realizing that the mikes were on. It was complete innocence, very touching really. And Paul was patting them on the back, saying they were great and were going to do fine. He wasn't being patronizing: it was almost like the Beatles passing on the mantle – at least some of it – and acknowledging the existence of a new generation of music.

'In my discussions with him, McCartney had always been convinced that there would be a new synthesis of electronic music and studio techniques and rock and roll. He didn't see the Beatles as being quite the vehicle for that. But the Pink Floyd, he thought, were the very stuff that we'd been talking about.'

'I'm sure the Beatles were copying what we were doing,' adds Peter Jenner. 'Just as we were copying what we were hearing down the corridor!'

When the Floyd received an advance copy of *Sergeant Pepper* from EMI, it was cause for a riotous celebration at Jenner's house on Edbrooke Road. As the Beatles' psychedelic masterpiece was played over and over, the joints were smoked as fast as the multi-talented June could conjure them. Though she never herself indulged, preferring to 'feel in control', nobody could roll those joints like June.

For the Pink Floyd, however, the party that much of the rest of the turned-on tuned-in world would remember as the Summer of Love was apparently doomed to end almost before it had begun. The night after *Sergeant Pepper*'s release, on June 2, the Floyd returned to UFO for the first time in two months. ('MY WATCH STOPS. MY RADIO IS

SILENT . . . BUT WHAT DO I CARE . . . at UFO?' the ad in *IT*
beckoned.)

Unsurprisingly, in light of all that had happened since their last
performance there, the club was as packed as it had ever been, with
the likes of Jimi Hendrix, Pete Townshend, and a flock of Yardbirds
and Animals joining a mob of eager new fans, would-be hippies, and
plain old tourists. Yet the Floyd were obliged to use the same entrance
as everyone else, before fighting their way through the crowd to their
dressing room.

On their way in, they passed Joe Boyd (who was still seething from
his ouster as their producer but had never held it against the boys
themselves). Nine years later, he was to recreate the scene in a
conversation with Miles: 'It was very crushed, so it was like faces two
inches from your nose. They all came by – "Hi, Joe!" "How are you?"
"Great!" I greeted them all as they came through, and the last one was
Syd.

'And the great thing with Syd was that he had a twinkle in his eye;
he was a real eye-twinkler. He had this impish look about him, this
mischievous grin.

'And he came by, and I said, "Hi, Syd!" And he just kind of looked
at me. I looked right in his eye and there was no twinkle. No glint. It
was like somebody had pulled the blinds – you know, *nobody home.*'[9]

The next issue of *IT* charged that the Floyd 'played like bums' that
night. Only in retrospect did it become apparent that Syd Barrett was
beginning to crack.

For a number of other prominent underground Londoners, the
Summer of Love turned out more like the Season of the Witch, to
borrow a phrase from Donovan, who was among those on the receiving end of an intensifying crackdown by the Powers That Be. This was
certainly true for UFO and *IT* founder John Hopkins, who marked
Sergeant Pepper's release with his first night in jail.

'The English system *works,*' he says. 'If you're putting yourself
about, making a lot of noise against the system or the establishment,
they'll get you on something.' They got Hoppy on pot, and threw the
book at him: nine months. 'I was very young and naive. I didn't
understand that if you stand up in public, they didn't like it. I wasn't
very careful. It was like walking into a brick wall with my eyes shut. If
I had been a little more hip, I wouldn't have gone down.'

Hopkins's remarkably philosophical attitude notwithstanding, his
incarceration deprived underground London of one of its foremost

catalysts and free spirits; without Hoppy, things were never quite the same. When he finally emerged from jail, moreover, the old spark appeared to have been crushed out of him, and he seemed virtually a broken man.

The long arm of the law also removed from the UFO stage the Soft Machine's Australian electronics wizard Daevid Allen. According to Pete Brown, 'The authorities knew the whole scene was kind of drug-orientated, so when he went to Paris they wouldn't let Dave Allen back in the country. That's why the Floyd took the lead – because the Soft Machine couldn't work anymore.'

The most notorious bust of 1967 involved Mick Jagger and Keith Richards of the Rolling Stones, whose rebellious and sexually charged image, always a thorn in the authorities' side, had lately acquired a psychedelic dimension. The Stones had been targeted by the sensationalist *News of the World* after Jagger served the tabloid with a libel writ following its 'exposé' of his alleged drug escapades. As it happens, the story *did* contain some kernel of truth; only the Stone in question was the less discreet Brian Jones, whom the reporter had mistaken for Jagger.

In a preemptive strike, the powerfully connected *News of the World* (which later asserted that providing 'information to the police . . . was our plain duty') helped arrange a raid on a pot party in Richards' home, at which Jagger was present. All that the Drugs Squad could pin on Mick were four pep pills for which he lacked a prescription; but even after his doctor testified on his behalf the Stones' singer was sentenced to three months in jail. Richards got a year and Jones was subjected to a separate series of arrests and trials that were literally to kill him.

The sentences were so brutal, and the violations of the defendants' civil liberties so egregious, that even much of the establishment was appalled; *The Times* protested with a famous editorial headlined '*Who breaks a butterfly upon a wheel?*' The two Stones were freed after serving only three days, during which they briefly renewed their acquaintance with John Hopkins. 'The people you meet,' he quips, 'in the strangest places . . .'

In the meantime, Hoppy's former colleagues at UFO had organized a protest march on the *News of the World* to focus attention on its role in framing the Stones. Joe Boyd reminisced that, following an early set by Tomorrow, 'The whole club virtually cleared out and we all went down and picketed the *News of the World*, and then came back at like four a.m.'

72

When Tomorrow reclaimed the stage, 'The place was just jammed, it had never been that full. It was five o'clock in the morning, and you couldn't move! The atmosphere was incredible because . . . they'd turned the police dogs loose on a couple of people, and the whole thing had been really exciting. And Twink ended up crawling through the audience with a microphone on a long lead, chanting "Revolution! Revolution! Revolution!" and Steve Howe was playing some amazing guitar feedback riff . . . Very stirring stuff.'[10]

The *News of the World* did not take such provocations lying down, and retaliated with a series of 'Shock Probe' articles about UFO itself which, from the standpoint of the reactionary scandal sheet, would have provided an irresistible target in any case. The 'hidden dangers' thereby brought to light for millions of clucking readers included 'frenzied music', 'flower motifs', 'oblivious faces', 'fanatical members of the cult [who] eat only macrobiotic food', and 'weirdly dressed . . . men dancing with men, girls dancing with girls'. These reprehensible characters, it almost went without saying, indulged in 'Free Love – sex for sex's sake with whoever takes their fancy'. Not to mention drugs . . .

One irony in all this was that UFO had become considerably less wild and freewheeling since Hopkins's imprisonment left the club under the direction of the relatively business-minded Boyd. As UFO lights man Mark Boyle recalled, 'Hoppy had been running it largely for love, and also to help finance *International Times*. Joe ran it for profit.'[11] This is an assessment with which Boyd does not argue.

Nonetheless, the muckracking publicity had an instant effect on the police stationed down the road, who were almost by definition *News of the World* readers. Up to then, they had treated the underground mecca in their midst more or less with benign neglect, greased by the whisky that the venue's genial Irish owner provided by the caseload at Christmastime. But when they warned him that firm measures would now have to be enacted should this den of vice continue to operate with impunity, he took the hint and summarily terminated UFO's lease at 31 Tottenham Court Road.

Boyd and Miles attempted to perpetuate the Friday night tradition in the far larger and more impersonal setting of the Roundhouse. But despite a couple of performances by the Pink Floyd, the revamped club with its swelling crowds and the bouncers hired to keep them in line (not to mention the requirement that one's hand now had to be stamped at the door!) was barely recognizable to old-timers as UFO. What's more, says Miles, 'The Roundhouse's rent was gigantic, and groups like the Move and even Arthur Brown started to charge huge amounts of money. Some nights the thing only made about sixty quid profit. So in the end we stopped it.'

Thus did the nerve-centre of alternative London die: done in on the one hand by its own musical standardbearers' growing popularity and commercial clout and on the other by the rigid hostility of politicians, the police, and Fleet Street.

To many, a sixties underground without pot and acid is a contradiction in terms, but Pete Brown was among the few to identify such substances as its Achilles heel. Not only did their illegality provide the authorities with a pretext to mobilize the full force of the law against the John Hopkinses (and, ultimately, the John Lennons); the drugs also dissipated their users' push to effect fundamental, permanent changes in the larger culture. 'Everyone should have been going, "Give us this! Give us that! Let's change society!" ' laments Brown. 'Instead, it was, "Yeah, man . . . change society . . . wow." And the police would come, and they'd say, "Have a flower, man . . . take me away." I wanted to see more *resistance*.'

And so the cutting edge of the underground was blunted, even as its more surface trappings – the long hair, the clothes, the less threatening aspects of the music – were taken up by, and increasingly sanctioned among the 'overground' masses until those too could be discarded as the mere trends to which they had been largely reduced. (As if to illustrate this point, a half-hour-long *Nightline* TV programme I happened to catch in a break from writing these pages included *three* catchy commercial jingles based on late-sixties counterculture anthems: one each by Graham Nash, John Sebastian, and Pete Townsend. All of the above starred at the Woodstock Festival, a distinction that at the time was thought to represent the absolute antithesis of hawking appliances, home insurance, and Pennzoil in 30-second TV spots.)

'Whenever we do something good in England,' says Brown, 'if we're not careful, it will be written off as nothing but a fashion. It will be dismissed, its credibility destroyed. That's what happened with most of the sixties ideals: "Oh, well, that was just the fashion." Not true. It was more than that, but it's been reduced to the level of clothes. There were a lot of breakthroughs then, but they're largely gone – and that's why people go back to the sixties, because they vaguely remember that there *were* ideals. Nowadays, it's just money. Not that we weren't involved in money – everyone is; you can't help it. But we were trying to do constructive things.

'A lot of it was destroyed by the press and the Powers That Be because they recognized that it *was* a threat. So Jagger got busted, then Lennon got busted. Because in those days, it was still a "family audience" – with parental control over what their children purchased. Especially outside London. The Beatles – working-class boys writing lovely songs – everyone got into it. Mums, dads, everyone.

'But the minute that, say, Lennon got busted, there was a complete cooling in that area. There's that weird, uneducated Victorian hypocrisy: "Lennon's a junkie, we can't take him seriously any more." Eccentricity is one thing that was sort of tolerated here, but politics and drugs were different.'

Though the Pink Floyd didn't get busted, that special milieu which had given rise to the band was nonetheless effectively destroyed even as the Floyd were being swept inexorably into the very different world of the *Top of the Pops*. It was not a transition to which Syd Barrett easily adapted.

Chapter 7

Interstellar Overdrive

'It was all so easy then,' says Peter Jenner of Syd Barrett's artistic flowering and the Pink Floyd's initial success. 'The question is why it then became so hard. Money? Fame? People coming up and asking Syd the meaning of life and giving him loads of acid? I blame the acid, but I think it would have been something else if it hadn't been the acid.'

'Certainly acid had something to do with it,' says Rick Wright. 'The point is, you don't know whether the acid accelerated this process that was happening in his brain, or was the cause of it. No one knows. I'm sure the drugs had a lot to do with it.

'I think Syd just got involved with particular people who were trying to turn him on. The whole thing in the late sixties was like – taking acid, and it was a whole new world. He got caught up in it.'

In this regard, Barrett's next move – to the most notorious underground address in South Kensington – was stepping from the frying pan into the fire. One Cambridge friend remembers 101 Cromwell Road, already home to much of their old crowd, as 'an extraordinary building full of extraordinary people – very talented and high-flying painters and musicians. It was heavily drug-orientated; international acid dealers would stop off there for three days.' 'Cromwell Road, man,' as Donovan warbled, on 'Sunny South Kensington', 'Gotta spread your wings . . .'

The centre of gravity in this brave new world was, for a time, the New Zealander turned LSD evangelist John Esam. Hippie aristocrat Prince Stanislaw Klossowksi de Rola (who was himself known as 'Stash') renamed Esam 'the Spider' because 'he lived in a sort of warren, a windowless sort of gallery he'd made in a corridor.' Esam is described by Virginia Clive-Smith – a fellow 101-er who helped design his magazine The Image – as an 'incredible character who laid everything that moved and had the most extraordinary magic about him. He would take people over totally. He would create such energy around him that he was fascinating, almost the way a cobra fascinates a bird.'[1]

Esam became a *cause célèbre* after the authorities decided to investigate the strange goings-on at 101 Cromwell Road. Though the Spider had the presence of mind, when the police arrived, to fling hundreds of acid-laced sugarcubes out of the window, the garden had already been staked out by a constable who caught the incriminating bag. The case was brought to trial, only to founder on the fact that the British government had not yet got round to declaring LSD illegal. In an attempt to build an alternative argument that Esam should be charged with conspiring to manufacture controlled poisons, the prosecution then produced Albert Hoffman, the Swiss inventor of LSD, to testify that his hallucinogen was a derivative of the toxic substance ergotamine. But the defence won the day with expert testimony from penicillin pioneer Ernest Chain, to the effect that the ingredient in question was a synthetic ergot rather than the actual poison. Spared a lengthy prison sentence by this technicality, the Spider was nonetheless sufficiently spooked by the ordeal of his show trial to renounce acid forever.

Syd Barrett, however, proceeded to give every indication of having been launched into a permanent LSD orbit. Back at Earlham Street, says a friend, 'Barrett would take acid in very protected circumstances – with people we knew very well, in familiar surroundings. But Syd began taking it on his own and getting well freaked-out.'

In this he was now constantly (if unwittingly) aided and abetted by the likes of another new roommate named Scotty, characterized by Floyd underling John Marsh as 'one of the original acid-in-the-reservoir, change-the-face-of-the-world acid missionaries' and 'a desperately twisted freak' to boot. According to Marsh, Syd's more earthbound visitors would decline all offers of refreshments at 101 Cromwell Road, down to and including a glass of water – 'unless you got it yourself from the tap, and even then you'd be desperately worried, because Scotty's thing was spiking everything.'[2]

After Barrett, who adored cats, adopted one of the Jenners' brood, she too was fed LSD. Yet Peter Jenner and John Marsh, like almost everyone around the band, continued to keep to themselves any misgivings about Syd's excesses. It was, after all, the Summer of Love, when nobody – least of all a manager of the Pink Floyd, or a Mod kid privileged to help run their psychedelic lights – wished to be so *boring* as to suggest that the acidmania might be getting out of hand.

Not that Barrett's lapses could yet be perceived as symptoms of an irreversible metamorphoses or even of anything that went much beyond the general insanity of the times. For June Bolan, the alarm bells began to sound only when Syd kept his girlfriend under lock and key for three days, occasionally shoving a ration of biscuits under the door. After Juliette Wright and June succeeded in rescuing the badly bruised and shaken prisoner, Barrett locked *himself* in the room and refused to show his face for another week.

And yet, June stresses, there was no overnight change from 'Syd as we'd all known and loved him – and in comes the lunatic. Because it didn't work like that. It was very gradual. One day he'd be freaked out, for no apparent reason, but then none of us lived with him, so we didn't know what went on at home. Then maybe he'd be all right for a couple of weeks, and then he'd be funny for a couple of days and it would transpire that he was taking a lot of acid. He knew the volume of the acid, the tabs he was taking himself. But then "friends", when he had a cup of tea, would drop one in and not tell him so that halfway through a trip he'd be on another trip. And perhaps they'd do that a couple of times a day, for two or three weeks. And that's when his hold on reality became very tenuous – and very, very difficult to deal with for people that didn't live around him.

'I'm still convinced that a lot of it was acid-based. It may have happened without, but it probably would have taken longer. If people with schizophrenic tendencies have drugs, that accelerates those tendencies. It's very difficult when you do it on a daily basis to come back down to the other bit of you: the day-to-day having to go to photo sessions, having to do *Top of the Pops*. You never actually really come down, because you have all those flashbacks. So OK, he hadn't had any for a day – but the next day maybe he had to do a photo session and it would all be with him still.'

One of Barrett's peers detects in the very intensity of Syd's artistic vision a paradoxical clue to his problems with LSD. 'I often found that the people least able to cope with acid were those who had the strongest imaginations,' says Pete Brown, who hasn't had so much as a puff of pot or a whiff of whisky since 1967, when he was very nearly overwhelmed by LSD himself. 'For people who had no imaginations, acid provided them with the illusion that they had one. For people who were already out there, it pushed them too far out in many cases.'

Like Brown, Peter Wynne Willson renounced LSD forever in the wake of a bad trip which ended with his incarceration in a mental hospital. Barrett, recalls Susie, 'was the only person I could think of to come and get Peter out. He borrowed an ancient mini-car from somebody, and we drove round and round trying to find this hospital. Syd was very frightened to come in, because he was under the impression that they wouldn't let him out. Everyone was very, very on the edge then.'

Syd's year-long acid trip began to go haywire just when the Floyd's career was shifting into overdrive. Some of his friends attribute part of Barrett's deterioration to the pressures of 'pop stardom' and the attitudes of the rest of the Floyd: others, conversely, maintain that the personality conflicts within the band, along with Syd's inability to handle his success, essentially arose from his acid-fuelled derangement. A fair conclusion might be that all these factors – the drugs; the fame; personal and artistic differences; and some long-dormant disorder within Barrett's psyche – interacted with one another to increasingly nightmarish effect.

Peter Jenner is the first to concede that the Floyd's professional life 'suddenly stopped being fun. All these people were asking, "What's the next single? We need another hit now." And we were thinking, "Blimey, what's a hit?" It was all becoming a *business*.' And Syd, says Mick Rock, 'was a totally *pure* artist; he could not deal with the business at all. That kind of vision – when it's that out of stage-left, that original – can only come out of a state that has a tenuous hold on boring day-to-day reality.'

Contributing to the pressure-cooker effect was the relentless touring to which the Floyd (whose new found status as 'a hit parade group' triggered an avalanche of relatively lucrative offers) were committed throughout the rest of 1967: over eighty shows from May to September alone. Some were what June Bolan calls 'double-headers – two gigs in one night. Which meant driving to one gig, setting up, doing the gig, dragging it all out, loading it in the truck and getting to the next gig – and doing the late night show there.'

What's more, the strong-arm promoters of that era, Peter Wynne Willson says, 'paid no regard to the routes that we would take. It would get to the stage that the roadie would *have* to get some sleep – but we still had to get to the next place. There was very little traffic on the motorways at that time, they were fairly recently built. He would jam his foot on the accelerator and go to sleep. And whoever was sitting next to him, Susie or myself, would actually steer.'

Susie specifically faults Bryan Morrison for routinely making 'a booking up in the north of England, then one in the south, then one way up north again without thinking of how one got from A to B. I remember steering the wheel, because I didn't have a driving licence, sitting next to a driver who was fast asleep. We were all completely stretched.

'As you approached something, and you *knew* that you had to wake him, he wouldn't register properly for a moment or two and *then* he'd click into what the situation was – travelling at ninety miles per hour in a Ford transit motor!'

'Imagine what it was like,' her partner chuckles, 'waking up from a deep sleep to find yourself in the driver's seat rapidly approaching some disaster. It really would have been safer had we changed positions, and not worried about the police finding some non-licensed driver.'

Logistics aside, the British provinces – apart from a few hip pockets in the north – tended to be ill-prepared for Barrett's twenty-minute feedback soliloquies, Wynne Willson's cosmic bubbles, and the group's wilful lack of danceable rhythms or traditional showmanship. Conspicuously absent from most sets, moreover, was the one tune, 'See Emily Play', that the punters were likely to have heard, or to want to hear. The Pink Floyd and their ballroom audiences mixed like oil and water: 'Very middle-class intellectual boys playing for very working-class yobs,' says Jenner. 'But there was no circuit then for "good" rock music: very few college gigs, hardly any concerts. It was easier to work in Holland or France than in most English cities.' Years later, Roger Waters quipped to a friend that the '67-model Floyd 'earned the record for clearing ballrooms faster than any other band'.

Sometimes, however, audiences expressed their displeasure more forcefully. At one Bedfordshire ballroom earlier in the year, Waters reminisced, 'They were pouring pints of beer onto us from the balcony. That was most unpleasant, and very dangerous too.' As close to home as the Feathers Club, in the London suburb of Ealing, a heckler armed with pre-decimalization British pennies 'made a bloody great cut in the middle of my forehead. I bled quite a lot. And I stood right in front of the stage to see if I could see him throw one. I was glowering in a real rage, and I was going to leap out into the audience and get him. Happily there was one freak who turned up who liked us, so the audience spent the whole evening beating the shit out of him.'[3]

A decade later, Nick Mason described a typical out-of-town Floyd venue, circa 1967: 'There would be this revolving stage, and the audience out front all hoping to hear "Arnold Layne" and "See Emily Play" and a host of other hits which we couldn't, of course, play. We had a repertoire of strange things like "Interstellar Overdrive" which carried us through about half the set. I just remember the stages going round and the whole audience just appalled by what they saw in front of them. The whole thing was fantastic anyway, because what was then considered to be "our" audience could never get into these places because you had to have a tie. And there was this whole business of not letting us drink at the bar because we hadn't got collars and ties, and various outrages which used to drive us all mad.'[4]

As the Floyd, in Mason's words, 'trudged around for a daily dose of broken bottle', they were heralded with little more fanfare than squibs such as this from a small-town Scotland newspaper – tucked beneath an account of the Morayshire Farmers' Club annual fruitcake competition: "And at the Red Shoes ballroom, Columbia recording stars the Pink Floyd. This is the group that brings its own lighting to set the scene oscillating and vibrating with WAY OUT SETS."

When *Disc and Music Echo* clambered aboard for the Floyd's July swing through Scotland, its coverage noted not only the grind endured by our 'four unpretentious, easygoing, and unaffected boys' but also the recreational activities still favoured by at least three of them:

Maybe there are only four trains out of town each day . . . but even Elgin has its moments.

Which is why four Pink Floyds – Roger Waters, quiet and seemingly cultured, Syd Barrett, quiet and seemingly shy, Rick Wright and Nick Mason – pile into a car at Great Yarmouth at darkest night on Wednesday and drive through the night to arrive near Elgin at a seaside hotel in Lossiemouth at 4 p.m. on Thursday.

Snatch a few hours' sleep, order horses for the following morning's riding, check the local fishing scene and inquire about a round at the local golf club.

Then into Elgin for the gig . . . [5]

In the event, the audience at least saved their beer for their own gullets, and left their pennies in their pockets. Audience reaction at the Red Shoes ranged from 'do ye ken I could sing better in ma wee bath' to 'not bad . . . the Cream were better'.

Cream's lyricist, however, was and is keenly sympathetic to Barrett's predicament at this juncture. 'When he was at the height of his powers and when they had these pop hits, "Emily" and "Arnold Layne" ' Pete Brown recalls, 'the whole psychedelic thing was a very London-based phenomenon; it didn't spread for a long time. And they were putting them out on the road playing ballrooms to audiences who'd only heard R & B bands and didn't know what the fuck was going on.

'Also the British music business in those days was really silly. There was this element which said, *"The whole thing's gonna end tomorrow and we gotta grab what we can right now"*. And if the artist is left in the shit, it doesn't matter. It was very hard for them to understand what was going on with the Floyd. There was no real alternative structure, except these few places where peope would play in London to very supportive fans. The rest of it wasn't there. Nobody realized that the Floyd would be one of the biggest-selling acts in America. When they started breaking out with these hits, the record company didn't know what to do with them.

'And of course Syd was probably the last person in the world who could deal with those structures. He was out there giving 100 per cent and not getting very much back except in London where people understood him. That was a big strain; the audiences could be very philistine when they had something as difficult and demanding, in a way, as the Floyd. On the road, Syd had to compensate by taking it as far as it would go. And I'm sure he was taking a lot of stuff – everybody was.

'They didn't go down terribly well in the provinces because the audiences hadn't been educated and the media didn't know how the fuck to do it. The media weren't sure for a couple of years whether the whole underground movement wouldn't get banned. And therefore the steps that they took towards featuring it and understanding it were very slow.

'Nowadays they're in there instantly, no matter how weird or subversive it is. You've got this clip-on weirdness-kit syndrome: "What are we going to be tomorrow? Something out of the sixties? Something with a Syd Barrett influence?" They clip it all on, and straight away the media's in there.

'*Then* they were afraid of it politically – not that the Floyd were at all political, except in their veiled advocation of getting somewhere out of your mind. There were unbelievable amounts of incomprehension.'

New Musical Express greeted the Floyd's rising star with the request that each member list for the mainstream pop weekly's readers such vital information as his height and weight; brothers' and sisters' names; pets and hobbies; 'age entered show business'; and favourite colours, foods, and actors. NME's Life-lines of the Stars was, after all, a venerable rite of passage through which the Beatles, Stones, and Kinks – not to mention the Dave Clark Five and Herman's Hermits – had all proceeded on their way to the top. Now it was the Pink Floyd's turn.

The individual Floyds' responses to this exercise were nonetheless arguably revealing. Rick Wright was by far the most conscientious and earnest, confiding, for instance, that his 'professional ambition' was 'to hear my own symphony performed at the Festival Hall'. Nick Mason turned his questionnaire into a good-natured jest; to wit, *Biggest influence on career*: 'Fear and rum.' Roger betrayed a hint of impatience, writing 'Mum and Dad', 'none', and 'multi!' under (respectively) *Parents' names*, *Hobbies*, and *Favourite colour*, yet was evidently quite willing to play the game. (He even followed the traditional pop star practice of bringing his birthdate forward one year.) Syd, by contrast, beyond allowing that he had a 'cat named Rover', tended simply to answer 'haven't got one' or 'everything' or leave his entries stark raving blank.[6]

Depending on the observer's perspective, such recalcitrance could be regarded either as a principled protest or as a manifestation of incipient psychosis. The notorious *Top of the Pops* episodes, with Barrett appearing on TV in escalating states of sartorial disarray, may be viewed along similarly divergent lines.

The success of 'See Emily Play' had qualified the Pink Floyd to appear on the programme as many times as the single placed in the weekly Top Ten – three, as it turned out. The rest of the band, like their managers, regarded such TV exposure as a valuable windfall. But Syd cringed at the very thought of showing his face on such a tacky show; to him, doing *Top of the Pops* was a sell-out. Five years later, Rick Wright conceded that '*Top of the Pops* was definitely one of the worst things I did. It was horrible to be on it . . . a real drag.' On a subsequent *Saturday Club* BBC radio programme, Syd went even further and walked out, saying, 'I never want to do that again.'

Whatever Barrett's motives, an ever-widening rift developed between Syd and at least two of his fellow Floyds. According to one insider, 'Roger was always intensely ambitious. The others obviously liked the idea of being pop stars, but Roger was constantly trying to drive the group into more commercial situations – in the way of the press, in the way the gigs were structured, in the numbers they put out. Nick Mason went along with that.

'Rick was a much lower-key personality, very much more in tune with Syd in the early days. They played a lot together, worked a lot together. Basically they were the two smokers, and Roger and Nick were the two drinkers. There was a bit of a split. But Rick eventually swung towards the stronger personalities in the group.'

Peter Jenner, on the other hand, his own differences with Waters notwithstanding, feels the bassist was largely motivated by a desire 'to get the whole thing organized and make it more manageable'. And he, at least, remembers Mason as the Floyd 'who could always talk to everybody, the one who had nothing to prove. He deserves enormous credit for keeping the band together over the years.'

June Bolan attributes some of the friction to Barrett, the charismatic singer and songwriter, having naturally been singled out for special attention. 'It always happens, the singer in the band gets more pictures. He was also the most photogenic. Syd was the motivating force in the band, and that's basically, initially, who people wanted to see.

'I think it's indicative of fame – it could be just one record, something like "See Emily Play", and your first *Top of the Pops* – and then things change,' she says. 'Before, they were four people who'd grown up together, or gone to college together. It became separate camps of people: your smokers and dopers, and your drinkers. The drinkers weren't extreme, by any manner of means, but they preferred doing that to rolling joints and taking acid, and whatever else one did in those days. But it was a very gradual split.'

As for the artistic differences, June fingers LSD as the main culprit: 'The more acid one takes, in one's mind the music sounds tremendous – but outwardly it sounds like a heap of shit. People who aren't taking the same stuff as you aren't hearing the same thing you're hearing in your head. That's when all the bones of contention came, because it wasn't working as a whole. That's when it all started to fragment.

'That's when the others began to assert themselves in their own musical rights. Richard would have opinions about how the keyboards ought to go; Roger would have quite positive feelings about things. Nick least of all – at least not in front of everybody!'

Peter Wynne Willson remembers the dynamics a bit differently: 'There was always a lot of pressure on him from Nick and Roger, to conform to their picture of what a pop group should do – that they should always play the current single at a concert, and selected tracks from the album. And that just wasn't in Syd's reckoning at all. He was very much wanting to develop the music, because of that experimental altruistic feeling among likeminded people at that time. But Nick and Roger saw the possibility of big commercial success for the band.

84

'They put a lot of pressure on me, too. Roger would often complain that he was not illuminated as a star. I specifically didn't illuminate any of them as "rock stars" because I did the lighting to blend with the music rather than accentuate somebody as a personality.'

'The Floyd tours,' says Susie Wynne Willson, 'were frantic and competitive and they hassled each other. Roger had a very heavy way of playing, as if there had to be a winner. They didn't have the same living attitudes; they only lived together because they were on tour together. They didn't even eat the same food. Syd, Pete and I were vegetarian and smoking vast quantities of dope. Everyone else was into drinking beer and eating big juicy steaks. We were in a completely different space, worlds apart.'

As Barrett's behaviour on the road turned increasingly erratic, the other Floyds took to needling him with a vengeance. During one trip, for instance, he was moved to buy himself not one but twelve sandwiches from a roadside stand. These he proceeded to cram into his mouth in rapid succession, oblivious to the mess on his face and hands, while his fellow band-members egged him on in a mounting chorus of sarcasm and contempt. Amazingly, he wasn't sick.

June Bolan says, 'Once Syd lost his grip, in the sense that he was a very volatile member of the band, they were really wicked to him. With Syd behaving like a complete cretin, they would send him up on long car journeys where you're all stuck in one vehicle, and there's nowhere to go because you've got to end up at the gig.

'Perhaps had they been kinder, in those early days of his breakdown or cracking up or whatever you want to call it, he may not have been hit so hard by it all. But that is speculation. It may have happened anyway, in exactly the same way, or it may not have happened so badly – but I do feel that they were horrider to him than they need to have been.'

On 29 July the Pink Floyd appeared at a second Alexandra Palace extravaganza, second-billed only to Eric 'San Francisco Nights' Burdon and his new set of psychedelic Animals – three months to the day after the euphoria of the Technicolour Dream. In the event, the International Love-In was not quite the triumphal return Peter Jenner and Andrew King had hoped for.

'The main attraction,' Keith Altham reported in *NME*, 'was the audience itself, aged between seventeen and twenty-five . . . with faces painted blue, yellow, or green (streaked by the torrential rain outside). Some wore floral jackets, some robes and brightly coloured scarves. Some wore beads and threw carnations about.'[7]

As the Floyd's big moment approached, June Bolan remembers, Barrett was nowhere to be seen. She finally located him in a dressing-room, 'Absolutely gaga, just totally switched-off, sitting rigid like a stone.'

She tried to shake him out of his trance while the other Floyds changed into their stage gear – which was unnecessary in Barrett's case because he was already so flamboyantly attired. 'Syd!' she cried. 'It's June! Look at me!' His blank stare registered not a flicker of recognition.

As the milling audience grew restless, the stage manager kept knocking on the door with his increasingly urgent summons: *'Time to go! Time to go!'* 'And we're trying to get Syd up,' June recalls, 'and get him together to go and play. He couldn't speak, he was absolutely catatonic. Roger and I hoofed him onto the stage, and en route put his guitar around his neck, and stood him in front of the vocal mike.

'That's when you have to give Roger credit for what he did: he actually got the other two together and made a sort of half-arsed version of a set. Peter and Andrew were frantic – they were pulling out their hair.'

The two managers' relief when Syd at last let rip with his white Stratocaster proved short-lived; according to June, the discordant, yowling notes bore little connection to what the other three were playing. Mostly, Barrett 'just stood there, tripping out of his mind'.

Fortunately for the Floyd, June had had the foresight to collect their fee from the Love-In's promoter before he sussed out what was going on. Upon ascertaining that she had the money in her handbag, Peter Jenner shouted at her through the din: 'Go out to the car – now! Leg it!'

'I whizzed out,' says June, 'and sat in the car until the end of the gig, saying, "Please don't let them find me, because they'll hit me on the head and take the money!" Apparently in the interim the promoter, the bouncers, and the stage manager were all looking for "the chick with the money". We knew that we probably would never get paid afterwards – we weren't that daft! It was something like a thousand pounds – a lot of money to them in those days. And I had it all in, like, ten pound notes in my bag.

'They all ran out with their guitars, and we just shot off, and went *"Whew!"* '

The next issue of *Melody Maker* announced that, 'Syd Barrett is suffering from nervous exhaustion and the group have withdrawn all engagements booked for the month of August. As a result they have lost at least £4,000 in work.' In keeping with the band's newfound prominence, this report appeared on page one under the banner headline 'PINK FLOYD FLAKE OUT!'[8]

Chapter 8
Paranoid Eyes

By the summer of 1967, the conquest of America had begun to loom large in Jenner and King's game plan. Ever since the Beatles launched the British Invasion of 1964, it had become obligatory for all English recording stars worthy of the name to attempt to duplicate (if not exceed) their UK success in the far larger Stateside market. English bands, says Peter Jenner, 'are often made or broken by their first trip to America.' In the case of Pink Floyd, their status as the premiere British underground band could only enhance their status at a time when such American kindred spirits as Jefferson Airplane were actually cracking the U.S. top ten.

Accordingly, Jenner travelled to New York to lay the groundwork for the Floyd's breakthrough. Thanks to the Joe Boyd connection, he received a warm welcome at Elektra Records' offices from producer Paul Rothchild. 'If you want to see the underground,' Rothchild admonished him, 'you must go to San Francisco. When Jenner confessed that such junkets were beyond his limited budget, the producer insisted on flying him across the continent, first class, at Elektra's expense.

'Such a nice thing to do,' says Jenner, 'but very much a part of the spirit then. I was like a brother hippie from England.' At the Fillmore West, however, he was shocked at how 'lame it was compared with UFO, and how ordinary the bands were compared with the English psychedelic bands'. In Los Angeles, Jenner sat in on a recording session with Rothchild's hottest new act, the Doors.

Such gestures notwithstanding, Elektra boss Jac Holzman had already passed on the Pink Floyd before their signing with EMI. The group ended up by default with EMI's American sister label, Capitol, which in turn banished the Floyd to one of its more obscure satellites, Mike Curb's Tower Records. (Curb was the man who subsequently launched a much-hyped campaign to purge the record industry of 'drug-oriented' artists, and went on to be elected California's

Lieutenant-Governor.) In a departure from its biker movie sound-tracks and cut-price versions of Broadway musical scores orchestrated by Curb himself, Tower released a version of *The Piper at the Gates of Dawn* to coincide with the Floyd's live U.S. debut at the Fillmore West on 26 October.

Capitol, as it happens, was not a company known to put much stock in such notions as value for money or artistic integrity. It had milked its foremost cash cow, the Beatles, to the extent of routinely squeezing at least three numbers off each British LP up to 1966 so that the leftovers might be combined with stray single hits and B-sides to create twice as much album 'product'. Though at long last *Sergeant Pepper* had been spared this treatment, no such deference was due the little-known Pink Floyd. In the event that these English hippies somehow became the next teen sensation, the Capitol brass reasoned, three cuts withheld from *Piper* might be thrown together with a handful of singles for an instant second Pink Floyd album.

The upshot was that the British *Piper*'s opening and closing tracks – 'Astronomy Dominé' and 'Bike' – were both slashed from the Tower records version, along with 'Flaming', which was earmarked for a future single release. The rest of the line-up was reshuffled without regard for the organic flow of the original cycle. Rick Wright later complained that no one from Capitol had bothered to advise the band of these changes.

Such was the record company that welcomed 'the light kings of England' (as it labelled the Floyd) with, of all things, a midday reception at a tinselly Mafia-style nightclub. While Capitol employees attempted to exchange pleasantries with Syd and the others, drinks were served up by hapless go-go girls in leotards and fishnet stockings whose bleary eyes suggested that they had been roused from their customary sleeping shifts for the occasion.

This surreal scene might be viewed as an augury of the monumental fiasco in store. 'The American tour was when Syd was beginning to get seriously eccentric,' says Jenner, who let Andrew King handle the honours for this trip. 'That was when it became unarguable that it was a real problem.'

In San Francisco, the Floyd played not only the Fillmore but a few dates at Winterland, where they opened for their old acquaintance Chet Helms's protegees Big Brother and the Holding Company. Though disappointed that Big Brother and the other Haight-Ashbury bands proved to be so much less 'extraordinary and mindblowing and trippy' than he anticipated, Waters – along with Mason – was initiated backstage by lead singer Janis Joplin into the joys of Southern Comfort. Helms, for his part, had few complaints about a Floyd set 'absolutely dominated by feedback, which was very novel and very innovative at that time. As far as I'm concerned the Hendrix feedback thing came from Pink Floyd.'

'Syd was OK at Winterland – just,' says lighting director Peter Wynne Willson, who accompanied King and the Floyd to the States. 'But when we went on to Los Angeles to play at a little club, Syd became almost catatonic, partly because we weren't sleeping very much. We were constantly being taken up by ravishing California girls who asked us our star signs and then plied us with everything you can think of. Very seductive for somebody from England, particularly in that sunshine.

'I don't know that Syd was taking acid there. There were certainly prodigious quantities of grass being consumed by all except Roger and Nick, who were consuming prodigious quantities of Southern Comfort.'

Any party atmosphere was rather abruptly dispelled after the Floyd took the Cheetah Club stage, where the silence from Barrett's guitar proved positively resounding. Clutching at its neck, Syd stared blankly off into farthest space, his right hand dangling inertly by his side. When he also failed to deliver any of his lyrics, Waters and Wright struggled to cover for his vocals. 'It wasn't unnatural that Roger got very pissed off,' says Wynne Willson. 'I seem to remember that he was actually demanding of Andrew that Syd be dismissed on the spot.'

A decade later, Nick Mason spoke revealingly of his own emotional response to Syd: 'It's easy now to look back on the past and try and give it some shape and some form. But at the time you're in a total state of confusion, muddling about because you're trying to be in this band and be successful and make it work – and things aren't working out. You don't really understand why, and you can't believe someone's deliberately trying to screw it up: and yet the other half of you is saying, "This man's crazy – he's trying to destroy me!" Destroy me, you know – it gets very personal. You all get very worked up into a state of extreme rage.

'I mean, obviously there were some incredible moments of clarity, like the wonderful American tour, which will live forever. Syd detuning his guitar all the way through one number, striking the strings and detuning the guitar, which is – very modern [laughs], but very difficult for a band to follow or play with. Other occasions he more or less just

90

ceased playing, and would stand there, leaving us to muddle along as best we could. At times like that you think, "What we need is someone else – or at least some help."'[1]

'At the time,' says Wynne Willson, 'you always expected he would suddenly snap out of it. I was very close to Syd, and in a way felt personally responsible for him. There were some intensely embarrassing situations.

'Syd was a bit frightening to look at – and frightening to be with. You'd say something as you would normally say to someone, and just get this totally paranoid stare back.'

Adding to the macabre picture was Barrett's grotesque new hair-do. 'We all went down to Vidal Sassoon and had our hair permed.' Wynne Willson recalls. 'But Syd's went very badly. And he had on an awful flowery shirt with a braided collar and wide sleeves which you could just get by with if it was a very fluid scene and you were laid back and smiling. But if you're fantastically uptight and paranoid it makes those clothes somehow a bit dreadful.'

Capitol, meanwhile, obliviously continued to lay on its brand of hospitality. After ushering the Floyd round Beverly Hills to gawk at the homes of the stars, the A & R man trumpeted, 'Yes, and here we are, the centre of it all – Hollywood and Vine!' At which the glassy-eyed Barrett momentarily seemed to snap out of his trance, gushing, 'It's great to be in Las Vegas!'[2]

Another eager host in Los Angeles was Alice Cooper, who invited Syd and the others to dinner with his own band – thus enabling rock's most ersatz psycho to come face to face with a more authentic specimen. Cooper guitarist Glen Buxton came away convinced that 'Syd was definitely from Mars'. Though Barrett said hardly a word all evening, Buxton did not find him altogether uncommunicative.

'All of a sudden I'd pick up the sugar and pass it to him,' he recalled, 'and he'd shake his head like, "Yeah, thanks . . ." It's like telepathy, it really was. It was very weird. You would find yourself right in the middle of doing something, as you were passing the sugar or whatever, and you'd think, "Well, damn! I didn't hear anybody say anything." That was the first time in my life I'd ever met anybody that could actually do that freely. And this guy did it all the time.'[3]

The intended highlights, and actual nadir, of the Floyd's stay in Tinseltown were their legendary televised encounters with Pat Boone and Dick Clark (on 5 and 6 November, respectively), during which Syd mutely responded to Boone's fatuous questions with his most zombie-like stare and then kept his lips sealed when it came time to

91

mime 'See Emily Play' on *American Bandstand*. In the wake of these mortifying episodes Andrew King decided to cut his U.S. losses and put everyone on the next plane home, obliging the TV show *Beach Party* to scramble for a suitable replacement. The Floyd had also been booked at New York's Cheetah Club for 12 November; under the circumstances, however, even the Big Apple would have to wait.

During their unscheduled week off, some of the group found that they did after all have some urgent business to take care of in London. 'They came back from the States with gonorrhoea,' recalls one of their female friends, 'They were all frantically getting injections.'

Had all proceeded to plan, the Floyd would have performed in Rotterdam, Holland, the night after New York, only to launch yet another gruelling tour of Britain the very next evening! Such was the mill to which aspiring 'pop stars' were routinely subjected in those days – *welcome, my son, welcome . . . to the Machine!* – and for which Syd Barrett had already proved singularly ill-suited from both a psychological and an artistic standpoint.

And yet, now that the starmaking machine had been activated, one could hardly switch it off – or even put it on hold or slow it down for very long. There were endless bills to be paid, especially large ones because of the Floyd's multi-media shows. The music rags wanted interviews; the fan mags demanded pictures; the record company was clamouring for a new single. And the other Floyds were certainly not about to be robbed of their chance to become big stars, just because Syd was fucking up. *The show must go on . . .*

And so the Floyd went right back on the road as a supporting act for the Jimi Hendrix Experience. The format was the old-fashioned fifties-style 'package tour' – seven acts playing twice a night, and each night in a different town – but the music was strictly 1967-model progressive rock. The show's premiere, at London's Royal Albert Hall on 14 November, was even dubbed, in best underground fashion, 'The Alchemical Wedding'.

It was at this concert, Peter Wynne Willson recalls, that he unveiled his new ultra-high-speed colour-change effect. 'I would run the two units up to speed, then fade the lights in them, and you'd just get a slightly shimmery white light. But as I then brought the speed down, any rapid movement would trail rainbows behind it. So the first thing you'd see was that Nick's hands would become a bit coloured, given that he was moving faster than the others. And then as the speed came further down, the rainbows would broaden out until the whole stage area was pulsing with colour. But you couldn't actually figure out what colour, because it was changing so fast.

'That was a wonderful effect. It could give all the entrancing qualities of strobe but without that heavy jerking that sets people off into unpleasant situations. I very rarely used strobes on the Floyd because I always felt it was a bit violent for the music we were into.' Wynne Willson was gratified to learn that only one fan was known to have thrown up as a result of this latest effect: 'not a bad score' in light of the mass queasiness that conventional strobes could trigger among a crowd of acid freaks.

At the Royal Albert Hall the scintillating visuals and a sense of event carried the band through their short third-billed set. A credible if undistinguished performance from Barrett proved, however, to be the briefest of remissions.

Above and beyond the Hendrix tour's punishing schedule, its format encapsulated everything that Syd had long resisted about the packaging of his muse – and inevitably intensified the conflicts with the rest of the band. At each gig, the headlining Hendrix was allotted exactly forty minutes in which to do his thing. The Move, who preceded him onstage, had just half an hour. And the Floyd were expected to sum up what they were all about in precisely *seventeen* minutes! Which, from the standpoint of Waters and Mason, required that the band play a selection of tested favourites – and keep them as short and snappy as possible.

To Barrett, however, music had always been an act of spontaneous combustion, and repetition was simply redundant. As he wilfully resisted his colleagues' attempt to display a modicum of profession-alism, they in turn became ever more intolerant of his idiosyncrasies. 'It seems to me that they were grossly insensitive to the kind of psychosis Syd was going through – they didn't have an inkling,' says Susie Wynne Willson. 'He was so hypersensitive to atmosphere; he couldn't even walk into a room that had the faintest jar of bad feeling or heaviness.'

Syd's friend Storm Thorgerson, however, takes a more sympathetic view of the others' position during this period. 'He played a different tune literally and metaphorically from the rest of the band, and became impossible to work with. Now I may on hindsight believe that they should have taken more care, but it's very hard when you are that young, and may not have much of a handle on your own problems; it's asking a lot.

'Maybe Roger and Nick were more commercially minded, but Syd was by far the strongest, musically, and I don't have any recollection to think he was a *weed*. You must give people credit for their own autonomy – or lack of it.'

As the Hendrix tour wore on, Barrett appeared increasingly morose and depressed. 'Syd got very starey at that time, with dark rings under his eyes,' says Susie. 'But he was looking actually very very beautiful. He put a lot of make-up on, and it suited him very well.'

Sometimes, however, Barrett couldn't be persuaded to go on stage at all, and Dave O'List, lead guitarist of the Nice (who were fifth on the bill) would stand in for him. In the swirl of Wynne Willson's psychedelic lights, the difference was seldom apparent to the fans. 'The girls at the front would scream, "*Syd! Syd!*" with their arms out and the tears streaming down their faces,' says Susie. On at least one such occasion, she recalls, Barrett was in actuality speeding away on a London-bound train, leaving it to Peter Jenner to chase after him and drag him back. (Fourth on the bill, incidentally, were the mod combo Amen Corner, whose singer Andy Fairweather-Low would twenty years later become Roger Waters's guitarist.)

Jimi Hendrix, unaware as almost everyone else of the underlying seriousness of Syd's condition, took to addressing him ironically as 'laughing Syd Barrett'. Hendrix himself had cause to smile: his star was exploding into worldwide renown, and his guitar pyrotechnics were rapturously received throughout the tour. 'The girls were throwing themselves at him like there was no tomorrow,' says Wynne Willson. 'I remember two girls coming down from his room, absolutely shaking. One of them had had a severely physical time with him, and her friend took her off to the loo to try to repair the damage.'

At one point the Hendrix entourage was augmented by that colourful clan known as the Plaster Casters – groupies whose mission in life was to mould casts of rock and roll's most eminent hard-ons. After crowning their legendary collection with a Jimi Hendrix replica, they arranged an exhibit of their trophies on a shelf backstage for the viewing pleasure of the entire touring party. The Casters evinced little interest in preserving a Pink Floyd phallus for posterity: 'A, because they were not very well known,' says Wynne Willson, 'and B, they were not a sexy act. They were supposed to be Art.'

Three of the band, moreover, were already hooked up with wives or fiancées. In Roger's case, his engagement to Judy Trim was partly in reaction against his possessive mother, who had actually encouraged

him 'to go out and look for dirty girls'[4] in the hope that he wouldn't
settle down with one clean one. The new Mrs Waters nonetheless had
much in common with the older version: both were schoolteachers
and radical left-wingers, and couldn't bear rock and roll. (Rick's
Juliette and Nick's Lindy, by contrast, were themselves both
musicians.)

For Syd, however, one of the compensations of pop stardom had
always been the constant supply of nubile bodies thrown at his
disposal; as with the drugs, he was hardly one to stint himself. Storm
Thorgerson feels that this 'wantonness with women' may have played
a part in Barrett's breakdown, insofar as 'being a good-looking and
charismatic guy, and all the chicks liking it, doesn't necessarily do
your sense of reality any good. Often times it wears off, it's not the
whole story. I think that was quite confusing for him – a bit of an
overload, too. That was another catalyst.'

Despite everything, Syd did enjoy one idyllic interlude amid the
Hendrix whirlwind. When the tour reached Manchester, he, Susie,
and Peter Wynne Willson resolved to pay their respects to the poet
Neil Oram (author of *The Walk*), who had recently settled a few miles
away in Haworth, the windswept hillside village best known as the
home of the Brontë sisters and the setting for *Wuthering Heights*. Since
his days as a Free School habitué and a frequent caller at No. 2
Earlham Street, Oram's own underground odyssey had achieved
legendary status among his former comrades. He is fondly described by
Wynne Willson as 'one of the most unwholesome-looking people you
could meet – one felt, despite his wonderful poetry, that he was always
dropping headlice everywhere.' Oram had gone to study biodynamic
farming at a special commune on the moors where, it was said, the
vegetables dispensed advice at sunrise to all who were spiritually
attuned enough to hear.

'I think a cabbage told Neil to leave, and the direction to go in,'
Susie laughs. 'He went miles, found an empty cottage backing on a
steep hillside – a wonderful little cottage without electricity. And he's
been living there ever since, guarding an intersection of some ley-
lines.' Though Roger and Nick had no time for such nonsense, 'The
freak contingent from the Pink Floyd of course had to go and visit
Neil.'

The poet's cottage did seem to live up to its magical reputation
when Barrett, in Susie's words, 'actually relaxed, and felt at home and
very rooted, and very wholesome and together'. For a too-brief
moment, far from the motorways and the grind of the tour, Syd

95

reverted to his old charming self as they all sat around a crackling fire, eating Oram's buckwheat pancakes.

Back on the road, however, the spell was shattered when the rest of the band engineered Wynne Willson's abrupt replacement by his longtime deputy John Marsh, who had ably taken charge of the lights when Peter was indisposed. Ever since the Floyd's concert fees swelled to three and four figures, Roger and Nick had begrudged Wynne Willson the five per cent of the nightly gross to which he was automatically entitled on top of his £20-a-week retainer: with the mounting overheads, this often resulted in Peter taking home more than any of the four musicians. Marsh was happy to accept Wynne Willson's job for a flat weekly wage of just fifteen pounds.

This arrangement also suited Jenner and King, whose house Marsh had long shared. Given the sorry state of Blackhill Enterprises' balance sheet, the repossession of Wynne Willson's five per cent could only be a plus.

Wynne Willson, for his part, says he might just as soon have moved on anyway: 'Syd's degeneration, and the attitude of the rest of the band to him, was probably as instrumental to Susie and I leaving as anything else.' Marsh, however, while a sympathetic figure, was a former Mod who took a dim view of the acid scene and made no pretense of operating on Syd's special wavelength.

Between the ongoing grind of a road show now purged of two close friends and allies, and the acid-addled ambience of his South Kensington flat, Syd Barrett could only go from mad to worse.

Chapter 9

The Thin Ice

A third Pink Floyd single – Syd Barrett's 'Apples and Oranges' paired with Rick Wright's vinyl debut as a composer, 'Paint Box' – was released during the Jimi Hendrix tour. The kaleidoscopic suburbia of Barrett's lyrics, encompassing supermarket stalls and duck-feeding by the riverside, evokes a madcap return to the Beatles' 'Penny Lane'; the shout of *'We thought you might like to know!'* is an apparent nod to *Sergeant Pepper*.

Unlike its two predecessors, however, the hurriedly recorded 'Apples and Oranges' is not only bereft of Beatle-like hooks, but glaringly out-of-tune, and with each manically sped-up verse set to completely different music, hardly the recipe for a pop smash. Though *NME* pronounced it 'the most psychedelic single the Pink Floyd have yet come up with', it made not the slightest impression on the British charts. (Long unavailable, the record is now a rarity commanding up to £50 among collectors. 'Apples and Oranges' was never even released in America.)

Years later Roger Waters pinned the blame on Norman Smith: '"Apples and Oranges" was destroyed by the production. It's a fucking good song.'[1] Syd's own public reaction to his single's failure was 'couldn't care less'.

Be that as it may, the Pink Floyd's 'hit parade group' status was suddenly imperilled; with word also spreading of Barrett's unsteady performance on stage. Their stock with promoters plummeted. Peter Jenner defends his own role in this debacle by saying, 'EMI told us we needed another single, and that was the only song we had. So we had to put it out, hadn't we? Another example of our naivete and inexperience. There wasn't anything else lying around.'

As a matter of fact, there were three more Barrett compositions in the Floyd pipeline, next to any of which 'Apples and Oranges' sounded almost commercial. The one Syd reportedly favoured for a single release was the shatteringly disjointed 'Jug Band Blues' whose middle section featured, at Barrett's insistence, a guest appearance by a Salvation Army sextet whom he instructed to 'play what you want'. Citing phrases like '*I'm wondering who could be writing this song*', Jenner describes 'Jug Band Blues' as 'possibly the ultimate self-diagnosis on a state of schizophrenia'.

'Jug Band' was at least to surface the following summer on the second Pink Floyd album, a distinction denied the similarly autobiographical 'Scream Thy Last Scream (Old Woman with a Casket)' and 'Vegetable Man', though both have since become standard contraband among Floyd bootleg freaks. 'Syd wrote "Vegetable Man" in my house,' Jenner recalls. 'It was really uncanny. He sat there and just described himself, what he was wearing and doing at that time.' '*In yellow shoes I get the blues . . . blue velvet trousers make me feel Pink . . . in my paisley shirt I look a jerk.*'

'After he left the band, they all thought those songs were too intense. They couldn't handle them. They were like words from a psychiatrist's chair – an extraordinary document of a serious mental disturbance.

'I always thought they should be put out, so I let my copies be heard. I knew that Roger would never let them out, or Dave. They somehow felt they were a bit indecent, like putting out nude pictures of a famous actress: it just wasn't cricket. But I thought they were good songs and great pieces of art. They're disturbing, and not a lot of fun, but they're some of Syd's finest work – though God knows, I wouldn't wish anyone to go through what he's gone through to get to those songs. They're like Van Gogh.'

Van Gogh or no, Jenner and his partner were confronted with 'an economic crisis developing in the band. The initial flood of money was drying up, and tax bills were beginning to loom on the horizon. We were all thinking, "Fucking hell, how are we going to keep this whole thing going and pay everybody's wages?" ' At one Floyd meeting Jenner counted thirty-three faces, including assorted girlfriends and wives – a lot of mouths to feed.

'At the end of the week,' Roger Waters recalled, 'we'd all go in to get our cheques, and week by week people would start to go in earlier and earlier. They'd collect their cheque, dash round to their bank, and have it expressed because there wasn't enough money to pay everybody, so whoever got their cheque first got their money. Cheques were just bouncing all the time . . .'[2]

One solution was for Blackhill Enterprises to diversify: indeed, Jenner had long entertained Apple-like fantasies of a hip business empire. Blackhill's first non-Floydian client was to be an act that could have arisen only in London and only in 1967: Marc Bolan's Tyrannosaurus Rex.

Bolan had initially made his diminutive presence felt on the fringes of Swinging London as a razor-sharp Mod hustler named Mark Feld: but, in Jenner's words, 'Back then you could transform, you could see the light, be born again and become a hippie.' To his small underground cult following, the elf-like Bolan had been reincarnated as a messenger from another time and place – wrapped in a cape, strumming an acoustic guitar, and warbling about mythical creatures from the far shore of his fertile imagination. His 'group' boasted but one other member: the bongo-playing Steve 'Peregrine' Took, who had renamed himself after a character in Tolkien's *Lord of the Rings* before linking up with Marc through an ad in *IT*.

The ragtag duo's most influential booster was former Radio London deejay John Peel, adopted by the BBC as its token hippie after the government shut down the offshore pirates in August 1967, who took to airing Marc's pre-Rex singles 'Hippy Gumbo' and 'The Wizard' on his late-night radio show. Intrigued by the bizarre voice and lyrics, Andrew King had June drive him in the Rolls-Bentley to a lunch-hour gig at Ealing College.

June was instantly smitten, perceiving in Marc that otherworldly 'illumination' she had heretofore thought unique to Syd, of 'a candle that was about to be snuffed out any minute'. A few days later Bolan dropped by Blackhill's office to charm Jenner with his earnest 'hippie buttercup sandwich' raps, as the manager recalls them, and a deal was struck. 'What the Pink Floyd do electronically,' Marc announced in the pop press, 'we do acoustically.'

In those days Rex's work usually drew comparison with that of Donovan and that other mystical duo, Joe Boyd's protegés the Incredible String Band; if Bolan boasted little of their musical facility and grounding in traditional folk idioms, he made up for it with sheer style and chutzpah. But according to someone who was soon in a position to know. Marc's true underground hero was Syd Barrett.

'He came to Blackhill because Blackhill managed Syd Barrett,' states June. 'It was a recognition of a kindred spirit, that there existed another one of him, another lunatic who didn't know where he fitted in, but knew he was special.

'Marc called himself a wordsmith, and that's what he thought and knew Syd was. Someone was doing something that he was doing, but getting some recognition for it. He'd never met him then, but he totally knew all his songs and his words – so he came to what he thought was the horse's mouth. He thought, "If they can deal with Syd Barrett, they're the right people to deal with me."

'It was like magnets. He felt wonderful that he'd been in the office that managed Syd Barrett. It was a regular ordinary office with telephone, typewriter, two rooms, and he was very happy to know that Syd had been there.'

Magnetic might also be the word for the attraction between Marc and June. Within days of the meeting, June had left her jeweller boyfriend and Marc his parents' Wimbledon prefab: the new couple shacked up in an old van June bought from Juliette Wright, before finding more permanent digs in a Notting Hill cold-water garrett.

'From when I met Marc,' says June, '*that* was where my loyalty lay. Syd still had access to me, which he would always have – even now, if he knew where to find me. But there was no way you could possibly encompass both. It took twenty-four hours a day to do one.'

Other sources contend that June's tenure at Blackhill ended on a sour note when Andrew King, returning from his honeymoon, was unamused to find her in his bed with the bopping elf. According to Peter Jenner, Marc reacted to June's dismissal by terminating his own association with Blackhill – albeit on the pretext that his managers were tampering with his art by advocating a more commercial, electric-pop sound for his Barrett-like stream-of-consciousness fantasies.

By the turn of the decade, Bolan had not only 'gone electric', but abbreviated his alias to T. Rex and jettisoned the hippie trappings (along with his hobbit-monickered sidekick) to take on another identity: that of glittering teen idol with a string of Number One hits. As with the Floyd, Jenner and King would be obliged to witness their protegé's big commercial breakthrough from the sidelines: T. Rex's management was now in the capable hands of sometime Floyd agent Tony Howard – and June Bolan. She and Marc finally married in 1970.

Well into his *Electric Warrior* period, however, the prototype for Marc's fey glamour, down to the eyeliner, pancake make-up, and corkscrew hair, was provided by Syd Barrett, whom Bolan still acknowledged as 'one of the few people I'd actually call a genius . . . he inspired me beyond belief'.[3] The 'glitter king' even *looked* just like the late-'67 model Syd. Says June of her late husband: 'Syd influenced him *tremendously* – we used to speak about it a lot after Syd had got ill and was no longer with the Floyd.'

The young David Bowie, destined to become Bolan's chief competitor in the early 1970s glam-rock sweepstakes, was no less smitten and shaped by Syd. The revelation that pop music and high art might be fused into one medium first struck him, Bowie told *Penthouse* many years later, when he wandered into a Pink Floyd performance at the Marquee Club. 'And there was Syd Barrett with his white white face and his black eyeliner all around his eyes – this strange presence singing in front of a band that was using light shows. I thought, "Wow! He's a bohemian, a poet, and he's in a rock band!"'

The chameleon's 'Barrett phase' was to manifest itself on the 1969 *Space Oddity* album, in compositions like 'The Cygnet Committee', as well as in the performing alias he adopted shortly thereafter – Arnold Korns, as in Syd's 'Arnold Layne'. When Bowie met Mick Rock in late 1971, their instant rapport, and Rock's selection as the rising star's semi-official photographer, had everything to do with the fact that he was a friend of Barrett; David told Mick at the time that Syd remained one of his three great inspirations (along with Iggy Pop and Lou Reed). In 1973, Bowie would feature his own interpretation of 'See Emily Play' on *Pin-Ups*.

Blackhill never was to turn much of a profit from Tyrannosaurus Rex or subsequent underground discoveries like Roy Harper (the future vocalist on the Floyd's 'Have a Cigar'). In the meantime, Peter Jenner attempted the imaginative ruse of applying for a £5,000 grant from the Arts Council of Great Britain. All concerned, however, seemed at a loss when pressed to explain how this money might actually be used. Roger Waters came closest with vague talk of 'a saga like *The Illiad* . . . telling a story like a fairy tale, a definite scene with good and evil' featuring music by the Floyd, narration by John Peel, and Arthur Brown performing the part of a Demon King.[4]

The Daily Express promptly did its editorial best to ensure that nothing of the sort might ever come to pass:

> The Pink Floyd according to some accounts reproduces the sound equivalent of LSD drug visions . . . It has taken part in those curious way-out events, simulating drug ecstasies. which are known as 'freak-outs', in which girls writhe and shriek and young men roll themselves naked in paint and jelly . . . I don't think the Arts Council should put any kind of approving seal on this sort of thing, do you?

The application was rejected.

In early January 1968, readers of *Fab(ulous)* were given little inkling that anything might be amiss with the merry foursome gathered around a birthday cake on the glossy teenybop magazine's cover. 'This month,' *Fab*'s breathless copy explained, 'not only is it our fourth birthday, but it is half the members of Pink Floyd's birthdays too.'

The feature article consisted mostly of a discussion with the two birthday boys – Barrett and Mason – on the subject of . . . birthdays. Syd recalled his own childhood celebrations: 'games that you play in the dark, when someone hides and hits you with a cushion. We also used to dress up and go into the street and throw stones at passing cars.' Nick and Syd went on to confide that 'when all this has worn off' they hoped to become, respectively, an architect and a painter.

'But as far as we are concerned,' concluded *Fab*'s Sally Cork (who must have caught Barrett on one of his better days), 'we are very happy if they stay the way that they are. And carry on being half of the very progressive and psychedelic group, called THE PINK FLOYD.'[5]

Behind such happy talk scenes, a campaign for Barrett's ouster from the Floyd was now being openly waged, with Roger (in Jenner's words) 'the leader of the Syd Must Go faction'. One insider remembers Waters presenting 'a whole list of complaints about Syd. Some of them seemed a bit petty; one was that Syd kept nicking Roger's cigarettes and never bought any of his own. Roger said that was the final straw.'

Storm Thorgerson, however, argues, 'It's not very fruitful being hard on Roger and Nick and Rick, or them on themselves. My recollection is that they really didn't know how to handle it. You don't cut off your nose to spite your face – he was the songwriter. That's ascribing to Roger vast degrees of egocentricity which he later had, but I don't think he did then. It was a very difficult time for them.

'I know they were very reluctant because they met in my flat and were talking about how difficult Syd was, and we had a big conversation about what to do. I was trying partially to act as arbitrator, cause they knew I knew Syd.

'I remember at some point his hair getting really matted and sticky, like pre-punk. If nothing else, he was definitely an innovator, even then – but with the innovation which would occur with a lot of artists, so akin to unsettled, unstable behaviour. It's one thing to admire in terms of the manifestations of an artist. It's another to live with it. That was the continuing dilemma for the Floyd – having to live with their main creative drive being fundamentally impossible.'

Andrew King, meanwhile, had installed Syd, Lindsay, and their cats Pink and Floyd in a flat owned by his dad at the top of Richmond Hill. But any hopes of providing Barrett with a more stable home environment were subverted by the ubiquitous hangers-on: drug freaks and groupies who turned up in such numbers that the place reminded some visitors of a railway station. 'The allegation,' says Thorgerson, 'although not founded, nor detailed or pinpointing any one person, is that forces unknown were lacing his coffee with small amounts of acid for months on end.'

Peter Jenner recalls that he and King 'fought like mad against Syd leaving the band. We went through a lot of grief trying to keep him in. Being an academic who knew a bit of sociology and psychology – a little knowledge can be a dangerous thing – I tried all sorts of things that I thought might be appropriate in relating to this person who was obviously under a lot of mental stress.

'But finally we had to agree it was just too much. They'd go on stage and they wouldn't know what songs he'd play. And you just didn't know where he was going to go with a song. He might do a solo which might go on for two minutes or five. He might just play the same song for forty minutes – and the same note all the way through it. They'd just have to keep waffling away while he'd play the same note, *boing . . . boing . . . boing . . . boing . . .* for ages and ages. As it became obvious that he was deeply disturbed, we had to accept that we couldn't reasonably expect the others to go on working with him as before.'

David Gilmour, in the meantime, had endured his own series of rather more down-to-earth frustrations, despite having received his first Fender Telecaster as a twenty-first birthday present from his indulgent parents. Jokers Wild had had little trouble mustering gigs and appreciative audiences on the Continent as a cover band, with Ricky Wills (the future member of Frampton's Camel and Foreigner) and John 'Willie' Wilson taking over on bass and drums, and the songs of the Four Seasons making way for those of Jimi Hendrix. Come 1967, they even changed their name to the Flowers.

Yet since the Sam and Dave debacle back in '65, no one had asked them to cut another record. In mid-1967 the Flowers disbanded, and Gilmour, Wills, and Wilson struggled on as a power trio called Bullitt.

In London one night, after David attended a typically catastrophic Floyd performance, Nick Mason approached him with a vague proposition: 'Keep it under your hat – but would you consider joining the band at some time in the future? Because we might need to get someone in . . .'

Barrett, however, had arrived at plans of his own for expanding the line-up with, according to Waters, 'two freaks that he'd met somewhere or other. One of them played the banjo and the other played the saxophone. We weren't into that at all, and it was obvious that the crunch had finally come.'[6]

Gilmour's call came at Christmastime. 'They just said, Did I want to? and I said, Yes, and it was as simple as that.' The initial inducement for Dave had less to do with new artistic horizons than with the prospect of 'fame and the girls'.

His rock and roll acquaintances suspected something was afoot when Dave strode into a Cambridge music shop they frequented, and grandly requested the custom-made Fender Stratocaster that they had all coveted. Future Sex Pistols chronicler Lee Wood watched agog as Gilmour then produced a wad of notes totalling 'a hundred and something pounds. They took this yellow Stratocaster off the wall and he bought it and said cheerio and walked out. We were all thinking, "*How did he get all that money?*" Nobody paid cash for a guitar. About three days later in *Melody Maker* I read that Dave Gilmour had joined the Pink Floyd.' The Stratocaster was to remain Gilmour's guitar of choice throughout his career with the Floyd.

Another aspiring local guitarist, Tim Renwick, vividly recalls hanging out in a 'fusty little club in Cambridge called the Alley Club when Dave arrived, and said he'd just been taken on as a member of the Pink Floyd. I remember thinking, "Oh, what a day! I wonder if this would ever happen to *me*."' Nearly twenty years later, it finally would. In the meantime, Renwick would team up with Bullitt's Willie Wilson in the band Quiver.

Blackhill officially announced Gilmour's addition in January, 1968, alleging the Floyd's desire 'to explore new instruments and add further experimental dimensions to its sound'. One of Dave's first assignments was to pretend to play a guitar on an 'Apples and Oranges' promotional film – with Roger faking the recalcitrant Syd's vocal. Gilmour, says a friend, found such episodes 'really spooky'.

And how did Barrett react to finding his old mate in the spotlight with him? 'It was fairly obvious,' Gilmour recalled years later, 'that I was brought in to take over from him, at least onstage, [but] it was impossible to gauge his feelings about it. I don't think Syd has opinions as such. He functions on a totally different plane of logic, and some people will claim, "Well yeah, man, he's on a higher cosmic level" – but basically there's something drastically wrong.

'It wasn't just the drugs – we'd *both* done acid before the Floyd thing – it's just a mental foible which grew out of all proportion. I remember all sorts of strange things happening – at one point he was wearing lipstick, dressing in high heels, and believing he had homosexual tendencies. We all felt he should have gone to see a psychiatrist, though someone in fact played an interview he did to R.D. Laing, and Laing claimed he was incurable.'[7]

Gilmour, for his part, brought to the Floyd a musicality as harmonious and adaptable as his character. 'He came into a very difficult situation,' says Peter Jenner, 'and he handled it very well. He was also a great guitarist – the best musician the Floyd ever had.' In a conversation with superfan Andy Mabbett, the manager recalled 'Dave playing in the studio for the first time . . . doing a terrific imitation of Jimi Hendrix. He could also do a great imitation of Syd Barrett. He was a technician in a way that none of the others were . . . He started off playing in a very simple Syd-y style, and through the years it's become his own.'[8]

Yet Jenner, sceptical of the rest of the band's creative talent, continued to insist that Barrett be involved in some capacity. 'If you told me that without Syd they were going to be the biggest working band in the world . . . with Syd I could've believed it, but without Syd where's it going to come from? Nobody else could write very well: Rick could do a bit of a tune, and Roger could knock off a couple of words if necessary under pressure. But [Waters] wrote only because Syd wrote and we encouraged everybody to . . . Rick wrote before Roger.'

The Floyd proceeded to play a handful of gigs as a five-piece – until the day that the others decided not to bother to fetch Barrett before their performance. 'The idea,' says Jenner, 'was that Dave would be Syd's dep. and cover for his eccentricities. And when that got to be not workable, Syd was just going to write. Just to try to keep him involved, but in a way where the others could work and function.' Accordingly, Barrett was left, in Gilmour's words, 'to stay home and write wonderful songs, become the mystery Brian Wilson figure behind the group.'[9]

But Syd's new material turned out to be more than the band was willing or able to handle, especially the taunting 'Have You Got It Yet?' with its ever-changing melody and chord progression. His bemused colleagues had simply had enough.

'They came to Andrew and me,' recounts Jenner, 'and said, "You don't believe in us, you don't think we could do it without Syd, do you?" We said no. So they wandered off to Bryan Morrison, and we agreed that we'd go on looking after Syd.' In April, with the byzantine process of dismantling the original six-way Blackhill partnership already underway, the press was advised that Syd Barrett had 'left' the Pink Floyd.

But, says Jenner, 'Syd never really understood that, because he always thought of them as *his* band. He just drifted back to the Floyd always.'

Then again, in a figurative sense, with *Dark Side of the Moon*, *Wish You Were Here*, and *The Wall*, the Floyd would end up drifting inexorably back to Syd.

Chapter 10

Shine On You Crazy Diamond

Exactly one month after the official announcement on 6 April 1968 that Barrett had 'left' the Pink Floyd, Peter Jenner steered him back to Abbey Road. Eager to prove that Blackhill had been right to place its bets on Syd over the rest of the band, Jenner did indeed produce a solo album's worth of material that spring. But the tracks, which ranged from the tuneless free-associating American Indian saga 'Swan Lee' to the wordless (and tuneless) guitar freak-out 'Lanky', were deemed entirely too, well, *inaccessible* for public consumption.* EMI's displeasure was compounded by the smashed microphones and 'general disorder' that Barrett left behind at Abbey Road.

Syd, meanwhile, moved into Storm Thorgerson's flat in the Egerton Court mansion block opposite the South Kensington underground station. He inherited his room from another old Cambridge friend, Nigel Gordon; the current roster of resident bohemians included Mick Rock (who romanticized Barrett during this period as 'a doomed flying force'), Storm's fellow student at the Royal College of Art and Hipgnosis design partner Aubrey 'Po' Powell, and one Harry Dobson.

For all Jenner's relief that his star client was now in the custody of the 'supportive' Storm and Po, others remember life at Egerton Court as less than salubrious. According to the writer Jonathan Meades, Barrett 'was this rather weird, exotic, and mildly famous creature . . . living in this flat with these people who to some extent were pimping off him both professionally and privately. I went there to see Harry and there was this terrible noise. It sounded like heating pipes shaking. I said, "what's that?" and he sort of giggled and said, "That's Syd having a bad trip. We put him in the linen cupboard."'[1]

'I do *not* remember locking Syd up in a cupboard,' retorts Thorgerson. 'It sounds to me like a pure fantasy, like Jonathan Meades

---

* The backing track for 'Late Night' was subsequently salvaged for *The Madcap Laughs*; 'Swan Lee' and 'Lanky' finally surfaced twenty years later on the *Opel* collection.

was on dope himself. But we *might* have, as we might easily have done all sorts of playful and not so playful things. There was a lot of dope around, so people would be in various states of "travelling" and "exploring". There would be occasions where everybody in the flat, not just Syd, would have been somewhat disorientated.

'By the time he got there, he was fairly far gone. He'd fluctuate – states of reason, states of not so reasoned behaviour. I was not particularly cognizant of psychology at that time, nor was I able to cope with it. But Syd being generally deranged didn't necessarily register, particularly. We were all grooving around London at the height of Psychedelia, an extremely exciting time, and half the people were out of their minds half the time.

'We *all* went loopy in our own ways. Half of us were with shrinks or running off to India. There was a very high degree of unsettled behaviour, to put it mildly.' In any case, Storm points out, 'One was very loath turning around and describing a friend that one had grown up with as *loony*. Unless they froth at the mouth and beat up people, one refrains from doing it.'

Thorgerson says Barrett came closest to meeting these criteria on one 'markedly horrible' occasion, when he began smashing his girl-friend's head with a mandolin: 'She lying on the floor screaming and him straddled across her, pinning her down. We had to pull him off and take the mandolin away from him.' This was but the most memorable of the many 'horrendous rows' that augured the end of the couple's relationship.

Some evenings, a desire for alternative companionship would lead Syd to the Youth Hostel in Holland Park, a veritable nest of young acid freaks from around the world. When his trips went hay-wire, he would then sometimes crawl to the nearby flat of a trusted former associate. Though Roger Waters then occupied the floor above her, June Bolan recalls that 'Syd would never go up and knock on Roger's door, but he'd always knock on me. I was still June, and "Office" had always made things right; it meant stability, it meant wages on Friday, and if you needed something done you'd phone Office.

'He'd arrive covered in mud at five in the morning, looking absol-utely manic, and rambling on about how the police were chasing him and all sorts of people were after him. I'd say, "Come in, sit, do you want a cup of tea, would you like a bath?" "No – have you got any wages?" He hadn't been on wages for a year!' June would, however, give him the cabfare before sending him home to Egerton Court.

108

Always restless, Barrett never seemed to stay in any flat for long. He also had a certain knack for wearing out his welcome. His next move was to the home of the Pink Floyd's longtime friend Duggie Fields in Earls Court. A generation later, it seems ironic that the former Floyd star once taunted his new flatmate, destined to become a successful artist, with the words 'Duggie, you're twenty-three and you're not famous!' Syd still was, leaving Fields, by his account, 'speechless at the number of people who would invade our flat, and how they would behave towards anyone who was in the group . . . Some of the girls were stunning, and they would literally throw themselves at Syd.'

And yet, according to Fields, Barrett was excruciatingly ambivalent about both his fame and his physical attractiveness. 'People kept coming around, and he would actually lock himself in his room . . . He'd have these girls pounding on his bedroom door all night, literally, and he'd be locked inside, trapped. He did rather encourage this behaviour to a certain extent, but then he didn't know what to do with it; he would resent it.'[2]

Barrett was in fact haunted by his perception that he was ending up a failure. The underlying problem, according to Fields, was, 'He had the world at his feet, all the possibilities, and he just couldn't choose. He had great problems committing himself to doing anything for any length of time, he was the kind of person who'd change in the middle. He'd set off, lose his motivation, and start questioning what he was doing, which might just be walking down the street.' Syd's moods were mercurial: paranoid, brooding, or catatonic one moment, he was perfectly capable of coming across as 'bright, charming, and jolly' the next.[3]

While Fields tried with limited success to encourage his friend to resume painting, Bryan Morrison attempted to return Barrett to the public eye by drumming up some press coverage. For all Jenner and King's struggles on his behalf, Syd no longer viewed them as his managers; the Pink Floyd, after all, were now managed by 'Morrie', and Barrett never fully recognized his separation from the band. Morrison, who had long controlled the publishing to Syd's Floyd songs, was happy to take charge of Barrett's earthly affairs, such as they were.

Jonathon Green, then a staffer for *Rolling Stone*'s short-lived British edition, remembers being sent to interview Barrett at the manager's new offices at NEMS Enterprises. 'He didn't have an album out, and I didn't know why I was doing it,' Green says. 'I went into this big white room, and there was Syd, dressed all in white clothes. It was really very sad. Syd spent the whole time looking at the top corner of the room, saying, "Hey man . . . hey . . . right." '

Morrison tried to coax Barrett into sharing his religious insights with *Rolling Stone*'s readers, but the Piper would have none of it. 'Right, right,' he mumbled dismissively. 'Now look up there – can you see the people on the ceiling?' In the end, Green decided to scrap his article.

In March 1969, the unpredictable Barrett nonetheless took the initiative in leaving word at Abbey Road that he wanted to record again. The message reached EMI's Malcolm Jones, a former rock musician in his twenties who had signed up the likes of Deep Purple and Marc Bolan, and had recently persuaded his bosses to let him launch a 'progressive' EMI subsidiary called Harvest Records (to which Pink Floyd themselves would be rerouted). An admirer of Syd's work with the Floyd, Jones was thrilled at the thought of adding him to the Harvest roster. He lost no time in setting up a meeting, during which Barrett seemed almost his old charismatic self.

Despite their misgivings over Syd's previous solo abortion, Jones's superiors Roy Featherstone and Ron White proved willing to gamble that the former Floyd star might indeed be back on track. Barrett had, after all, been responsible for the group's only two hit singles – a commodity nowhere in evidence on his ex-colleagues' work-in-progress, *Ummagumma*. Featherstone and White did, however, insist that someone accountable to them be hired as producer. After Norman Smith begged off, Jones, who had already produced a Love Sculpture LP, landed the job himself.

His enthusiasm mounted when Syd serenaded him with the likes of 'Terrapin' and 'Clowns and Jugglers', later renamed 'Octopus' and released as a single, whose lyrics were to yield the album's title, *The Madcap Laughs*. The Harvest boss was particularly impressed by 'an extremely haunting song' called 'Opel', an impressionistic *'dream in a mist of grey on a far distant shore'* that turned increasingly stark and personal before ending with the heartfelt cry *'I'm drowning . . .'* Jones immediately booked Abbey Road for a series of sessions beginning on 10 April 1969.

Barrett initially seemed enthusiastic and on the ball as he put down solo guitar and vocal tracks for six numbers, of which the first on the agenda was 'Opel'. Inexplicably, however, Syd would end up abandoning perhaps the strongest of all his post-Floyd compositions, almost as if 'Opel' was just too good for him to cope with in his generally fragmented state. In the second week, Barrett brought in Quiver's Willie Wilson and Humble Pie's Jerry Shirley to accompany him on 'No Man's Land' and 'Here I Go'.

Working with drums and bass, Syd's guitar playing turned, in his producer's words, 'extremely erratic. He would frequently switch from rhythm to lead, setting the meters well into the red and requiring a re-take. It was a matter of having too many ideas and wanting to record them all at once.'[4] But Jones was truly given pause only when Barrett then insisted on spending an entire day overdubbing home recordings of a friend's motorcycle onto an 18-minute conga-drum doodle from the Peter Jenner sessions, called 'Ramadhan'.

Some rather more productive overdubbing was accomplished in early May, when the Floyd's old UFO rivals the Soft Machine – then comprising Mike Ratledge on keyboards, Hugh Hopper on bass, and Robert Wyatt on drums – came in to fill out Syd's unaccompanied recordings of 'It's No Good Trying' and 'Love You'. According to Wyatt, the Softs 'thought the sessions were actually rehearsals. We'd say, "what key is that in, Syd?" and he'd reply, "Yeah," or, "That's funny".'[5]

Because Barrett had punctuated the music-hall patter of 'Love You' with instrumental breaks variously running to eight, seven, and six-and-a-half bars, the band found it excruciating to follow. In keeping with his 'spirit of the moment' philosophy, however, Syd insisted that the ragged first take was perfect, and wouldn't let them try it again. (For contractual reasons the Soft Machine could not be credited on the *Madcap Laughs* sleeve.)

By this time, the EMI brass were having second thoughts about the mounting costs of an album that was still only half complete. The ever-protective David Gilmour, meanwhile, had been spending a lot of time with Barrett and monitoring his progress in the studio; now he informed Malcolm Jones that Syd wanted him and Roger Waters to produce the rest of the record. Jones, having achieved his original goal of getting Barrett back to work, readily bowed out in the hope that a collaboration with his former colleagues might not only provide Syd with a more comfortable ambience, but generate some inspired Floydian productions. The catch for Gilmour and Waters was that they were only allowed three increasingly hurried sessions to complete *The Madcap Laughs*, which Dave then mixed in its entirety.

Most of their tracks consisted of little more than Syd's voice and acoustic guitar; the Floyd boys' only real productions were 'Octopus' and 'Golden Hair', an early James Joyce poem that Barrett had set to music in his late teens. For *The Madcap Laughs* it was subtly embellished with bass, cymbals, vibes, and organ, the latter reportedly played by Rick Wright. But Dave and Roger saw fit to undermine this display of musical polish with the *audio verité* of Syd stumbling unaccompanied through the ensuing acoustic tracks, complete with his false starts and studio babble – leaving the listener, whether by chance or by design, with an album almost as unsettlingly fragmented as its featured artist.

Issued in the first days of 1970, *The Madcap Laughs* was warmly received (*Melody Maker* rather unwittingly called it 'a fine album full of madness and lunacy'), and despite the lack of airplay sold a respectable 6,000-plus copies in Britain within eight weeks. Reassured that he had not, after all, been forgotten by his fans, Syd embarked on a round of relatively lucid press interviews. He even talked about the Floyd, and 'the progress the group could have made. But it made none, none at all, except in the sense that it was continuing. To make my album was a challenge as I didn't have anything to follow.'[6] And he immediately began planning another solo record with Dave Gilmour and EMI.

The second album, to be called simply *Barrett* and released in November 1970, benefited from, if nothing else, consistent personnel and some semblance of structure. This time Gilmour shared production duties with Rick Wright, Waters having gasped, 'I can't cope with *that* again!' The band featured Jerry Shirley on drums, with Rick doubling on keyboards and Dave (who insisted that Syd take all the guitar solos) on bass. Yet, beyond the sprightly, *Piper*-esque 'Baby Lemonade' and 'Gigolo Aunt', *Barrett* often suffered from Syd's growing inability to perform or even write coherently; much of it scraped the bottom of his barrel of Pink Floyd rejects. In the best 'Have You Got It Yet?' tradition, moreover, Barrett seemed determined never to play a song the same way twice.

Gilmour heroically nursed his old friend through the project, patiently reviewing the material with him before each session, then translating Barrett's aspirations to Wright and Shirley. As often as not, Dave would end up simply coaxing a presentable solo performance from Syd, over which he and Rick would subsequently overdub an arrangement. So if the ending of the sublime 'Dominoes' sounds like something from the Floyd's 1969 *More* soundtrack, it is because Barrett stopped playing so abruptly that Wright and Gilmour felt obliged to supply their own coda.

112

For that song, Syd also became so stuck for a lead guitar part that Dave, acting on a weird brainstorm, put the tape in reverse. With his 'Dominoes' coming at him backwards, Barrett suddenly returned from limbo, reeling off, in Jerry Shirley's opinion, 'the best lead he ever played. The first time out and he didn't put a note wrong.'[7] Incidents like this convinced some acquaintances that Syd, for all his disabilities, was indeed possessed of, or by, unusual psychic powers.

Working with Barrett nonetheless 'tortured Dave's ass' says Storm Thorgerson. 'He wouldn't turn up to recording sessions when he was supposed to, he'd play the wrong song, he'd forget the lyrics, it was a nightmare. It's amazing they got a whole album recorded at all.'

In the midst of the project, Barrett did actually perform – with Gilmour and Shirley – on two live BBC radio broadcasts, and even agreed to sing at London's 'Extravaganza '70 Music and Fashion Festival' in Olympia, on 6 June. But then Syd got cold feet, and Dave and Jerry virtually had to haul him onstage. Barrett rushed through 'Terrapin', 'Gigolo Aunt', and 'Effervescing Elephant', then hit his stride with a dynamite 'Octopus', only to bring his first post-Floyd public appearance to an abrupt and premature end.

Four years later, Rick Wright was to say of the Barrett albums, 'I can't imagine anyone liking them; musically, they're atrocious. Most of the songs were great but it was impossible to get any sound because of the state Syd was in at the time. At least it tells people how Syd was when he made them.'[8]

The songs on *The Madcap Laughs* and *Barrett* are similar in content and structure to Syd's Pink Floyd work, only much of the method seems to have gone out of his madness; next to *Piper*, they often sound flat, listless, offhand, and awkward. 'It's all going on his head,' Shirley said, 'but only little bits of it manage to come out of his mouth . . . Sometimes he'll sing a melody absolutely fine, and the next time round he'll sing a totally different melody, or just go off-key.'[9]

Barrett's later material still yields brilliant flashes of fantastic imagery – or (to use his own phrases) '*clover honey pots of mystic shining seed*' and '*moaned magnesium proverbs and sobs*'. But the visions have turned desperately bleak: '*Cold iron hands clap the party of clowns outside . . . Light misted fog, the dead waving us back in formation . . . A broken pier on a wavy sea . . .*' And every so often the phantasmagoria gives way to insightful commentary on Syd's own confused psyche: '*Inside me I feel so alone and unreal . . . Please lift a hand . . . I tattooed my brain all the way . . .*'

113

While the insects that incongruously adorn the *Barrett* sleeve were a product of Syd's art school days, the *Madcap* jacket was created by his former flatmates Storm Thorgerson and 'Po' Powell (who had already furnished his ex-band with two covers), and Mick Rock (whose own career as a photographer was, he says, entirely sparked by the experience of snapping Barrett strictly as a friend). The trio agreed to photograph the artist in his current Earl's Court digs, whose floorboards Syd painted for the occasion with festive orange and purple stripes.

But Thorgerson says that the nude Oriental loitering in the background was no mere prop. 'The whole place had a scuzzy, suspiciously drug-ridden vibe to it, added to which this girl was wandering around at eleven in the morning, starkers. Not that it's *that* amazing, nor do I have a moral view about it; it's just not particularly . . . *typical.*'

As ever, the demands sycophants made on Syd, together with his own inability to say no, mitigated against any semblance of a stable home life. He began to talk yearningly of someday getting married and settling down in the suburbs, and studying medicine to become a doctor like his late father. For a time, his new girlfriend, Gayla Pinion, rented another of Duggie Field's rooms at Earls Court; but when she moved out, Barrett allowed a trio of his young admirers to requisition her tiny cubicle. Three soon turned into five, and they were always underfoot, along with the unending stream, of visitors – all competing for their idol's attention, and constantly bringing him offerings of drugs.

Unable to cope any more, Syd fled to his mother and Cambridge, leaving Fields instructions that he had to get rid of the hangers-on. This was finally accomplished by invoking Barrett's 'violent side', which anyone who had spent much time with him was anxious to avoid at all costs.

By 1971 Syd was living in Cambridge, where at one point Mrs Barrett reportedly had him committed to a sanitorium for several months. Though his solo LPs would go unreleased in America until 1974, *Rolling Stone* ran a profile, uncredited, but in fact written by Mick Rock, who had tracked Syd down in his mother's cellar. Rock reported that Barrett looked 'hollow-cheeked and pale, his eyes reflect[ing] a permanent state of shock. He has a ghostly beauty which one normally associates with the poets of old.'

Like his own songs, Syd seemed alternately lucid and elliptical. He told Rock he felt 'full of dust and guitars', and, at twenty-five, afraid of getting old. 'I think young people should have fun, but I never have any.' Yet, he insisted he was 'totally together', adding: 'I'm nothing that you think I am anyway.'

In early 1972, Syd's neighbour Twink, former drummer for Tomorrow, the Pretty Things, and the Pink Fairies, talked him into forming a new, locally based band called Stars. Apart from a coffee-bar gig or two, the trio's first (and only) public performance was at the Cambridge Corn Exchange, second-billed to the MC5. Barrett, Twink, and bassist Jack Monck had rehearsed a Syd retrospective that included the Floyd's 'Lucifer Sam' and highlights from the solo LPs, but then the PA rendered the vocals inaudible; Monck's amp malfunctioned; and Syd, who had somehow managed to cut his finger open, freaked out.

Among the shocked witnesses was the drummer from Syd's very first band. 'He looked completely at a loss – stumbling and stammering to sing,' recalls Clive Welham. 'The applause from the audience was only in sympathy, because the music was poor quality, like some drunk performing.' When Welham dropped by the dressing room, Barrett didn't even seem to remember who he was. Some devastating press accounts hardly assuaged Syd's paranoia, and he never played with Twink again.

Around this time Barrett looked up his childhood sweetheart, Libby Gordon, who, says Storm Thorgerson, 'has a rather sad tale to tell of him staying at her house; everything seemed fine for a day or two, and then she found him early one morning with a pair of scissors, having cut off the flower heads in her garden. This is not the sort of thing that is designed to endear you very easily, so she threw him out.'

And yet, as always with Syd, there were times when the madcap could confound his old friends' diminished expectations. Pete Brown was in for a surprise when he arrived at a Cambridge club for a reading of his poetry. 'I'd arranged for Jack Bruce to meet me there,' Brown remembers, 'and after the gig we were going to go to his place in Colchester to work. I got there very late, and there was this insane band on stage, playing this interesting, weird kind of jazz. Somebody had recognized Jack and handed him a double-bass, which he was playing, and there was a guitarist who I vaguely recognized.

'Then during my set, I said. "I'd like to dedicate this poem to Syd Barrett, because he's here in Cambridge and he's one of the greatest songwriters in the country." At which point, the guitar player from that band, who was sitting in the audience, got up and said, "No I'm not." That was *him*. And that he could get up and play with Jack Bruce was something.'

For the next two years, Barrett divided his time between Cambridge and a penthouse room at London's Park Lane Hilton Hotel. He kept an exceedingly low profile and accomplished absolutely nothing, only to see his ever-growing legend fanned by one of the most zealous cults ever known to rock and roll. To some degree it resembled that of Jim Morrison, vicariously feeding upon the bizarre escapades of a brilliant and charismatic countercultural icon who evidently let himself be ruled – and ultimately destroyed – by the weirder implications of his own art and public image. Only Syd didn't die.

The appearance in 1972 of a Syd Barrett Appreciation Society, which sponsored a publication called *Terrapin*, brought Syd freaks out of the woodwork in countries as far-flung as Brazil, Israel, and the Soviet Union. Even the mainstream pop weeklies took to reporting Barrett 'sightings' in breathless tones worthy of a UFO landing. A more substantial tribute was paid by *NME*'s Nick Kent in 1974, in the form of a 5,000 word account of Syd's rise and fall.

But for all its increasing reliance on fan artwork and poetry and Syd Barrett crossword puzzles, *Terrapin* was doomed to run out of old clippings and lyrics to reprint. As editor John Steele felt obliged to note in one of his last (and slimmest) issues, 'The Society cannot keep functioning if there is nothing new to report, and people tire of old records, no matter how amazing they might be.'

And yet by 1974 Barrett was earning more royalties than ever before, thanks to David Bowie's recent recording of 'See Emily Play' and the repackaging of the first two Pink Floyd LPs as *A Nice Pair*. Tired of Cambridge, he resumed full-time residence in London, where Bryan Morrison installed him in two rooms at Chelsea Cloisters, an imposing red brick residential hotel off the fashionable King's Road.

There one 'Syd sighting' had him popping into a chic boutique, trying on three different sizes of trousers and claiming they all fitted him perfectly. When he wasn't aimlessly roaming his Chelsea neighbourhood, Barrett could often be found at a nearby pub, guzzling Guinness alone in a corner.

Back at the aptly named Cloisters, with his windows permanently closed and curtains drawn, Syd, oblivious to the overpowering smell, spent his time ogling a giant TV suspended from his ceiling and compulsively raiding his refrigerator. Over the course of about a year, his slender figure ballooned to fourteen stone, at which point the psychedelic Andonis of yore completed his transformation (and, some would say, self-flagellation) by shaving his head. When John Marsh ran into Syd in the street – wearing a Hawaiian shirt and Bermuda shorts – the former Floyd lighting man was reminded of 'a picture of the middle-aged Aleister Crowley'.[10] Other acquaintances described him, more succinctly, as a fat slob.

For all his idiosyncracies – which included the occasional outing, Arnold Layne style, in ladies' clothing – 'Mr Barrett' endeared himself to the Chelsea Cloisters staff by indiscriminately giving them his guitars, TV sets, and stereo equipment. And at least one delivery boy was rewarded with a tip of several hundred pounds.

In the meantime, EMI decided to capitalize on Syd's growing cult legend and on his ex-band's runaway success with *Dark Side of the Moon* by repackaging *The Madcap Laughs* and *Barrett* as another 'two-fer' called, simply, *Syd Barrett*. Seeking a current portrait of the artist for his cover design, Storm Thorgerson, camera at the ready, tracked Syd down at Chelsea Cloisters, only to be shown the door. When he returned the next day, Barrett wouldn't let his old friend in at all.

'I still did the job as conscientiously as I could,' said Thorgerson, who ended up devising a rather touching arrangement of old Barrett photos and memorabilia. 'But it wasn't very pleasing to knock on his door and be told to fuck off – for something that I was doing for *him*.'

Peter Jenner had only slightly better luck in late 1974 when he attempted to rehabilitate Barrett's career with a new solo production. Syd did at least show up at a recording studio, but with no strings on his guitar. After a set was finally cadged from Phil May of the Pretty Things, someone handed Barrett a sheet of paper on which the lyrics had been typed to his new songs, which Jenner described as minimalistic 'sketches'. Unfortunately these had been typed up in red; and Syd, thinking he was being presented with a bill, angrily bit the bearer's hand.

The sessions stumbled on for three days, during which time the disorientated artist would often lose interest and wander outside to take the air. The engineer noticed that, invariably, when Syd turned right upon leaving the studio he would soon return, but when he turned left it would be the last anyone saw of him that day.

'It was very frustrating and upsetting, and very sad,' says Jenner. 'Glimpses of things would come through in the chaos and confusion, a bit of a melody line or lyric. From the doodlings of a sick mind, bits of clarity would emerge. In the undergrowth the flowers were still growing, but he couldn't get at them.' Although Jenner did manage to get some backing tracks on tape before abandoning the project as hopeless, the absence of any vocals left EMI with nothing to salvage of Barrett's abortive third solo album.

'He's a great artist, an incredibly creative artist, and it's tragic that the music business may well have a lot to do with doing him in,' Jenner subsequently said, adding that he and 'everyone else involved with' Barrett had 'a lot to answer for'. The 1975 Pink Floyd album, *Wish You Were Here*, revealed that Syd's former band was thinking along much the same lines.

Apart from materializing, as if steered by an uncanny sixth sense, at the studio where the Floyd were mixing their towering Barrett tribute 'Shine On You Crazy Diamond' (described in Chapter Eighteen), the Piper's only further contact with the rock world was when he dropped by Bryan Morrison's offices to collect his songwriting royalties. It had become, in the words of Barrett archivist Mark Patress, 'painfully evident that the adult world appeared too gruesome, too corrupt, and altogether too unreal for Syd Barrett'.

At the end of the decade, Roger Barrett – as he now insisted on being called – moved back to Cambridge, apparently for good. Susie Wynne Willson last saw him there in the early 1980s, when she rashly brought him to a Sat-San service. But any hope of at least ameliorating the fifteen-year-old trauma of Barrett's rejection by the religious group faded when a supercilious young disciple exclaimed: 'Oh look who's here – it's *Syd Barrett!*' The living legend instantly fled, leaving Susie to chase him down the road and drive him home.

By this time, 'sightings' in the rock press had dwindled down to a precious few. In 1982, two writers for the French magazine *Actuel* purportedly finagled a brief meeting with Barrett, with his mum hovering behind him, on the pretext that they were returning some laundry he had abandoned at Chelsea Cloisters. They quoted him as saying that he wanted to go back to London, but couldn't because 'there's a train strike at the moment'. (The strike had been over for weeks.) And as to what he was now doing with his life: 'I watch TV, that's all . . .' A photo said to have been snapped at the time showed a mousy, nondescript man with a receding hairline, looking very much older than his thirty-six years. The piece concluded with an incisive epitaph from David Gilmour: 'It's not romantic. It's a sad story. Now it's over.'[11]

Three years later, *Sounds* callously claimed to have been tipped off, by 'supposedly reliable sources', that Barrett was 'found expired in a

Above: Syd Barrett as a Cambridge teenager: 'a very up and easy guy.'
Below: Architectural Abdabs, late 1965: (from left) Nick Mason, Roger Waters, Syd Barrett, Bob Close, and Richard Wright.

Ticket and flyer for underground London's most legendary 1967 'happening': With only one single out, the Floyd were given the honour of closing the show.

Above: 'Straight to Heaven in '67': The Pipers at the gates of fame, all decked out for the Summer of Love. *Left:* The Flower Power turns sour beneath Syd's 'obligatory Hendrix perm.'

Two views of the
'Madcap' at his Earl's
Court Pad.

The Floyd (and their concert and LP sales) lift off towards the stratosphere with *Dark Side of the Moon*.

Dennis Żentek

Above: 'Comfortably Numb': 'Doctor' Waters claiming centre stage in his autobiographical magnum opus *The Wall. Below:* Dave Gilmour and Roger Waters rehearsing for *The Wall*'s London premiere, August 1980.

H. Knott, Hulton-Deutsch Collection

Knott, Hulton-Deutsch Collection

Andreas Kraska

Above: The famous Floyd pig after 'her' post-Waters sex change. *Below:* The Roger-less Floyd's *Momentary Lapse of Reason* 'comeback' is launched in 1987 with a bed over the River Thames.

Nils Jorgensen, RDR Productions

Left: The late-1980s model Floyd (from left, Mason, Gilmour, and Wright) at Red Square after staging the Soviet Union's biggest-ever rock concerts.
Below right: All-time Floyd stalwart Nick Mason in 1988: 'You don't want the world populated *only* with dinosaurs, but it's terribly good to keep *some* alive.'
Below left: 'General' Waters during his triumphant 1990 resurrection of *The Wall* in Berlin, art imitating life imitating art . . .

shop doorway late last year'. Actually, *Syd* Barrett had, for all intents and purposes, met his demise over a decade before that. *Roger* Barrett remained very much alive, if not entirely well, on the suburban dead-end street where he now lived all by himself.

Dave Gilmour says his contact with Syd throughout the 1980s was limited to 'a bit of checking on whether his money was getting to him properly, stuff like that. And I asked Rose, his sister, whether I could go and see him. But she didn't think it was a good idea, because things that remind him of that period of his past tend to depress him. If he sees me or other people from that period, he gets depressed for a couple of weeks. It's not really worth it.'

But the interest in Syd, it seemed, would never die. And when the punk New Wave splintered off into 'neo-psychedelia', Syd Barrett was all but canonized as the one figure who could be credited for having helped father both retro-rock movements.

The sublimely wacky singer/songwriter Robyn Hitchcock, who lived in Cambridge during the late 1970s, initially made his mark as an unabashed Syd soundalike. Robyn's first band, the Soft Boys, like Jesus and Mary Chain after them, went so far as to commit the elusive 'Vegetable Man' to legal vinyl; Hitchcock also wrote and recorded a Barrett tribute called 'The Man Who Invented Himself'. He is still wont to serenade his concert audiences with 'Dark Globe', yet protests that he wasn't '*that* much more influenced by Syd Barrett than a lot of other people were, like Bowie. I just *sound* more like him. I tend to wear my influences on my sleeve.' The band Love and Rockets acknowledged their own debt to Syd with a recording of 'Lucifer Sam'.

In 1987 a host of other latterday Barrett disciples, boasting day-glo names like the Shamen, the Mock Turtles, the Green Telescope, and Death of Samantha, teamed up on the British tribute album *Beyond the Wildwood* (another phrase from *The Wind in the Willows*). Their cover versions of seventeen Syd classics spanning 'Arnold Layne' and 'Baby Lemonade' are often slavishly imitative, but on tracks like Fit and Lemo's poignantly painstaking restoration, in the early Floyd's exact style, of the unfinished *Madcap* flake-out 'Long Cold Look', or Opal's conjuring of a wholly new song from the wreckage of 'Jugband Blues', or the Chemistry Set's imaginative update of 'See Emily Play' the Crazy Diamond's enduring legacy is indeed well illuminated.

Some of *Wildwood*'s contributers also boasted walk-on parts in the ongoing Barrett/Floyd story. The TV Personalities, whose 'Apples and Oranges' is even more out-of-tune than the original, had been dismissed as David Gilmour's London opening act in 1984 for the *faux*

119

pas of capping a performance of 'Emily' with an onstage recital of Barrett's home address. And Plasticland, who cover 'Octopus' on *Wildwood*, went on to collaborate with Syd's onetime co-star, Twink.

In post-punk America, meanwhile, Richard Barone's group the Bongos made 'Emily' a highlight of their live act, and members of the Feelies moonlighted in a lonely hearts club band, Gates of Dawn, whose repertoire consisted exclusively of Barrett and early Floyd material. The much-adored REM chimed in with their own recording of 'Dark Globe', and the French Canadian heavy-metal band Voi-Vod turned a remarkably faithful version of 'Astronomy Dominé' into the featured track of their fifth album, *Nothingface*.

The 1980s also brought a new generation of Barrett fanzines: *Opel*, *Dark Globe*, and *Clowns and Jugglers*. Paperback biographies of the lost hero popped up in the Floyd strongholds of Italy and France. An EP's worth of the 1970 John Peel BBC Radio One sessions, featuring Syd with Gilmour and Jerry Shirley (and the previously unissued 'Two of a Kind'), surfaced on Britain's independent Strange Fruit label. And finally, in the autumn of 1988, the ongoing clamour spurred EMI to release a 'new' Syd Barrett collection called *Opel*: a jumble of out-takes that (except for the unvarnished title demo) inevitably proved less satisfying actually to listen to than it had been for Syd freaks to fantasize about throughout the previous fifteen years. The compilers had intended to include 'Vegetable Man' and 'Scream Thy Last Scream', but couldn't obtain permission from the other Floyds.

All the while, the Piper himself remained conspicuous in his absence, though in 1989 Mick Rock, contemplating a limited collectors' edition of his best rock and roll portraits, was amazed when Barrett actually signed and returned a letter of permission. The closest anyone else in the music world came to re-establishing contact was in October 1988, when Radio One's Nicky Campbell persuaded a Barrett family spokesman to mark *Opel's* appearance by saying a few words on his show. Rose's husband, Paul Breem, let it be known that Barrett was pursuing 'a very ordinary sort of lifestyle', albeit one devoid of any regular human contact beyond an occasional shopping trip with his elderly mother. He 'doesn't play any musical instruments any more'.

As for Syd's musical career, that was a 'part of his life which he prefers to forget now. He had some bad experiences, and, thankfully, has come through all the worst of these, and is now able – fortunately – to lead a normal life here in Cambridge.'

Part Two

HEROES FOR GHOSTS

Chapter 11
Burning Bridges

With Syd Barrett out of the picture, 'the' Pink Floyd lost not only their lead singer and guitarist and the source of their original artistic vision, but also the sole figure in the band to resemble anyone's idea of a rock and roll icon. It gradually became apparent that the post-Barrett band was another proposition altogether: and though it would be a few years yet before the public and EMI's record labels dispensed entirely with the definite article, this would seem as good a moment as any to begin calling the group simply – Pink Floyd.

Along with the changes in personnel and artistic direction, the band was now under new management. While Peter Jenner concedes that Bryan Morrison's agency was better able to bankroll the multimedia Floyd experience, he smelt a conspiracy when the group's dry spell on the concert circuit suddenly ended as soon as its former booking agent took over from Blackhill Enterprises. From Jenner's perspective, 'Morrison was quite calculating. He nicked the band off us. He's a right old rogue.' But to John Marsh, who still ran the lights, the Floyd's 'switch from Blackhill to Morrison also underlined the direction they wanted to go: they believed that Morrie could set them up as big-time pop stars, not counterculture darlings.'[1]

If Roger Waters had also had his fill of Blackhill's psychedelic business methods, he was soon to receive a lesson in the music industry's more traditional *modus operandi*. In a 1987 interview, he claimed that Morrison, with whom the Floyd had not had a formal contract, persuaded them to sign one prior to their return to America in summer 1968. '"Just a legality, boys; we won't be able to legally book the American tour otherwise, so you'll never tour the States." The next day he sold the agency. One lives and learns.'[2] The buyer was NEMS Enterprises, originally founded by the Beatles' late manager Brian Epstein.

Morrison and his more intellectual associate Tony Howard were ultimately superseded by their junior partner Steve O'Rourke, whose greatest claim to fame heretofore had been a fleeting appearance in the Bob Dylan documentary *Don't Look Back* (during the scene showing an altercation with a waiter). NEMS inherited O'Rourke along with the Floyd, who were to take him with them when they escaped. According to Jenner, 'Steve O'Rourke went off with the band to gigs in Europe or wherever to collect the money and so on, because the office could get by without him, because he was a bit of a wanker. That's how he ended up as their manager, because he spent time hanging out with them.'[3] (And still does – Steve has made it a point to attend virtually every Floyd concert of the past twenty years.)

As managers go, O'Rourke was as circumspect and down-to-earth – and financially savvy – as the Blackhill boys were not. Roger regarded him as 'an effective hustler, a man in a man's world' (not to mention 'about ten times cheaper than a Robert Stigwood'); David Gilmour described him to a friend as 'the great deal-maker' whose lack of interest in matters aesthetic allowed the Floyd to take complete control of their artistic direction.

According to Nick Mason, the unflappable O'Rourke was also willing to absorb endless abuse that the Floyd might have otherwise directed at one another. Another close associate, however, says that Waters 'always regarded him as a glorified booker, rather than an actual career manager. He feels Steve O'Rourke shouldn't take any credit for the Floyd being where they are, and that his musical acumen is virtually zero.'

A supremely unconfident Gilmour, meanwhile, maintained a low profile as he alternated between playing rhythm guitar and 'to be honest, trying to sound a bit like Syd. But the numbers that they were doing were still Syd's, mostly. Consequently there was a kind of fixed thing in your head of how they had been played previously, and that makes it very much harder for you to strike out on your own.'[4]

Longtime associates and peers were almost unanimous in following the revamped Floyd's progress with an extremely sceptical eye. 'I couldn't see it happening without Syd,' says Peter Jenner. 'Which was one of my great lessons in show-biz – that what matters is the brand name.' But he hastens to add: 'I stick to my guns, mind you. I don't think they were ever as interesting after Syd left. They never had that wild excitement and innovation.

Peter Brown says he simply 'lost interest when Syd disappeared', and scathingly compares 'the charm and humility of Barrett's songs' with the latterday 'self-indulgence of Roger Waters doing the sort of misunderstood artist bit, almost in lieu of what Barrett went through'. And as far as David Bowie was concerned, 'When Syd Barrett left there was no Pink Floyd for me any more.'

In these circles, June Bolan was among the few to harbour much sympathy for the new Floyd. 'Having had two or three years of a band, and suddenly one member falls by the wayside,' she argues, 'why should your lifeblood, your livelihood, be stopped? Roger was determined that it wasn't going to fall apart because Syd wasn't there any more, and he would show everybody. And he bloody well did, didn't he?

'And he did it against all adversity, because nobody gave him credence for being a creator. Everybody was very Syd-oriented. Everybody said, "Oh with Syd gone, the Floyd will fall apart." They didn't – at all. Roger kept it all together. He was very much a motivating force.'

'It took an *enormous* amount of energy for Roger to get that together,' Sumi Jenner agrees, 'and he deserves credit for it. From then on, he always thought of the band as *his* baby.' Yet even June couldn't find it in herself to 'feel about David like I feel about Syd; I don't feel that specialness at all. He's lovely, a nice person, but he doesn't have that certain *je ne sais quoi*.'

Like many prominent undergrounders, Miles had felt a special personal affinity with Barrett – but very little with the other three. 'Syd was the most attuned to what was going on with *International Times* and the scene that I was involved with. He was the really exciting one. As far as I knew the other guys didn't even smoke dope; they were very, very straight indeed. They were just architecture students.

'I've always thought their music sounded deeply architectural. The change from the Syd Barrett period into the music of three architecture students was really quite dramatic.' Miles pursued this theme in his introduction to a book of Floyd sheet music: 'Mason, Wright, and Waters had all studied architecture and their architectural vision of music flowered into great cathedral constructions taking up whole albums and filling huge amphitheatres.'[5]

But Rick Wright, for one, contends that his architectural background had 'no effect on the kind of music *I* wanted to play or write. Maybe in terms of trying to structure an album into something, rather than just putting songs on –trying to make a meaning out of all the songs together – possibly architecture had something to do with that. But I didn't want to be an architect, I wanted to be a musician. I

123

wasn't aware of whether Nick and Roger actually wanted to be musicians – I think *they* wanted to be architects.'

Andrew King has observed that, in marked contrast to Syd, 'Roger's great strength was always structure, which I would imagine to some extent originates from his architectural training and is one of his innate characteristics. He is very structured.'[6] It was, in any case, not long before Pink Floyd's artistic ethos began to take a 180-degree turn, the anarchic spontaneity of the Barrett era giving way to meticulous and elaborate constructions in which little was left to chance.

This metamorphosis, says Nick Mason, 'started with recording. All the things that interested us in a studio were not the things that were involved with improvisation. Very quickly we found that what we were aiming for was to try and perfect things and then build them up, particularly in the early days when we were working with four and eight tracks. There was a hell of a lot of layering that went on, where things had to be sort of set in stone, because you then were going to overdub on them. So you became more and more conscious of trying to get something absolutely right, and that it was better if it was simpler and correct than a bit fancy and wrong. Because once you started layering things on them any little glitch that was there got worse and worse. You'd think, "We'll just put a guitar on," and every time it came to that lurch the guitar would lurch over it and emphasize it even more.

'So I think that started us on something else. And then, when we'd take those recordings into live performance, to work with staging and with lights and all the rest of it, it made life a lot easier and a lot better if we stopped being too free.'

Even Peter Brown concedes, 'The Floyd were one of the first bands to learn to use the studio properly. They had to, because otherwise they would have disappeared; they weren't players, they were kind of concept artists, really.'

The Syd-less Floyd first struck out on their own with 'It Would Be So Nice' – perhaps the most relentlessly upbeat (and unrelentingly vapid) entry in the band's entire discography. To Mason, 'Nice' was the outgrowth of 'being hustled about to make hit singles. There's so many people saying it's important, you start to think it is important.'[7]

Reminiscent of the 'Flower Power'-style hits then being hacked out by such formerly mainstream entertainers as the Hollies and the Bee Gees, this ditty penned by Rick Wright nonetheless signally failed to duplicate their commercial success, despite a well-publicized 'controversy' over the lyrics' mention of *The Evening Standard*. When the BBC objected to giving the newspaper free advertising, the Floyd obligingly spent an extra £750 in studio time to change the word 'Evening' to 'Daily' on deejay copies. (Funny – no one seems to have taken exception to the Beatles' invocation of the *Daily Mail* in 'Paperback Writer'.)

Disputing the implication that the Floyd thereby sold out. Mason said: 'If you're a rock and roll band and you've got a record that you want to be number one, you get it played, and if they say take something out, or whatever, you do it. In fact what you do is exactly what was done – you make as much press out of it as possible. You ring up *The Evening Standard* and say, "Did you know that the BBC won't play our record because it mentions your paper?"'[8] Yet even the ensuing free publicity in *The Standard* could not rescue 'It Would Be So Nice' from oblivion.

The B-side, meanwhile, illustrated another dead-end route for the post-Syd Floyd. 'Julia Dream' saw Waters trying as best he could to imitate Barrett in a psychedelic fairytale pitting misty monsters against 'the queen of all my dreams'. *'Will the key unlock my mind?'* the voice of Roger Waters quavers plaintively through a maze of echo chambers. *'Am I really dying?'* Some Floyd freaks even swear that the song ends with the whispered name *Sss-syd*.

Some rather more viable directions were explored on *A Saucerful of Secrets*, released on 29 June 1968. This second Pink album was basically a hodgepodge of possible Floyds, ranging from Barrett's psychotic 'Jug Band Blues' to the long instrumental title suite on which Syd was wholly absent in spirit as well as in fact. The one inescapable conclusion to be drawn from the album as a whole (and its successors through at least *Dark Side of the Moon*) is that the melody and the poetry in the Floyd went out with Syd Barrett, a deficiency for which the band, to its credit, found unexpected compensations.

Before getting the last word on the collection, with 'Jug Band' and its hauntingly jarring final line *'And what exactly is a joke?'* Syd is highlighted on slide-guitar in Rick's nostalgic childhood reverie 'Remember a Day' (an out-take from *Piper*), and appears to get in a few manic licks on Roger's 'Corporal Clegg'. Ostensibly an upbeat novelty number, the latter nonetheless foreshadows a future Waters songwriting obsession in its sarcastic portrait of a shell-shocked war hero.

Roger's other two contributions were more in keeping with the astral image the Floyd were to project over the next few years. for the incantatory 'Set the Controls for the Heart of the Sun', Waters found his title in a William S. Burroughs novel and his whispered stanzas in a book of Chinese verse. (Some Barrett guitar work is rumoured to be buried in the mix of this longtime Floyd concert staple, with subsequent overdubs from Gilmour.) On both 'Set the Controls' and his album opener 'Let There Be More Light', Roger's lyric gives way to one of the extended Johnny-one-chord cosmic space-out jams that were to become a Floyd trademark.

Rick Wright's songs – 'Remember a Day' and the almost catatonically sluggish 'See Saw' (whose working title was 'The Most Boring Song I've Ever Heard Bar Two') – are quintessential Flower Power artifacts, best appreciated in a cloud of incense and cannabis smoke. 'Remember a Day' specifically echoes the Rolling Stones' 'Dandelion' with its spacey 'blow away' bridge and the kind of drum fills Charlie Watts favoured during Their Satanic Majesties' short-lived psychedelic incarnation.

'They're sort of an embarrassment,' winces their author, a generation later. 'I don't think I've listened to them ever since we recorded them. It was a learning process. Through writing these songs, I learned that I'm not a lyric writer, for example. But you have to try it before you find out. The lyrics are appalling, terrible, but so were a lot of lyrics in those days.'

For all his subsequent contributions to the Floyd songbook, Gilmour's sole composing credit on *A Saucerful of Secrets* was attached to the long instrumental title suite (originally called 'The Massed Gadgets of Hercules'), a group effort that was built up from scratch in the studio. Gilmour, however, gives all credit to 'the architecture students in the band . . . drawing these peaks and troughs and things on a chart, working out where the piece was going to go.'[9]

It seemed to Dave that his colleagues were undertaking the aural equivalent of a war. 'The first part is tension, a build-up, a fear,' he ventured. 'And the middle, with all the crashing and banging – that's the war going on. The aftermath is a sort of requiem.'

The predominant instrument in the opening section, 'Something Else', was, Gilmour revealed, a closely miked cymbal stroked 'very gently with soft mallets. That actually produced a tone not a bit like a cymbal. The whole first section is basically a series of those tones, with lots of stuff tacked on top.' For the middle section, 'Syncopated Pandemonium', a Mason drum pattern was snipped and spliced into a loop over which Gilmour played his instrument 'turned up real loud and using the leg of a microphone stand like a steel bar running it up and down the guitar fingerboard. 'I remember sitting there thinking, "My God, this isn't what music's all about." I had just come straight out of a band that spent most of its time rehashing early Jimi Hendrix songs to crowds of strange French people. Going straight into this was culture shock.'

Gilmour, however, proved far more adaptable than the band's producer. Rick Wright recalls that Norman Smith 'was into the songs, but "Saucerful of Secrets" he just couldn't understand. He said. "I think it's rubbish . . . but go ahead and do it if you want."'[10] From that point onward, Smith's 'product' credit gradually turned into a polite fiction.

According to Wright, 'There wasn't a sudden break, or a bad feeling at all. It wasn't all of us one day saying, "Right, Norman, you're out!" We all realized what was happening, cause his good point, early on, was teaching us how to work in the studio.' After *Saucerful*, whose sound quality lacks the clarity and bite of its successors, the pupils had clearly outpaced their master.

Smith was incorrigibly 'staid', according to Gilmour, 'and tended to get in the way of invention some of the time. On one or two occasions he bugged me when I was trying to do something that sounded great to me but didn't fit the rulebook. But he was a nice guy.'[11] ('Hurricane' Smith, in any case, was soon to be a recording artist in his own right with middle-of-the-road pop hits like 'Oh Babe, What Would You Say?')

Nick Mason, for his part, ranks 'Saucerful' as a Pink milestone 'from the point of view of helping us sort out a direction we were going to move in. Just that piece itself contains ideas that were well ahead of that period, and very much a route that I think we have followed, on and off, quite a lot. Which is making something sound professional, really, even without using a lot of elaborate technique, without being particularly able in our own right – finding something that we can do individually that other people just haven't done, or haven't tried. We're not competing for who can play the guitar fastest. It's actually about finding that you can provoke the most extraordinary sounds from a piano by scratching about inside it, or something like that.'

The results often echo, however inadvertently, the electronic music then being produced by classically trained composers armed with arsenals of complex equipment and academic theory: one passage of 'Saucerful of Secrets', for instance, has a strikingly similar counterpart in *Animus* by Columbia University's Jacob Druckman (one time composer-in-residence at the New York Philharmonic).

'A Saucerful of Secrets' was to remain a Floyd concert centrepiece nearly three years after its conception, when *Rolling Stone* commented: 'The distance they have brought it even since the live *Ummagumma* recording is remarkable. The group, and particularly Wright, has achieved a complexity and a depth, building nuances into the main line of the music, far beyond what is on either the studio [version] or the live cut.'[12]

'The title track of A *Saucerful of Secrets* I still think is great,' says Gilmour. 'I really love it; it was brilliant. That was the first clue to our direction forwards, from there. If you take "Saucerful of Secrets", the track "Atom Heart Mother", then the track "Echoes" – all lead quite logically towards *Dark Side of the Moon* and what comes after it.'

Nonetheless, *Saucerful*'s reviews in both the alternative and the mainstream pop press were less than ecstatic. NME complained of 'basically good tracks being ruined by the now mandatory bit of extended psychedelic electronics.' Miles, meanwhile, wrote in *International Times* that 'there is little new here', specifically excoriating the title track for being 'too long, too boring, and totally uninventive, particularly when compared to a similar electronic composition such as "Metamorphosis" by Vladimir Ussachevsky, which was done in 1957 . . . In the same way as bad sitar music is initially attractive, electronic music turns people on at first – then as one hears more the listener demands that something be made and done with all these "new" sounds, something more than "psychedelic mood music." ' That said, the erudite sage of *IT* concluded his piece: 'A record well worth buying'![13]

With A *Saucerful of Secrets*, Pink Floyd became the second EMI act (after the Beatles, of course) to be granted permission to hire outside designers for an album sleeve. The job went to Syd Barrett's impecunious roommates Storm Thorgerson and Aubrey 'Po' Powell (who had recently co-designed the covers of some cowboy novels), with instructions to 'do something spacey and psychedelic'.

'We called ourselves Hipgnosis,' Thorgerson wrote in his book *Walk Away Renee*, 'after we'd discovered the word scrawled by some ingenious dope freak on the door of our flat. It was chosen because it sounded, of course, like ordinary hypnosis, and if we could design hypnotic visuals then that would be absolutely great. In addition, the misspelling possessed a nice sense of contradiction, of an impossible co-existence, from Hip = new and groovy, and Gnostic relating to ancient learning. The old and the new, cohabiting a world that implied bewitchment.'[14]

Thorgerson and company's bewitching artistic vision would be displayed on all but three of the band's subsequent albums, and become an integral part of the Floyd magic. Though Hipgnosis was eventually to attract a long list of star clients including Paul McCartney and Led Zeppelin, Storm still feels that his finest work was almost always in conjunction with Pink Floyd.

Simulating the effect of the band's light shows, Hipgnosis's first effort on their behalf superimposed thirteen images, ranging from the solar system and a zodiac wheel to old photos of an alchemist and his bottles of potions. (*Saucerful*'s cover also incorporated an all-but-invisible infra-red shot of the musicians themselves.)

Such imagery, in tandem with song titles like 'Set the Controls for the Heart of the Sun', tended to further the aura of science-fiction and fantasy (and even the occult) that swirled around the Floyd. This in turn led to specialized gigs (such as one at an American SF convention, for which the band reportedly flew all the way to Detroit before playing a gig in England the following night) that served to reinforce the Floyd's astral reputation.

By July 1969, this image had made Pink Floyd the obvious choice to score three televised celebrations of the Apollo 11 moon landing – one German, one Dutch, and the BBC's satirical 'What If It's Just Green Cheese?' – with their futuristic-sounding atmospherics. The SF/fantasy association, about which Mason now professes some bemusement, proved one that the Floyd, try as they might, could never live down.

'It's interesting,' says Nick, 'the way a band becomes established with a reputation that quite often has nothing to do with what they're really like. There was certainly an interest in science-fiction; particularly in the sixties we were all reading it like mad: Robert Heinlein and *Dune* and Ray Bradbury. There was an enormous interest in all that sort of "What does the future hold?" and concepts of how things might be.

'People *still* think of us as "music of the spheres" and all the rest of it, whereas, the last fifteen years we've been grinding away at very down-to-earth personality disorders rather than anything to do with aliens. None of us has ever really had much of an interest in the occult, and I don't think there are any references within our work to anything like that. I know Led Zeppelin always had a reputation for it. Lots of heavy metal bands seem to favour dressing up in heavily occult wardrobes. It's not something I think is terribly interesting, but obviously it does interest quite a lot of people. I don't think it's a very *useful* route.' (*Syd*, of course, had had a more than passing interest in the occult; in this respect, too, Pink Floyd could not easily escape his shadow.)

On the day of *Saucerful*'s release, Pink Floyd topped the bill at the first free rock concert ever staged in Hyde Park in London. Thus began a tradition subsequently made famous by the likes of the Rolling Stones and the short-lived Eric Clapton/Steve Winwood 'supergroup' Blind Faith. It was Peter Jenner and Andrew King who had originally conceived of the event and assuaged the Bailiff of the Royal Parks' fear of vandals: yet, Mason sardonically noted, it was music-biz tycoon Robert Stigwood who ultimately claimed 'some golden award for putting on free concerts in Hyde Park, because they thought that the Blind Faith concert was the first . . . That's the story of Blackhill in a nutshell. The whole thing had been started by Peter and Andrew.'[15]

The Floyd's triumph at Hyde Park did much to renew their credibility, not least with deejay John Peel, who had previously given short shrift to the Barrett-less line-up. 'In these harsher times it sounds a bit silly, but it was a religious experience,' Peel effused nine years later. 'It was marvellous. They were playing "Saucerful of Secrets" and things, and it just seemed to fill the whole sky . . . and to coincide perfectly with the lapping of the water and the trees and everything. It just seemed to be the perfect event, and I think that was the nicest concert I've ever been to in fact.'[16] (And few people on this planet, it might be added, have been to more rock concerts than Mr Peel.)

While the Hyde Park concert was a breakthrough, the key factor in the band's survival during this period, given their decidedly uneven vinyl output, was their success at making *any* Pink Floyd show, by definition, an 'event'. (The Floyd had long since overcome the provinces' resistance.) This achievement was all the more remarkable in the absence of a Barrett-like star figure; as Gilmour caustically put it (after his partnership with Waters unravelled): 'We didn't have a Roger Daltrey or a Mick Jagger. All we had was a bass-player that would stomp around scowling and making faces.'

They also boasted the best and most innovative sound system in rock and roll. Its most legendary component, the quadrophonic 'Azimuth Co-ordinator', transformed the music into a truly three-dimensional experience by systematically projecting sound effects and solos behind and around the audience, in the process giving even the

130

kid in the last row the sense that he was 'inside' the performance. (For a definition of Azimuth, Waters reached for his dictionary: '"Arc of the heavens extending from the zenith to the horizon, which it cuts at right angles." That's . . . vaguely relevant, isn't it?').[17]

Though the Floyd's financial straits were so dire by 1969 that they temporarily shelved the light show, their concerts were increasingly augmented not only by films but also a plethora of inventive visual effects. During the group's return to the Royal Albert Hall in July 1969 – dubbed 'More Furious Madness from the Massed Gadgets of Auximenes' – someone materialized in a gorilla's outfit, a cannon was fired, and the programme climaxed with the explosion of a pink smoke bomb. At this show the Floyd's old Cambridge friend Tim Renwick, whose own group Quiver was frequently enlisted as their opening act having joined Steve O'Rourke's select roster of clients, was especially impressed by a segment reminiscent of Peter Jenner's first band AMM.

'They built a table with rhythmic hammering and sawing,' recalls Renwick. 'When it was done the roadies came on with a pot of tea and switched on a transistor radio and put a mike in front of it, so the entire audience would be listening to whatever happened to be on the radio at the time while the guys were drinking their tea. It was tremendous, really good.

'I'd always been very interested in what they've done. I've seen so many of their different shows through the years. Every single one – even though sometimes it wasn't musically a knock-out – would always be an event, something very special. I've always really admired that.'

In concerts such as this, the Floyd were already structuring their performances in the guise of two album-length song-cycles called *The Man* and *The Journey*. The former was intended to evoke 'a day in the life' of a typical Briton. It began with a daybreak sequence, followed by work, a pause for tea (the scene described by Renwick) and culminated in nightfall, a bit of what the Fen-dwellers call *umma-qumma*, and finally sleep with its attendant dreams and nightmares.

Floydoids salivating at the prospect of two lost masterworks, however, are advised that both suites (apart from made-to-order instrumentals like Nick's bump-and-grind drum showcase, 'Doing It') were compiled mostly from past, present, and future album tracks. *The Man*'s 'Daybreak', for instance, is now better known as 'Grantchester Meadows', and 'Nightmare' as 'Cymbaline'. *The Journey* likewise presented a fantastic voyage through such realms as 'The Pink Jungle' ('Pow R Toch H' revisited, as it happens) and 'The Narrow Way'.

Turning (in their view) from the sublime to the ridiculous, at the end of 1968 Pink Floyd played the singles sweepstakes once more with Roger's 'Point Me at the Sky', which sounded more than a bit like the Beatles' 'Lucy in the Sky with Diamonds'. It was the B-side's throw-away jam, however, that survived as a minor Floyd classic, and was yet another milestone in the development of the band's distinctive sound.

Like other such Floyd efforts, 'Careful with that Axe, Eugene' consisted of, in Gilmour's words, 'basically one chord. We were just creating textures and moods over the top of it, taking it up and down . . . it was largely about dynamics'.[18] This time the predominant mood was that of menace and fear, which became increasingly pro-nounced and effective as 'Eugene' developed into another long-term concert staple. (Retitled 'Beset by Creatures of the Deep', it provided a key sequence for *The Journey* suite.) In comparison with the Floyd's subsequent eerie live renditions, the original track was, as Mason put it, 'extremely mild, jigalong stuff'.

Few heard it at the time; the single met with the same indifference as its predecessor. Even so, Mason said, the band 'never did feel that we'd had it when two singles slumped horribly – that it was all over. I don't know why not, because a number of people did think it was all over.'[19] (The A-sides of both 1968 Floyd flops would actually get second hearings a generation later in parody revivals of 'It Would Be So Nice' by the Damned's Captain Sensible, and of 'Point Me at the Sky' by the Acid Casualties, a Rhino Records cover band that special-ized in exactly that.)

After 'Point Me at the Sky', Pink Floyd simple ignored the 45 rpm market to become something almost unheard-of at the time: an *album band*. Never again would they record a song specifically for single release; in Britain, no LP track, not even 'Money', would even be issued in the seven-inch format until 'Another Brick in the Wall' eleven years later. As Waters has cracked, 'Our sense of snotty purity was so great that we wouldn't even have a single out.'[20] At the very least, this policy would spare them any prospect of another appearance on *Top of the Pops*!

Perhaps singles were simply too restrictive for a group dominated by former architecture students, destined to leave their mark with sprawl-ing constructions filling first one, then two, and finally four entire LP sides. In any case, Pink Floyd's no-singles policy did not detract from the sales of their albums and concert tickets, and finally became an inherent part of the band's mystique. It also opened the way for the likes of Led Zeppelin, who never made singles, period.

Chapter 12

Yet Another Movie

When Pink Floyd were invited early in 1969 to compose a full-length musical soundtrack for a movie, there was no need to ask twice. They had already provided background music, including an early version of 'Careful with that Axe, Eugene', for Peter Sykes's *The Committee*, starring Manfred Mann's Paul Jones. 'We would have done almost *anything* in terms of film.' David Gilmour later recalled. 'We wanted to have a go at it.' Hence the low-budget French-language youth-culture melodrama, *More*, directed by former Jean Luc Goddard associate Barbet Schroeder, and remembered today solely for having engendered the third Pink Floyd album.*

Between their longstanding involvement in multi-media performance and the cinematic feel of the music itself, the Floyd would have seemed a natural for this kind of work which, Rick Wright pointed out, promised to be far more lucrative and congenial than continuously gigging around Britain: 'Films seem to be the answer for us at the moment. It would be nice to do a science-fiction movie – our music seems to be that way oriented.'[1]

Roger Waters, yet to balk at the SF association, went so far as to say his 'greatest regret' was that they didn't do the score for *2001: A Space Odyssey*, parts of which, particularly in the long mind-blowing hallucinatory sequence near the end, nonetheless sound remarkably 'Floydian' (another instance of the group's affinity with the 'serious' electronic composers favoured by director Stanley Kubrick). The band's admirers are left to regret that the films to which the Floyd did add their distinctive magic were hardly on the order of that Kubrick classic.

Gilmour describes Pink Floyd's experience with *More* and its successors as 'contract work. You start in the studio without anything,

---

* Except in France, where *More* did achieve a reputation comparable to that of *Easy Rider* in the English-speaking world – and thus was to play a large part in advancing

and you work until you come up with stuff. You chuck things down and ask, "How about something like this?": then you work on it a bit. It's not the same process as making your own music for yourself: much more hurried, and less care tends to be taken.'

Yet because EMI viewed the album as a special project, *More* also allowed the band a freer artistic rein – and a higher royalty – than its predecessors. It was the Floyd's first major opportunity to demonstrate that they could produce their own recordings, without the constraints imposed by Norman Smith at Abbey Road.

Oddly enough, the *More* soundtrack features a higher proportion of actual songs to instrumental mood pieces than several of the Floyd's regular albums. Most are lightweight acoustic ballads by Roger Waters that make for pleasant enough listening even if the vocals, rarely Pink Floyd's strong suit since Syd Barrett's departure, sound almost painfully feeble on tracks like 'Green is the Colour'. The band nonetheless held this ditty and 'Cymbaline' in sufficient regard to include them in the Floyd's concert repertoire for the next two years.

The instrumentals, meanwhile, helped define Pink Floyd's 'distinctive brand of instant cosmic epiphany soundtrack Muzak' (in *New Musical Express*'s memorable phrase). The creative impetus here, says one Floyd associate, was provided by 'Gilmour basically stoned out of his box, going into these dream sequences'.

Those who regarded Pink Floyd as 'the band that ate asteroids for breakfast' were not surprised to learn that *More* depicted drug fiends on the scenic hippie island paradise of Ibiza – whose expatriate longhairs had given Syd and Rick a heroes' welcome during a 1967 holiday. Only the drug turns out to be heroin, and the message less than idyllic. 'It said the right things about drugs; I'm sure that if it were saying the wrong things about drugs we wouldn't have done it,'[2] Wright chided one space-cadet college-radio interviewer, with whom the Floyd nonetheless proceeded to share a joint.

In the year or two after Barrett's departure, the 'dopers and drinkers' divide that had once polarized the Floyd camp was effectively resolved: everyone was now doing both (albeit seldom to excess), with Dom Perignon the group's beverage of choice on the road. 'I didn't drink when I joined the band,' Dave observed. 'But I soon learnt the error of my ways.'[3] The input of Gilmour and (on the visual side) Storm Thorgerson, neither of whom were exactly strangers to the acid

the Floyd's extraordinary popularity in a market heretofore virtually closed to Anglo-American rock groups.

culture, further enhanced Pink Floyd's ability to maintain the aura of Britain's 'head' band *par excellence*.

The post-Barrett Floyd, says one longtime friend, 'inherited that acid generation image almost by default, and were often mystified by it. The Floyd did smoke a bit of dope here and there, but they were never heavily drug-orientated. They were a bit too balanced to go the whole way, and also seeing Syd so greatly affected by all the chemicals he pumped into himself was a lesson to be learned. Their attitude was: "Fair enough, they may *think* we're doing it, and we're very happy they think so, but we'll just carry on in our own normal way." Ultimately, they were well brought-up upper-middle-class college kids.'

'I've only used psychedelics twice in my life,' Roger Waters confessed in 1987. 'And on both occasions it was after our music got that label. The first time it was absolutely wonderful. It was on a Greek island, in very idyllic surroundings, and I don't know how much I did but it seemed to go on forever. It was very powerful, and strange. Whether it affected my music, I have no idea.

'I did some more acid a couple of years later, but in a vastly smaller quantity, and I remember crossing Eighth Avenue in New York, trying to get to Smilers to buy myself a sandwich and a bottle of milk, and I got stuck halfway across the road. I never did anything again.'[4]

If Pink Floyd, in Gilmour's words, took on *More* because they 'wanted to break into bigtime movie scores,' then Michaelangelo Antonioni must at first have seemed the answer to their prayers. *Blow-up* having won international acclaim for its evocation of Swinging London, the 56-year-old Italian director set out with *Zabriskie Point* to perform a like service for the California youth revolution. After hearing the anarchic strains of 'Careful with that Axe, Eugene', Antonioni (who had first encountered the Floyd back at the Roundhouse *IT* launch) summoned the boys to Rome.

The band wound up spending the better part of a month whiling away the days at a posh hotel, munching Crepes Suzettes and sampling vintage wines. 'We could have finished the whole thing in about five days,' Waters recalled. But Antonioni 'would listen and go – and I remember he had this terrible twitch – "Eet's very beautiful, but eet's too sad," or "Eet's too stroong." It was always something that stopped it being perfect. You'd change whatever was wrong and he'd still be unhappy. It was hell, sheer hell. He'd sit there and fall asleep every so often, and we'd go on working till about seven or eight in the morning, go back and have breakfast, go to bed, get up – and then back into the bar.'[5]

Antonioni, in any case, ultimately concluded that he required a more American-sounding score to accompany the adventures of his West Coast revolutionaries. The director substituted recordings by the Grateful Dead and the Youngbloods, plus Patti Page's 'Tennessee Waltz' and a bluesy Rolling Stones number, for all but three of the Floyd's contributions. One of the three, ironically, was a pale country and western imitation. Antonioni, meanwhile, turned thumbs down on a lyrical Rick Wright piano piece that subsequently evolved into the *Dark Side of the Moon* favourite 'Us and Them'.

From the standpoint of Pink Floyd's artistic legacy and credibility, however, perhaps this was all just as well. Even more than *More*, *Zabriskie Point* is the kind of film that, seen a generation later, almost makes one glad the sixties are long gone. To the extent that it can be said to have a coherent plot, it follows a young man suspected of shooting a policeman in a student riot as he commandeers a small plane and flees to the Arizona wilderness. There, the first person he chances to encounter is the obligatory leggy model-type, who wastes no time in initiating an ecstatic sexual union under the desert sun.

Our equally good-looking hero, played by Mark Frechette, then paints the plane psychedelic colours and attempts to return it to the airfield whence it came: whereupon he is himself shot dead by the 'pigs'. A new variation on 'Careful with That Axe', retitled 'Come In Number 51 Your Time Is Up', does at least provide an effective backdrop for the apocalyptic final fantasy scene, where a luxury desert resort is shown exploding in slow motion.

By the beginning of 1970 the Floyd had also become deeply committed to scoring a projected psychedelic cartoon series called *Rollo*, masterminded by the artist Alan Aldridge, perhaps best known for his two books of *The Beatles' Illustrated Lyrics*. 'It was a great story,' Waters recounted. 'The basic idea was that this boy Rollo is lying in bed and he starts to dream (or maybe it really happens), and suddenly his bed wakes up and these two eyes pop out of the bedpost and start looking around, and the legs grow . . .

'And then the bed leaps out of the house and goes out down the street, all in beautiful movements . . . and goes flying off into the sky. And when he gets up there . . . the moon is smoking a big cigar, which turns out to be an optical illusion – it's really a space ship.'[6] Accompanied by his new friend Professor Creator and a robot dog,

136

Rollo goes on to enjoy a series of extraterrestrial adventures, culminating in the trio's victory over a race of tunnel-dwelling giants.

'It really could have been so good,' enthused Roger, a man not noted for lavishing praise indiscriminately. But *Rollo* was not to be; despite a stunning pilot executed by a team of Dutch animators, Aldridge was never able to secure the considerable financial backing that the ambitious project required.

There was to be yet a third Floyd-related movie soundtrack (and album spinoff) within a period of about a year. This time, however, Roger Waters stepped out from the Pink Floyd collective to help his friend Ron Geesin score a cinematic adaptation of Anthony Smith's 1968 book *The Body*, a pop-biology primer enlivened with explanations of the rate at which hair grows and the monetary value of breast milk.

A feature movie along such lines was a whimsical (if not downright improbable) proposition, for which the idiosyncratic Geesin seemed ideally suited: he had worked extensively with film, and his compositions and performances interwove sound effects, electronic experiments, unlikely instrumental combinations, and lunatic speech fragments. But writer Tony Garnett and director Roy Battersby also wanted songs, which was the one thing Geesin could not supply. Accordingly, he introduced them to his new golfing (and intellectual sparring) partner, Roger Waters.

Though a semilegendary character in Notting Hill's mid-sixties artistic subculture, Geesin – who had initially made his mark as a jazz pianist – confesses to having remained oblivious to the Floyd during their underground heyday. 'I've never been in the rock scene – I'm me. I have these strange ideas about music and I try to execute them, more or less.' When a mutual friend brought Nick Mason down to Ron's Notting Hill basement flat in 1968, noting, 'He is of the Pink Floyd,' the electronics innovator responded in his Scottish lilt: 'Oh – and what do *they* do?'

Geesin nonetheless formed a warm friendship with Mason and his bride Lindy, for whom Ron originally composed a flute and organ piece on an LP tribute to Indian guru Meher Baba conceived by his other rock star pal Pete Townshend. 'She was quite a good flautist – but not quite good enough to actually get around it. So then I got a professional to record it on Pete's album.' He also composed the score for one of Nick's father's motor sport documentaries.

Geesin says that when he was subsequently introduced to Waters. 'I responded to *him*. I respond to individuals and not groups. He was very much his own being, with his peculiar ways.'

Peculiar ways? 'What makes art, what makes creativity? It's a sort of imbalance, I think. Roger had a need for acceptance and applause – the egocentric. And then a need to repel the very applause that's coming. I even experienced that as a close friend, where sometimes I'd turn up at his house, having made arrangements to get together at a certain time, and he'd be going off to a squash match. To me, that was calculating. It was like saying, "Come to my castle," and then when you get there you get a bucket of hot oil, or a cannon ball.

'With Roger, I learned to live with that switch, between closeness and farness. There was a certain abrasiveness; political arguments flaring up at dinner parties. But he's really a nice bloke if you don't put him on a pedestal.'

Geesin recalls enjoying 'sort of arty, intellectual affairs with *all* the Floyd, at one point. In other words, going round to their homes and talking about things, and listening to things, and looning about. The one thing I wasn't into was pot. I always said I preferred fresh air. The air around the Floyd was blue most of the time, but that's normal with musicians.

'Rick was comparatively untogether. He'd talk about doing ideas that would never quite make it. I'm saying this because I'm like that as well, so I recognize it in someone else. *If only* – "if only I had a bigger studio, if only I had more time . . ." He was probably considered by the rest of the group to be falling behind a bit.

'Roger was no great bass player, but he got through. It's the old thing of, it's not what you do, but how you do it. As Louis Armstrong would say, "It's not what you put in, but what you leave out."'

Some sense of the offbeat nature of Waters and Geesin's first musical endeavour can be gleaned from the selections' titles: 'Womb Bit', 'More than Seven Dwarfs in Penis Land', 'Dance of the Red Corpuscles', 'Piddle in Perspex'. *The Body* also introduced 'Breathe', whose lyric about industry's rape of the environment was to evolve, with different music, into a mainstay of *Dark Side of the Moon*.

The music heard in the actual film of *The Body* was essentially recorded, in early 1970, by each of the two men on his own – Geesin overdubbing his inimitable wacky instrumentals with the help of a lone cellist, while Waters separately nursed an acoustic guitar through a series of frail tunes reminiscent of his songs on *More*.

Roger, however, learned what he could from Ron's more extensive experience with film. 'I certainly helped him out with the tedium of measurements for film sequences, stuff like that,' says Geesin. 'The tailoring, I'm very much a craftsperson, I can fit things in. I've found over the years the average film sequence lasts exactly one minute and fifteen seconds.'

Geesin was also a perfectionist, and upon finding out that EMI wanted to release a soundtrack LP, insisted on rerecording the whole thing so it might hold together better as an album. During these sessions in September and October 1970 the pair worked much more closely, with Ron producing Roger's material and vice-versa.

The first Floyd 'solo' outing (apart from Syd Barrett's) ended on a note very different from more recent such endeavours, with Gilmour, Mason, and Wright trooping in to play on the finale, 'Give Birth to a Smile'. 'It was like the happy-family-helping-out-at-the-sessions bit,' says Geesin, adding that the Floyd asked for and received EMI's standard session musicians' fee for their services.

Chapter 13

The Amazing Pudding

The turn of the decade found Pink Floyd floundering for direction and undergoing something of an identity crisis. The next Floyd album, their first on EMI's 'progressive' Harvest label and a double-LP in the bargain, actually offered virtually no new music by the band as such. The first disc, recorded at Manchester College of Commerce and at Mother's Club in Birmingham (long a favourite Floyd venue), preserved superior live remakes of 'Astronomy Dominé', 'Careful with that Axe, Eugene', 'Set the Controls for the Heart of the Sun' and 'Saucerful of Secrets'. ('Interstellar Overdrive', still a concert mainstay, was dropped at the last minute.)

Much of the album's reputation rested on these tracks, particularly in America, where few listeners had ever been exposed to the originals and where *Ummagumma*, by dint of repeated airings on late-night free-format FM rock radio, soon gave the Floyd their first toehold in the top hundred. For all the legend that adhered to the band's concert performances, this was to remain the only official live Pink Floyd album until the release of *Delicate Sound of Thunder* over nineteen years later.

It was mainly on the strength of their shows that in September 1969, a month before *Ummagumma*'s appearance, the Floyd were voted sixth most popular group in *Melody Maker*'s annual poll. Their lack of individual recognition, however, was underscored by the failure of any of the band-members to match this showing in the categories for their respective instruments: a situation that even *Ummagumma*'s second LP was unlikely to rectify.

The studio record arose out of Rick Wright's disgruntlement with the limitations imposed by playing in a mere rock band: he wanted the opportunity to compose 'real music'. Accordingly, each Floyd was allowed half an LP side to indulge in solo experiments, where 'making weird music' seemed to become an end in itself.* It was an exercise for which only Roger was yet ready, as Rick – who now dismisses 'Sysyphus', his keyboard extravaganza in four movements, as 'pretentious' – would be the first to agree. Dave has admitted he 'just bullshitted' through 'The Narrow Way', whose lyrics were almost inaudible due to their author's insecurity about his poetic talents; Waters, who would later insist on writing the words to all Gilmour's and Wright's Floyd tunes, declined an invitation to do so here. The album climaxes with Nick Mason's electronically treated nine-minute drum solo.

Perhaps the most interesting of these pieces – or the least tedious – was Roger's acoustic Cambridge reverie, 'Grantchester Meadows', in which real swans could be heard taking flight while the nagging sound of a bee buzzing through one earphone and out the other sorely tempted listeners to swat the air with their *Ummagumma* sleeves. Waters also contributed the succinctly titled 'Several Species of Small Furry Animals Gathered Together in a Cave and Grooving with a Pict' whose rhythmically orchestrated menagerie puts the Beatles' 'Good Morning, Good Morning' in its place, before giving way to a maniacal Scottish-sounding rant.

'People always used to ask me if I did that,' says Ron Geesin. 'I was doing a lot of John Peel radio programmes at that time, doing pieces even further out. My variety of Scottish ranting may have jogged something in Roger, but it was probably coincidental. We both had Scottish mothers and English fathers, as it happens.'

SF-oriented Floyd-oids assumed that the album's cryptic title referred to the sages known as 'umma' in *Dune*; there was, after all, talk at this time of the band scoring a movie of the Frank Herbert epic. But Nick Mason confirms that 'ummagumma' was actually a 'slang expression for copulation' picked up in Cambridge by Syd, Roger, and Dave. 'It's just a name. It wasn't taken because it means anything, it was taken because it sounded interesting and nice. And it can be either made to sound like a chant or as a sort of exclamation.' *Ummagumma* also boasted one of Hipgnosis's most quintessentially 'trippy' covers, which depicted the Floyd posing next to a picture of the Floyd posing next to a picture . . . and so on, receding into infinity.

---

* The Waters song 'Embryo' was also recorded during these sessions: as a group performance, however, it could not be fitted into *Ummagumma*'s format. Though Roger claimed it was never actually finished, 'Embryo' finally surfaced in 1983, on Capitol's American compilation *Works*.

The first Floyd album for the seventies reflected both the band's own aimlessness and the trends then prevailing on the British music scene. At a time when trailblazers like the Who's Pete Townshend and the Kings' Ray Davies were touting Rock Opera and when it seemed obligatory for the likes of Deep Purple to inflict their 'concertos' on the Royal Philharmonic Orchestra, and Emerson, Lake, and Palmer to bludgeon *Pictures at an Exhibition* and *The Nutcracker Suite* in concert, Pink Floyd could hardly resist the temptation to weigh in with a work both monumental and Serious. Hence, *Atom Heart Mother*.

'That whole main theme,' says Dave Gilmour, 'came out of a little chord sequence I had written, which I called "Theme from an Imaginary Western" at the time. It sounded like *The Magnificent Seven* to me.' Hearing the guitarist toss it off during a rehearsal break. Waters was struck by the music's 'heroic, plodding quality', evocative of 'horses silhouetted against the sunset' like some 'very heavy movie score'.

He and Wright were inspired to supply further themes and variations in the same cinematic spirit, until the piece burgeoned into the longest Floyd composition to date (ultimately clocking in at close to twenty-four minutes). Recalls Gilmour, 'We sat and played with it, jigged it around, added bits and took bits away, farted around with it in all sorts of places for ages, until we got some shape to it.' Under the title 'The Amazing Pudding', an early version of the piece was premiered in Paris on 23 January 1970.

Increasingly at loggerheads over the production of their sprawling instrumental, the four Floyds finally agreed to bring their pal Ron Geesin to the rescue, and handed him the tapes with instructions to superimpose Something Grand – heavenly choirs, brass fanfares, whatever – while they went off on an American tour. 'They were pretty exhausted at that time due to getting famous and being pushed,' says Geesin. 'Steve O'Rourke was a heavy pusher. They just needed some other kind of input – another thinking being in there.'

For a full month, Ron, stripped to his underpants in the uncharacteristically sweltering London weather, worked feverishly on his score. 'Rick Wright looked over the choir section with me for maybe half a day, and Dave Gilmour suggested a riff for one part. Roger couldn't read music and just kind of accepted that this bloke Geesin was getting on with it. There was no great creative input from them.

'Given that their cards were set, the actual tunes and the harmonies were entirely mine. That again is part of my crafts area – having an existing concept, and having to fit and yet get something over. I

always felt that the one thing the Floyd lacked was a real sense of
melody, in those long pieces drifting along with the odd spiky bit here
and there. But that's why we worked so well, because I was giving
them melodies and tunes.

'There were problems with tempos because of the way they laid
down the original tracks. There were variations between sections that
weren't due to any progression, just to an accident. Dropping back in
tempo when it really should have increased a bit, maybe. Or it would
be better to have a sudden change, rather than a very slight change.

'But these were the things we were stuck with, because they had
recorded this slab of backing tracks, with all their usual – the long
organ chords, the droning bass lines, the flowing guitar. So it was a
problem, when it came to actually recording the live musicians on top
of the prerecorded tracks, to get the tempo right. It's normal anyway
for classical musicians to have problems with the beat. Classical beat
sense and rock beat sense are quite different.'

Geesin's troubles really began after he took it upon himself to
conduct the ensemble at Abbey Road studio. His first mistake, he
reckons, had been to let EMI hire the session musicians. The cellist
was congenial – they had worked together on *The Body* – but the ten
brass players, Ron found, 'were hard, uncaring types who certainly
weren't going to tolerate anyone green or naive. Brass musicians, I've
discovered, are the hardest and most belligerent of all; they've been
shit upon so much by primadonnas that they've formed this crust
that's covered up their gentle, helping core of being. One horn player
was particularly awkward – making little remarks, and asking questions he knew the answers to.'

The threat of physical retribution finally kept the man quiet, but
getting the ensemble to play what Geesin had in mind proved an
ongoing challenge. 'The first thing that happened was that what I
wrote for that very strange stuttery introduction was actually meant to
be far more stuttery, but to play it at the speed I'd written proved
pretty well impossible for those players. They had to regularize that
stutter to become a syncopation they could understand.

'Then when it came to the funky section, which has the choir in it,
I'd reckoned that beat number one was in a certain place, and had
written the whole section calibrating the inflections from there. It
turned out that from Nicky's point of view, beat number one was one
beat off that and he insisted that everything I'd written for that section
had to be moved one beat. So that whole part has all my writing one
beat away from where it should have been. I should have just rubbed

out all the bar lines and moved them one beat up, but I wasn't clever enough.'

Adding to the confusion, Syd Barrett, having heard that his band was cutting a new album, wandered into the sessions. 'I just thought he was a nutter,' says Geesin. 'He didn't know what was going on, and had suddenly become some kind of a Jesus figure. This is the fascinating thing about myth versus endeavour. By not doing anything, he was revered much more than if he'd done something.'

Ron, for his part, came close to cracking up himself midway through the recording. 'Having written this thing, I'd had a very heavy year, and was definitely pretty shattered. I couldn't cope any more. I daresay the group in the box were tearing their hair out, thinking, "Christ, is this bloke going to get through this? My God, *what* have we taken on?" All were agreed that the director of the twenty-voice choir, John Aldiss, should take over as conductor.

Geesin, however, suggests that the benefits of his replacement 'might have been outweighed by the rather puddingy quality of the beat from then on. Because John Aldiss was a classical choir person, and was definitely not into hot rhythms. The brass were all plonking along just a nudge behind the beat all the time. As a jazz appreciator I would tend to phrase slightly ahead of the beat – that's the essence of Hot. So the whole execution was kind of puddingy – a Scottish word, that.'

After they all listened to the playback, Geesin told Steve O'Rourke: 'OK – that's a good demo. We've had a good practice. Can we do it for real now?' One can imagine the groans this suggestion elicited.

Whatever the reason, the end product, for all its grandiose sweep and melodic richness, does often sound surprisingly conventional: more like stolid middlebrow 'classical' music – if not, indeed, an epic film soundtrack – than the last word from Britain's supposed high priests of cosmic rock. 'Underground' critical response ran the gamut from 'huge, timeless, sweeping, universal' (*Frendz*) to 'try freaking out again, Pink Floyd!' (*Rolling Stone*).

Nearly two decades later, Gilmour dismisses the Floyd's first magnum opus as 'a load of rubbish, to be honest with you. We were at a real down point. We didn't know what on earth we were doing or trying to do at that time, none of us. We were really out there. I think we were scraping the barrel a bit at that period.' Waters, for his part, wouldn't object if the suite were 'thrown into the dustbin and never listened to by anyone ever again'.

Nonetheless, *Atom Heart Mother* was enormously successful in

Britain, where it if nothing else resonated opportunely with the prevailing fashion for 'symphonic rock', and gave Pink Floyd their first number one record. And, as Nick Mason points out, it enabled them, to think on the scale of *Meddle*'s 'Echoes' and the subsequent concept albums.

The work also set a precedent with the mystery and mystique generated by a title and LP cover that, truth be told, bore little connection with one another – let alone with the music. The title materialized as the Floyd prepared to preview their still-unchristened suite on John Peel's BBC-Radio One concert programme. When the producer wondered how the piece should be announced, Geesin pointed to a copy of *The Evening Standard* and, he says, 'suggested to Roger that he would find a title in there'. Spotting an article about a pregnant woman with an atomic-powered pacemaker, headlined ATOM HEART MOTHER, Waters remarked, 'That's a nice name. We'll call it that.'

'We often pick titles which have nothing to do with the songs,' Wright subsequently noted. 'The name is just a way of marking it. We could have called our songs "Number One", "Number Two", and "Number Three". Except words are more interesting, and – like "Careful with That Axe, Eugene" – can create a nice sort of image.'

Storm Thorgerson says he and the band were determined that the *Atom Heart Mother* sleeve 'be as un-psychedelic as possible, as un-Floyd like and completely off the wall'. After toying with the 'really flat' images of someone diving into the water (later elaborated for *Wish You Were Here*) or walking out of a door, Storm heard his friend John Blake cite Andy Warhol's famous cow wallpaper as the ultimate in ordinariness. This conversation inspired him to drive through Essex and photograph the first cow he saw, in the manner of animal textbooks he remembered from school. The result was, in Thorgerson's phrase, 'the ultimate picture of a cow: it's just totally COW'.

All concerned delighted in the irony that on an album by any ordinary Top Forty act such an ordinary photo could – as Thorgerson puts it – 'never have carried the weight it carries on a Pink Floyd album. It looked great in the shops when it first came out. It was something completely different, and really did look completely different. Especially 'cause the group decided not to put their name on it, which was quite a risky thing to do at the time. I'm very fond of it.'

The cow motif, in fact, was to prove a stronger 'hook' than anything on the actual record. The Floyd played along by renaming individual segments of their suite 'Breast Milky' and 'Funky Dung', and titillating the music-press pundits with Mason's talk of 'a connection between the cow and the title if you want to think of the earth mother, the heart of the earth'. The pedigree Fresian's proud owner, Arthur Chalke, also got in on the act, milking Lulubelle III's new-found celebrity for all it was worth, though his claim that she received £1,000 for her services is dismissed by Storm, who can hardly imagine himself 'paying a farmer for his fucking cow'.

The new Harvest Records boss, Dave Croker, arranged a special photo opportunity at dawn in the Mall, in the heart of London, for which the police redirected traffic to make way for a herd of cows. Capital Records, in a long-overdue campaign to 'break' Pink Floyd in America, subsequently pasted the celebrated Lulubelle's image across forty-foot freeway boards, and furnished the nation's leading rock critics and disc jockeys with inflatable plastic udders.

The only people who weren't happy with the *Atom Heart* cover were the Geesins. 'My wife Frankie was pretty incensed that my name was missing from the acknowledements,' says Ron. 'My conscious self was saying, "I'm not concerned about having glory on a record sleeve, I'm concerned about having done a piece of work" – but it would have done me some good it they had given me the credit. I believe they were a bit embarrassed about not being able to see the thing through themselves. And so they weren't up to crediting properly who had done the work. But that is a minor ripoff to what goes on in the Business. And I am on a one-fifth royalty for that side.'

The LP's second side, meanwhile, offered a song apiece from Waters, Wright, and Gilmour. All three were lyrical and melodic, even if the rather limp execution caused *Rolling Stone* to dismiss them as 'English folk at its deadly worst'. Waters thought highly enough of his 'If' – wherein he holds a poetic mirror to his own ornery and contradictory character – to feature it in his 1980s solo tours. ' "If".' Geesin maintains, 'shows more of the real Roger than all that bloody political shouting his head off. Far more important than the Floyd's great astral wanderings. The line *'If I were a good man I'd understand the spaces between friends'* – that's the essence of the man.'

Dave, for his part, sounded on 'Fat Old Sun' like a dead ringer for the winsome falsetto of Ray Davies, but calls it sheer coincidence that the Kinks had previously released a strikingly similar piece called 'Lazy Old Sun', and had incorporated into their 'Big Jack Smoke' the same tolling church bells that open and close Gilmour's own ditty. 'Maybe I ripped it off subconsciously. Who knows? They've never sued me. One sometimes gets the feeling about something that maybe one pinched it from someone; you can't figure out where on earth it's from.

'The added coincidence is that there were only one or two tape libraries around: the EMI Abbey Road library and one or two others which mostly had the same sound effects. It can make a magical difference in a track if you put some bit of real atmosphere in the background, like church bells. Usually, you'd go and find the bells, and it's the only set on tape that anyone can use. You'd often recognize exactly the same bit of birdsong on different records from that period.' Gilmour says he actually conceived the pastoral 'Fat Old Sun' as a sequel to Waters's 'Grantchester Meadows', in a nostalgic reminiscence of the neighbourhood where he spent his early teens.

Atom Heart Mother concluded with a long sequence of kitchen noises, such as the sizzle of a frying-pan. 'I've always felt that the differentiation between a sound effect and music is all a load of shit,' said Waters. 'Whether you make a sound on a guitar or a watertap is irrelevant.'[4]

Speaking of watertaps, the original British pressings of *Atom Heart* had one dripping right into the run-off groove, so that the sound might be repeated *ad infinitum* on record players lacking automatic changers. 'Alan's Psychedelic Breakfast', titled in honour of roadie Alan Stiles, even served as the opening number for several Floyd concerts, enabling front-row fans actually to smell Alan's bacon and eggs. But, Wright told *NME*, 'It didn't work at all so we had to give it up . . . Quite honestly, it's a bad number.' Gilmour subsequently called it 'the most throw-together thing we've ever done'.

If some of the rest of the platter also seemed half-baked, at least most of the ingredients for the winning Pink formula were now in evidence. Once they learned to hone their writing skills, and to build their grand conceits from actual songs, – while at the same time integrating the sound effects more fully with the music, Pink Floyd would truly be in business.

Augmented by French horns, trombones, trumpets, tuba, and Aldiss's choir, Pink Floyd presented the new improved 'Atom Heart Mother' for the first time at the Bath Festival on 27 June 1970. Three weeks later they brought the production to London's Hyde Park for an enormous free concert produced by ex-managers Jenner and King where co-composer Geesin (evidently less impressed than the then-teenage author of this book) distinguished himself by actually walking out. 'In some ways it seemed such a big posture, this thing of having classical brass players,' Ron remembers. 'I didn't leave out of malice – I didn't think anyone would notice! It was a cold day and the instruments were all out of tune, and it sounded awful – like a great wet pudding. I just thought, "I'd rather be home listening to my early jazz records." '

Among the 20,000 other concertgoers was John Hoyland, whose essay 'Pink Floyd: Unquiet Desperation' recalls 'one of those strokes of imagination that have always lifted their live performances out of the ordinary. At one point, after the crowd had been reduced to hushed reverence by one of Rick Wright's ethereal organ solos, a little girl started laughing and everyone craned their necks to see where she was. It was some time before people realized that the laughter was coming from a tape and the Floyd were producing it as part of their act.'

During the American tour that autumn, Leonard Bernstein attended an equivalent Filimore East performance; the Floyd reciprocated by catching his concert with the New York Philharmonic. Wright, in particular, expressed effusive admiration and the hope that they might work together some day. Bernstein, for his part, allowed that 'Atom Heart Mother' was the one part of the Floyd's programme he *didn't* much care for. Nonetheless, 'Atom Heart' was soon to earn Pink Floyd the honour of becoming the first rock band ever to perform at the Montreux Classical Music Festival.

Their flirtation with the cultural establishment culminated in the autumn of 1970 with French choreographer Roland Petit's proposed ballet, based on Marcel Proust's *Remembrance of Things Past* and featuring Rudolf Nureyev plus sixty other dancers, which was to have incorporated Floyd compositions performed by the band and a 108-piece orchestra. 'Pretty amazing!' Gilmour gushed to *Melody Maker*. 'Something nobody in our field has ever done . . .' 'Freakier and freakier,' announced *Rolling Stone*. 'Pink Floyd is now into ballet . . .'

Prior to their lunch in Paris on 4 December with Petit, Nureyev, and Roman Polanski (who hoped to direct a film of the ballet), the Floyd dutifully attempted to familiarize themselves with Proust's eight-volume classic. All found it slow-going, especially Dave, who gave up after eighteen pages. Only Roger managed to struggle past the first book.

By the time Waters, Mason, and Steve O'Rourke got to Paris, however, Petit had decided to set aside Proust in favour of *The Arabian Nights*. 'Everyone just sat there drinking this wine and getting more and more drunk,' Roger recalled, 'with more and more poovery going on around the table, until someone suggested *Frankenstein* and Nureyev started getting a bit worried . . . I was just sitting there enjoying the meat and the vibes, saying nothing. . . .

'And when Polanski was drunk enough he started to suggest we make the blue movie to end all blue movies, and then it all petered out into cognac and coffee and we jumped into our cars and split. God knows what happened after we left!'[6]

Over two years later, Roland Petit finally would choreograph a Pink Floyd ballet. Though Nureyev, Polanski, and the 108-piece orchestra were conspicuous in their absence, the Floyd gamely appeared at performances in Marseilles and Paris to provide live renditions of 'Careful with that Axe, Eugene' and three newer works in which the Syd-less Floyd had at last discovered its *raison-d'etre*: 'Echoes', 'One of these Days', and 'Obscured by Clouds'. The ballet climaxed with a typically Floydian flourish: ten cans of oil exploded like fireballs from the front of the stage.

Chapter 14

Return of the Son of Nothing

'I'm bored with most of the stuff we've done. I'm bored with most
of the stuff we play . . . There isn't much new stuff, is there?'
Roger Waters, early 1971[1]

For all their multi-media dabbling and ever-accelerating popularity,
Pink Floyd's creative motor was running on empty. Such artistry as
they could muster went into perfecting the stage spectacle on whose
strengths the group rose to second place in *Melody Maker*'s 1971
readers poll (behind Emerson, Lake, and Palmer, but ahead of Led
Zeppelin, the Rolling Stones, and the Who). In America, where the
Floyd now directed much of their live firepower (and flabbergasted
promoters with their insistence on taking the stage for the entire
evening, with no warm-up act), each album generally charted a few
notches higher than its predecessor. For the first time in the band's
history, the Floyd were actually turning a profit – only to find
themselves, Nick Mason confessed, 'in acute danger of dying of
boredom'.

Pink Floyd had the Federal Bureau of Investigation, of all people, to
thank for salvaging the first of two 1970 U.S. marathon tours.
Following the theft in New Orleans of equipment worth $40,000
(including four guitars, Mason's drums, Wright's electric organ, and
the Floyd's 4,000-watt PA), Waters recalls, 'We sat down at our hotel
thinking, well, that's it – it's all over. We were pouring out our
troubles to a girl who worked at the hotel, and she said her father
worked for the FBI. The police hadn't helped us much, but the FBI got
to work, and four hours later it was found.'

'We'd all rather stay at home than tour America,' moaned Mason.
'We're all too domesticated and much too old for all this!' Indeed,
both he and Rick Wright had become fathers, and now that the Floyd
were actually making money, they began buying houses in different
parts of London. David Gilmour (the last of the band's bachelors)

150

abandoned the city altogether for Essex, where he shared his secluded nineteenth-century farm with an army of cats and horses and a rout of antiques and musical equipment.

Waters, by contrast, established his Shangri-La on a proleterian main thoroughfare in the north-east London borough of Islington. Visiting journalists invariably noted their astonishment that a rock star should choose to dwell in such dreary surroundings, even if the interior did testify to the owner's unostentatious good taste with the Scandinavian furniture and bare polished wood floors over which his Burmese cats reigned supreme. (Beyond their Cambridge roots, a love for cats was one thing Barrett, Gilmour, and Waters always had in common.) A converted toolshed in the garden served both as Roger's home recording studio and as a workspace for his wife, Judy Trim, who was to establish herself as an accomplished potter.

She was also the one person known to boss *him* around. 'On the one hand,' observes Peter Jenner, 'Roger was extremely tough and strong, and held the band together after Syd left. At the same time, he was weak – always very influenced by his women. His first wife Judy was a very extreme leftie, a Trot. When he was with her, Pink Floyd money was spent on buying rows of houses to be let at economic rents to the deserving poor, in the best tradition of the English upper-middle-class benefactor.'

During this period, the idealistic Waters even found himself (he confessed in *Melody Maker*) unable to reconcile 'socialist principles and compassionate feelings about people who are less well off than you are' with his ownership of an E-type Jaguar, which he duly relinquished in favour of a Mini. In this regard, at least, Nick, Rick, and Dave flatly refused to follow Roger's lead.

In any case, the 'boys', as Waters resounded some fifteen years later, were growing up and apart. 'In the early days of the group, we did mix socially. There is something rather appealing about a *group* together *on the road*. But that soon palls. And things like families make sure that cycle comes to an end.'[2] On the road, the genteel Floyd strove to keep themselves amused with football matches, sightseeing excursions, Monopoly and Backgammon, and long afternoons reading by the pool. They were rather more circumspect about groupies and drugs than most of their fellow 1970s superstar travellers, from whom they tended (with the exception of Dave Gilmour) to hold themselves aloof.

The Who were among the few groups with whom Pink Floyd chose to socialize when their tour itineraries happened to cross. The late

151

Keith Moon they found 'incredibly amusing', his penchant for demolishing his hotel lodgings notwithstanding. 'He's a very sophisticated smasher,' Waters says, 'He's got it down to a fine art.'[3] Mason deemed his fellow drummer 'very good company to sit and have a drink with. A lot of [rock] people are just drunken maniacs, just lurching around being boring.' The Who's singer, Roger Daltrey, however, made himself scarce at these get-togethers after committing the faux-pas of mistaking Rick Wright for Eric Clapton.

For Waters, at least, a primary impetus for staying on the rock-concert treadmill was the prospect of transforming the medium even more radically than the Floyd already had. As early as 1970, he was citing 'a complete theatrical show in a theatre in London' as his ultimate ambition for the band. In the meantime, Roger was not shy about driving Pink Floyd further in that direction.

'There was always a great battle in the band [between] "the architects" and "the musicians," ' he sardonically recalled in 1985. 'Nicky Mason and I were relegated to this inferior position of being the architects, who were kind of looked down upon by Dave and Rick, who were [laughs] *the musicians*. There was a lot of opposition from "the musicians" to doing anything theatrical at all. So you could say it was by virtue of the forcefulness of my nature that we went on to do those shows.'[4]

Among the Floyd's more memorable 1971 shows was a 'Garden Party' at London's Crystal Palace on May 15, where they introduced a new work that at last ended their creative logjam. Conceived as the centrepiece for the band's next record, and every bit as long and ambitious as the 'Atom Heart Mother' suite – only this time the four Floyds were creating all the sounds with their own instruments – it still went by the title 'Return of the Son of Nothing.'

The performance climaxed with the emergence of a fifty-foot inflatable octopus, shrouded in dry ice, from the little lake separating the audience from the stage, while fireworks exploded overhead. Unfortunately, the music's volume was such that the real fish in the lake expired from the trauma.

Strange to say, the post-Syd Floyd heretofore had not even attempted to make a truly representative album. Barrett had remained a partial presence on the transitional *Saucerful*; *More* was a film soundtrack; *Ummagumma* paired live retreads with solo experiments; *Atom Heart Mother* was in large part a collaboration with Ron Geesin and the

152

session hacks. *Meddle*, released in November 1971, would be the record that finally began to define Pink Floyd.

This largely reflected the input of David Gilmour. The group's most accomplished musician, and the only one who still bothered to keep abreast of current pop trends, Dave was at last beginning to feel fully at home in the Floyd. 'He'd gone from one band, Jokers Wild, which was much more conventional,' says his old friend and one time drummer Clive Welham, 'to another that was totally different – revolutionary, you might say, as opposed to musical. I'm sure he found that rather strange at first.

'When people are trying to be experimental with music it doesn't always come off. The early Pink Floyd were amateurish, and I think Dave Gilmour would admit that himself. I'd probably compare it to modern alternative humour, which is getting very good now, but in its early days some of the acts didn't quite score. A person struggling to become a comedian, some of his jokes aren't beautifully timed. You have to go through that period until something really emerges and gets tacked together.

'Dave was very responsible for the melodic side of Pink Floyd. When he first joined them they were in a form that wasn't really to his liking. I think it's Dave who put the form into their music, made them a more mature band in that sense.'

Yet the origins of the new album's main attraction – retitled 'Echoes' on the eve of its live broadcast on John Peel's show – could hardly have been more experimental. At the time, Mason called it 'a specific attempt to do something by a slightly different method'. Without having composed anything in advance, the Floyd booked Abbey Road for the month of January 1971 and 'anytime that anyone had any sort of rough idea, we'd put it down'. Inspiration was not long in arriving, and they ended up with 'thirty-six different bits and pieces that sometimes cross-related and sometimes didn't. "Echoes" was made up from that.'

An especially auspicious fluke literally set the tone for the entire project, when the rest of the band were hanging out in the control room while Wright doodled at a piano that had been mixed through a Leslie amp. Every time Rick hit a certain note, his colleagues were transfixed by, in Gilmour's words, 'a strange resonance . . . kind of a feedback thing . . . *Ping!* A complete accident. We said, "That's great!" and we used it as the start of the piece.'[5]

If many of the original musical ideas came from Dave and Rick (who also harmonized the vocal sections), it was 'the architects' who

153

structured the myriad fragments into a more or less cohesive whole. As Lenny Kaye has noted, 'Each segment responded to and mixed into one another in a continuum of motifs and themes. At times a formal song might bob to the surface, only to be captured by the tides and borne away again.'[6] In the classic Floyd manner, 'Echoes' is replete with slow 4/4 tempos gradually building up to dramatic crescendos that then veer off on unexpected tangents, demonstrating the band's growing mastery of, in Kaye's phrase, 'the art of the segue'.

In early live performances, the lyrics seemed almost calculated to perpetuate the sci-fi Floyd stereotype, until Roger was inspired to change the drift of his imagery from outer space to underwater. (The opening line *'Planets meeting face to face'*, became, *'Overhead the albatross . . .'*) Also stirring beneath the surface of the aquatic dreamscapes of 'Echoes' were intimations of the 'alienation theme' in Waters's subsequent work.

The 'epic sound poem' (as Roger then described it) was rerecorded in July, along with material for the reverse of the album, at AIR Studios, where for the first time the Floyd had sixteen tracks at their disposal. All the previous LPs had made do with four, except *Atom Heart Mother*, which used eight. Despite its unorthodox composition, 'Echoes' proved to be, said Rick, 'an easy number to play live . . . "Echoes" on the album and on stage is exactly the same.'

Like 'Atom Heart Mother', 'Echoes' was paired with an LP side's worth of unrelated songs. The most popular of these began life as a Roger one-note bass riff filtered through the Binson repeat-echo unit that the Floyd still retained from the Syd Barrett era. 'You sort of make a rhythm between yourself and the echo . . .' Gilmour explained. 'Originally it was just that sound; then later on when we'd recorded that thing, it didn't sound like it held up on its own as a whole number, and we did another piece with . . . a heavy vibrato – the whole middle section, which we then cut in. And then we started laying on all the other boogaloo, all the organs and fast guitars.'[7] Not to mention the howling wind.

This ominous mood piece was christened – in best 'Careful with that Axe' style – 'One of these Days (I'm Going to Cut You Into Little Pieces)'. Once again, the proceedings are entirely instrumental save for the brief spoken incantation of the title – which represents Nick Mason's sole 'lead vocal' in the entire Floyd canon.

The best of the rest was the hauntingly melodic 'Fearless' (words by Roger, music by Dave), with its inspired juxtaposition of a crowd of Liverpool soccer fans bellowing their anthem 'You'll Never Walk

Alone' while lines like '*Fearlessly the idiot faced the crowd*' hint at the Barrett predicament. At the end of these sessions, Waters was inspired to write another song, 'The Dark Side of the Moon', that alluded even more powerfully to Syd. He decided, however, to save it for a new project that was only beginning to percolate from his unconscious. (The song itself would be renamed 'Brain Damage'.)

Meddle is not without its dispensables: the cocktail-hour jazz of 'San Tropez' and – a perennial contender for Worst Song Ever in Floyd fanzine polls – the 'blues' called 'Seamus' whose lead vocals literally showcase a yowling dog. 'I guess it wasn't really as funny to everyone else,' conceded Gilmour, 'as it was to us.' Again, however, the Floyd were later, on the *Animals* album, to put the botched experiment to much more effective use.

Meddle's physical appearance is also far less striking than that of its predecessor, and evinced little of the care and imagination that would go into packaging *Dark Side of the Moon* and *Wish You Were Here*. Bob Dowling's cover photo, which looks at first glance like a random shot of a psychedelic blob show, actually depicts an ear picking up waves of sound, represented here by ripples of water. *Meddle* remains Storm Thorgerson's least favourite of all Hipgnosis's Floyd album designs, though he demurs that the concept was essentially dictated by the band. His original suggestion, vetoed by the Powers That Be, had been a close-up of a baboon's anus.

'It was a very strange time, the titling and putting together of it,' says Gilmour, 'because we were actually on tour in Japan when it was about to come out. The cover was being done by telephone, from Japan to England, and the picture of the submerged ear was not as good as we thought it would be. Believe it or not, there is an ear in there! We never quite managed to put the right energy in right at the end of the record, for getting the cover and the little detail stuff done. It's not my favourite cover.' The title's rather feeble pun – 'a play between "medal" (the thing that you wear for achieving something) and "interfere" ' – likewise materialized at the eleventh hour while the Floyd were brainstorming in a Japanese hotel room.

Meddle got a mixed reception from the critics. *Rolling Stone* called it 'killer Floyd from start to finish', *Record Mirror* 'marvellous' and *NME* 'an exceptionally good album' – specifically citing 'Echoes' as the 'zenith which the Floyd have been striving for'. *Melody Maker*'s Michael Watts, however, shrugged off the record as 'a soundtrack to a non-existent movie' and Pink Floyd generally as (quoting Shakespeare) 'so much sound and fury, signifying nothing'. In re-

155

sponse, the waggish Mason sent Watts a gift box containing a boxing glove mounted on a spring. Waters, for his part, would soon do his utmost to insure that no critic could ever again dismiss the Floyd in such terms.

Meddle was shortly followed by Pink Floyd's second soundtrack to a film by their friend Barbet (*More*) Schroeder – this one about French hippies 'going native' in New Guinea whilst searching for a hidden valley and the meaning of life. Though the movie was called *La Valée*, the album was retitled *Obscured by Clouds* after the pulsating instrumental theme that provided an irresistibly atmospheric opener for the Floyd's concerts as well as the record and film.

Obscured by Clouds hardly suffers from having been cooked up in little over a week, at the Chateau d'Herouville outside Paris, better known to Elton John fans as the Honky Chateau. Indeed, on several numbers the lack of studio polish reveals a seldom-heard side of Pink Floyd: the tightly-knit band of rock and rollers who simply get down and *play*. 'I thought it was a sensational LP, actually,' Nick Mason confessed years later.

The dominant instrument in these relatively raw and funky performances is the lead guitar of David Gilmour, whose vocals have also acquired considerable resonance. To this day, he cites as a particular favourite his bond-crunching 'Childhood's End' (named after Arthur C. Clarke's SF classic), even though the lyric was still minus one verse when the Floyd recorded it. Henceforth Roger would relieve Dave of the responsibility for writing his own words.

Roger's most important lyric on *Obscured by Clouds* was unquestionably 'Free Four', which could hardly have had less to do with the exploration of space – or even New Guinea. The title comes from the jokey 'one-two-free-fowah!' count-off, and the tune itself is just as irrepressibly jaunty and, in the context of the words, absurdly incongruous. For 'Free Four' – a milestone on the road to *The Wall* and *The Final Cut* – turns out to be the ramblings of a senile man babbling on his deathbed, of a life that went by '*In a twinkling of an eye*', even as he surrenders to his '*long cold rest*'. The only sci-fi thing about it is that the old geezer is unmistakeably G. Roger Waters, ruminating about the yet shorter life of his own father, who was '*buried like a mole in a foxhole and everyone's still on the run*'. Note this first appearance of the phrase *on the run* – 'run' to become a virtual byword, in the Waters songwriting lexicon, for 'paranoia'.

156

In the macabre light of 'Free Four', the imperatives of the 25-year-old Roger's existence (e.g. *'all aboard for the American tour/ . . . maybe you'll make it to the top'*) are made to seem suddenly rather hollow. Rarely, in fact, had the form of the three-minute-plus pop song ever encompassed a world view of such breathtaking cynicism. The overall effect of this catchy little tune is that of a man smiling genially in the act of delivering a death sentence which in this case happens to be his own.

America's FM-radio programmers responded to 'Free Four's' snappy tempo and succinct running time by giving it more airplay than any previous Pink Floyd track. Ironically, the hurriedly-recorded film score which spawned it became the first Floyd album to crack the top fifty on *Billboard*'s American charts.

Soon after scoring *La Valée*, our heroes starred in a film of their own. *Pink Floyd at Pompeii* was a live concert in which the audience consisted exclusively of ghosts: the two-millennia-old faces on the ancient ampitheatre's frescoes and statues. The band's customary props and pyrotechnics likewise deferred to Roman ruins and the volcano Vesuvius during a recital of 'Echoes', 'One of these Days', 'Set the Controls', 'Careful with that Axe', and 'Saucerful of Secrets'.

In so eldritch a setting, the Floyd's eerie atmospherics truly seemed to resonate, in the words of Mr Poe, *'From a wild weird clime that lieth, sublime./Out of space – out of time'*. Originally conceived for continental European television, this cosmic tour-de-force was screened to considerable acclaim at the Edinburgh Festival in September 1972. Legal complications, however, were to postpone its general release for nearly two more years.

Performing to scenic historical backdrops would become a Floyd speciality, culminating on 15 July 1989 in a free concert on a floating stage in Venice for a crowd of 200,000. About a year earlier on that neverending *Momentary Lapse of Reason/Delicate Sound of Thunder* tour in a bustling dressing room just moments before a concert in Pittsburgh the author of this volume shared a table with an ever-shifting coterie of Floyd lighting technicians, bodyguards, and auxiliary singers and musicians. Finally, for a minute or two, the three people sitting with me happened to be none other than Messrs. Gilmour, Mason, and Wright – at which point the conversation turned to *Pink Floyd at Pompeii* and its recent dissemination on videocassette.

'It's the kind of film,' said Dave, 'that they should just show once on late night television. I don't think it holds up on videotape.' 'It's a very interesting film, actually,' countered Nick. Rick then got in the last word: 'The only problem was the director!' Whereupon the three Floyds were summoned to the stage, and the opening strains of 'Shine On You Crazy Diamond' washed across that twentieth-century coliseum called Three Rivers Stadium.

In early 1973, amid torturous deliberations over the fate of his film, the said director – Adrian Maben – interspersed additional footage of Pink Floyd at work in the recording studio, eating lunch, and disputing the popular belief that their music was created by machines:

> *David Gilmour*: It's all extensions of what's coming out of our heads. You've got to have it inside your head to get it out. The equipment isn't actually thinking of what to do any of the time. It couldn't control itself . . . It would be interesting to see exactly what four people who didn't know anything about it could do. Just give them the equipment, and tell them to get on with it. It would be an interesting experiment. I think [broad grin] we'd come off better.

> *Roger Waters*: It's like saying, 'Give a man a Les Paul guitar and he becomes Eric Clapton.' But it's not true. And give a man an amplifier and synthesizer – he doesn't become us.

The works-in-progress heard in these studio scenes are 'On the Run', 'Us and Them', and 'Eclipse', which last was also then the working title for the album that millions would come to know and love as *The Dark Side of the Moon*.

Chapter 15
Eclipse

'I've been mad for fucking years . . .'

So mutters the lunatic, over the steady beat of the human heart. *Ba-bump, ba-bump, ba-bump* . . . the beat is taken up by the relentless ticking of a clock, and by a pair of rhythmically synchronized cash registers: time and money, two of the forces that can drive a man to the brink. *'I've always been mad, I KNOW I've been mad . . .'* Demented cackles, unearthly screams; and then the tension gives way to release, in the familiar form of Rick Wright's celestial chords and David Gilmour's echoing slide guitar, sweeping the listener off to the dark side of the moon.

Thus begins the masterpiece, the album Pink Floyd were *meant* to make: that hypnotic evocation of alienation, paranoia, madness, and death that has transfixed several generations of listeners, and claimed a place in the record books for remaining on the charts literally years longer than its closest competitor.

'I think every album,' says Wright, 'was a step towards *The Dark Side of the Moon*, in a sense. We were learning all the time, the techniques of the recording, and our writing was getting better.' In its masterful blending of sound effects and speech fragments with musical atmospherics and studio technology, *Dark Side*, released in 1973, represented the apotheosis of five years of hit-or-miss experimentation, and of five years of coming to grips with the madness of the man who had given Pink Floyd their name, and their fame. The title itself was nothing to do with astronomy but, as Gilmour put it, 'an allusion to lunacy'. To Peter Jenner – often his ex-clients' most exacting critic – '*The Dark Side of the Moon* is undoubtedly one of *the* great rock records. Though it was largely about him, that was the record where they escaped from Syd.'

Even as it consolidated and came to terms with the Floyd's musical and personal history, *Dark Side* marked a deliberate break from the past. As early as 1971 Roger Waters had publicly expressed his determination to 'come down to earth a bit, get a bit less involved with flights of fancy and a bit more involved with what we as people are actually involved in'. Additionally, this architect manqué could hardly resist the challenge of taking the structure of 'Atom Heart' and 'Echoes' one step further, and organizing an entire album – the lyrics no less than the music – into a single cohesive statement. 'We thought,' he explained to author Michael Wade, 'we could do a whole thing about the pressures we personally feel that drive one over the top . . . the pressure of earning a lot of money; the time thing, time flying by very fast; organized power structures like the church or politics; violence; aggression.'

The Floyd already had in hand various bits and pieces that seemed to lend themselves to such a concept: a total rewrite of 'Breathe', from *The Body*; 'Us and Them', which they informally called 'The Violence Sequence' in reference to the *Zabriskie Point* scene for which the original version had been written; the song Roger had written during the *Meddle* sessions, 'Brain Damage', with its pivotal couplet, '*And if the band you're in starts playing different tunes/I'll see you on the dark side of the moon.*' Gilmour and Wright, moreover, had recently come up with some inspired melodic ideas.

After long nights of brainstorming over his 'list' of pressures with Nick Mason, Waters finally psyched himself up 'to sit down with pencil and paper and start writing the fucking words'. Gilmour subsequently recalled that, 'Roger tried definitely, in his lyrics, to make them very simple, straightforward, and easily assimilable – easy to understand. Partly because . . . people read things into other lyrics that weren't there.' And this time round there was no question of any of the other Floyds getting a line in edgewise.

The Dark Side of the Moon was thus the album on which Waters decisively appropriated Pink Floyd not only as a vehicle for his conceptual ambitions, but as a mouthpiece for his personal world view. This last may broadly be said to combine withering cynicism and righteous anger towards 'the system' with a passionate advocacy of more humane values that might ultimately enable people to realize their lives' potential rather than to withdraw in alienation, or break down altogether. In the process, the *Dark Side* cycle naturally incorporated allusions to Roger's life story as well as Syd's, thus beginning the fusion of their biographies into the character of 'Pink', star of *The Wall*. 'Us and Them', for instance, lambastes generals playing their game of war, oblivious that '*the lines on the map moved from side to side*' are comprised of fellow human beings, – like Roger's late father.

160

Yet *Dark Side* was equally the record on which David Gilmour came into his own in Pink Floyd, asserting his musicality to give Waters's message a more mainstream appeal. Having established himself as the band's best vocalist, moreover, Gilmour was now singing lead even on songs that he didn't have a hand in composing, such as 'Money' and 'Us and Them'. (In later years, this was to be an ace up his sleeve when he presumed to reconstitute a Roger-less Floyd.)

Visiting his old friend just prior to its release, former Jokers Wild drummer Clive Welham – no great Floyd fan – didn't expect much when David insisted on playing a master tape of their new album. Yet he was bowled over, and over the following days and weeks found himself compulsively listening to the advance copy Gilmour had pressed upon him. 'That was the first Pink Floyd album that I had liked, that I thought was a total package. To me that was the emergence of four years of Dave being with them, and having got their music a bit more rounded, a little less esoteric. And the lyrics were marvellous, real one-liners which really strike home.' To Nick Griffiths, subsequently the band's recording engineer, the secret behind the Pink Floyd magic is simply this: 'Dave made people enjoy it, and Roger made them think. The combination worked really well.'

Not least of the reasons why *The Dark Side of the Moon* sounded so much more polished than its predecessors was the Floyd's decision to perfect the cycle in live performance before committing it to 24-track (with which the Abbey Road studios had finally been equipped). 'It was a hell of a good way to develop a record,' says Nick Mason. 'You really get familiar with it, you learn the pieces you like and what you don't like. And it's quite interesting for the audience to hear a piece developed; if people saw it four times, it would have been very different each time.' ('Time', for example, was originally much slower even than on record, with Gilmour and Wright singing throughout in strained, low-pitched harmony; in the final version, Dave sings the main section and Rick the bridge.)

The Dark Side of the Moon was premiered on 17 February 1972 – over a year before the album's release – at the first of four rapturously received sold-out concerts at London's Rainbow Theatre. Some of the atmosphere at that historical event was captured by Derek Jewell's review in *The Sunday Times*:

It looks like hell. The set is dominated by three silver towers of light that hiccough eerie shades of red, green, and blue across the stage. Smoke haze from blinding flares that have erupted and died drifts everywhere. A harsh white light bleaches the faces of the musicians to bone . . .

If all this sounds like *The Inferno* reworked, you would be only partly right. The ambition of the Floyd's artistic intention is now vast. Yet at the heart of all the multi-media intensity, they have . . . an uncanny feeling for the melancholy of our times . . . In their own terms, Floyd strikingly succeed. They are dramatists supreme . . .[3]

Despite such accolades, Roger sensed that the Floyd's Big Statement lacked a suitably stirring finale and went back to his drawing boards to compose 'Eclipse'. This in turn briefly became the name of the entire cycle after the Floyd were irked to learn of a new album, by the band Medicine Head, called *The Dark Side of the Moon*. Only when it proved a commercial dud did they feel free to reclaim their original title.

Recording finally commenced at Abbey Road on 1 June 1972, continuing throughout most of that month and (during time off from lengthy tours of America and Europe) the months of October and the following January. Though Roger remembers it as rock's 'first completely cohesive album', *The Dark Side of the Moon* made no attempt at a sustained narrative on the order of 1979's *The Wall* (or even the Who's 1969 'pop opera' *Tommy*). Rather, each song tackles a different topic – such as 'Time', 'Money', and 'Brain Damage', to cite three of the more self-evident titles – that Waters considered pertinent to the overall theme of a young man driven to madness.

Some of these topics are explored without benefit of Roger's lyrics. In 'On the Run', airport announcements of an imminent flight (with footsteps frantically racing from speaker to speaker) are all the words needed to frame its synthesized study in paranoia. And the spectre of death is eloquently invoked by Rick's wordless 'Great Gig in the Sky', featuring guest vocalist Clare Torry.

At the sessions, the gospel singer initially seemed nonplussed by the Floyd's explanations of the concepts behind the album and the song, not to mention the absence of lyrics for her to sing. But she rose to the challenge with a performance that, said Wright, 'sends shivers down my spine . . . No words, just her wailing – but it's got something in it that's very seductive.'[4]

Clare Torry's is not the only female voice heard on *The Dark Side of the Moon*, the first of several Floyd albums on which the band's vocal

162

harmonies are sweetened by soulful girl singers: a format eventually adopted by other major British bands, up to and including the Stones and the Who on their 1989 reunion tours. Insofar as none of the Floyds was exactly a Jagger or a Daltrey to begin with, the girls' discreet presence contributed to *Dark Side*'s well-rounded, mainstream appeal. As did the saxophone of Dick Parry, which introduced an alternate lead instrument to the standard Floyd keyboards and guitar. ('Atom Heart Mother', to be sure, had boasted *lots* of female voices and brass, but both figuratively and literally, those were playing on top of rather than with, the band.)

In another concession to the commercial, the Floyd brought in veteran producer Chris Thomas to supervise the final mix, largely on the strength of his work with other art-rockers from Procol Harum to Roxy Music. Like subsequent Floyd producers, Thomas found that much of his role was to abitrate between Waters (to whom the lyrical concept was paramount) and Gilmour (who was more interested in the music for its own sake).

But if any one person can be credited with the superlative *sound* of *The Dark Side of the Moon*, it would have to be the Floyd's longtime engineer Alan Parsons, whose achievement was ratified with a Grammy award for best-engineered album of 1973 (one of the few such awards that Pink Floyd ever garnered, even indirectly). Like Norman Smith before him, Parsons had not only hooked up with the Floyd after cutting his teeth with the Beatles, whom he served as apprentice engineer on *Abbey Road*, but would also go on to make the unusual transition from studio technician to recording star in his own right. (All those years around Pink Floyd must have persuaded both Smith and Parsons that one needn't be a born entertainer or a glamorous personality to have hit records!)

Again and again on *The Dark Side of the Moon*, one can hear echoes of the Beatles, especially *Abbey Road*: the 'Sun King' vocal harmonies in 'Us and Them'; the 'Dear Prudence' guitar riffs in 'Brain Damage'; and 'I Want You (She's So Heavy)' guitar riffs in 'Eclipse'. Gilmour says none of this was 'a conscious tribute', though he does acknowledge a general Beatles influence, particularly in the recording techniques the Floyd and their wonderboy engineer adopted at the Abbey Road studios.

'No one ever thought about it,' he recalls. 'That's just the way one did things, probably because the Beatles had started it. If you listen to loads of records from that period, there's the style, the current fashion, for the type of sounds that you could do given the limited equipment that was available. Those "Dear Prudence" guitar sounds were done by knowing how to do it with an oscillator on one tape machine, wobbling it. There was also putting two microphones out of phase next to each other to get those thin, crackly, telephoney sounding backing vocals.'

The Beatles connection aside, Parson's most remarkable feat on *The Dark Side of the Moon* was the immaculate reproduction of the album's myriad sound effects – the heartbeats and footsteps, the aeroplanes and explosions, the recurring clocks and cash registers – and their seamless integration into the music. On Roger's sarcastic paean to 'Money' – which Capitol released as a single in America, where it became Pink Floyd's first top forty hit – Waters's home-made numismatic sound effects, cleverly synchronized to the unusual 7/8 meter, were the hook.

Parsons was also directly responsible for the clocks at the beginning of 'Time'. These he had originally recorded at an antique shop for a demonstration tape showcasing the quadrophonic sound that, partly thanks to the Floyd's own efforts, was then being hyped to consumers as the heir apparent to stereo. (*Atom Heart Mother* had already been released in a 'quad' edition, as *The Dark Side of the Moon* and its sequel *Wish You Were Here* would also be.)

The contributions of Waters and Parsons notwithstanding, the compiling of the Floyd's sound effects had over the years gradually become the special province of Nick Mason, who received a rare solo composing credit for 'Speak to Me' – the 'color sound montage', as he calls it, that launches the album to the beat of the human heart. At the time, Gilmour said, 'The heartbeat alludes to the human condition and sets the mood for the music, which describes the emotions experienced during a lifetime.'[5] Some critics have faulted Pink Floyd for being a tad obvious and overliteral in their deployment of such effects – so unlike the inspired randomness of those on, say, Barrett's 'Bike' from the first Floyd album. The difference, of course, was the difference between a conscious exploration of madness by observers themselves fundamentally sane, and the visionary delirium of an artist who was actually going mad.

Far more imaginative is the interspersing throughout *The Dark Side of the Moon* of spoken passages, often barely audible or intelligible, which were gleaned by asking people who happened to be at Abbey Road at the time to speak into a microphone on such pertinent topics as madness, violence, and death. One interviewee whose remarks weren't used was Paul McCartney, whose cautious philosophizing proved no match for the inspired spontaneity of Abbey Road doorman Jerry Driscoll and the late Floyd roadie Pete Watts – or even his own Wings guitarist Henry McCulloch.

These subjects were shown a series of flash cards posing such questions as, 'When was the last time you were violent?' and, 'What do you think of death?' An interview with 'Roger the Hat', a stoned-out road manager for a rival band, provided the Floyd with a particular wealth of material (for his maniacal laughter no less than his demented commentary). In the original taped conversation, Roger Waters can be heard prompting his namesake (in a decidedly patronizing tone) about a violent act committed only three days previously, after a fellow motorist called the roadie 'a long-haired git'.

Waters: And you think you were justified? You put one on him?

Hat: Definitely. Because the thing is, man, is like when you're drivin' on the road, I mean, like, you get a person 'oo's that rude. I mean they're gonna kill ya, so if you give him a quick short sharp shock, they don't do it again. Dig it? I mean, he got off light 'cause I could 'ave given 'im a frashing. I mean, I only 'it 'im once *ha ha ha ha ha ha ha ha ha ha ha* . . .

Waters: Right, now another thing that we're interested in, 'cause again there's a track on the album that's supposed to be about it, is peggin' out . . .

Hat: Death? Wow! . . . Doesn't bovver me in the slightest. Live for today, gone tomorrow, that's me . . .[6]

It is doorman Driscoll, however, who gets the album's unsettling last word, as a reprise of the heartbeat fades into the run-off groove: 'There is no dark side of the moon, really; matter of fact, it's all dark.' *Ba-bump, ba-bump, ba-bump* . . .

Like many rock 'classics' – *Sergeant Pepper* springs instantly to mind – *The Dark Side of the Moon* boasts a physical package so strikingly apt that nowadays one can hardly imagine the album otherwise. After the Floyd's original vision of a box containing the record and an assortment of posters and stickers was deemed too expensive, Hipgnosis prepared seven different sleeve mock-ups for the band's contemplation. Storm Thorgerson credits Rick Wright for inspiring – with his request for something not only 'simple, clinical, and precise' but pertinent to the Floyd's light show – their ultimate selection of a pyramid-like prism transmuting a thin white beam into a rainbow.

Roger Waters subsequently came up with the idea of having the spectrum carried through the inner sleeve design; then on the back of the cover, the rainbow reverts through an inverted prism to reemerge as the original ray of light, thus fostering a continuous Mandala-like effect. This, of course, is in keeping with the music itself, which begins and ends with the same heartbeat.

Pursuing the pyramid motif to its irresistible conclusion, Thorgerson travelled in person to Giza in Egypt, to photograph one of the poster inserts. 'That was very spooky,' he says. 'Going up to the pyramids at night, under a full moon. *Very* scary. But great . . .'

Some well-meaning hack at EMI conceived the notion of unveiling the new album at a press party in London's Planetarium, where the band, in a spacier incarnation, had once expressed an urge to perform. But the Floyd's self-image had since changed; Waters said they deemed the event 'so daft that we tried to get it stopped, and when they refused to stop it we refused to go . . . The only point of the reception was to make a really first-class presentation with a quadrophonic mix, so that it was something special.'[7]

The 'quad' version, however, was not yet ready; and the Floyd were further irked by EMI's choice of an inferior sound system. When all but Rick Wright boycotted the reception, the guests were greeted instead by a quartet of life-size Pink cut-outs.

No matter; the press accorded *The Dark Side of the Moon* the most favourable notices in the Floyd's career. Steve Peacock's review in *Sounds* concluded: 'I don't care if you've never heard a note of the Pink Floyd's music in your life, I'd unreservedly recommend everyone to *The Dark Side of the Moon* . . . In every sense of the word, this is great music.'[8]

To nobody's surprise, *The Dark Side of the Moon* was an instant number one in Britain and throughout Western Europe. But it was its accession to the same exalted slot in the USA on 28 March 1973 in the wake of a full-tilt American tour that finally sealed Pink Floyd's reputation as a global attraction, a megaband on the order of the Rolling Stones or the Who.

The Floyd's midnight concert at New York's Radio City Music Hall on 17 March was attended by a buzz unmatched at any of the group's Gotham shows, before or since. Everybody was there, from scraggly-haired survivors of the East Village's Summer of Love to the new rock glitterati, and Andy Warhol himself. All rose to their feet when the lights finally dimmed at 1.30 a.m. and vents in the stage began spewing clouds of pink steam as four statuesque Floyds, discharging the opening gusts of 'Obscured by Clouds', slowly emerged on a platform elevator through the floor at the rear of the stage. A trio of lighting towers, with a reflecting dish mounted on the central one, bathed the band in shades of red as the elevated stage section attained its full height before sliding forward towards the cheering audience.

Credit is due here to the group's early-seventies lighting designer, Arthur Max, who styled himself 'the Fifth Floyd' but was rarely recognized as such by the public. On 'Set the Controls for the Heart of the Sun', the Floyd seemed to be performing in a firestorm as Max's lights coloured the rising smoke yellow and orange, and strobe sparks showered off Nick's drumkit. Setting down his bass, Roger lit with a white spotlight, lunged into a giant gong which duly burst into flames at the song's climax.

After the intermission, the house lights dimmed once more to reveal an enormous floodlit balloon moon hovering overhead. *Ba-bump, ba-bump* . . . From the back of the hall ricocheted the amplified throb of the human heart. *'I've been mad for fucking years . . .'*

Highlights of *The Dark Side of the Moon*'s Big Apple debut included an aircraft launched from the back of Radio City Music Hall at the end of 'On the Run' which crashed into the stage in an explosion of orange smoke – followed by the transformation of the home of the Ziegfeld Follies into a vast panorama of watches and clocks for 'Time'. The presence of saxophonist Dick Parry and a female duo called the Blackberries (fresh from a stint with Leon Russell) furthered the band's near-flawless reconstruction of the sound of the album. When the cycle had been performed in its entirety, and the Floyd had exhausted their supply of encores, the sky outside was already turning pink. For 6,000 New Yorkers, it had been a night that few would ever forget.

With Pink Floyd on such a roll in the States, Steve O'Rourke brought them back for yet another tour two months later. This one focused on the great American heartland, where, Gilmour marvelled, 'We have been able to sell out ten to fifteen thousand seaters every night on the tour – quite suddenly. We have always done well in New York and Los Angeles, but this was in places we had never been to before.'[9]

Yet superstardom also ushered into the Floydian temple a heretofore unfamiliar element', that breed of 'fan' who take any lull in the decibel level as an opportunity to chatter about their favourite TV shows, or to screech out the titles of the performers' greatest hits. Gilmour's overriding memory of the period after *Dark Side* was, he recounted, 'The incredible annoyance at these gigs . . . We were used to all these reverent fans who'd come and you could hear a pin drop. We'd try to get really quiet, especially at the beginning of "Echoes" or something that has tinkling notes, trying to create a beautiful atmosphere, and all these kids would be there shouting "Money!" ' [10] And Roger didn't like it one bit. The Pink Floyd cult had finally been eclipsed by the band's popularity.

Though they knew from the start that *The Dark Side of the Moon* would be their most successful record, the Floyd professed themselves bemused by the staggering scale of its success. 'When it was finished,' Nick Mason later recalled, 'everyone thought it was the best thing we'd done to date, and everyone was very pleased with it. But there's no way that anyone felt it was five times as good as *Meddle* or eight times as good as *Atom Heart Mother* – the sort of figures that it in fact sold . . .' [11]

That *The Dark Side of the Moon* should hit number one in America, where no previous Pink Floyd album had come anywhere near the top twenty, was much in keeping with the pattern set by other British groups like the Who, who had struck the jackpot with their magnum opus, *Tommy*, after first establishing themselves as a legendary concert draw by dint of relentless Stateside touring. And that *The Dark Side of the Moon* should still ride the *Billboard* charts a year or two after its release – like *Tommy* and a mere handful of Beatles albums – seemed only to confirm its status as a genuine popular 'classic'.

But unlike those records, or any other, before or since *The Dark Side of the Moon* simply wouldn't go away. With a tenacity that seemed every bit as spooky as the album itself – and certainly constituted a unique phenomenon in the history of recorded music – *Dark Side* continued to sell steadily, week in and week out, in sufficient numbers to keep it on the charts three . . . six . . . ten . . . fourteen years after its debut.

In so doing, it usurped the niche in the record books long reserved for *Johnny Mathis's Greatest Hits*, issued almost a generation earlier, in a pre-Beatles era before albums became a multi-billion-dollar industry, and when a place on the charts meant far less in terms of sales. The

Mathis LP finally disappeared in 1968, after 490 weeks on the *Billboard* listings: *Dark Side* surpassed that total in 1983, and was still going strong five years later. (Unlike the Mathis disc, however, it did slip off for several brief stretches, only to bounce right back.)

For even the most 'classic' album, the time must come when almost everyone likely to buy a copy has already done so; hence the end of its chart run. People don't generally purchase records they already own – except, it seems, in the case of *The Dark Side of the Moon*, when many thousands did exactly that. Some evidently did so because its state-of-the art production and engineering techniques (especially in conjunction with the sound effects) helped establish *Dark Side* as the album with which to showcase the high-tech stereo systems that proliferated in baby boomers' homes during the 1970s and 1980s. For such purposes, even a mildly scratched copy would simply not do.

But audiophiles alone cannot float an album on the hit parade for fifteen years; the words and music must also have an extraordinarily enduring appeal. Along with its relatively commercial sound, *The Dark Side of the Moon* certainly boasts a far stronger melodic content than any Floyd album since *Piper*; beyond all the concept-mongering and future-shock electronics, nothing can capture the popular imagination like a good tune.

The record also coincided with the rise of AOR (album-oriented radio), whose programmers were often seduced by *Dark Side*'s brilliant segues into playing more than one selection at a time. (*Billboard*'s charts, it bears noting, reflect airplay as well as the sales thereby generated.) Over the years, moreover, *The Dark Side of the Moon*'s appeal has cut across all the usual demographic boundaries. Someone who grew up with Pink Floyd can, for instance, still relate to Roger's relatively adult lyrics, even as the albums's morbidly depressed sensibility captivates new generations of angst-ridden adolescents.

All these factors, however, *still* don't quite add up to a 700-week-plus chart phenomenon. While on tour with the Floyd in 1988, I felt obligated to ask Rick, Dave, and Nick if they could muster any insights into *The Dark Side of the Moon*'s astounding longevity. Each politely suppressed a groan while pondering this question for the umpteenth time.

'No idea at all,' shrugs Rick Wright. 'After we'd made it, actually sitting down listening to it for the first time in the studio, I thought, "This is going to be big. This is an excellent album." Why it goes on and on selling, I don't know. It touched a nerve at the time. It seemed like everyone was waiting for this album, for *someone* to make it.'

169

'It hit a chord, obviously,' David Gilmour agrees. 'It still doesn't sound dated; it still sounds good when I listen to it. But I can't really say why it should achieve that longevity over some of the other great records which have been out.

'We always knew that it would sell more than we had sold of anything before. Because it was better than anything we had done before, more complete and more focused. A better cover. Every detail was well attended to.' Gilmour nonetheless now feels that the sound could have been even better, particularly with respect to the drums.

'I don't think there is a clear reason for it,' says Nick Mason. 'It's almost certainly a number of different things, which comprise the record itself and what's contained in it. Plus being the right record at the right time, and generating its own momentum because it was in the charts for so long, people start to think, "Oh that's the one that's been there awhile."

'We haven't suffered from any misapprehension that it's the best album ever made. I think it's a very good album and I'm very proud of it, but there are other albums that equally deserve that longevity – Dylan albums, *Sergeant Pepper*.

'It's a variety of things that just happened to pack well into the bit of luck. A message that the storyline, or ideas, contained, has lasted very well. That short of peculiar sixties message.'

The man who almost singlehandedly crafted most of that message has, of course, often been invited to shed his own light on the *Dark Side* phenomenon. Most of Roger's explanations tend to echo his ex-colleagues', for example, 'It's very well-balanced and well-constructed, dynamically and musically, and I think the humanity of its approach is appealing.' But he did once go out on a limb and venture that the album may be 'comforting to people because it gives you permission to feel it's all right to be going crazy' and 'because it's a musical version of that kind of truism, "Today is the first day of the rest of your life." There's all this stuff in it about how this is your life and it's all happening now, and as each moment passes that's it. It talks about the illusion of working towards ends which might turn out to be fool's gold. The philosophy that's embodied in it has got a little meaning for a lot of human beings. It deals with the Big Picture.'[13]

Rock scribe Chris Charlesworth, who often covered Pink Floyd for *Melody Maker* during their *The Dark Side of the Moon* phase, has a more down-to-earth explanation for the album's unique appeal. 'It's a great record to fuck to,' he reports. Especially Side One, climaxing as it does with 'Great Gig in the Sky' and Clare Torry's orgasmic shrieks, sobs, and moans. Indeed, the Floyd opus once topped an informal *Sounds* survey of the most prevalent soundtracks to live sex shows in Amsterdam's red-light district. 'Millions of people across the globe,' Charlesworth contends, 'have fucked to *The Dark Side of the Moon.*'

And will doubtless continue to do so, though with the advent of the unscratchable compact disc, whose sonic clarity proved an ideal match for the Floyd's legendary production, aficionados no longer found it necessary to keep replacing their copies. After enjoying a renewed sales spurt in the new format – nearly a million of the shiny five-inch discs, many of them originating in a German factory that produced nothing but *The Dark Side of the Moon* CDs – the fourth best-selling album of all time* (24 million worldwide, 11 million in the U.S. alone) finally dropped off *Billboard*'s charts on July 23, 1988, in the wake of its 736th week, apparently for good.

---

* *Dark Side of the Moon* is the fourth best-selling album after *Thriller* (Michael Jackson), the *Saturday Night Fever* soundtrack, and *Rumours* (Fleetwood Mac).

Chapter 16
Comfortably Numb

After *The Dark Side of the Moon*, much about Pink Floyd was utterly changed. The band had now acquired the clout in the music industry to proceed entirely on its own terms along with the wherewithal to take up the lifestyles of the landed gentry. And yet – for at least a year or two, anyway – the unlikely new superstars didn't seem to know quite what to make of it all.

'At that point,' Roger Waters recalled in 1976, 'all our ambitions were realized. When you're fifteen and you think, "Right, I'm gonna start a group," the pinnacle that you see (apart from very vague thoughts about rather smart bachelor flats and not having to get up till four in the afternoon) . . . is the Big Album. The number one in *Billboard*. And once you've done that, a lot of your ambitions have been achieved.'[1]

But with no more professional or material goals to strive for, the Floyd felt hard put to motivate themselves to keep on creating. Roger's sense of bitterness and alienation, moreover, was tempered not at all, as would become amply apparent when he finally *did* conquer his writer's block. 'Yes, it does feel wonderful for a month or something,' he went on, 'and then you begin to start coping with [the realization] that it's not going to make any difference really to how you feel about anything, and – it doesn't work. It doesn't mean changes. If you're a happy person, you were before and you will be afterwards, and if you're not, you weren't before and you won't be afterwards. And that kind of thing doesn't make a blind bit of difference to how you feel about anything. But even though you know that, it still takes you a long time to assimilate it.'

As far as some of the band's longtime friends and associates were concerned, the ultimate cost of the Floyd's new sports cars, yachts, and stately homes was the group's old enthusiasm and idealism. 'The whole atmosphere around the Floyd seemed to change profoundly,'

172

remembers Ron Geesin, 'when the money began pouring in, when it became such a Business.'

Rick Wright all but conceded as much in 1974. 'Suddenly one was aware that Pink Floyd was becoming a product, and a lot of our time and energy was spent hassling about the business side of running a group, rather than playing. Which is not a good thing . . .'[2]

The Pink Floyd coffers were further swelled by a reported million dollar advance from America's Columbia Records, a CBS affiliate, with which the band publicly signed at the beginning of 1974. (In Britain and Europe, Pink Floyd continued to record for EMI's Harvest label.) The Floyd's defection from Capitol had actually been engineered over a year earlier by Columbia's then president Clive Davis, who could claim much of the credit for bringing his once stodgy label into the rock age with acquisitions ranging from Donovan to Janis Joplin to Bruce Springsteen. Davis's new team of hip young A & R men included the likes of Kip Cohen, who knew Pink Floyd from his days as the Fillmore East's manager. Around the time of *Obscured by Clouds*, Cohen appraised his boss of the Floyd's powerful effect on American rock-concert audiences and of their dissatisfaction with Capitol's inability to generate commensurate record sales.

The flamboyant Davis lost no time in assiduously courting Steve O'Rourke, even inviting the Floyd manager to one of his weekly 'singles meetings', at which Columbia's department heads and A & R men would gather to hear new product and plot sales strategies. The enthusiasm and professionalism on display at this New York pow-wow contrasted so impressively with the sluggish operations at L.A.'s Capitol Tower that O'Rourke was willing to come to terms with Davis over a year before his clients' commitment to Capitol was due to expire. Never even given the opportunity to make a competing bid, Capitol was effectively kept in the dark about the Floyd's plans. By the time Pink Floyd could officially join the Columbia roster, however, Davis – who had pushed the deal through against the advice of conservative business advisers – was ousted for such indiscretions as financing his son's bar mitzvah with CBS funds.

With *The Dark Side of the Moon*, of course, Capitol finally did realize Pink Floyd's superstar potential, only to see the golden goose bolting the coop after years of neglect. The company was left with little choice but to exploit its existing catalogue (no small consolation, as it turned out, with *Dark Side* continuing for years to sell like a brand new release). Capitol's first Floyd repackage was the budget priced *A Nice Pair*, which coupled the *Piper** and *Saucerful* LPs – hard to find in America – and ended up charting higher Stateside than any previous Floyd title save *The Dark Side of the Moon* itself.

The *Nice Pair* sleeve, meanwhile, became the subject of a farcical saga quite disproportionate to such a minor release. To begin with, Hipgnosis devised so many design alternatives, none of which leapt out as the obvious choice, that Storm Thorgerson hit upon the grand concept of using them all (and then some). The result was a gallery of eighteen miniature LP covers, many of them jokey visual depictions of such phrases as a fork in the road', 'A frog in the throat', 'laughing all the way to the bank', 'a kettle of fish', and 'a nip in the air'. (The latter, for instance, is represented by a drawing of a levitating Japanese.)

Storm also planned to include a similar pun on 'Pink Floyd' – a photo of Floyd Patterson in which the boxing star was coloured pink. 'Quite a funny picture, I thought,' says Thorgerson. 'But he wanted $5,000 – an outrageous sum of money – so we told him to fuck off.' He hastily substituted a rare shot of the Pink Floyd Football Team – consisting of the band, the roadies Steve O'Rourke (in the upper right corner), and Storm himself (posing between Rick and Dave) – contemplating their recent 4–0 defeat by a contingent of North London Marxists.

Capitol, for its part, took exception to a visual pun on the title itself. In America, the 'nice pair' of female breasts was duly changed to an unarguably nice *pear*. Then, after the album's release in Britain, the photo of a London office bearing the sign W.R. PHANG DENTAL SURGEON also had to be replaced (by one of a gargling Buddhist monk, as it happens) when Mr Phang objected that it might be construed as advertising – a serious breach of professional ethics.

All this, however, was merely a sideshow to the pressing business of conceiving a *new* album. Yet the Floyd had poured so much of themselves into *The Dark Side of the Moon* and the pressures inherent in following up such a blockbuster were so intense that they found themselves locked in a state of creative paralysis. 'Yes, that was the hardest thing,' says Rick Wright. 'What do we do after *this*? At one

---

* While this U.S. permutation of *Piper* did restore the original British track listing, the live *Ummagumma* rendition of Astronomy Dominé was somehow substituted for the Barrett-era studio version – a mix-up that was corrected in other countries where the double-LP was subsequently marketed.

174

point, the band determined to break out of the trap with a departure so radical – if not downright whimsical – as to preclude any comparisons whatsoever with *The Dark Side of the Moon*: an album of music performed on everything *but* instruments.

Accordingly, the Floyd set aside all their usual musical equipment during a series of recording sessions in autumn 1973 devoted to experiments with *Household Objects*, as the album was to be called. 'If you tap a wine bottle across the top of the neck,' Dave Gilmour explained at the time, 'you get a tabla-like sound close up.' Stretching rubber bands between two tables, he aded, yielded 'a really good bass sound'. And for a touch of melody, the boys found that a roll of adhesive tape could be pulled out to different lengths; 'the further away it gets, the note changes'. [3]

The Floyd actually completed three tracks with these and other household objects, including aerosol spray cans, buckets of water, and drinking glasses, before conceding that few of the sounds, when heard out of context, couldn't in fact be bettered on their own drums, guitars, and synthesizers. Even so, one does almost regret the abandonment of *Household Objects* – if only for the expressions that might have crossed the faces of the CBS execs upon contemplating the first fruits of their seven-figure investment in Pink Floyd.

Rather than attempting to devise more suitable product, the Floyd devoted much of 1974 to spending their money and getting on with their personal lives. 'There was a point after *Dark Side*,' Nick Mason later confessed, 'where we might easily have broken up . . . we were a bit nervous about carrying on.' Apart from a couple of European dates, the group's sole concert appearance was at a benefit at the Rainbow Theatre on 4 November 1973 that raised £10,000 for Robert Wyatt, the drummer for the Floyd's UFO-era rivals the Soft Machine, who had fallen out a window, permanently paralyzing his back.

Dabbling with a second career as a record producer, Mason further helped out the indomitable Wyatt on a new solo album called *Rock Bottom* (which Nick has singled out as the record he most enjoys listening to of all those he ever worked on, and a campy remake of the Monkees' 'I'm a Believer'). He also produced an LP for Principal Edwards' Magic Theatre, a folk-rock-drama ensemble.

Dave, meanwhile, sat in on several shows by Sutherland Brothers and Quiver (as the band was now called) when Tim Renwick fell ill, played guitar with Roy Harper at Blackhill Enterprises' annual free

175

Hyde Park concert and did some producing of his own on *Blue Pine Trees* by the group Unicorn, to whom he had been introduced by an old Cambridge friend, Ricky Hopper.*

Also through Hopper, Dave first took up the cause of an unknown fifteen-year-old singer/songwriter named Kate Bush, going so far as to invite her to his farm to record a clutch of demos in his home studio. One of these, 'Passing through Air', featuring Gilmour on guitar, together with members of Unicorn, would surface on the B-side of her 1980 single, 'Army Dreamers'.

Gilmour, Mason and Wright also pursued more private hobbies – collecting vintage guitars, cars, and Persian carpets respectively. (Dave was soon to crown his hoard of over a hundred instruments with the very first Fender Stratocaster ever made, sporting the serial number 001.) All three spent much of the mid-1970s basking in the sunshine of their new holiday homes on the south coast of France (Mason) and the Greek island of Rhodes (Gilmour and Wright). Both Nick and Rick cultivated a passion for sailing, and each now had two young children needful of time and attention (Chloe and Holly Mason, and Gaia and Jamie Wright). Music was no longer an overriding priority for either of them.

Though that could never be said of David Gilmour, he too was settling down – with a vivacious blonde American rock fan and painter named Ginger, who was to bear him three daughters (Sara, Clare, and Alice) and then a son (Matthew) following their marriage in 1975. In the meantime, the couple busied themselves doing up Gilmour's new Notting Hill town house. 'I tried living in London for a short time and hated it,' Dave said later. 'I'm a country boy at heart.'

By contrast, Rick Wright – the band's lifelong Londoner – resettled just outside Cambridge. There he generated one of the post-*Dark Side* season's few Floydian news stories with a birthday bash in his custom-restored manor house that featured marquees on the lawn, bathing beauty contests around the pool, and cream teas served up by the local Women's Institute.

Despite a handy arsenal of synthesizers and state-of-the-art recording equipment, Wright admitted that those days he felt more motivated 'to jump on my lawnmower and shoot round the garden'. He was not, he added, going to let the pleasure he derived from success's

---

* Gilmour would go on to produce the band's other albums, *Too Many Crooks* and *One More Tomorrow*, and to record 'There's No Way Out of Here', by Unicorn keyboards man Ken Baker, on his own first solo LP.

material rewards be affected by anyone else in the band's 'guilt about having a lot of money when there's penniless people walking around outside'.[5]

One may safely venture that Rick was referring primarily to Roger Waters – the odd man out in this picture of genteel contentment. In the wake of *The Dark Side of the Moon*, Water's ongoing preoccupation with the sorry state of the world was eclipsed by more personal troubles. Still ensconced in their £5,000 Islington terraced house, he and Judy, for all their desire to have children, had been unable to produce any; now their marriage was going to pieces.

Roger's own take on the circumstances that culminated in their bitter divorce in 1975 would provide another brick or two for *The Wall* – in which, for instance, 'Pink' places a transatlantic phone call to his hard-as-nails wife during an American tour, only to have another man hang up on him.

With the advent of a less ideological girlfriend from California, however, Socialist principles would no longer appear to preclude the Waters lifestyle from becoming at least as upscale as the other Floyds'; his taste in collecting ran to French impressionist paintings. As he himself was to quip, 'You go through this thing where you think of all the good you could do by giving [the money] away. But, in the end, you decide to keep it!'

In the meantime, Roger channeled his fiercely competitive spirit into sports – and, above all, golf. To some of Pink Floyd's constituency at the time, golf – that favourite sport of solicitors and stockbrokers, not to mention statesmen like Vice-President Spiro Agnew – might have seemed an unlikely diversion for the author of 'Set the Controls for the Heart of the Sun' and 'Us and Them'. Its Establishment image notwithstanding, Ron Geesin, who had long served as Roger's regular golfing partner, extolls their shared obsession as 'The most complex, multi-layered microcosm of life known as a game. You're dealing with individuals, out in an expanse of grass. You're having to deal with their characters, what they tell you and what they won't to tell you. You're having to deal with yourself, trying to do something perfectly and failing.

'Of course the lay person would say it's only a game – you're hitting a wee ball from there to here with a piece of wood or iron – but the problems you get into exactly parallel life itself. I've always said that at least once in every round I play I give up the game of golf, and again that parallels life. Maybe in my case I'm trying to make an album, or some idea that's deep inside, and I can't quite pull it out. And I feel I must give this up, but then something else says – *no, you must carry on.* The idea involved with hitting this tiny ball 250 yards down a narrow strip and hoping that it lands on the strip when it finishes, and not in someone's garden – it epitomizes the lonely journey of the individual.'

The lonely journey of the individual in a cold and brutal world was to provide a pervasive theme for nearly all of Roger's subsequent Floyd lyrics. The first of these were written for three long meandering pieces, which would surface in vastly different form on *Wish You Were Here* and *Animals*, that the Floyd finally worked up in a North London rehearsal studio, to supplement *The Dark Side of the Moon* on a mid-1974 mini-tour of France. One was a brooding meditation on the disintegration of Syd Barrett ('Shine On You Crazy Diamond'); the other two (then titled 'Raving and Drooling' and 'Gotta Be Crazy') were tirades against a social order that leaves its children '*empty and angry and spaced*'.

The Floyd's conflicting response to their newfound superstardom was perhaps most vividly illustrated by an agreement to let a French soft drink company sponsor the six-city tour. Over a decade before corporate sponsorship of rock and roll became epidemic, many French Floyd freaks were startled by the sight of the astral foursome shame-lessly touting Gini bitter lemon in glossy magazine ads. According to Nick Mason, the Floyd had naively imagined that they were taking Gini for a ride; the fans, after all, would supposedly be charged less for concert tickets, and the band would make an extra bundle. It simply never occurred to anyone that Pink Floyd's integrity might seem compromised.

'In the beginning it was as if we were winning a prize,' Roger told Philippe Constantin, the resident Floyd buff at their French record company. 'They wanted to give us £50,000 to take our photograph. Good God, fantastic! It was only later that I told myself: Who needs that?'[6]

The Floyd's belated sense of guilt over the bitter lemon episode was such that they ended up donating their windfall to charity. Waters was also moved to write a song about selling his soul in the desert (a reference to the setting of the band's Gini ads) called 'Bitter Love', but it was Gilmour who had the last word on the subject: 'We never tasted the fucking drink anyway.' Though 'Bitter Love' was never released, Roger Waters and the rest of Pink Floyd would henceforth keep their distance from corporate sponsors.

178

The French dates served as a dry run for a long-awaited twenty-concert British tour at year's end – the Floyd's first since *The Dark Side of the Moon*'s release a year and a half earlier. Much of the autumn was spent filming and editing scenes for projection on the band's new giant circular screen: including one that fostered the illusion of prominent 'lunatic' politicians ('*the paper holds their folded faces to the floor*') singing along with the Floyd on 'Brain Damage' and, for 'Eclipse', a series of solar flares erupting from the sun's rim.

There was also an animated sequence by the mordant political cartoonist Gerald Scarfe. His initial effort in the genre – a 1971 parody of America's overconsuming lifestyle called *Long Drawn-out Trip* – had deeply impressed Waters, who had been courting him ever since. Scarfe's first Floyd animations, depicting nightmare creatures lumbering across a ravaged fantasy landscape, were soon to attach themselves to the brand-new 'Welcome to the Machine'.

Other embellishments included the most sophisticated mixing-board in rock and roll, and a huge revolving mirror-ball devised to spray the audience with pencil-thin jets of light during 'Shine on You Crazy Diamond'. All told, the cost of mounting the tour topped £100,000 – some of it earmarked for the wages of an equally unheard-of 35-strong crew, including one sound mixer, three lorry drivers, four film men, five 'external hands', and thirteen roadies.

In yet another innovation, the Floyd, displaying a sense of humour rarely apparent in their music and live performances, trashed the institution of the vacuous and overpriced glossy concert programme. At Nick Mason's suggestion, Hipgnosis created a comic-book pastiche that could be printed on pulp paper and sell for only 15p. Along with a wacky Floyd trivia quiz, Roger's new lyrics, and a Scarfe cartoon, the booklet featured four comic-strip adventures starring the individual band-members in swashbuckling roles that parodied their respective extramusical interests. 'Rog of the Rovers' was cast as a champion soccer player, 'Dave Derring' as a hellraising motorcyclist, 'Captain Mason, RN' as a naval war hero, and 'Rich Right' as a globetrotting playboy. (There was also a send-up of the old *New Musical Express* 'Life Lines' feature, in which the still-married Waters gallantly cited 'Jude' as his Favourite Person.)

In other respects, too, the band served notice on the '74 tour that henceforth Pink Floyd could – and would – do things strictly Their Way. The itinerary was planned to coincide with key football matches around the country, enabling the Floyd to attend the games in the afternoon before facing their own fans in the evening. Waters also directed that their hotels be located as near as possible to a golf course.

More importantly, the band implemented a new policy towards – or, rather, *against* – the media. Since the days of Jenner and King, the Floyd (one of the few groups of their stature never to have employed a publicist) had rarely gone out of their way to fraternize with the press; now they made it icy clear that reporters were unwelcome in their company. Henceforth, requests for interviews would be routinely denied – except in the case of authorized special projects like Capital Radio's 'Pink Floyd Story' series in 1976 – and journalists and critics could count themselves lucky merely to receive a ticket to one of the London shows.

'We took on this slightly precious feeling,' Nick Mason recalls, 'that there wasn't much point in doing interviews. It generally became: "Well, we're not going to do interviews because we always get slagged off," and them thinking, "Well, they won't do interviews so we'll just slag them off." '

British music journalists certainly did not take kindly to the Floyd's high-handed treatment of them. The London pop world was a very small and clannish one, where the writers and stars traditionally ate and drank together – fed off one another, some might say – at the same clubs and pubs. The musicians were expected to accept the writers' occasional barbs as part of the game.

But it was a game that the Floyd – particularly their touchy and none-too-sociable chief songwriter – had never felt very comfortable playing. 'They were middle-class kids,' says Miles, 'who didn't have much in common with most rock writers circa the early seventies – let alone most other rock bands. Most English rock and roll was very much a working-class phenomenon, and the Floyd came from an utterly different kind of life. They weren't part of it – *couldn't* be part of it.'

From the Floyd's perspective, one beneficial aspect of the press ban would be the shielding of their individual personalities from the public eye, facilitating a degree of privacy that few other rock superstars have ever enjoyed. 'We really don't want to become public property . . .' Gilmour said in 1978. 'I hate the thought of walking around like anyone else you care to mention and having people continually staring at me and tormenting me. A lot of people are happy to trade that [for] their privacy – but I'm not, and we're not as a group.'[7]

Yet it gradually became apparent that the main architect of the Floyd's official near-silence was Roger Waters, who regarded most journalists as fifth-rate hacks, and bitterly resented their presumption in intruding into his life and passing judgement on his work. The rock critics incurred his displeasure most of all. 'I get a little fed up with what they tell me,' Waters told the favoured Philippe Constantin. 'It hurts me because I see it all written in black and white. I don't like the feeling of being attacked. Even if, with a handful of exceptions, they don't really get to the bottom of things . . .

'Plenty of people in the press have come down really hard on us saying the lyrics are awful. Sometimes I think those people couldn't do any better themselves. They tend to forget that people who buy records and get into the music haven't all got degrees in English Literature . . .'[8]

Nonetheless, reporters who managed to make unofficial contact with Dave, Rick, or Nick often found them perfectly affable – and sometimes quite talkative. 'It was a question of hanging around long enough and not being obtrusive,' says the writer Chris Charlesworth, 'and you would maybe gain their confidence and they'd talk to you.'

Charlesworth, on assignment for *Melody Maker*, put this strategy to the test at the beginning of the 1974 UK tour. Installing himself at the Floyd's posh hotel in Edinburgh, he descreetly shadowed the band until finally, on the morning after the show's British premiere, Rick Wright proved in the mood to chat. 'Just the fact that I was there showed sufficient interest to get me an interview. I really wanted to interview Roger, but he went off to play golf.'

Among the very few writers who succeeded in earning Roger's trust and respect was Charlesworth's *Melody Maker* colleague Karl Dallas. It helped that he was nearly a generation older than the Floyd and most of their critics, and that his relationship with the group had started out on a purely social footing: UFO had served as Dallas's neighbourhood hang-out during Syd Barrett's hey-day, but he never thought much of the band's music at the time. He liked it far more after Barrett's departure – 'the best thing that ever happened to the Floyd' in his unfashionable opinion – and, uniquely among journalists, remained a friend and confidant of both Gilmour and Waters. (Until he published a book about their music, anyway.)

While a select handful of commentators like Dallas would continue to give Roger's views a periodic airing, those bulletins from 'the horse's mouth' (in Waters's phrase) were increasingly few and far between. Yet, somewhat paradoxically, with the Floyd's popularity already such that they had little need of additional press coverage, their determined remoteness only served to enhance their anonymous mystique among the record-buying public. Years later, Dave quipped that the Floyd were anxious not to let their astral image be compromised by giving 'the fans too much information about us sitting at home watching television and drinking beer'.[9]

The lack of personal access notwithstanding, there would always be fawning writers like Derek Jewell of *The Sunday Times*, who proclaimed Pink Floyd 'the symphonic overlords of today's popular hierarchy' after attending the first of their four concerts at London's Wembley Arena. Jewell pronounced it, 'A performance with musical textures so ravishing and visual accompaniments so surprising that, for once, the thunderous standing ovation was completely justified.'

The Young Turks of the rock press, however, were having none of it. An anti-Floyd backlash was especially evident in the pages of the increasingly iconoclastic and incendiary *New Musical Express*, which the underground-London crowd had once scorned as a vapid fan sheet. In a 5,000-word *NME* broadside, Nick Kent and Pete Erskine blasted as 'utterly morose', 'incredibly tired', and downright 'Orwellian' the very extravaganza Jewell had so effusively praised. Automaton Rock, Erskine called it: 'Non-participatory, non-thinking music, where all the audience has to do is walk in, sit down, and watch it all exploding in front of them.'

The new material, Kent charged in his turn, was 'indolent musical deadwood' whose 'ranting' anti-Establishment message seemed highly suspect in light of the Floyd's own 'desperately bourgeois' private lives. Especially 'offensive' was the line *'gotta keep everyone buying this shit'*, which struck him as all too germane to its author's bored and disdainful onstage demeanour – not to mention the shoddy quality of the music. According to Kent, Waters and Mason were rock's 'dullest ever' rhythm section, and Wright and Gilmour merely 'adequate'. His critique extended even to Dave's 'filthy' hair, 'anchored down by a surfeit of scalp grease and tapering off below the shoulders with a spectacular festooning of split ends' – yet further evidence of the 'facile, soulless' Floyd's indifference to their performance and their fans:

One can easily envisage a Floyd concert in the future consisting of the band simply wandering on stage, setting all their tapes into action, putting their instruments on remote control and then walking off behind the amps in order to talk about football or play billiards.

182

I'd almost prefer to see them do that. At least it would be more honest.

Still, the Floyd can content themselves on one score. They are definitely the quintessential English band. No other combine quite sums up the rampant sense of doomed mediocrity inherent in this country's outlook right now . . . And there's absolutely nothing 'cosmic' about any of it, really, now is there?[10]

The usually placid Gilmour felt sufficiently stung to corrall Pete Erskine and rebut his and Kent's article point by point – thus engendering yet another *NME* epic. 'I don't think we're remotely close to that thing about tapes,' Dave insisted; he took his guitar playing very seriously indeed, 'and I don't need to have clean hair for that'. Yet even he conceded that the new material had yet to be thrashed into palatable shape, and that he had felt 'definitely dispirited' at Wembley, where some of the stage props had failed to activate on cue: 'It gets very depressing when you're fighting against odds like dud equipment. Energy soon flags.'[11] Which only seemed to corroborate *NME*'s point about the spirit of rock and roll getting snuffed out by all that high-tech machinery.

If nothing else, the *NME* inquisitions served notice that Pink Floyd's status among the rock community's trendy tastemakers was plummeting in inverse relation to the group's soaring popularity in the world at large. It seemed equally apparent that both developments had caught the Floyd very much by surprise, and that the band had yet to get a grip upon its radically changed circumstances.

Chapter 17
The Hero's Return

During the first week of 1975, Pink Floyd finally returned to the Abbey Road studios to come to grips with the problem of their next record. At least the band now had three substantial compositions to work with, one of which – 'Shine On You Crazy Diamond' – seemed by general agreement a promising centrepiece for any new Floyd album.

A mostly instrumental twenty-minute-plus suite in the tradition of 'Atom Heart Mother' and 'Echoes', 'Shine On' had originally evolved, nearly a year earlier, out of the four-note Gilmour guitar phrase that was to figure so prominently near the start of the finished recording. To Roger Waters, these notes resonated with a profound melancholy that brought the spectre of Syd Barrett inescapably to mind. And when Roger began tackling the lyrics, all his long-blocked feelings of sadness, guilt, and regret over his erstwhile partner seemed to come flooding to the fore. The result, which incorporated music by Rick Wright as well as David Gilmour, was Pink Floyd's epic tribute to that piper and prophet, stranger and legend of whom Waters said: 'It couldn't have happened without him but on the other hand it couldn't have gone on *with* him.'

Having proved themselves so convincingly with *Dark Side*, the band at last felt able to confront Barrett's shadow head-on. Roger took exceptional pains to get every word just right, he told Philippe Constantin, 'Because I wanted it to get as close as possible to what I felt . . . that sort of indefinable, inevitable melancholy about the disappearance of Syd. Because he's left, withdrawn so far away that, as far as we're concerned, he's no longer there.'[1] A case could be made that, both musically and lyrically, 'Shine On You Crazy Diamond' was the Floyd's finest single achievement since its protagonist *wore out his welcome with random precision*.

Even so, Rick Wright says, 'It took us a long time before we actually got into really getting down and making the album. There was a lot of

184

sitting around. I think all of us were playing half-heartedly as well. It was a difficult period, after *The Dark Side of the Moon*.'

According to Waters, those early sessions 'became very laborious and tortured, and everybody seemed to be very bored by the whole thing. We pressed on regardless of the general ennui for a few weeks, and then things came to a bit of a head'. At a stormy group meeting, he announced that, 'The only way I could retain interest in the project was to try and make the album relate to what was going on there and then, the fact that no one was really looking each other in the eye, and that it was all very mechanical . . .'[2]

Roger, in other words, was beginning to discern in Pink Floyd's predicament glimmers of another Concept Album. But Dave just wanted to get on with it: knock their existing material into shape, stick 'Shine On' on Side One and 'Gotta Be Crazy' and 'Raving and Drooling' on Side Two and leave it at that. As far as Gilmour was concerned, the real obstacle was his colleagues' self-indulgent unprofessionalism.

Much of Dave's impatience was directed at Nick Mason – no virtuoso at the best of times – whose marriage was now going the way of Roger's, and whose 'alarming despondency', by his own admission, 'manifested itself in a complete, well, rigor mortis . . . I didn't quite have to be carried about, but I wasn't interested. I couldn't get myself to sort out the drumming, and . . . that of course drove everyone else even crazier.'[3]

'I felt,' Waters said, 'that at times the group was there only physically. Our bodies were there, but our minds and feelings somewhere else. And we were only there because this music allows us to live and live well, or because it was a habit, to be in Pink Floyd and operate under that banner.' So he wanted 'to write something about it all, cutting "Shine On You" into two and projecting my feelings about what was going on.'[4] And in the end, of course, Roger got his way.

The upshot was three new songs, to be sandwiched between the two halves of the main piece. On one level, 'Welcome to the Machine' and 'Have a Cigar' addressed the record-industry pressures exerted upon Pink Floyd to crank out more hit product on the order of *The Dark Side of the Moon* – even as 'Machine' also related to the mechanical nature of the actual sessions, and 'Wish You Were Here' to the band's own lack of commitment therein. ('It could equally have been called "Wish *We* Were Here."' Waters quipped.)

On another level, the new lyrics dovetailed neatly with 'Shine On You Crazy Diamond', insofar as all three were also thoroughly applicable to the rise and fall of Syd. And Barrett's plight, in turn, struck Waters as symbolic not only of the latter-day Floyd's 'fragmented' state, but of twentieth-century alienation generally: 'All the extremes of absence some people have to indulge in because it's the only way they can cope with how fucking sad modern life is – to withdraw completely.' And so *Wish You Were Here*, as it came to be called, coalesced into a concept album no less cohesive – albeit rather more subtle – than *The Dark Side of the Moon*. (Like its predecessor, *Wish You Were Here* also inadvertently recycled the title of an album released a year earlier by a rather less successful band – in this case Badfinger.)

At the time, however, no one was entirely happy with the format of *Wish You Were Here*. Rick Wright allowed that 'Roger's preoccupation with things such as madness and the Business is something that I didn't feel nearly so strongly about';[5] Waters, in turn, fretted that his message was diluted by 'the very drawn-out nature of the overture bits that go on and on and on and on . . . I think we made a basic error in not arranging it in a different way so that some of the ideas were expounded lyrically before they were developed musically.'[6]

Such remarks suggest that already the Floyds, whether they realized it or not, were artistically at cross-purposes. Gilmour and Wright were content that Pink Floyd's music should keep on transporting listeners into advanced states of REM. Waters was now determined, by his lights, to wake them all up.

Yet *Wish You Were Here* turned out to be so effective precisely because it struck such an inadvertent balance between Roger's growing conceptual obsessions and Dave and Rick's refinement of the classic Floyd atmospherics that attracted most listeners to the group in the first place: the album thus ended up capturing the best of both worlds. 'I particularly like that record,' Wright says now. 'I think that's my favourite album that the Floyd ever did, I like the feel of it – and in it. It's the kind of music – *Dark Side* as well – when all three of us were writing, together sometimes. I feel the best material from the Floyd was definitely when two or three of us co-wrote something together. Afterwards we lost that: there wasn't that interplay of ideas between the band.'

Even after it acquired its new form, *Wish You Were Here* did not come easily. The recording sessions were twice interrupted by three-week-

long American tours (in April and June 1975)'* after which, said
Roger, 'I hadn't got an ounce of creative energy left in me.' And when
the Floyd finally did get 'Shine On You Crazy Diamond's' instrumental
arrangement just right, the take was spoiled by an inexperienced
engineer who had accidentally overloaded some of the tracks with
echo. The band had no choice but to do it all over again.

The music for 'Welcome to the Machine' – as close as Pink Floyd
ever came to living up to their 'electronics wizards' stereotype – was
built up in the studio from the relentless throb of a VC3 synthesizer
hooked into a repeat echo unit. The band then imaginatively softened
the edges with Dave's shimmering acoustic guitar and some nice
tympani flourishes from Nick Mason. This scorching indictment of
the Music Biz begins with the opening of a door – which Waters has
described as an ironic symbol of the sense of musical discovery and
progress that is ultimately betrayed by a 'Rock Machine' driven far less
by artistic considerations than by greed and empty dreams of 'success'.

At the song's end, the industrial throb gives way to the (more or
less) human sounds of a party. 'That was put there,' Roger explained,
'because of the complete emptiness inherent in that way of behaving –
celebrations, gatherings of people who drink and talk together. To me
that epitomizes the lack of contact and real feelings between people.'[7]
That protagonist, in other words, steps outside the dehumanizing
Rock Machine, only to find that 'the people there are all zombies' too.
For a sensitive rock star, it would seen, there ain't no way out.

'Have a Cigar' makes even more explicit Roger's resentment and
contempt for the industry that had recently made him a millionaire.
The lyric malevolently incorporates just about every crass cliché that a
hot new star is liable to hear from a record-biz fat cat so delighted with
the sales figures he 'can hardly count'. A personal touch is added by
the song's most famous phrase – *By the way, which one's Pink?* – which
had actually been addressed to the Floyd on at least one occasion.

Musically, 'Cigar' is to *Wish You Were Here* what the similarly
sarcastic 'Money' was to *The Dark Side of the Moon*, opening Side Two
with a shot of rhythm-and-blues and some crackling Gilmour guitar.
CBS picked it as the company's first Pink Floyd single.

But when it came time to record 'Have a Cigar', Roger's admittedly
limited voice was in shreds from his struggles with the 'Shine On You

---

* Capitol Records attempted to turn these visits to the advantage of its own back
catalogue sales by sending radio stations *Pink Floyd Tour '75* (Capitol SPRO 8116/7):
a new compilation of 'The Gold It's in the . . .', 'Wots . . . Uh the Deal', 'Free Four',

Crazy Diamond' lead vocal. That, he confessed, had proved 'incredibly difficult and fantastically boring to record because I had to do it line by line – over and over again just to get it even sounding reasonable'.[8] After Gilmour demurred at singing such 'complaining' lyrics, Waters invited the Floyd's friend and longtime Harvest labelmate Roy Harper to take the mike on 'Cigar'. A topical singer/songwriter and Jenner-King client whose hippie credentials (and subterranean sales figures) had never been overly compromised by the Rock Machine, Harper was recording his own album, *H.Q.* to which Dave had already contributed some guitar licks, in another of the Abbey Road studios.

At the time, Waters was 'hoping everybody would go, "Oh no, Rog, *you* do it" – but they didn't. They all went, "Oh yeah, that's a good idea." [Roy] did it and everybody went, "Oh terrific," so that was that. I think it was a bad idea now, I think I should have done it. Not that I think he did it badly – I think he did it very well – it just isn't *us* any more.'[9]

Uniquely among Pink Floyd's songs, the album's title track originated as a Roger Waters poem that Gilmour, who also sings it, then set to music. Usually the tune materialized before the words. One of the few truly classic Pink melodies, 'Wish You Were Here' is also just about the only Floyd number you're ever likely to hear performed by street troubadours in places like New York's Washington Square Park.

Though the lyric relates both to Syd and to the current Floyd, Roger has said that it was most of all about 'the battling elements' within his own contradictory character: the compassionate idealist and 'the grasping, avaricious, selfish little kid who wants to get his hands on the sweets and have them all. The song slips in and out of both personae' with the ambitious, arrogant Roger plaintively asking his more admirable alter ego to reassert his presence. A sense of shifting perspective is also fostered by the production trick in the opening bars, which sound as if they are being broadcast from afar over a cheap little radio. (Just the sort of thing Floydophobes used to call 'contrived'.)

'Wish You Were Here', too, boasts a guest performance of sorts. Upon learning that the master violinists Stephane Grappelli and Yehudi Menuhin were recording a duet down the hall at Abbey Road, the Floyd decided to pursue Gilmour's whim that his folky tune should

---

'Fat Old Sun', 'One of these Days', 'Astronomy Dominé', and 'Careful with that Axe, Eugene' – none of which the Floyd actually performed on the '75 tours.

conclude with the sound of a fiddle. For a price, Grappelli was induced to overdub a violin solo – only to get virtually drowned out, in the end, by a more typically Floydian coda of howling wind. 'We decided not to give him a credit, 'cause we thought it might be a bit of an insult,' said Waters. 'He got his £300, though.'[10] (Then again, Nick Mason's name was not to appear anywhere on the album, either.)

On 5 June, yet another legendary guest materialized, unannounced, at the Abbey Road studio. It was Dave and Ginger's wedding day – as well as the eve of the band's second 1975 U.S. tour – and the Floyd were frantically trying to wrap up a final mix of 'Shine On You Crazy Diamond'. With the voices of Roger and Dave summoning the spirit of Syd Barrett from the studio monitors, who should lurch in but . . . an obese man with shaven head and eyebrows, wearing a white trenchcoat and white shoes, and clutching a white plastic bag. Gilmour was the first to notice him sniffing around the Floyd equipment but, preoccupied with other matters, figured that the odd-looking character was some EMI minion.

'He came into the studio,' remembers Rick Wright, 'and no one recognized this person. I remember going in, and Roger was already in the studio working. I came in and sat next to Roger. After ten minutes, Roger said to me, "Do you know who that guy is?" I said, "I have no idea. I assumed it was a friend of yours." He said, *"Think, think."* And I kept looking at him – and I suddenly realized it was Syd!' Waters, by his own account, was 'in fucking tears' upon divining the identity of 'this great, fat, bald, mad person'.

Another visitor from the past, Andrew King, thought Barrett looked like nothing so much as a chef at some Middle-American burger joint. King tried to break the ice by asking his former star client how he'd put on so much weight. 'I've got a very large fridge in the kitchen,' Syd explained, 'and I've been eating a lot of pork chops.' Barrett then reportedly let it be known that he was now ready for the Floyd to make use of his services once again.

As his ex-colleagues applied themselves to the onerous task of mixing 'Shine On You Crazy Diamond', replaying it over and over, Syd fell silent, giving no sign of understanding that he was the hero of this stirring tribute. Finally, when they asked for the track to be played yet another time, he interrupted: 'Why bother? You've heard it once already.'

Barrett subsequently joined the others at the EMI canteen for the Gilmours' wedding reception. After unnerving unsuspecting guests –

some of whom mistook him for a Hare Krishna fanatic – with his maniacal laughter and penetrating stares, Syd vanished into the night without saying goodbye.

The following day, the Floyd left for America without him. None of them has ever seen him since.

No Pink Floyd LP was ever to boast a more elaborate package than *Wish You Were Here* – nor one whose artwork was so closely synchronized, in ever detail, with the record's musical and lyrical content. Indeed, it was Storm Thorgerson who selected the album's title.

In providing the Floyd's recordings with a visual complement, Thorgerson had never felt any lack of inspiration. 'The atmospheric thing,' he says, 'seems to me what the Floyd did better than anybody else, I'm not just saying that 'cause I worked with them: I actually do think that they are masters of evoking a mood in an auditorium with about two notes. The beginning of "Shine On" is only about two notes and it just works a treat. It is very moody and atmospheric, and it has this sense of wide open spaces of the inner mind, or of some unknown terrain. Most of my pictures reflect that.'

Yet Storm was never content merely to provide 'decorative embroidery' for an album. He made it a point to glean from its songs some 'meaning' that might then serve as 'a stepping stone towards getting an image. Because my job, as I see it, is to invent an image related to the music'.

In his book *The Work of Hipgnosis: Walk Away Renee*, Thorgerson recalls pondering Roger's new lyrics while accompanying Pink Floyd on their April U.S. tour: 'They seemed to be about unfulfilled presence in general rather than about Syd's particular version of it – and he certainly had his own unique brand. The idea of presence withheld, of the ways that people pretend to be present whilst their minds are really elsewhere, and the devices and motivations employed psychologically by people to suppress the full force of their presence, eventually boiled down to a single theme – absence; the absence of a person, the absence of feeling.'[11]

Following the tour, Thorgerson spent long nights brainstorming with the Floyd, 'Searching for a powerful metaphor or symbol of absence. We were especially interested in the aspect of absence which involved pretense, something supposedly genuine but that was in reality as phoney as a Nixon denial.'[12] The anti-Music Biz themes of 'Welcome to the Machine' and 'Have a Cigar' finally suggested a

190

handshake: a physical presence and an ostensibly friendly gesture that often amounts to little more than an empty and meaningless ritual. Rather like the socializing heard at the end of 'Machine.'

While in America, meanwhile, Storm had noticed that in record shops there, copies of Roxy Music's latest LP, *Country Life*, were packaged in an opaque green cellophane to shield innocent browsers' eyes from the two topless maidens adorning its cover. This inspired the conceit of concealing the *Wish* artwork inside a similar black or blue shrink wrap, so that the sleeve itself would be 'absent'. There would, in effect, be two covers: one for the Pink Floyd audience, and one for the trade. On the latter, the title and artist would be identified only by a sticker created by Hipgnosis graphics designer George Hardie, which would also feature the album's ominous logo of two mechanical hands shaking – to a backdrop quartered into the elements of fire, air, water, and earth. In a touch of the mysticism that, despite Roger's best efforts, was still associated with Pink Floyd's music, these represented the sun signs of the four astrologically well-balanced band-members: fire for Wright's Leo, air for Mason's Aquarius, water for Gilmour's Pisces, and earth for Water's Virgo.

The package structure having thus been determined before the imagery on the actual cover, Thorgerson felt free, just for once, to separate art from commerce clearly – to do the sleeve without any commercial considerations in mind whatsoever (no writing, no name, etc.) because it couldn't be seen . . . This "personal" design could be composed of very arty pieces, pertinent to the record, yet as obscure as we liked – hence studies in absence.'[13]

The photo on the front of the jacket was inspired by Storm's simple observation that people withdraw their presence from others, concealing their true feelings, out of fear of 'getting burned'. With the handshake motif also in mind, George Hardie came up with the idea of a businessman consumed by flames, obliviously shaking hands with his lookalike. It was no coincidence that 'getting burned' was also a phrase commonly heard in the Music Biz – especially among artists who'd been cheated out of their royalties.

The equally surrealistic back cover – pursuing a theme reminiscent of Roger's unreleased song 'Bitter Love' – shows a faceless 'Floyd salesman', in Thorgerson's words, 'selling his soul' in the desert. (Note the briefcase bedecked with stickers from *Obscured by Clouds*, *The Dark Side of the Moon*, and, of course, *Wish You Were Here*.) This suave hustler's lack of genuine presence is emphasized by the absence or wrists and ankles: he is, after all, little more than an empty suit.

Two further 'studies in absence' adorn the inner sleeve. One depicts a veil in a windswept Norfolk grove: the other, a splashless diver. Storm's own favourite piece, this was duplicated on the giveaway postcard packaged – fittingly enough – with *Wish You Were Here*.

Once all this had been accomplished, both of the Floyd's record companies objected strenuously to the dark shrink wrap – and not only because it cost far more than the customary transparent cellophane. In America, CBS – blissfully oblivious to the package's anti-Record Biz symbolism – couldn't fathom why the band should want to conceal 'such great' graphics. EMI, on the other hand, expressed concern that Pink Floyd weren't identifiable on the cardboard sleeves, which British retailers would be using for display purposes.

Having 'moved' several million 'units' of their last 'product', how-ever, the Floyd could now insist on indulging their every whim. And when Thorgerson and company ceremoniously presented the group with a mock-up of the *Wish You Were Here* package – complete with black shrink wrap – the four Floyds accepted it with a spontaneous round of applause.

Wish You Were Here had its live British premiere on 5 July 1975 at a huge open-air pop festival in Knebworth. For Waters the event's most memorable episode was a tantrum thrown by Roy Harper prior to his own set, when he discovered that his stage outfit had disappeared. Harper proceeded to demolish one of the Floyd's vans – tearing up the upholstery, hurling bottles through every window, and cutting himself quite badly in the process. This scene was eventually to form the basis of yet another brick in *The Wall* (where 'Pink' destroys his hotel room).

It also contributed to an unfortunate delay in properly setting up and testing the top-billed Floyd's sound system. At any other gig, the band would have held off until all was ready, but arrangements were already in motion for the Knebworth crowd to be buzzed by a pair of low-flying World War II Spitfires at the exact moment of the Floyd's own liftoff – just the first in a series of spectacular effects that would end with a crescendo of flares and rockets. When Rick Wright hit the opening notes of 'Shine On', however, he found his keyboards hope-lessly out of tune – their note-producing generators having been put out of phase by the Floyd's overloaded power supply. Sweating profu-sely, his hands shaking, Rick fell to pieces – and the band with him.

After the intermission, the Floyd were more or less back in form for *The Dark Side of the Moon*. The fans cheered, but the critics – few of whom took kindly to getting banned from the backstage area – already had enough ammunition for some of the most savage press attacks of the group's entire career. Pink Floyd were to play no further concerts in Britain, or anywhere else for that matter, until 1977.

Not that *Wish You Were Here* was to require any live promotion when it was finally released just over two months after the Knebworth fiasco. In America, the album hit number one in its second week on the *Billboard* charts; in Britain, where it went directly to the top on the strength of a quarter-million advance sales, EMI was unable to keep up with the unprecedented demand. Even with its pressing plants working overtime, the company had to inform retailers that only 50 per cent of each order could be filled.

While the fastest-selling of all their albums topped record charts the world over, Pink Floyd themselves remained 'studies in absence', having retreated back into their anonymous cocoons. Little more would be heard from any of them for at least another year, during which time the British music scene was to change almost beyond recognition.

Chapter 18
Pigs on the Wing

If 1967 had given London a Summer of Love, 1976 might almost be said to have brought the city a Summer of Hate. With Britain's crumbling economy wracked by plant closures, strikes, double-digit inflation and unemployment, a record 100,000 teenagers graduated that June to an idle and aimless life on the dole. Even the weather seemed to be conspiring against an England wilting under a rare and protracted heat wave, as nearly three months passed without a rain shower. By August the dry, sunny weather – initially welcomed as a heaven-sent antidote to the country's woes – had joined the long list of national crises, inducing failing crops, water rationing, and a specially appointed Minister of Drought.

That month, moreover, the annual Notting Hill Carnival, initiated ten years earlier by the Pink Floyd's Free School sponsors, exploded in racial violence. For British TV viewers, it was a rude awakening indeed when the images of brick-throwing black youths chasing policemen down sweltering streets originated not in faraway Johannesburg or Detroit, but in *London*! The chickens of the old Empire had come home to roost in the guise of a growing immigrant population frustrated by lack of opportunity in the mother country, even as underemployed working-class whites vented their resentment at the newcomers – manifested at its most extreme in rabble-rousing fascistic movements like the National Front, which Pink Floyd were to skewer on *The Wall*.

From this cauldron of anger, tension, and disillusionment, a new youth movement – and musical revolution – erupted in the summer of '76. 'They wear torn and ragged clothes held together with safety pins,' warned one London tabloid. 'They are boorish, ill-mannered, foul-mouthed, dirty, obnoxious, and arrogant. They like to be disliked. They use names like Johnny Rotten, Steve Havoc, Sid Vicious, Rat Scapies . . .' The Punks had arrived.

Punk Rock started out (before it broadened its musical base and popular appeal under the less threatening label 'New Wave') as a nihilistic howl against not only the prevailing socio-political conditions, but the complacency and nostalgia in which mid-seventies rock – and its reigning 'Boring Old Farts' – appeared to be mired. Promising to return the music to the streets, to the kids, and to the moment, the Punks stripped the music of all niceties, subtleties, and frills: back to rock and roll's three primal chords, thrashed out with the volume and treble controls of battered amps dialled past the threshold of pain. Anyone could play Punk Rock, and anyone did. Thousands of bands arose almost overnight, recharging those three magic chords in a machine-gun volley that threatened to level the superstars' vaunted pedestals, reconsecrate rock as a force for subversion and anarchy, and put fear and loathing back into the hearts of respectable citizens.

Of the seventies' megaplatinum legends, Pink Floyd – with their studied lack of spontaneity, auro of remoteness, and predilection for both bombast and lethargy – gave the spike-haired safety-pin brigade an especially tempting target. '*Hanging on in quiet desperation*' was certainly not the punk way. The Floyd's psychedelic heritage and image, moreover, were anathema to Punks who preferred speed to pot or acid, and who pronounced the word 'hippie' with the utmost disdain.

Indeed, the Floyd played an unwitting role in Chelsea bondage-boutique owner (and Rock Biz hustler) Malcolm McLaren's discovery of the notorious Johnny Rotten. In the words of Julie Burchill and Tony Parsons, McLaren recruited the 'teenage amphetamine hunchback with green hair and rotted dentures to match' as the Sex Pistols' lead singer largely on the strength of Rotten's 'sadistically mutilated Pink Floyd T-shirt with the words I HATE scribbled in a biro trembling with furious loathing above the Dodos' moniker.'[1] (Dave Gilmour quipped that the Floyd at least represented 'a target with substance', pointing out that Johnny Rotten could never have got so much mileage from an I HATE YES T-shirt.)

In view of their own subterranean beginnings, and their early penchant for demolishing traditional pop structures, there was a certain irony in the Floyd being subjected to such abuse. McLaren did at least voice a high regard for Syd Barrett, whom the Pistols subsequently tried to smoke out at Chelsea Cloisters. The madcap, however, remained resolutely locked in his room.

Nick Mason insists he never took the anti-Floyd rhetoric personally, and actually welcomed the Punk Rock insurrection. The Floyd, says Mason, had enjoyed 'a marvellous youth in the sixties when we were the darlings of the underground, and were in the magazines as the extraordinary underground band and all the rest of it. And that very quickly dried up: we became fairly put down and disliked in the rock press. We were quite used to not being particularly loved by everyone; you learn to live with it. You get some people who like you and some people who don't.

'The Punk thing, I felt – and still do – was an inevitable healthy cycling of the whole rock and roll business. Because rock had become complete techno-flash overkill, both in the business and on stage. The worst thing about it was the record companies were becoming bigger and bigger and going public; they were much more worried about their figures. They wouldn't take risks, and the bands were more and more expensive to promote and maintain. They would rather outbid each other for a million-dollars-plus to buy the Rolling Stones than invest in new bands. It's totally understandable – you pay a million dollars for an established act, the odds are you're going to make it back. You could try eight new bands at $100,000 a throw and lose the lot.

'The business had changed – in the early sixties, the record companies seemed to sign anything with long hair; if it was a sheepdog, so what. But there was this problem whereby the thing had become Emerson, Lake, & Palmer, and Pink Floyd, and Yes – huge massive dinosaurs rumbling across the earth. There was fuck all else for anything else; and also it was "Yes, trained at the Rock College of Music." What Punk did was say we can make records for twenty quid again; it was about energy and wanting to perform, not about who's the greatest musician in the world. It was absolutely necessary.'

'Of course,' Nick wrily adds, 'you don't want the world populated *only* with dinosaurs, but it's a terribly good thing to keep *some* of them alive.'

Mason went so far as to produce the second album by the Damned – who had originally sought the services of their boyhood hero Syd Barrett, but settled for his former drummer as the next-best thing. (No matter that Mason had been the least close to Barrett of anyone in Pink Floyd.) 'It was such an off-the-wall idea that it was gonna be either completely brilliant or totally diabolical,' Damned drummer Rat Scabies recalled a decade later. 'I tend to think of it as the latter.'[2]

One of the first products of the Floyd's own Britannia Row studios, *Music for Pleasure* also marked Nick Griffiths' initiation as house engineer. 'The studio was absolutely awful then,' he concedes, 'and I don't think the album turned out as well as we'd hoped.' Mason, however, insists it was 'fun to do' and 'quite illuminating in terms of watching people rediscover the roots of rock and roll' – even if he and Griffiths felt thwarted by the punk hellraisers' refusal, as a matter of principle, to do overdubs.

The scabrous foursome, for their part, quickly concluded that their producer was – in the words of guitarist Brian James – 'in a different world from us'. Further sabotaged by personality conflicts within the band, the outcome of this Pink-Punk encounter was cordially detested by critics, the buying public, and the Damned themselves.

Pink Floyd had originally acquired their converted chapel in Britannia Row, a little side street in Islington, primarily as a place to store all their sound and lighting equipment between tours. It also provided the group with office space and, for good measure, a demo and rehearsal studio. By 1976, with a new album looming up on the Floyd's agenda, the band began to upgrade the Britannia Row studio to a higher professional standard, so that they might record at their leisure without the scheduling constraints imposed at the likes of Abbey Road.

The studio was initially overseen by Brian Humphries, who had engineered *Wish You Were Here*. Nick Griffiths, then a novice engineer in his early twenties, was hired as his assistant, only to find himself left to run the shop when Humphries and the rest of the staff went off with the Floyd in January 1977 for a six-month world tour. At that time, the studio was equipped with 'off-the-shelf' MCI tape machines, and lined with Lignacite brick, whose acoustical properties left much to be desired. Part of Griffiths's brief was to help outfit Britannia Row with custom-made, state-of-the-art equuipment.

The Floyd planned in principle to defray the enormous cost by making studio time available to other artists on an hourly basis. However, their desire to keep Britannia Row free for their own use whenever they needed it tended to limit the studio's viability as a commercial venture. What's more, says Griffiths, 'The accounting procedures weren't all they could have been. The petty cash tin went through about five grand a day. It was a bit like the Apple situation with the Beatles.'

Not that the Floyd appeared much to care – yet. After all, the money still seemed to be rolling in almost faster than Steve O'Rourke could count it.

As if to signal that Pink Floyd were returning from the outer (or inner) limits to take on the here and now, the cover of their own first

197

Britannia Row production, *Animals*, conceived by Waters, depicted the grimy edifice of no less down-to-earth a vista than London's Battersea Power Station. 'I like the four phallic towers,' allowed Roger. 'And the idea of power I find rather appealing in a strange way.'[3]

The picture, however, was completed by a flourish of trademark Floyd/Hipgnosis surrealism: wafting through the smokestacks was a forty-foot inflatable pig destined to become a fixture of all subsequent Floyd performances. During the photo sessions, the pig drifted out of control, and – to the surprise and consternation of air traffic controllers – was carried by prevailing winds over Heathrow Airport before finally crashing some twenty miles southeast of the capital.

In pointing out a new direction for the band, Water's anthropomorphic vision of the human condition furthered an impression, at the time, of the Pink Floyd dinosaur breaking out of its comfortable rut. Ultimately, however, Roger's preoccupation with the lamentable state of the national and world political order (not to mention his own psyche) would leave Pink Floyd's music transformed beyond recognition, to the point (with parts of *The Wall* and all of *The Final Cut*) where a few veteran Floyd freaks would question whether it even *was* Pink Floyd music. Conspicuous in their near-absence on *Animals* (and its successors) are the dreamy tempos, celestial organ backdrop, and ethereal vocal harmonies that had long virtually defined the Pink Floyd sound.

'That was the first one I didn't write anything for,' says Rick Wright, whose jazz-inflected doodlings often sound almost gratuitous amid *Animals*'s slashing aggro-rock. 'And it was the first album, for me, where the group was losing its unity as well. That's when it was beginning where Roger wanted to do everything. There are certain bits of music that I quite like, but it's not my favourite album of the Floyd.'

By the same token, however, the making of *Animals* was dogged by little of the artistic conflict that had stymied the *Wish You Were Here* sessions. That it still took ten months to complete was mainly attributable to the Floyd's struggles to match their usual sonic standards at their own relatively makeshift studio.

Somewhat in the manner of George Orwell's classic *Animal Farm*, Roger's allegorical song-cycle carves up the human species into three categories, each heralded by the title of one of the album's main pieces. The pigs are moralists, self-righteous and tyrannical, yet ultimately pathetic; the dogs, cutthroat pragmatists out to claw their way

198

to the top of the heap. The sheep comprise a mindless and unquestioning herd (Roger's vision of Pink Floyd's audience?) – dim dreamers whose sole function in life is to be used and abused by the dogs and pigs. A far cry indeed from the whimsical anthropomorphic fauna of Barrett's beloved *Wind in the Willows* (albeit not so far, perhaps, from the post-Floyd Syd's predatory 'Rats').

Yet unlike David Bowie's earlier *Diamond Dogs*, which was directly inspired by *1984*, Pink Floyd's animal trilogy was not an outright adaptation of Orwell's book. For one thing, the model for Orwell's allegory was plainly the Soviet Union, while Roger's target is his own society's dog-eat-dog capitalistic system. And where Animal Farm ultimately yielded to the pigs' unchallenged control, the Floyd opus climaxes with an uprising of vengeful sheep, aroused at last from their complacent stupor. (Maybe they started listening to Waters's new songs instead of to *Ummagumma*!)

Not that Roger exempts himself from this misanthropic formulation. In 'Pigs on the Wing',* a tender two-part acoustic confessional in the 'If' tradition that briefly opens and closes the album – and without which, he ventured, *Animals* 'would have just been a kind of scream of rage' – Waters allows that he, too, is something of a 'dog'. (He also allowed – for the first and virtually the only time in his career as a Floyd songwriter – that he was in love. Roger had finally found a permanent replacement for his Red Judy in the blue-blooded Carolyne Christie, the niece of the Marquis of Zetland.)

Though none of Waters's animal caricatures is presented in a remotely flattering light – for positive role models, the listener is advised to search elsewhere – 'Pigs (Three Different Ones)' generates its considerable energy through sheer, unbridled contempt. The piece specifically lampoons Mary Whitehouse, the self-appointed guardian of British morals: a counterpoint of heavy breathing implies an underlying prurient interest in the 'filth' she so vociferously condemns and so desperately fears. '*All tight lips and cold feet*', this grim crusader had reportedly denounced the Floyd as early as 1967 for their sinister links with advocates of LSD.

To music composed by David Gilmour ('not one of my real favourites,' he says now), 'Dogs' takes on the unquestioningly materialistic superachiever – the 'yuppie' of a decade later – '*who was fitted with collar and chain/who was given a pat on the back . . .*' The highly

---

* Collector's note: In the then-popular 8-track-tape format, the two parts of 'Pigs on the Wing' were linked together by an otherwise unreleased guitar solo.

effective literary device of beginning each unrhymed line with the word 'who' takes after Allen Ginsburg's famous poem 'Howl'.) The dog's ultimate fate is to die alone of cancer dragged down by the weight of his own self-importance. Intones Dave:

So have a good drown . . . dragged down by the stone.

Following this cheery advice, the endlessly repeated echo of the word 'stone' is electronically distorted to the point that it comes to resemble a cry from the primaeval slime, even as the accompanying noise of barking dogs is filtered to chilling effect through a Vocoder box, gradually taking on a more musical and even 'human' quality.

A similarly ominous moment occurs in 'Sheep'. Where Animal Farm had its Seven Commandments (including the famous, '*All animals are equal, but some animals are more equal then others*', Water's sheep hark to a parody of the Twenty-Third Psalm, again distorted through the Vocoder: '*The Lord is my shepherd . . . With bright knives He releaseth my soul . . .*' 'Sheep,' deadpans Gilmour, who awards himself much of the credit for the musical end result, 'was always good fun.'

It might be tempting to view *Animals*'s vitriolic angst and social commentary along with its relatively lean arrangements, low-gloss production, high-voltage music, and 'Sheep's bond-crunching power-chord climax as Pink Floyd's answer to the Punk Rock insurrection, had 'Dogs' and 'Sheep' not consisted, essentially, of those 1974 concert warhorses 'Gotta Be Crazy' and 'Raving and Drooling'. The band was already in the throes of reworking them at Britannia Row, together with the freshly conceived 'Pigs', when Waters discerned the canine and ovine implications of those earlier lyrics, and – serendipity! – the gist of another Concept Album.

But because the concept was stuck together at the eleventh hour from largely pre-existing material, *Animals* doesn't (as Roger himself later admitted) entirely gel. The three main pieces don't always sustain their respective metaphors; many passages seem hardly relevant to the overall context. And even when they are, Waters often contents himself with clusters of crusty platitudes, unleavened by the sardonic wit of a Ray Davies or the poetic language of a Bob Dylan.

Nevertheless, *Animals* is in some respects one of the Floyd's more powerful albums. Lyrically, it offers the first 100 per cent proof distillation of Roger's socio-political venom, even as it marks the last instance of Waters, Gilmour, Mason and Wright working together as a tight four-piece unit, without any overlay of outside musicians. (Even if, like the citizens of Animal Farm, some Floyds were already rather more equal than others.) Musically, Pink Floyd have never (before nor since, in any incarnation) rocked out so uncompromisingly, or with more conviction.

Animals was also uncompromising – courageous, even – in its format. Pink Floyd had, of course, always been renowned for their long and winding compositions ('Atom Heart', 'Echoes', 'Shine On'); *Animals* consisted, pretty much, of nothing but. This left few openings even for 'progressive' FM radio programmers; no readily excerptable choice five-minute 'bites' like 'One of these Days', 'Welcome to the Machine', or the individual tracks from *The Dark Side of the Moon*. In consequence, there was little chance the latter's sales phenomenon could remotely be matched this time around.

Especially after Waters and company had stripped *Animals* of most of its predecessors' lush and soporific textures, thus denying Floyd freaks the luxury of spacing out during Roger's misanthropic tirades. This, too, could be viewed as courageous, but also foreshadowed a time when Waters would stress his increasingly strident message to the detriment of the medium provided by Pink Floyd's distinctive music.

Waters has said that he was endeavouring 'to push the band into more specific areas of subject matter, always trying to be more direct. Visually, I was trying to get away from the blobs . . . [so] there isn't much left for you to interpret.'[4] By the same token, however, it might be argued that much of the attraction of Pink Floyd's compositions and performances had always been that they enabled the listener to give free rein to his or her own imagination. Beginning with *Animals*, Roger Waters often seemed more interested in simply telling his audience what to think.

This self-important streak was also manifested when journalists were summoned to Battersea Power Station in the second week of 1977 for a preview of the album – and then forbidden to take notes. Nevertheless, *Animals* did salvage Pink Floyd's credibility among critics who had made common cause with the Punk revolution. In *NME* – now a fully-fledged New Wave rag – Angus Mackinnon, 'still reeling from the aural evidence before me', pronounced *Animals* not only the Floyd's best-ever album, but 'one of the most extreme, relentless, harrowing, and downright iconoclastic hunks of music to have been made available for public perusal this side of the Sun'.[5]

201

Though the sales figures were nothing like those for its two predecessors, *Animals* did give Pink Floyd yet another British number one.
In America, the album 'only' got to number three.

On the day of its release – 23 January 1977 – Pink Floyd took *Animals*
on the road for a six-month marathon covering nine countries on both
sides of the Atlantic. In at least one respect, this tour distanced the
band still further both from the fans and from the new Punk Rock
ideals: for the first time, the Floyd's itinerary encompassed stadiums.

Pink Floyd – In the Flesh (as the tour was dubbed) is remembered
largely for its enormous inflatable props, notably the flying pig, which
Waters described at the time as 'a symbol of hope'. A decade later he
recalled that the other Floyds 'thought I'd gone the way of Syd when I
said we needed a giant inflatable family' – depicting the corporate
compromisers of 'Dogs' – 'and a load of inflatable animals'.[6]

The preparations and logistics entailed by a show of this scale were
staggering. The Equipment and Technical Riders in the promoters'
contracts, providing detailed specifications on the stage, lighting, and
power requirements, included literally dozens of clauses along the lines
of these:

(c)   Three scaffolding towers will be required of rigid construction
. . . 2 metres high by 4 metres long by 2 metres deep, with 3 metres
overhead clearance. The area directly below these towers will
contain highly valuable equipment, so each tower should be surrounded by 1.20m security barriers.

(d)   An area no less than 6 metres wide by 5 metres deep on the
ground floor audience level at the exact centre of the house, ie
equidistant from stage front and house rear, left and right, must be
reserved for the sound and light mixers. Contained in this area is to
be a platform 5.50m wide by 1.50m deep and with a height of 75
cm. This platform must be able to support equipment weighing 500
kg. Behind this platform, seating must be supplied for Pink Floyd's
technicians who will be operating the sound and lighting for the
duration of the concert. It is essential that the whole area is
surrounded by a secure barrier (1.20m high) . . .

The Floyd, in turn, were in constant danger of being ambushed by
equally exacting bureaucrats enforcing compliance with local power
and safety regulations.

Lesser mortals (and Floyds) might have wilted under the grind of such minutiae, but Roger seemed to revel in every detail. Backstage before one show, his *Melody Maker* friend Karl Dallas overheard him instructing the crew: 'I want the smoke to begin at the words "*all tight lips and cold feet*", at the beginning of the second verse of "Pigs". And I want as much smoke as you can give me. I don't want the audience to see the pig until the loud solo from Dave that comes after the verse . . .'[7]

Waters applied himself with equal intensity to the accompanying film footage. 'Roger edited it and oversaw it and made sure it fitted the bill,' says Nick Griffiths. 'He can walk into a film cutting room, sit down with the editor, and take control very knowledgeably of the whole proceedings. He knows the technology, doesn't really need to rely on anyone else to come up with the ideas. He has his own ideas. The only problem is if anyone argues with him.'

A quadrophonic complement of bleats, barks, and grunts notwithstanding, *In the Flesh*'s musical content seemed less imaginative: the whole of the *Animals* album in the first half and *Wish You Were Here* in the second (albeit with their songs' running order rejuggled), plus an encore consisting of 'Us and Them' and/or 'Money' (and, on exactly one occasion, 'Careful with That Axe, Eugene'). Apart from the predictability of it all, 'Sheep' hardly seemed the strongest possible choice with which to begin Pink Floyd's biggest-ever show.

There were other problems, often stemming from the sheer complexity of the production. At each gig, *something* was almost bound to go wrong, and throw the band (augmented for this tour by second guitarist Snowy White as well as the familiar sax and keyboards player Dick Parry) out of whack and out of sorts. To keep them in synch with the films' 'click track' Waters felt obliged to ensconce himself in earphones throughout each performance – which only served further to insulate him from his audience.

In Frankfurt, West Germany, the smoke was so thick that irate fans, unable to view the show, were moved instead to rain the stage with bottles. Come March, the Floyd's London dates at Wembley were frostily received by critics like *Sounds*'s Tim Lott:

Disappointment. I am left cold. They have acted as machines. No acknowledgement of the crowd. Minimum enthusiasm. Ragged instrumental approach . . . the Floyd have never been virtuosos, but they always achieved *effect*. This time, no . . .

> The main destructive, ruining, hopeless, avoidable, grating flaw
> is still Waters' vocal stumblings. The obvious thing to do would be
> to have Gilmour's relatively strong voice handling all lead singing
> with Waters occasionally chipping in for a bit of strained harmony
> . . . maybe it didn't occur to him just how inept a singer he is.[8]

True to form, Derek Jewell of *The Sunday Times* was more sympathetic, calling the show 'the ultimate in brilliantly-staged theatre of despair' and an 'all-engaging (or all-deterring) musical and visual experience.'[9] In *Melody Maker*, however, Michael Oldfield snidely proposed that 'the next logical step for them is to hire a bunch of puppets to stand on stage with Floyd masks on'.[10] Roger, as it happens, was beginning to think along similar lines.

As the tour proceeded, Waters increasingly showed signs of what associates variously termed paranoia or megalomania. He kept largely to himself, shunning the Floyd's festive pre- and post-concert dinners and receptions. A disapproving Peter Jenner remembers Roger arriving at gigs in a helicopter, having relegated the other three to a limousine.

The fans, meanwhile, puzzled over his habit of always shouting out a single numeral in the midst of 'Pigs' (e.g. '*Twenty-one*' or *Forty-six*' or *Fifty-four*') until someone noticed that it would generally correspond to the number of *In the Flesh* gigs the Floyd had weathered thus far. It was as if Waters could hardly wait for the ordeal to end.

Much of this alienation stemmed (and to his credit) from profound misgivings about the dehumanizing venues in which he had allowed the Floyd to play, and his inability under such circumstances to feel any sense of community or communication with his audiences, 'most of whom' he later contended 'were only there for the beer'. And, he added, 'It's very difficult to perform in that situation with people whistling and shouting and screaming and throwing things and hitting each other and crashing about . . . but I felt at the same time that it was a situation that we have created ourselves, out of our own greed.'[11] From Roger's perspective, the band was no longer merely a victim of the Rock Machine, but had become an active collaborator.

Waters was horrified at the recognition that something so personal as his own songs had gradually been transformed into 'a circus and a meaningless ritual'. As he was to tell the writer Timothy White: 'Rock and roll is becoming greed disguised as entertainment, just as war has become greed disguised as politics.'[12]

Any such twinges of conscience, however, could not mitigate Roger's perception of his audiences – thirty, fifty, sometimes *ninety* thousand strong – as one monolithic, insensate, roaring, flailing *beast*. It was at the very last show – at Montreal's Olympic Stadium, on 6 July – that he finally cracked.

During the course of the evening, Roger's baleful gaze zeroed in among the fans up front revelling in the Floyd's 'space cadet glow', to one particular kid he didn't like the looks of – a little worm writhing upon the belly of the beast. Waters began directing his entire performance at this hapless boy, luring him ever closer, as the teenager reached new heights of mindless ecstasy with each glance and gesture from his contemptuous idol. Finally, Roger leaned into the fan's face – and let fly a great gob of spit.

Summoned back by thunderous applause for the obligatory encore, a ravaged-sounding Roger announced: 'We can't do any more of our old songs, so we're just gonna play some music to go home to.' No one noticed that Dave Gilmour was no longer even on stage: the exasperated star guitarist had slipped unrecognized into the audience, leaving his fellow Floyds and Snowy White to improvise a slow, sad blues.

Returning to England, Waters was consumed by the ultimate conceit of his entire career, something that he had been idly fantasizing about for years. In view of what he was to recall in *Rolling Stone* as 'this enormous barrier between *them* and what I was trying to do, [which] had become almost impossible to clamber over'[13] Roger vowed that if ever Pink Floyd were to perform another concert extravaganza, it would literally be from behind . . . a Wall.

Chapter 19

Another Brick in the Wall
Part 1

Animals behind them, Pink Floyd all but disbanded again. From September 1977, Roger Waters secluded himself in the countryside to build his *Wall* – whether for a group or solo project, no one could yet be certain. Left to their own devices, the Floyd's other two songwriters sought refuge in solo debuts, to be released in May 1978 under the titles *David Gilmour* and *Wet Dream*.

The former reassembled Gilmour's Summer of Love power trio, Bullitt: indeed it was bassist Rick Wills (lately of Foreigner) and drummer Willie Wilson, together with Ginger Gilmour, who had talked Dave into attempting an extra-Floyd showcase for his Fender benders. Another longtime colleague, Roy Harper, cowrote the record's standout track 'Short and Sweet' (which the pair would also rework, along with several more such collaborations, for Harper's next LP).

On Italian radio, Gilmour said that he approached his album as an antidote to Pink Floyd's policy of 'complete perfection': 'At home, I sometimes catch an acoustic guitar and begin to play, aimlessly. My recording was born from a crazy desire to express myself, wanting to be as natural as possible.'[1]

This exercise's most inspired dividend came only when it was too late to make immediate use of it. While adding the album's final touches at the Floyd's new favourite studio in the south of France – Super Bear in Miravel – Gilmour popped up with the tune that the world would come to know and love as 'Comfortably Numb.' But with Wills and Wilson back in England, Dave contented himself with a rough demo, to be saved for some future project.*

---

* In the meantime, 1978 also saw the release of *The Kick Inside*, the debut LP by Kate Bush, who had finally been signed to EMI largely through Gilmour's selfless efforts. These had included financing and arranging a 1975 Bush recording session, from

Richard Wright's *Wet Dream*, also recorded at Super Bear, featured the Floyd's second guitarist on the *In the Flesh* tour, Snowy White. The material, which included lyrics by Juliette Wright, had been composed at Rick's villa near Lindos in Rhodes, where he now lived full-time as the first of the Floyd's tax exiles. In contrast to *David Gilmour*'s heavy rock sound, *Wet Dream* offered a light, middle-of-the-road jazz-flavoured pop. The two records, however, had much in common beneath their stylish Higpnosis jackets. Both were long on instrumentals and short on originality – tasteful and competent, yet also rather pedestrian and forgettable.

It seemed (and not for the last time) as if individual Floyds who ventured outside the magic Pink circle were fated to forfeit their special powers, and expose themselves as '*only ordinary men . . . men . . . men . . .*' In a showing that also reflected the Floyd boys' lack of personal name recognition, *David Gilmour* sold fairly modestly, and *Wet Dream* hardly at all.

They could actually have used the money at that juncture. In September 1978 the Floyd woke up to the realization that they were the victims of a multi-million-pound scam.

They had been brought to this pass by a dapper young accountant named Andrew Oscar Warburg. At the age of twenty-nine, around the time *The Dark Side of the Moon* came out, he and six colleagues had left the insurance brokers Scott Warburg and Partners to found a City-based financial advice organization called Norton Warburg Group. Warburg's personal flair helped him attract a clientele of sports and show-biz stars like cricketer Colin Cowdrey, Barry Gibb of the Bee Gees – and Pink Floyd. By 1976, NWG had been appointed the Floyd's collecting agents, and handled all the band's secretarial, financial and insurance broking, for fees amounting to some £300,000 a year.

Warburg proceeded to gamble between £1.6 million (his estimate) and £3.3 million (the Floyd's) of the group's income in high-risk venture capital operations, on the grounds that most of it would otherwise be claimed by the taxman. The promising new businesses thus bankrolled ranged from the Willows Canal chain of floating restaurants (in which the Floyd bought a 60 per cent stake for

which two tracks would surface on the album. The poetic pop enchantress credited Dave for having 'done the biggest thing for me that anyone's done in my life'.

£180,000) to Benjyboards, a skateboard importer and distributer (55 per cent Floyd-owned, at their cost of £215,000). The biggest of all the band's venture capital vehicles was Cossack Securities, a Norton Warburg Group creation that was wholly owned by Pink Floyd, for which privilege they paid about £1.5 million. The band also acquired an indirect stake in a constellation of other new business ventures when they shelled out a further £450,000 for a 20 per cent share of a separate company called Norton Warburg Investments.

NWI did pick one winner in the London pizza chain My Kinda Town; the Floyd's own stakes in a carbon-fibre boat manufacturer and a property deal in London's Cadogan Gardens also turned handsome profits. But by mid-1978 it began to dawn on the Floyd and Steve O'Rourke (who had also invested in Andrew Warburg's ventures) that the bottom line was sinking ever deeper into the red; within a year the floating restaurants and skateboard company would be declared insolvent, with many of the others, including Cossack Securities, soon to follow suit.

'It wasn't only that they lost money,' Nick Mason would recall, 'By losing the money they also cocked up all the tax planning, so that we could have been liable for all sorts of money not only that we'd lost, but money that we'd never received.'[2] And in those pre-Thatcher days, Britain's Inland Revenue hit taxpayers in the Floyd's income bracket to the tune of 83 per cent.

In his company's September 1978 report Warburg remained upbeat, noting, for instance, that while 'the skateboard market in the UK has not lived up to expectations . . . a large quantity of slow-moving/dead stock is expected to be sold to Arab countries at good prices within a month'. Before that month was out, however, the Floyd resolved to cut their losses, ending their agreement with Norton Warburg Group and demanding the return of all uninvested Floyd cash on deposit, amounting to £860,000 (of which they actually salvaged £740,000). They subsequently sued NWG for £1 million, charging fraud and negligence.

After the company finally crashed in 1981, Andrew Warburg fled to Spain, leaving hundreds of less exalted clients (including old-age pensioners) bereft of their life savings. Norton Warburg Investments, in which the Floyd retained their share, acquired a new name (Waterbrook) and a new chairman, who proceeded to sell of most of its holdings at losses ranging from 60 to 92 per cent. And in June 1987 Andrew Warburg, having returned from exile and pleaded guilty to fraudulent trading and false accounting, was sentenced to three years in jail.

These sorry circumstances helped persuade all concerned that Roger's *Wall* should indeed be pursued as a Pink Floyd album. Offers of record-shattering advances from CBS and EMI, ultimately amounting to a reported £4.5 million, no doubt sweetened the deal.

In late '78, the London music weeklies revealed that the Floyd had booked their Britannia Row studio for six straight months and Rick Wright told a Canadian deejay that his band was in the throes of 'a big project. It's going to take us a year to record the album, work out the show – all the theatrical effects – and we're doing a film as well: a feature film based around the music of the album.'[3] *The Wall* promised to be rock's most ambitious and multi-faceted epic since Pete Townsend's *Tommy* had successively spawned a Who double-album, an all-star stage show, and a Ken Russell movie.

That July, Waters had actually returned from his self-imposed exile in his country house with two song cycles: *The Wall* and *The Pros and Cons of Hitchhiking.* 'He presented them to the band,' Nick Griffiths recalls, 'and said, "Which one does the Floyd want to do?" They chose *The Wall.*'

After falling out with his partner years later, Gilmour claimed that this was not such an easy decision, insofar as both homemade Waters demos were 'unlistenable' and 'sounded exactly alike'.[4] Griffiths, however, begs to differ: 'I heard the *Wall* demos. They were seriously rough, but the songs were there.'

In any event, the original understanding was that *Pros and Cons* might be used for a subsequent Floyd album: the band, according to Dave, 'put a hell of a lot of work into that' as well. But the guitarist never much warmed to it, in the end agreeing with Nick Mason that it was 'too personal to be a Pink Floyd album. *The Wall* had something universal. But *Hitchhiking* . . .'[5]

From its inception, *The Wall* was truly a multi-media proposition, with Waters simultaneously developing his ideas for the album, concert, and movie. All, he said, arose from that last *In the Flesh* stadium concert in Montreal, when the 'notion of expressing my disgust by building a wall across the front of the stage came to me in a flash, and I was so thrilled with the theatricality of that'. The wall image suggested, in turn, 'the idea of each brick being a different bit of the life, and the whole autobiographical number that developed out of it.'[6]

'It was like, "How *far* can I take it?" ' Griffiths chuckles fondly. 'He can be very perverse. Can you imagine trying to explain it to somebody – "people are going to be coming onstage throughout the concert to build a wall totally obscuring the band." It's a pretty extreme idea to suggest.'

Then again, extreme ideas were Roger's stock-in-trade throughout the construction of *The Wall*. 'I wanted to make comparisons between rock and roll concerts and war,' he later told *Rolling Stone*. 'People at those big things seem to like being treated very badly, to have it so loud and distorted that it really hurts.' His original film script even called for 'a rock and roll audience being bombed and, as they were being blown to pieces, applauding, loving every minute. 'As an idea, it is quite pleasing. But it would look silly to actually do it . . .'[7]

War's further significance in *The Wall*, of course, is the pop star protagonist's loss, in his infancy, of his father to World War II – a tragedy that had scarred the life not only of Roger Waters, but others of his generation of young Britons. (The very first line in *Tommy* was '*Captain Walker didn't come home, his unborn child will never know him*'.) This fundamental trauma is then compounded by smothering mother love, a dehumanizing educational system, marriage to a faithless shrew, and, finally, the pressures of 'success' in the Rock Biz – whose shortcomings had already been so eloquently delineated in *Wish You Were Here*.

'On the simplest level,' Waters would explain to his new deejay friend Jim Ladd, 'whenever something bad happens, he isolates himself a bit more, i.e., symbolically he adds another brick to his wall to protect himself.'[8] Most of the earlier 'bricks' are chunks of Roger's own autobiography; but then, in an elaboration of *The Dark Side of the Moon*'s lesson that the only exit from the maze is madness, his character 'Pink Floyd' increasingly takes on the likeness of Syd Barrett.

By the time the first half ends with 'Goodbye Cruel World' (based, as it happens, on a riff from 'See Emily Play'), Pink is completely bricked in (metaphorically) as indeed would the Floyd be (literally) at the climax of the stage performance's first act. 'He then,' said Waters, 'becomes susceptible to the worms. The worms are symbols of negative forces within ourselves, [of] decay. The worms can only get at us because there isn't any light or whatever in our lives.'[9]

All this material is structured as a series of flashbacks from the opening number, 'In the Flesh?' (titled after the Floyd's 1977 tour) – a bloated 'dinosaur rock' parody intended to convey the crass and alienated persona of a fully 'bricked in' Pink. (And should some of the Floyd's more casual fans actually enjoy the tune at its face value, that would only illuminate Roger's point about his band's failure to communicate with its post-*Dark Side* audiences.)

210

In the second half, which chronicles Pink's breakdown, the flash-backs seem to flip into reverse, the Sixties (and Syd Barrett) references of the Randy Newman-influenced 'Nobody Home' giving way to the World War II imagery of 'Vera'. This is followed by what Waters called 'the central song on the whole album' – 'Bring the Boys Back Home' – equally applicable to soldiers at the front or rock and rollers on tour.

At this point, having scared even his groupie away, the hallucinating star is revived by a doctor's injection, and (emerging from behind the Wall in the show) reclaims the stage for a goose-stepping reprise of 'In the Flesh' (no question mark this time) – its words transmuted into a racist and homophobic diatribe. The concert itself becomes a 'rock Nuremberg' with the crowd's chant of 'Pink Floyd! Pink Floyd! (from the left – get it? – stereo channel) turning into 'Hammer! Hammer! (on the right). 'The idea,' said Waters, 'is we've been changed from the lovable old Pink Floyd that we all know and love [into] our evil alter egos.'[10]

Originally, he told Karl Dallas, 'The plan was just to build the Wall and leave it. But that was *too* tough . . . too "Fuck You."' [11] Instead, the rock and roll demagogue's overloaded defences explode and his Wall comes crashing down, leaving him exposed as a vulnerable and feeling human being, after all.

The *Wall*'s exposition would ultimately require four sides of long-playing vinyl and twenty-six lyric-laden songs – more individual tracks than on all Pink Floyd albums of the previous seven years combined. In view of the project's complexity and scale, and his own tendency to clash with Gilmour over Floyd musical policy, Waters resolved to bring in an outside collaborator and coproducer. This would also free him to spend his evenings with his new common-law wife Carolyne and their infant sons Harry and India; Roger was determined that his own kids should be spared the 'absent father' syndrome that he had made a key theme in *The Wall*. His first and final choice was Carolyne's nominee Bob Ezrin, for whom she had once worked as secretary.

Though best known for producing hellraisers like Alice Cooper and Kiss, Ezrin had served as midwife to Lou Reed's 1973 masterwork *Berlin*, whose status as the most harrowingly cheerless concept album in rock history would be rivalled only by *The Wall* itself. Not least of Ezrin's qualifications was that he had accompanied Roger and Carolyne to the Floyd's traumatic last concert in Montreal, and witnessed the famous spitting scene firsthand.

211

The 29-year-old Canadian dynamo was in for a surprise when he arrived in London to take the measure of his new star clients. 'Their lifestyle,' he observed, 'is interchangeable with the president of just about any bank in England; it's anything but rock and roll madness. If you bumped into Roger on a Sunday afternoon with the kids . . . you wouldn't know that this guy wasn't a wonderfully successful executive marching his family into the park.'[12]

Pink Floyd, agrees Griffiths, were 'a completely different sort of band than any Who or Rolling Stones – a law unto themselves. They don't live the life of rock and roll. Roger lives the life of a gentleman landowner who's very happy to pay people to do the work, and he'll look after them.'

'You can write anything you want,' Waters assured Ezrin at the outset of their partnership. 'Just don't expect any credit.' Ezrin, who used to write for *Atlantic Monthly*, found the literate Waters a refreshing change from all those 'turkeys who can't put four words together in a nice sentence'.

At Britannia Row, Ezrin and Gilmour subjected Water's demo to intensive analysis. 'We went through it,' Dave recalled, 'and started with the tracks we liked best, discussed a lot of what was not so good, and kicked out a lot of stuff. Roger and Bob spent a lot of time trying to get the story line straighter, more linear conceptually. Ezrin is the sort of guy who's thinking about the angles all the time, about how to make a shorter story line that's told properly.'[13]

'In an all-night session,' Ezrin recalled, 'I rewrote the record. I used all of Roger's elements, but I rearranged their order and put them in a different form. I wrote *The Wall* out in forty pages, like a book . . . I acted as Roger's editor, and, believe me, his lyrics are so good they didn't need much.' Among the casualties of Bob's red pencil were 'dates in the lyrics that put him at thirty-six years old. Kids don't want to know about old [sic] rock stars. I insisted we make the record more accessible, more universal.'[14] To that end, he also persuaded the Floyd to reconsider their no-singles policy, and aim for at least one *Wall* hit.

The Floyd, Ezrin claimed, had never considered themselves at war with top forty radio: 'They just weren't really conscious of radio programming needs and formulas. So they did what they do best, and it put them in a very special class of their own. But in things like what a good tempo would be for a single, and how to get an intro and an outro – I know all those things, and they were quite open to trying them.'[15]

According to Gilmour, Waters was 'sent away to write other songs

. . . Some of the best stuff, I think, came out under the pressure of saying, "That's not good enough to get on – do something!" '[16] Despite Roger's resistance to anyone else getting a credit in edgewise, Dave finally did cowrite Pink's final encore,' 'Run Like Hell', as well as an adolescent flashback that Waters had originally envisaged as a sequence about 'hanging around outside porno movies and dirty book shops . . . being very interested in sex but too frightened to get involved'.[17] In Gilmour's hands 'Young Lust' became instead a swaggering 'cock rock' pastiche, by way of 'The Nile Song' from *More*.

Dave's shining moment, however, intended to evoke Pink's narcotic trance following his doctor's injection, was 'Comfortably Numb', which evolved from an out-take from *David Gilmour* into *The Wall*'s most characteristically Floydian (and universally adored) track. And though Gilmour was later to cite 'Is There Anybody Out there?' as an example of an Ezrin composition that Waters appropriated as his own, Bob would also in the end be yielded one credit, on 'The Trial' – the Gilbert and Sullivan-esque, Roger-plus-orchestra finale that Ezrin himself had largely conceived with the aim of bringing together all the major characters in *The Wall* story.

'Ezrin was very good in *The Wall*,' says Nick Griffiths, 'because he did manage to pull the whole thing together. He's a very forceful guy. There was a lot of argument about how it should sound between Roger and Dave, and he bridged the gap between them. Even if both of them did have some rather rude things to say about him.'

The Warburg debacle, meanwhile, had reduced the Floyd's assets to little more than their houses, cars, and art collections – and, of course, their £3 million office and studio complex. One of the participants recalls Steve O'Rourke striding into a Britannia Row session with the announcement: 'Right, guys, we're going to have to do this one overseas.' The album would be completed at Super Bear and then in America; to reduce further the Inland Revenue's claims. Britannia Row was not to be mentioned in *The Wall*'s credits. And all the Floyd were obliged to pack up on short notice, and live abroad as tax exiles, with Waters officially domiciled in Switzerland, and the others at their holiday homes in the south of France (Mason) and the Greek islands (Gilmour and Wright). Unlike such compatriots as Ringo Starr, Rod Stewart, and David Bowie, the thoroughly English Floyd with the exception of Rick, had always resisted any temptation to trade their homeland for a tax break; now they had no choice.

Given the band's egregious 'lack of rock and roll energy' Bob Ezrin ultimately felt that the Floyd's uprooting from their London routines and office hours at Britannia Row did them a world of good. Especially after they moved their operations from France to Los Angeles, where *The Wall* was completed at the Producers' Workshop, and Roger (who installed Carolyne, kids, and nanny in a rented Beverly Hills mansion) befriended such natives as the Beach Boys and KMET's 'outlaw' deejay Jim Ladd.

There were even plans afoot for the Beach Boys to harmonize with the Floyd on 'The Show Must Go On' and 'Waiting for the Worms', for which purpose the two groups booked studio time in Dallas. But then Waters cancelled on the day of the session, in the end settling for a sole Beach Boy, Bruce Johnston, paired with Toni Tenille. Johnston (who had already sung on some other tracks) savoured the irony that the Beach Boys were know for 'saccarine' and the Captain and Tenille for 'fluff' – yet 'there we are, singing songs about worms'. Johnston found it no less ironic when the author of those songs proved so 'normal' and 'ultra-civilized'; Waters even invited him to play a game of tennis.[18]

For *The Wall*'s orchestral arrangements, the Floyd tapped Michael Kamen, the ex-New York Rock Ensemble leader whose 'legitimate' musical credits included a Broadway show and a La Scala ballet. (Waters had presumably forgotten his 1970 *Melody Maker* 'Blind Date' assessment of a Rock ensemble record as 'very weedy' and 'something Pete Townshend might have written – when he was four'.) Kamen overdubbed his 55-piece scores at CBS's New York studios, an ocean away from his secretive new bosses who were still in France at the time, and whom he didn't even get to meet until after his work had been completed and approved.

Another important component of *The Wall* – even more so, if possible, than on other Floyd albums – was the sound effects: from bomber planes and helicopters to babies' cries and schoolyard voices, ringing telephones and dialtones, and subliminal snatches of dialogue. The rhythmic repetition of some of these recorded snippets amounted to virtual leitmotifs. As with everything else on *The Wall*, their sound quality was superlative.

While the more seasoned James Guthrie engineered the overseas sessions, Nick Griffiths, back at Britannia Row, was assigned the task of gathering many of the sounds effects. 'I was given a list,' he says, 'of various bits and pieces to record, one of which was a big explosion. So I went around the country recording factories getting blown up, which was quite good fun. And we got a lot of crockery in the studio, set the microphones up, and got the 24-track going. And smashed everything in sight, threw it against the wall. Which was actually used on the film, but not on the album in the end.'

His most memorable contribution to *The Wall*, however, was a recording of a group of schoolkids. 'Another Brick in the Wall (Part 2)' began life as a single verse plus chorus on the order of Parts One and Three: in view of its lines about 'sarcasm in the classroom' and 'thought control'. Roger and Dave decided it might be a nice touch if some actual schoolchildren could be heard singing along with them. Griffiths's initial assignment was merely 'to record a couple of kids singing the song. But I went to the local school round the corner from Britannia Row, and asked the music teacher if the whole class of kids would like to come to the studio and do some singing. He was thrilled to bits. We made an arrangement that in return if he ever wanted the school orchestra or something like that recorded, they could just come down the road and we'd do it for them.'

Chaperoned by their teacher, Alan Redshaw – who entertained visions of a free professional studio recording of his own *Requiem for a Sinking Block of Flats* – twenty-three Islington Green School fourth formers soon found themselves gathered before the absent Floyd's microphones. Mr Redshaw initially blanched at the lyrical content of Roger's 'We don't need no educa-shun' chorus, but, says Griffiths, 'I leapt up and down getting the kids in the right spirit, and everyone had a whale of a time. It wasn't something I'd thought about beforehand; a lot of the best things happen that way. It took just half an hour to do; then I tracked the voices about a dozen times.'

When the Floyd received the tape in LA, they were so pleased that they decided to bring the children's voices to the forefront. 'But we didn't want to lose our voices,' Gilmour said, 'So we wound up copying the tape and mixing it twice – one with me and Roger singing, and one with the kids; the backing is the same. And we edited them together.'[19]

The backing, as it happened, also boasted a contemporary dance rhythm right out of *Saturday Night Fever* and Dave capped the whole thing off with a scorching double-tracked solo on his 1959 Gibson gold-top. The high-gloss discofied sound blended miraculously with the novelty appeal of the schoolkid chorus – to engender one of those instant-classic runaway number one hits such as comes along only once every few years.

In Britain 'Another Brick in the Wall (Part 2)' topped the charts

215

within a week of its release on 16 November 1979, having already sold over 340,000 copies; by January, the figure exceeded one million – meaning that one in fifty British citizens actually went out and bought the record (a phenomenon that was to be repeated for the expensive double album). In the United States, the single remained at number one for four consecutive weeks. Almost overnight, the band that 'didn't make singles' had on its hands one of the biggest hit singles of 1979 *and* 1980.

And one of the most controversial. In South Africa, 'Another Brick in the Wall (Part 2)' was even adopted by nonwhite protestors as the anthem of their nationwide school boycott. The Government's Directorate of Publications retaliated by prohibiting the Floyd single and album's sale or broadcast in the land of apartheid.

In London, meanwhile, the right-wing tabloids *News of the World* and *The Daily Mail* sniffed out an irresistible opportunity to embarrass not only the band behind the subversive hit, but also the school's young headmistress, whom the *Mail* had previously exposed as an ex-Communist. The multimillionaire rock stars stood accused of exploiting the poor schoolchildren, who hadn't even received complimentary copies of the record – let along a fee for their services. 'Which', says Griffiths, 'was all down to me trying to set up this little cottage industry between the studio and the school down the road. Next thing I knew I was having to climb out of the back window to avoid the reporters at the entrance to Britannia Row.

'In the end, the school was given an awful lot of money. Of course the kids individually didn't get any of it.' Roger Waters, however, did see to it that each child received a free copy of *The Wall*.

As early as 1982, Gilmour acknowledged mixed feelings about the lyrical gist of *The Wall*, which he deemed 'a very strong concept' but largely 'irrelevant' to his own concerns. 'I don't feel the pressure of a wall between me and my audience; I don't ever think there's something there that doesn't get through to them. I don't think a lot of the things that happened to me in my early years, some of which weren't so wonderful, adversely affect *my* life to the extent that Roger feels some of those things affect *his* life.'[20] But, as he would put it on a later occasion, he could 'get into it as fiction'.[21]

Even at the time, there were clues that *The Wall* was not built in a spirit of perfect Floydian harmony. Several published reports hinted at Dave, Nick, and Rick's restlessness under Roger's domination; in

Melody Maker, on a lighter note, Ezrin contrasted Mason's penchant for 'dancing his buns off' and Waters's disdain for such activities. Gilmour also seemed to Bob too reserved to boogie, but would bring current dance hits into the recording studio for the others to hear. 'The taste of some of the boys runs to the eclectic,' Ezrin observed. 'Now Roger's very difficult – he hates everything.'

But even the loquacious Canadian could not yet say – as he would years later – that 'under that English, left-handed, adversarial stance they take, with the smiles on their faces and soft voices . . . the war that existed between those two guys [Waters and Gilmour] 'was unbelievable.'[22]

'Out of the conflict,' submits Nick Griffiths, 'some good things occurred. Roger thrives on conflict – same with Bob Ezrin. Roger is a very competitive individual, and likes a good argument – no question about it. And chances are he'll win because he has a very good understanding of the English language.

'He can be very difficult to work with, but he has probably the most integrity out of anybody I know. What he believes in, he sticks by it, and feels it very strongly. His records always have a twist to them that he's absolutely adamant about. People will go, "you can't say that," and he'll say. "I feel it, so I should do it."

'Dave Gilmour was probably pissed off he had to go to *such great lengths* to get his point across. It was too much like hard work; he'd rather sit back and let it be. And a lot of resentment built up because David's a very easygoing guy, but he also knows what he likes and doesn't like. It became very difficult for him and Roger to actually be in the same studio together, because they were at loggerheads most of the time.

'The attitude Dave adopted was that the best way to maintain an even keel and one's sanity was only to be in a room with Roger when they needed to do a bit of work. Their paths no longer crossed on a social level at all.'

In that regard, it didn't help that the elegant Lady Carolyne had precious little in common with the down-to-earth American Ginger. 'What happened to the Floyd,' one friend suggests, 'was very similar to what happened with the Beatles. When the band was just four individuals, any problems were containable. But when they got married, it was obligatory that the wives got on as well. And Ginger Gilmour and Carolyne Waters came from opposite ends of the spectrum, with very different outlooks on life. There was a lot of friction between them – like Linda McCartney and Yoko Ono.'

The tensions within the group, however, had little to do with *The Wall*'s radical stylistic departure from the classic Pink Floyd sound. Gilmour has said that he shared Waters's goal of 'making things *say* what they're trying to say, quite snappily and not waste the time. That was the mood we were in, and certainly Bob Ezrin helped.'[27] A decade later, Nick Mason remains adamant that 'any band is entitled to try to follow any route they wish. The most ghastly thing is ever to feel constrained to "be like Floyd"' and so on.'

Dave's more resonant lead vocals alternate prominently with Roger's nasal histrionics on 'The Thin Ice', 'Mother', 'Goodbye Blue Sky' and 'Hey You', written solely by Waters, and Gilmour yields to no one of his musical contribution to *The Wall*. 'Whatever anyone says, I was there,' he maintains. 'I have my money on that record, tons and tons of stuff. Myself and Ezrin. I know lots of people think of that as the first Roger Waters solo album, but it ain't. Roger wouldn't have been able to make that by himself, no way. He's had three other gos at making solo records, and you can judge for yourself the difference.'

Be that as it may, there can be no question that *The Wall* was entirely Roger's idea – and would always remain, as far as he was concerned, *his* baby.

As if he didn't have enough on his hands wrangling with Gilmour, Waters proceeded to write Richard Wright out of Pink Floyd altogether. The crunch came when Rick elected to stay in Greece during the final sessions in the autumn of 1979, and Roger persuaded Dave and Nick to ratify the truant's dismissal. Though no public announcement was made, Wright was bought out of the Floyd partnership, and placed on a salary pending the completion of the various *Wall* projects.

'Roger and I couldn't get on,' Rick comments. 'It was a personal thing. Whatever I tried to do, he would say it was wrong. It was impossible for me, really, to work with him.

'We had to leave the country for a year, hopefully for *The Wall* to earn enough money to pay off the taxes. He said, "Either you leave after the album is made, or I'll just scrap the whole thing."

'I was in an impossible situation. It was a game of bluff, but knowing Roger he might have done what he was threatening to do, which would mean no royalties from the album. So I had to say yes. And in some ways I was really happy to get out, because I was so fed up with the whole atmosphere.'

218

Ezrin has told much the same tale, characterizing Wright as 'a victim of Roger's almost Teutonic cruelty. No matter what Rick did, it didn't seem to be good enough for Roger. It was clear to me that Roger wasn't interested in his succeeding.'[24] And Peter Jenner has discerned disturbing parallels with the bassist's hounding, over a decade earlier, of a certain other vulnerable Floyd member.

As Nick Griffiths saw it, however, 'By the time of *The Wall* Rick Wright had lost interest in the idea of the Floyd. He was more interested in his leisure time – sailing round the Greek islands and enjoying the life of a rich rock and roll star. Consequently, Roger felt that if he wasn't going to pull his weight, he should go.'

Waters has contended that Wright was too 'burnt out' to play, leaving Ezrin and an uncredited sessionman named Peter Wood to handle most of *The Wall*'s keyboard duties. There is even the suggestion that in 'Nobody Home' (which Waters said was 'about all kinds of people that I've known'), the passage culminating in the line '*I've got a grand piano to prop up my mortal remains*' was conceived as a vignette, not of Roger or Syd, but of Rick. Other observers acknowledge at least a few grains of truth in the widespread story that (as one puts it), 'Rick Wright was lobbed out because he was doing far too much coke, and he was *out of it*.'

It now seems ironic – in light of his own subsequent split with Waters and realignment with Wright – that on this issue at least, Dave was then in full accord with Roger. Rick 'wasn't doing the job he was paid to do,' Gilmour later said. And he minced few words with Karl Dallas: 'He got the boot because he wasn't contributing in any way to anything. Now, I argue vehemently with Roger about the way we want to do things, but I still see it as something I want to contribute to in a large way.'[25]

At the time, Dave seemed not altogether displeased that he was at least playing *second* fiddle in the Floyd hierarchy. Given that Roger's artistic and personal dominance still seemed an unavoidable fact of life, Gilmour had the consolation of knowing that no one else had more input than he in bringing Waters's ideas to fruition. Maintaining a functioning relationship with his prickly partner thus took precedence over any consideration of the group's also-rans.

'Roger made all the policy decisions in the Floyd,' observes Griffiths, 'and both Dave and Nick were grateful he was making them. After a couple of number one albums, they seemed the right decisions – until Roger became too difficult and perverse.'

Insofar as Gilmour still accepted that his job largely consisted of

investing Waters's creations with as much musical interest and
commercial appeal as possible, the guitarist would hardly have
minded working with musicians more attuned to his own high professional standards than the disaffected Wright – or, indeed, the
'playboy drummer', Waters has since claimed that Gilmour actually
agreed to the Wright purge with the words, 'Let's get rid of Nick
Mason, too!'[26] If Roger wasn't yet prepared to go that far, he in
turn was dissuaded by Dave and Nick from ousting Steve O'Rourke
(whom Roger is said to have held partly responsible for the Norton
Warburg fiasco).

While conceding that he 'contributed far less than on other albums
in terms of having a say', Mason felt that Ezrin's supervision 'benefited
my drumming and my drum sound enormously'. (Bob even taught him
to read rudimentary drum scores.) Waters nonetheless signalled his
own impatience with Nick by omitting the drummer's name, along
with Rick's, from *The Wall*'s almost biblical roll-call of sleeve credits.

'They were basically lazy,' Roger would contend, years later. 'Not
that I'm saying I did it all, Dave was contributing as an arranger and
an occasional advisor. He's a musican of note, and I don't want to
belittle his input. But the others had *no* input.'[27]

In one respect, however, Rick Wright was to have the last laugh.
Thanks to his recently arranged salary, he would end up the only
member of Pink Floyd to make money from the subsequent live
performances of *The Wall*; the cost of the show (like everything else
about it) was so spectacular that Roger, Dave, and Nick would lose a
fortune.

In any event, the Floyd organization's reputation for secrecy was
never so richly merited as in the mysterious Rick Wright affair. Many
of the group's fans would remain unaware that one of its founding
members had 'left' until nearly four years after the fact, with the
arrival of a *Wall* sequel in a sleeve listing but three names under the
words Pink Floyd.

Wright was not the only longtime Floyd pillar to fall from Roger's
graces at this juncture. Storm Thorgerson, after eleven years of
fashioning the band's universally acclaimed album artwork, was mystified when all of a sudden his lifelong friend would barely deign to
speak with him, let alone allow him a part in the *Wall* cover design. In
Storm's case, Dave would intervene in 1981 to the extent of securing
him the consolation prize of a CBS 'greatest hits' package that the
Floyd sardonically titled *A Collection of Great Dance Songs* (and for

which, incidentally, Gilmour would produce a new version of 'Money' to circumvent Capitol Records).

'Roger wasn't interested in that compilation,' Thorgerson recalls, 'so he actually let me get on with it. It was a fun cover, the couple "dancing but not dancing"; I liked it a lot. Roger never liked it, but by that time I don't think he would have liked anything I would have done. Which seems so silly 'cause the covers he had were so fucking awful. There are plenty of people who do good covers; why he didn't get any of them to work for him, I have no idea.'

Though hardly in the Hipgnosis class, Waters's choice of a faintly outlined pattern of plain white bricks for the *Wall* cover was if nothing else striking – much like the Beatles' white album – in its stark simplicity. In any case, the colourless packaging did not deter over half a million people in Britain alone from purchasing *The Wall* within a month of its release on 30 November 1979 (a deadline that the Floyd had struggled mightily to meet, in keeping with the terms of their promised £4 million-plus advance).* In America, it would top *Billboard*'s LP charts for all of fifteen weeks.

The Wall would eventually rank second only to *The Dark Side of the Moon* as Pink Floyd's all-time bestseller; as a double album, it actually sold more individual records. No doubt some of the sales were sparked off by the fluke phenomenon of the single, 'Another Brick in the Wall (Part 2)'; *The Wall* itself, as Kurt Loder concluded in his *Rolling Stone* review, was 'very tough stuff, and hardly the hallmark of a hit album'. Yet he also recognized it as 'a stunning synthesis of Waters's by now familiar thematic obsessions' that 'leaps to life with a relentless lyrical rage that's clearly genuine and, in its painstaking particularity, ultimately horrifying'.[28]

Many listeners found *The Wall* hard to stomach, and not just because it was such a downer. Some were repelled by the relentless self-importance, self-absorption, and self-pity; others dismissed the album as terminally contrived. For all its ingeniously elaborate symbolism and structure – the last words on the second disc, for instance, begin a sentence completed at the very beginning of the first – its main architect stood accused of being too clever by half. His

---

* Even after the LP sleeves had gone inexorably to press, Waters was still tinkering with the running order, moving 'Hey You' from the end of Side Three to the beginning; dropping 'What Shall We Do Now' altogether from an overlong Side Two in the interest of sound quality; and turning its slot over to 'Empty Spaces' which had much the same tune and was originally planned as a subsequent reprise. Hence the discrepancy between the LP sleeves and the actual record.

actual writing on *The Wall*, however ambitious and literate, is more prosaic than poetic – radiating little of the distinctive originality of, say, a Syd Barrett, that some would call the stamp of true genius.

Indeed, Allan Jones, the original Floyd fan from circa-'66 *Melody Maker*, now wrote that 'Waters might wear his heart bravely on his sleeve, but he often ends up with his feet in his mouth, choking on his own platitudes' and called *The Wall* 'finally more tiresome than moving'.[29] Yet even among the rock scribes, some *were* deeply moved. 'I felt Roger took the top off his skull,' says Timothy White, 'and invited the world to peer into the engine room of his subconscious. It's the vulnerable, courageous, and very necessary act of a serious artist, one who seeks community and solace by sharing the essence of his spiritual hopes and hungers.'

Love it or loathe it, the one thing everyone could agree about *The Wall* was that it was almost impossible to ignore. 'I'm not sure whether it's brilliant or terrible,' wrote *Melody Maker*'s Punk-generation critic Chris Brazier, 'but I find it utterly compelling.'[30] In the case of Roger Waters, *The Wall* would remain an all-consuming obsession for a further three years.

Chapter 20

Another Brick in the Wall
Parts 2 & 3

In bringing *The Wall* to the stage and the screen, Roger Waters found the ideal collaborator in Gerald Scarfe, whose drawings and sculpture were almost the visual equivalent of Pink Floyd's post-*Animals* music. Like Waters, Scarfe was an incorrigible cynic, whose nightmarish vision of the world was nonetheless fired by a passionate social conscience. Many of his concerns paralleled Roger's; as early as 1964, one of his famous cartoons had anticipated *The Wall* in its lampooning of the British school system; the artist, moreover, was haunted by memories of his wartime London childhood – such as the Government-issued gas masks that would provide the visages of the 'frightened ones' in his 'Goodbye Blue Sky' animations. And if both men were also 'megalomaniacs' (Scarfe's word), the simple fact that Waters 'deals entirely with music and words and I deal entirely with pictures' would keep their egos from clashing unduly.[1]

Scarfe set up a studio in the Fulham Road for the express purpose of directing his *Wall* animations, which were executed by Mike Stuart, Jill Brooks, and some forty other animators and took a year to complete. Scarfe was also obliged to adapt his style 'from *Sunday Times* scratchy-pen approach to something that could be copied by other artists'. In his book *Scarfe by Scarfe*, the artist himself offers a good a description as any of the resulting footage:

Walls scream and flowers turn to barbed wire. The dove of peace explodes and from its entrails a terrible eagle is born. This menacing creature tears great clods from the countryside with its gigantic talons, destroying whole cities. Swooping low it gives birth to the War Lord, a gargantuan figure who turns to metal, and sends forth bombers from its armpits. The bombers turn to crosses as the frightened ones run to their shelters. The ghosts of soldiers fall and rise again continuously and on a hill of bodies a Union Jack turns to a bloody cross. Blood runs down the cross and through the corpses and pointlessly trickles down the drain. Cathedrals are crushed and reform as glittering gods, and gigantic hammers march smashing all in their paths.[2]

Early on, Scarfe persuaded Waters to focus first on staging the *Wall* concerts, then use these as a springboard for the film. The original plan had been for the Floyd to tour with their own custom-designed transportable concert hall, which they dubbed the Slug – an inflatable worm-shaped canvas tent 354 feet long and 82 feet high, with a total area of 40,000 square feet and a seating capacity of up to 5,000.

'The halls in Britain,' Steve O'Rourke explained in a rare press comment, 'just cannot take the band's 45 tons of equipment and 45,000-watt PA system. The only way we can play to audiences in Glasgow, for instance, is to take our own hall on the road. It will take about a day to set up the tent in each city, but it should be worth it.'[3]

Problem was, the staging of *The Wall* itself, as it developed, promised to take far longer to set up than the tent; and the blueprints for the Slug were left in a Britannia Row file. The Floyd would settle in the end for extended runs at a small handful of existing venues: the Los Angeles Sports Arena and Greater New York's Nassau Coliseum (both in February 1980); London's Earls Court (August 1980 and again in June 1981); and Westfalenhalle in Dortmund, West Germany (February 1981). All four were arenas rather than *In the Flesh*-style stadiums which, Waters told Karl Dallas, 'makes a hell of a difference. You can cater to 15,000 people, with the technology that's available now, if you take it seriously enough and get the right people in, and spend enough . . .'[4] The Floyd would end up spending over $500,000 on props and equipment alone.

In addition to Scarfe, the 'right people' included set designers Mark Fisher (who supervised the actual design) and Jonathan Park (responsible for the engineering), both of whom had worked with the Floyd on the *In the Flesh* tour. The pair's greatest logistical challenge was the great white wall itself, over 160 feet wide and 35 feet high, to be erected during the concert's first half by an army of roadies, brick by cardboard brick (340 all told). This operation entailed, among other things, the installation, behind the rising wall, of discreet hydraulic

224

lifts from which the crew might hoist the bricks into place. Fisher and Park also had to work out how these would all come tumbling down at the conclusion of 'The Trial' and devise protective nets to spare the Floyd themselves any bodily harm.

Such vintage Floyd totems as the aeroplane and the pig were joined in the *Wall* show by giant grotesque Scarfe puppets representing the villains of the piece – the schoolmaster, mother, and young Mrs Pink. The familiar circular screen was also requisitioned for the programme's first half, after which Scarfe's animations could be projected, in tryptych, upon the Wall itself.

Once all these components were at hand, the Floyd reportedly rehearsed the show ten times at a Culver City movie soundstage, and spent several weeks setting it up at LA Sports Arena. 'We were all working furiously up until the first night,' Roger would recall. 'And the first time we had the Wall up across the arena with some film on it was four days before the first show. I walked all the way around the top row of seats at the back of the arena – and my heart was beating furiously and I was getting shivers right up and down my spine. And I thought it was so fantastic that people could actually see and hear something from everywhere they were seated.'[5]

The day before the opening on 7 February, however, the lighting effects were still in some disarray, causing the Floyd to summon an outside expert. 'I got called in twenty-four hours before their opening,' recalls Marc Brickman. 'Biggest theatrical thing I've ever seen in my life – and they're saying "We need it organized by tomorrow night." Trial by fire!' Gilmour was so impressed that seven years later he hired Brickman to design the lighting for his Floyd 'comeback' tour.

When the most spectacular of all Pink Floyd shows kicked off to the bombastic strains of 'In the Flesh?' the Floyd themselves were actually still backstage. In their place was a 'surrogate band' comprising bassist Andy Bown, guitarist Snowy White, drummer Willie Wilson, and keyboards player Peter Wood who completed the impersonation with masks of their equivalent Floyds' faces.

'They were meant to be what we *became*,' Waters told Dallas, 'i.e. at that juncture Pink was like a gestalt figure, the whole band turned into this kind of Nazi apparition [from] the end of the thing. That was really a kind of theatrical shock tactic, because people would assume that it was us . . . and suddenly realize that it wasn't.'[6] (Some of the audience, in fact, never realized any such thing – any more than their enjoyment of the song itself was clouded by much awareness that 'In the Flesh?' was meant as a crude self-parody.) During most of the rest of the show, the four 'imposters' would serve to fill out the Floyd's own sound, with Bown's bass freeing Waters to concentrate on his vocals, and act out the part of Pink. Roger later contended that Wilson was also needed throughout because Nick Mason was incapable of keeping proper time.

The opening night at LA's Sports Arena included a further, unintended, irony, when fireworks launched during 'In the Flesh' ignited some overhead drapes, eventually causing pieces of burning cloth to fall on the real Floyd and the fans in the front rows. In a scene reminiscent of Roger's discarded 'bombed audience' film scenario, the cheering crowds assumed the blaze was part of the show until Waters called a halt to the programme, and the fire brigade arrived.

Premeditated highlights included 'Goodbye Cruel World' when Roger, disappearing behind the wall's last remaining chink, personally inserted the final brick. Then, after the intermission, a trapdoor in the wall fell open for 'Nobody Home' revealing him isolated in a neon-lit motel room, complete with flickering TV and the actual sign of the Tropicana Motor Hotel (LA's home away from home for many top rock bands, including the Floyd themselves). On 'Comfortably Numb' a back-lit Dave Gilmour ascended via hydraulic lift to the top of the wall, his enormous shadow bleeding across the rapt faces of the audience during his dazzling solo.

The eight musicians were further augmented by four male back-up singers and the prerecorded orchestral scores of Michael Kamen, who was never even advised of their use beforehand. Helping James Guthrie supervise the U.S. concerts' sound was the producer Chris Thomas, whose last Floyd project had been *The Dark Side of the Moon*, and whose manager was now Steve O'Rourke. Roger had banished Bob Ezrin from the Floyd camp for the crime of shooting his mouth off to the press – 'and hasn't spoken to me since' Bob plaintively told *Melody Maker*'s Michael Watts in 1980 (thus compounding his offence). 'Honest to God, he's that sensitive. And we had a very good relationship too, after working cheek to cheek for a year.' Ezrin was not invited to help out on *The Wall* film soundtrack, either.

At the time of the American concerts, the wall between the Floyd and the media seemed higher and more impenetrable than ever. Even Gerald Scarfe was instructed not to discuss his animations with reporters without special dispensation. Michael Watts heard instead from, of all people, a 'very low' Waters extending him 'the courtesy of personally telling you no so that you knew that was the case from the horse's mouth rather than from some minion'. Photographers, meanwhile, routinely had the film gouged out of their cameras; Jill Furmanovsky's was personally seized from her bag by Steve O'Rourke. It was almost as if the fascistic impulses that *The Wall* ostensibly deplored were asserting themselves willy nilly.

Then again, that rock-star-turned-fascist routine, which some critics deemed especially preposterous, even though David Bowie had recently manifested just such a phase, was more or less a projection of the dark side of Roger's own personality: 'An attack on parts of myself that I disapprove of,' he acknowledged to Karl Dallas. One might even perceive Pink's manic totalitarianism as the flip side of the grandiosity that Waters evinced in creating *The Wall* in the first place. Peter Jenner, for one, was repelled by the entire show, which he branded 'the ultimate Roger Waters ego trip'.

In at least one instance, however, Roger's intransigence was entirely based on principle. After it became clear that the Floyd's twelve instantly sold-out American arena dates could accommodate a mere fraction of the fans who desperately wished to see the show, promoter Larry Maggid approached the group in New York with a $2 million guarantee for a pair of performances at Philadelphia's RFK Stadium. Everyone was eager to take up the offer – except Waters, who coolly reminded his colleagues that the original point of *The Wall* was to make a statement against stadium rock. Reluctant to kiss $2 million goodbye, Gilmour, Mason, and O'Rourke even contemplated doing the shows without Waters, and getting Andy Bown to sing his parts. But (in Roger's words) 'they didn't have the balls to go through with it' – not yet, anyway.[7]

Gilmour's role in the *Wall* shows was nonetheless crucial. Billed as 'musical director', he served as both guitarist and conductor, cueing everyone from the musicians to the stage hands throughout the concerts, which he remembers as 'brilliant and very effective, really good fun to do. But we were bored with the *Wall* shows as players by the time we got through the thirty-five we did. It was so choreographed, such a theatrical production, and I am fundamentally first a musician. It was just too much following cues and listening to little things on headphones – whamming people here and stopping dead at the right moment.

'The first ten shows we were terrified, there were ten to twenty dates that were fantastic, then after a while it was starting to get mechanical. I'd know when to do things, and I'd do them – with very few moments when you'd actually enjoy just singing and playing for their own sake.'

At the time of the *Wall* concerts, Roger still envisioned the film as an extension of the show, combining live Floyd footage and Scarfe animations with additional scenes and narration. He also pictured himself as the movie's star.

For all the album's enormous success, however, EMI's film people were baffled by the whole idea and gave Waters the runaround. But then Alan Parker – the young British director of *Midnight Express* and *Fame*, and a longtime Floyd fan – happened to inquire, while calling EMI on business of his own, whether anyone was planning to make a movie of *The Wall*. EMI's Bob Mercer gave him Roger's number.

Though Parker's original intent had been only to offer encouragement and advice, it wasn't long before Waters invited him to direct the movie. But Parker, then preoccupied with directing *Shoot the Moon*, demurred, proposing instead that he produce the film with Roger, with his cinematographer Michael Seresin handling the actual direction in collaboration with Gerald Scarfe.

In February 1981, Parker and Seresin flew to Germany to survey the Dortmund performances of *The Wall*. Parker was transfixed by the 'weird psychopathic quality' of Scarfe's copulating flowers and marching hammers and, he told Karl Dallas, by 'Roger's primal scream, the fears of madness, oppression, and alienation cutting through the giant theatricals. You couldn't fail to be astonished by the sheer scale of the mechanical undertaking and the colossal engineering problems that had been overcome to present it. Coming from the slow, almost archaic film process, to see *everything* – every sound fader pushed correctly, every hoist, every light, every one hit on time, was wonderfully impressive.' Parker was equally impressed by the atmosphere backstage – 'ultra-cool and professional' albeit 'a little edgy' – and by 'Roger's almost demonic control of the proceedings'.[8]

Waters, for his part, attempted to meet the film world halfway by studying a how-to book on screenplays. He and Scarfe then closeted themselves in the latter's Cheyne Walk studio for weeks on end, writing and drawing scenes for a 39-page script and a storyboard. This last in turn formed the basis of a lavish oversized full-colour book, privately printed in a very limited edition as a prospectus for potential investors. Alongside the lyrics for each song were one or more Scarfe illustrations, and a detailed description of what was to take place on

228

screen during that segment. One of the briefest of these, for 'Another Brick in the Wall (Part 2)', read:

> The teacher puppet has now arrived very close to Roger who sings the first few lines of 'The Happiest Days'. After the line 'hurt the children any way they could', we use animation of the teacher forcing children into a mincing machine built in the shape of a school. The children emerges as worms.

Throughout, the book referred to 'Pink' in the context of the proposed animation scenes, but to 'Roger' when the protagonist was to appear, so to speak, in the flesh. Lest there be any further doubt who would claim that starring role, Scarfe's 'In the Flesh' illustration of *The Wall*'s megastar-turned-megalomaniac clearly bore the features of Roger Waters. Elsewhere, Steve O'Rourke and rock concert promoter Harvey Goldsmith were also depicted in their hoped-for cameo roles as roadies.

One problem with this entire scenario was that Waters, as his screen tests soon made all too plain, was no actor. Among the first of Parker's challenges was to ease him into an off-screen role, and find a suitably charismatic figure who could act out Roger's story. Viewing some vidoes by the Irish New Wave band the Boomtown Rats, whose popularity had peaked, at the time of *The Wall*'s own chart reign, with the British number one 'Rat Trap' and 'I Don't Like Mondays', Parker was mesmerized by the 'dangerous quality and physical unpredictability' of lead singer Bob Geldof.

The Boomtown Rats' manager was delighted by Parker's subsequent overtures, and the prospect of a major film role to revive Geldof's sagging career. But the singer, who subscribed to the New Wave view of the Floyd as 'overblown and old hat' and disdained Roger's latterday lyrics as 'social-conscience-stricken millionaire leftism', was initially reluctant to recast himself in the guise of Pink. The 'idea of the pop star as incipient fascist' particularly struck him as 'a load of bollocks'. Geldof would finally relent because doing *any* film presented him with a new challenge; he also liked Parker and admired his work – and 'the money was good'.[9]

In the meantime, the Floyd staged *The Wall* at Earls Court in June 1981 expressly to have the five shows filmed for scenes in the movie. But the shooting was, in Parker's words, 'a total disaster . . . five chances, all muffed.' Not that this would, in the end, much matter:

after the decision was made to showcase someone else in the dramatic role of Pink, Waters also reluctantly had to agree with Parker that it would be too confusing for *The Wall* to remain both a Scarfe cartoon and a Floyd concert film. All the band-members were thus squeezed out of the picture entirely – though not, of course, from its sound-track, about a quarter of which would be specially recorded for the movie.* A further casualty would be Scarfe's puppets, but not before thousands of pounds had been squandered on a giant electronically-controlled schoolmaster robot.

Parker, driven to chainsmoking for the first time in his life by the project's mounting complications – not least of them the bad chemistry between his protegée Michael Seresin and Gerald Scarfe – decided to take over *The Wall*'s direction after all. 'I threw Michael the ball and expected him to run with it,' he subsequently groused to friends, 'but instead he just looked at the stitching and bitched about it.' Parker had in any case decided he 'wasn't really very good at walking around smoking my Marlboro in the background whilst other people were getting on with it' and that 'it would be much better for me to get on and do the job I'm supposed to do: direct.'[10] Scarfe's role was redefined as *The Wall*'s 'designer': Alan Marshall took over as producer; and Serensin dropped out altogether.

The British film world, however, remained unreceptive. Parker has said that when he would describe *The Wall* to the cinema moguls as 'a fragmented piece with no conventional dialogue to progress the narrative, with music as its main driving force, they would stare back at me incredulously'. The people at EMI, unmoved by memories of the million-plus *Wall* albums shipped by their record division in the UK alone, continued to tell him that 'this is something we can't go with right now.'[11] Despite his desire to keep the project all-British, Parker finally reached out to Hollywood. *The Wall* would be distributed by MGM, with the Floyd themselves underwriting most of its budget of some $12 million.

Given his enormous creative, emotional, and financial stake in *The Wall*, Waters was jealously possessive of the film. Working with him, the new director soon found, was 'a very unpleasant experience' –

---

* Along with the album out-take 'What Shall We Do Now?' and the all-new 'When the Tigers Broke Free' the film includes orchestrated remakes of 'Mother', 'Bring the Boys Back Home' (with a Welsh choir), 'In the Flesh' (with Geldof singing), and 'Outside the Wall'. The Floyd also devised a *Tommy*-style 'Overture' that, along with the album's 'Hey You' and 'The Show Must Go On', never made the final cut.

230

quickly adding that 'just because Roger and I didn't necessarily get on, it doesn't mean to say we didn't do a good piece of work.'[12]

Waters, for his part, recalled the filming of *The Wall* as 'the most unnerving, neurotic period of my life, with the possible exception of my divorce in 1975. Parker is used to sitting at the top of his pyramid, and I'm used to sitting at the top of mine. We're both pretty much used to getting our way.'[13] Before shooting started in earnest on 7 September 1981, Parker squeezed yet another concession from Waters, perhaps the most wrenching one of all: that he take a six-week 'holiday' during the actual filming, and let the director get on with it without further interference.

The first day's scenes were shot at the residence of a retired admiral, which served as the home of young Pink. While Parker worked with his actors indoors, an exterior crew rustled up footage for the sequence leading into Scarfe's 'Goodbye Blue Sky' animations, where a 'dove of peace' eludes a stalking cat and takes flight. Fifty doves and twenty pigeons were lost by the time they got a few usable frames.

Much of the subsequent filming was done at Pinewood Studios, outside London. A special set was created for the motel room, complete with penthouse swimming pool and computerized LA skyline; there was also a mammoth made-to-order wall that would ultimately be blown to bits with an air cannon previously deployed in a James Bond film. According to Geldof, the ambience itself was like 'a mine field which had been sown with exploding egos'. Resolved to ignore all the 'childish recriminations' between the director and producer on the one hand, and Waters and Scarfe on the other, the Boomtown Rat 'just put my trust in Parker who, I reckoned, knew what he was doing'.[14]

He would sometimes have his doubts, as in the scene where the pool's water turns to blood around a floating Pink. Not only did Geldof have 'a phobia about blood' but Parker had wrongly assumed that his leading man knew how to swim. The director finally hit upon the solution of using the transparent body mould in which *Superman*'s Christopher Reeves had lain to do his 'flying' while fast-moving scenes were projected behind him; but to Geldof's further shame he was too scrawny to fit the Superman mould and had to settle for Supergirl.

Bob also damaged himself physically, drawing real blood, when he shredded his hand on a Venetian blind during the room-smashing sequence inspired by Roy Harper for 'One of My Turns'. To the astonishment of the crew, the bleeding star refused to cease his demented demolition job until Parker had the scene all wrapped up.

As the filming progressed, Geldof began relating to Roger Waters's epic far more than he had ever thought possible – or desirable. By his own account 'the dense moods which *The Wall* brought down on me carried an insight into depths which were normally buried'.[15] The future 'Saint Bob' even sensed he was turning into 'an evil megalomaniac'.

Geldof's newfound identification with the subject matter enabled him to portray Pink all the more convincingly – not least in the Syd-inspired episodes of *The Wall*'s third quarter. Though Geldof had never met Barrett, June Bolan attests to the authenticity of Bob's impersonation: 'I was absolutely shell-shocked; it was so close to Syd I couldn't bear it. When he was looking in that bathroom mirror and shaving himself. I just had tears, and was sitting rigid in the cinema, because it was ever so close to home. I could feel for Syd totally.'

Geldof, who would add Barrett's 'Arnold Layne' to the Boomtown Rats' live repertoire, still balked at the notion of singing one of Roger's songs in *The Wall*. For a price, he finally did agree to record his own 'In the Flesh' voice-over at Gilmour's 24-track home studio (in the sixteenth-century Henley manor house Dave had bought from Alvin Lee, and would later sell for £850,000). At first, Geldof mischievously brayed Pink's neo-Nazi manifesto in a heavy Irish accent, 'like a drunken farmer at a Kerry agricultural show'. The singer delighted in the 'look of horror creeping over the faces' of Gilmour and engineer James Guthrie, but after tormenting them through several takes finally sang it the way they wanted it. As soon as he had done so, Dave's voice resounded over the studio monitors: 'You bastard!'[16]

In the film, Geldof is shown performing 'In the Flesh' to a crowd of skinheads at London's New Horticultural Hall, accompanied by a choir and brass band worthy of 'Atom Heart Mother' plus an elite 24-strong 'Hammer Guard' comprised of southeast London's hardened Tilbury Skins. Their Scarfe-designed uniforms (complete with crossed-hammer insignia) were so realistic that patrons of a local pub visibly blanched when the jackbooted guards marched in for a few lunchtime pints. The Tilbury Skins were also deployed to smash up a 'Paki' café for a sequence in 'Run Like Hell' – a task that they executed with disconcerting relish.

At moments such as these, Parker had to wrestle with the paradox that, in an intended statement against bigotry and violence, not only were his extras enjoying their role all too literally, but some of the film's audience might react likewise. (Scarfe, too, also had 'nightmares about meeting people in the street who've taken up the Hammer Look'.)[17] During the shooting of riot scenes at a disused gasworks in Becton – later recast as a school and destroyed for the climax of 'Another Brick in the Wall (Part 2)' – the skins seemed unable to grasp that their adversaries were merely actors dressed as policemen: the fighting, said Parker, 'always seemed to continue long after I had yelled out 'Cut!'[18] One band of punks enacted the lynching of a black Romeo and gang-rape of his white girlfriend so convincingly that in the end the director felt obliged to leave most of the footage out of his 'Run Like Hell' sequence.

There was much else that Parker would have to leave out; the sixty days of shooting yielded sixty hours of film, which needed to be polled down to a 99-minute feature under the auspices of his brilliant editor Gerry Hambling. It was then that Roger Waters returned to active duty and the tensions erupted full-force. 'That film had become *mine*,' Parker recalled, 'and then Roger came back to do it, and I had to go through the very difficult reality of having it put over to me that it actually was a collaborative effort.'[19]

In his BBC-TV documentary *Scarfe on Scarfe*, Roger's closest ally in *The Wall* drew a picture of 'three megalomaniacs shut in a room together, each one trying to get one's point across before the other one did. The whole film rose to a point of hysteria because of that.'

From his own experience with Waters, Dave Gilmour was not about to pin all the blame on Parker. One friend remembers him 'saying to Roger, "Man, just open up to the guy and apologize." But Roger won't let anyone beat him at anything.' Waters (together with Gilmour and James Guthrie) was at least given free rein on the soundtrack, painstakingly dubbing directly from the Floyd's original master tapes to insure the highest fidelity.

Upon its appearance, many film critics found *The Wall* self-indulgent at best, though it broke box-office records during its initial run, and would resurface as a longtime number one videocassette release that would earn back for the Floyd all the money they had lost on the concerts and then some. As a feature-length MTV-style music video, the film was surely several years ahead of its time, and certainly boasts many moments of perverse grandeur; but, like most music videos, it also often diminishes its soundtrack by robbing listeners of the free use of their own imaginations. In the case of *The Wall*, the album's more dubious aspects – Pink's nauseating self-pity, his preposterous self-importance – seem all the more glaring when amplified on screen. The heavy-handed symbolism becomes positively inescapable: all those worms, entrails, barbed wire, fanged vaginas – and blood, blood, and more blood.

Five years after the fact, Waters himself gave a remarkably insightful and dispassionate verdict: 'When it was finally put together, I watched the film, and I'd been dubbing it for the previous three weeks, reel by reel. Each reel on its own I thought was quite interesting, but when I saw all thirteen reels together, I felt that it lacked any real dynamic. It seemed to start bashing you over the head in the first ten minutes, and it didn't stop until it was over: there was no quiet time.

'But my most serious criticism was – although I thought Bob Geldof acted very well and that Alan Parker directed the film with great technical competence – at the end of the day, I felt, who gives a shit. I wasn't interested in this Pink character; I didn't feel any empathy for him at all . . . And if you can't care about Pink, then you can't care about his concerns about the totalitarian nature of the iconography of rock and roll . . . [or] even about the dead father in the war and all . . . And if I go to the cinema and I don't care for any of the characters, it's a bad film.'[20]

The world premiere of *The Wall* on 14 July 1982 at the Empire Theatre in London's Leicester Square was a gala event with tickets priced at £30 and £50 (all proceeds went to the Nordoff-Robins Music Therapy Centre for handicapped children). In attendance were Geldof, Parker, and Scarfe; rock stars like Pete Townshend and Sting; and three Pink Floyds, whose appearance in the Royal Box was accorded a standing ovation. Floyd fanatic Andy Mabbett, who had won a ticket in a *Sun* competition, observed that each band-member's attire appeared to reflect the extent of his commitment to the group: Roger was in formal evening dress, Dave sported a jacket but no tie, Nick wore jeans and a T-shirt – and Rick was nowhere to be seen. Mason, too, would be absent at the New York Ziegfeld Theatre opening a few days later with Scarfe, though in town, off playing pool because he couldn't 'bear to see the film again'.

Chatting with Andy at the Empire Theatre bar, the T-shirted drummer parroted the party line that Rick was 'on holiday' – a pretence that would finally be dropped by Dave in subsequent interviews promoting the film. Wright was in fact licking his wounds at his Rhodes retreat in the wake of his acrimonious divorce from Juliette, his wife of nearly fifteen years. ('That's when he *really* went to pieces,' says an old friend.) Rick disappeared into 'semi-retirement' while attempting to regain his personal equilibrium; after all, as he points out, 'There's other things in life apart from music.' Over the next few years he would rarely return to England – let alone to the world of rock and roll.

Mason's involvement on the Pink front had, of late, been little greater than Wright's. 'At least,' he quipped, 'I'm not a frustrated Floyd composer.' To help pass the time, he nonetheless became the last in the group to try the solo route with an experimental jazz/pop fusion that was called *Nick Mason's Fictitious Sports*, but bore the indelible stamp of its composer and pianist Carla Bley. Mason, who coproduced and played drums – and paid the bills – decided that her music would get a wider hearing if packaged under his own name; Pink Floyd's CBS and EMI contracts, moreover, guaranteed a substantial advance for any Floyd solo album. Also prominently featured on the 1981 release were the vocals of Nick's onetime Soft Machine rival (and longtime hero) Robert Wyatt, the guitar of Chris Spedding and the trumpets of Carla's husband Mike Mantler.

Mason had previously worked with both Bley and Mantler (as well as Wyatt, who had introduced him to the jazzy American couple) on Mike's 1976 LP *The Hapless Child and Other Stories*, set to the whimsically macabre verse of Edward Gorey; Nick would go on to drum on two further albums by the Mike Mantler Project. His other recent production clients had included, along with the irascible Damned, the more compatibly 'progressive' Gong (founded by another ex-Soft Machinist, Daevid Allen) and that band's guitarist Steve Hillage, whose revival of the Beatles' 'Getting Better' received some favourable notice.

'His forte as a producer is really organization,' says Nick Griffiths. 'People who've worked with Nick have really enjoyed it, because he'll make sure everything gets done at the right time. If it's an artist who knows musically what he's doing, the album will turn out well – on time, within budget, and sounding good. But he never looks at things from a musical point of view. He won't talk notes and arrangements.

'Nick Mason is not really into making works of art, musicwise. He regards himself as reasonably lucky tht he was around at the right time and the right place. His *cars* are works of art. He's very good at owning and racing cars, and has the most beautiful garage full of the most wonderful cars. He is probably better at that than at music and drumming.'

235

By 1979, Nick's collection of over twenty racing and historic cars was appraised at £500,000 (a fraction of its value a decade later, when his 1962 Ferrari GTO would alone be worth over £1 million). He also acquired a fleet of motorcycles. To generate some return on his investment, Mason founded a company called Ten Tenths to promote the photographing of his Ferraris and Bugattis for magazines, books, films, and TV commercials, in some of which Nick himself could be spotted behind the wheel. He also became a partner in Britain's largest Ferrari dealer, Modena Engineering, and in 1980 won Donnington's first-ever Bugattis-only race, driving his own 1927 model.

By 1982 he had placed first in seven more races, and set the Donnington lap record for historic cars. Ever the dedicated amateur, Mason foreswore any aspirations as a professional racing driver. Yet he acknowledged that his diminishing Floyd workload had freed him to pursue his time-consuming 'second love'.

By the same token, his Floyd affiliation – much though he tried to play it down – inevitably made his races a media curiosity. Nick's entry in the 1983 Le Mans – partnered by fellow enthusiast Steve O'Rourke – was covered on British national TV: a year later Mason became the subject of a *Penthouse* profile, in which he waxed almost poetic about his first Le Mans race in 1979: 'Out on the circuit at night, the experience was magical – the sheer speed, the lights of the fairground as the car just about took off under the Dunlop bridge and then swooping down to the Esses. The smell of brake pads and then the incredible Mulsanne straight.

'In the pits, the team spirit was marvellous. You'd finish your stint and come in to hand over the car, and with every hour that went by the excitement in our pit grew. Then you'd walk out to the back of the pits for a rest, hearing the French commentator and the roar of the engines – and smelling frying onions from hundreds of barbecues . . .'[21]

The Wall, meanwhile, would spark a real-life 'Trial' after a Kentucky public high school teacher named Jacqueline Fowler was fired in 1984 for corrupting her students with the R-rated film. A Federal judge, ruling that Fowler's First Amendment rights had been violated, ordered her reinstatement (with $10,000 compensation for 'emotional distress') – but was overturned by a panel of the 6th U.S. Circuit Court of Appeals. In 1987 the justices of the United States Supreme Court, in their wisdom, let the second ruling – and Ms Fowler's sacking – stand.

Chapter 21
Terminal Frost

On 2 April 1982, a puffed-up Argentine military dictator named Leopoldo Galtieri, seeking to distract his subjects from the ill effects of his junta's misrule, directed his Navy to invade and occupy the Falkland Islands. A British Crown Colony 250 miles off the coast of southern Argentina, the desolate, windswept Falklands were home to over a million sheep but fewer than 2,000 people (and hardly one tree). Confounding Galtieri's assumption that Britain was too distant, dispirited, and decadent to fight back, Prime Minister Margaret Thatcher dispatched a modern English Armada and clapped a total air and sea blockade around the South Atlantic islands.

After six weeks of pitched battles, the Argentines finally capitulated on 14 June, leaving the disputed rocks under the permanent protection of British troops whose numbers far exceeded those of the islanders they had been sent 10,000 miles to rescue. Back home, the 'Argie'-bashing media whipped the masses into an orgy of flagwaving nationalism, in which Maggie Thatcher was acclaimed for having put the 'Great' back into Britain (and, in the process, acquired the political clout that would enable her to dismantle its post-World War II socialist trappings). The deflated Galtieri, meanwhile, tendered his resignation, bringing to an end the international crisis that Argentina's eminent writer Jorge Luis Borges likened to 'two bald men fighting over a comb'.

It would have made for a fine comic-opera war – as deliciously ridiculous as *The Mouse That Roared* – but for one detail: the clash between General Galtieri's vainglory and the Iron Lady's patriotic principles was played out at the cost of over a thousand young British and Argentinian lives. As Roger Waters would sing in a recurring chorus on his next (and last) Pink Floyd album, '*Oh Maggie, Maggie what have we done?*'

It is not hard to see how Waters might have felt deeply affected by the Falklands War. For nearly five years now, his life had been taken over

by *The Wall*, that monument of alienation for which his own father's
wartime death had provided the first, underlying 'brick.' *The Wall*'s
film incarnation, which was being readied for release even as the
Falklands exploded, focused on that pivotal trauma far more unflinch-
ingly than had the original album or the stage show: its one all-new
song, 'When the Tigers Broke Free', explicitly chronicled the circumstances of Eric Fletcher Waters's untimely death.

This powerful albeit intensely personal elegy was released as a Pink
Floyd single in July 1982, pointedly coupled with a new extended
version of *The Wall*'s 'Bring the Boys Back Home'. The Floyd's original
plan had been to prepare a full-length soundtrack album (which the
film's closing credits actually trumpeted as 'available on CBS Records
and Tapes') or, at the very least, an LP's worth of material that had
been specially written or rerecorded for the movie, to be called *Spare
Bricks*.

But something happened on the way to the studio – that splendid
little South Atlantic war, for which young men very much like Eric
Fletcher Waters paid with their lives. The spare bricks took on a life of
their own, and became *The Final Cut*. (The title came by way of
Shakespeare, a reference to Julius Ceasar's stab-in-the-back by Brutus:
'This was the most unkindest cut of all.')

'I got on a roll, and started writing this piece about my father,'
Roger recalled. 'I was on a roll, and I was gone. The fact of the matter
was that I was making *this* record. And Dave didn't like it. And he
said so.'[1]

Gilmour asserts that his initial objection was not so much that 'he
didn't think we should criticize a Conservative government's action in
the South Atlantic' (as Waters was to claim in a 1986 London *Sunday
Times* story), but that some of Roger's new song-cycle (e.g., 'Your
Possible Pasts' and 'The Hero's Return') sounded all too familiar:
'Songs that we threw off The Wall, he brought them back for The
Final Cut – same songs. Nobody thought they were that good then,
what makes them so good now? I bet he thought I was just being
obstructive.' Dave wanted to take a month off to develop some new
musical ideas of his own, but Roger was adamant that the Floyd press
ahead with what *he* had already written.

If Waters seemed more possessive and defensive about his work than
ever before, it was partly because his 'requiem for the post-war dream'
(as the album would be subtitled) was so close to his own heart – at
once a cry of pain over his father's sacrifice, and a scream of rage
against the generals and politicians who were *still* sending the boys off

to die. And this time round there was no Bob Ezrin to mediate between him and Gilmour – or to help shape Roger's writing, let alone persuade him that some of it might not be up to scratch.

'I think Roger was becoming just too autocratic: he had to control everything,' remarks Dave's old friend and drummer Clive Welham. 'Now, Gilmour is just not the sort of person to live with that – not for long. There would come a point when he would stand his ground. David and Roger are *both* people who liked to lead.' The result, says Welham, 'was a Mexican stand-off between Roger and Dave'.

With *The Final Cut*, this took the form of Waters reviving his Rick Wright ploy, and threatening to ditch the project unless Gilmour abdicated as co-producer. Dave finally did agree to relinquish his position – but not his final cut of the producers' royalties. And Waters was left, in his words, 'to do it more or less single-handed, working with Michael Kamen',[2] who now served as his co-producer, pianist, and both arranger and conductor of Roger's special guest stars with National Philharmonic Orchestra. Even the LP cover was designed by Waters, with photos by his wife's brother, *Vogue* photographer Willie Christie.

The other two Floyds, meanwhile, were reduced to the role of mere sidemen, alongside the likes of top session percussionist Ray Cooper and *The Wall*'s surrogate bassist Andy Bown, now on organ. According to Gilmour, 'It reached the point that I just had to say, "If you need a guitar player, give me a call and I'll come and do it." ' As a vocalist, Dave, once the Floyd's dominant singer, found his services even less in demand. Except on the 'Money'-esque verses of 'Not Now John' (which CBS earmarked for an expletives-deleted single that would sink without trace). Gilmour's voice is conspicuously absent from *The Final Cut*.

Nick Mason, who shared many of Roger's political views, did make a valuable contribution with his suggestion that the cycle's several reprises of the opening track's '*Maggie, what have we done?*' chorus should be rendered minus the words, to give them more resonance and universality. But on the downbeat finale, 'Two Suns in the Sunset', a 'premonition' of the world's incineration in a nuclear holocaust, Mason was actually replaced altogether by the ace studio drummer Andy Newmark (lately of Roxy Music) when it seemed that nothing Nick could do with the song would satisfy Roger. Whether out of sheer egomania or in tacit acknowledgement that *The Final Cut* was indeed a solo album, its official billing would read 'by Roger Waters performed by Pink Floyd'.

Though Waters and Mason had for many years enjoyed the closest friendship within the Floyd (even recently, Roger had chosen Nick as godfather to one of his sons), the drummer found himself in growing sympathy with Gilmour's position, on both personal and artistic grounds. 'I think *The Wall* and even more so *The Final Cut*,' says Mason, 'very clearly indicate Roger's increasing control, and increasing interest in lyrics. There is no doubt in my mind that his strongest suit has always been writing. He works very hard at that, and he's less interested, I think, in the music.

'Roger will happily use the same piece of music four times, with different lyrics to make a new point in the story. Which is sort of corner-cutting in a way, but the approach would be, "*This* needs to be said but we can hang it onto a reprise of *that* just as easily, rather than worry too much about the music." Whereas Dave would probably try and find four different pieces of music – and hang the same lyric on it!'

But as Gilmour's input was now kept in check, *The Final Cut*'s melody count was lower than anything Pink Floyd had done since the days before Waters and company first began to focus on writing actual songs; only now the drone consisted not of dreamy Muzak-of-the-spheres, but a strident antiwar broadside. The singer's declamatory tone was hardly mellifluous. Even Roger has conceded that his vocals leave something to be desired – 'You can hear the mad tension running through it all' – and that the making of *The Final Cut* was 'absolute misery' and 'a horrible time'.[3]

He nevertheless remains fiercely proud of the album, which was recorded during the last six months of 1982 at eight different English studios. Britannia Row was not among them, Waters, like Wright, having sold his stake to Gilmour and Mason: eventually Nick would become the sole owner. In some ways *The Final Cut* qualifies as Roger's equivalent of John Lennon's highly acclaimed 'primal scream' LP, released in the wake of the Beatles' 1970 disintegration. Waters has cited 'Isolation' from that album as one of his all-time favourite tracks, adding, 'If I were to list fifty songs I wish I had written, very few of them would not be by Dylan or Lennon.'[4]

John Lennon/Plastic Ono Band, too, had constituted a bitter, anguished, and politically charged exorcism of the writer's most private demons – which, in Lennon's case, harked back to the violent death of his mother – and had made for anything but easy listening. *The Final Cut* saw Waters no less determined (as he put it in the title track) '*to bare my naked feelings*' and '*tear the curtain down*'. On 'The Gunner's Dream' Roger even lets rip with a primal scream of his own –

which magically metamorphoses into a wailing tenor saxophone solo from Raphael Ravenscroft (the man who had played the famous sax obbligato on Gerry Rafferty's 'Baker Street').

Plastic Ono Band, however, had not – Ringo Starr's presence on drums notwithstanding – masqueraded as a Beatles album. Waters has claimed that he was in fact perfectly willing to drop the group moniker from *The Final Cut*, but Gilmour and Mason 'didn't want that, because they know songs don't grow on trees. They wanted it to be a Floyd record'.[5]

Unlike Lennon's raw and minimalistic statement, moreover, *The Final Cut*'s production values represented the state of the art (and then some). To give extra presence to his continuous parade of sound effects, Waters even applied an experimental new technique – 'Holophonics', created by the Argentine physiologist Hugo Zuccarelli (and previously used only on an album by the band Psychik TV) – through which quadrophonic sound could purportedly be simulated on stereo equipment, by encoding into the recording process the dimensions of the human skull. The missile that launches 'Get Your Filthy Hands Off My Desert', for instance, is said to blast off in front of the listener, pass overhead, and explode behind. At the very least, effects such as these do seem to come fairly leaping out of the headphones.

Apart from Gilmour's several brief solos, it is the sound effects that provide the album's most recognizable echoes of the Floyd's former sonic glories. The wind from *Meddle*, the footsteps and clocks and madcap laugh from *The Dark Side of the Moon*, and radio babble and party gabble of *Wish You Were Here*, the howling hounds from *Animals* and the nightmare screams and martial megaphone voices from *The Wall* – all are recycled on *The Final Cut*. Now, however, these are pressed into the service not of surreal atmospherics, but of a harsh and claustrophobic realism.

Much of *The Final Cut* is narrated (in the histrionic vocal style Waters had introduced on the least 'Floydian' passages of *The Wall*) from the perspective of a serviceman who, unlike Roger's dad, did survive the horrors of World War II. Now, in his '*alcohol soft middle age*', he is employed as a schoolteacher, vainly trying '*to clout little ingrates into shape*' and repress his memories of the battlefront. (This complex and compassionate portrait certainly redresses any slight to the profession inflicted by *The Wall*'s too-wicked-to-be-true schoolmaster.) After dark, however, while the teacher's wife slumbers peacefully at his side, the '*bullet-proof mask*' slips, leaving the veteran tormented by nightmares of his wartime experiences.

241

On *The Final Cut*, these are interspersed with scenes drawn from the world stage of both the mid-1940s (when Britain, the US, the USSR and everyone else *'agreed with hand on heart to sheath the sacrificial knives'*) and the early 1980s (when at least three wars were being simultaneously waged by, or with the blessing of, those very powers). Waters thereby develops his premise that not only the death of his father, but also the 'post-war dream' of the survivors, had been profoundly betrayed. (Note Christie's back-cover photo of the World War II serviceman with a can of film under his arm and a knife in his back – also said to be a comment on Roger's own 'betrayal' by a certain movie director.)

In a 1984 interview, Waters cited the paranoia of 'powerlessness' as another of *The Final Cut*'s underlying themes: 'The door opens suddenly, and you find you're face to face with blokes in jackboots in a country like South America or Algeria, or France during the Occupation . . . You cry, "No, you can't do that to me. I'll call the police." And they reply, "We *are* the police." Your life slips into a nightmare. The most precious thing in this world is that your life is not controlled by someone else.'[6]

The album grows increasingly personal as it progresses. On 'Fletcher's Memorial Home' Waters describes his fantasy of gathering into one playpen such *'colonial wasters of life and limb'* as Russia's Leonid Brezhnev and Israel's Manachem Begin (who had recently executed their own bloody invasions of Afghanistan and Lebanon) – together with, of course, the Iron Lady and various *'Latin American meat-packing glitterati'* – and turning on the gas. By 'The Final Cut' itself, Roger is explicitly baring his own intimate fears and vulnerabilities.

At the end, these fuse with the topical themes as Roger confronts the ultimate fear of us all – and the ultimate consequence of his Fletcher's Memorial Home inmates' policies. He first conceived 'Two Suns in the Sunset' while driving home one evening, and imagining what it would be like if some madman pushed the button then and there: his windshield melting; his tears evaporating; and everything turned to charcoal:

> *Ashes and diamonds,*
> *foe and friend,*
> *we were all equal in the end.*

All in all, pretty strong stuff – not exactly your usual Top Forty teenybop treacle, let alone anything to be listened to on acid. It was hardly to the taste of most casual Floyd fans – or David Gilmour, who never made any secret of his displeasure with *The Final Cut*. Barely a year after its release, he was belittling most of its contents as 'cheap filler of the kind we hadn't put on a Pink Floyd album in years.'[7]

The ensuing years have hardly softened his aversion to the album. On the 1988 tour, when I mistakenly cited *Animals* as the only post-*Dark Side* LP excluded from the Roger-less Floyd's repertoire, he interjected: 'And *The Final Cut*.'

'Oh, yes – I forgot about that.'

'We like to,' Dave shot back, not missing a beat.

Moments later, though, he allowed that three of the tracks – 'Gunner's Dream', 'Fletcher's Memorial Home', and 'The Final Cut' itself (each of which, as it happens, features a remarkable, blistering guitar solo) – are 'really great. I wouldn't want to knock anything that's good, whoever it's by. And I didn't, at the time, knock anything because of any personal problems that one was going through.

'It could have been a great album, but it's unbalanced. There's too much filler, meandering rubbish inbetween songs.'

Though the sales were unspectacular by Floydian standards, some people thought *The Final Cut* was a great album. (From a literary standpoint, if nothing else, it surely qualifies as Roger's most mature accomplishment.) At the time, *Rolling Stone* awarded it the maximum five stars, with resident Floyd critic Kurt Loder calling it 'a superlative achievement' and 'rock art's crowning masterpiece'. 'Not since Bob Dylan's "Masters of War" twenty years ago,' the reviewer declared, 'has a popular artist unleashed upon the world political order a moral contempt so corrosively convincing, or a life-loving hatred so bracing and brilliantly sustained.' (Why then, one wonders, would the magazine neglect, at decade's end, to include this 'crowning masterpiece' among its Hundred Best Albums of the 1980s?) The editors of the Floyd fanzine *Amazing Pudding* have rated *The Final Cut* the band's best-ever album – even as their readers voted it the all-time worst.

Waters himself liked to counter criticism with the story of being approached in a greengrocer's by a well-dressed woman in her forties, who told him that *The Final Cut* had reduced her to tears, and was 'the most moving record she had ever heard. Her father had also been killed in World War II, she explained. And I got back into my car with my three pounds of potatoes and drove home and thought, *Good enough*.'[8]

Each Floyd album within memory had given rise to a new stage show, and at first *The Final Cut* was expected to follow the pattern: tentative concert dates were even announced for November, 1983. Ironically, however, the underemployed Gilmour and Mason were far more enthusiastic about the idea than Waters, who abruptly scuttled the plans – leaving his colleagues in the lurch, and yet further embittered.

Roger produced instead a relatively low-key (and low-budget) 'Video EP'. Directed by his brother-in-law Willie Christie, it featured visuals for 'The Gunner's Dream', 'The Final Cut', 'Not Now John', and 'Fletcher's Memorial Home'. Waters was shown baring his soul to a heedless psychiatrist named A. Parker-Marshall (another subtle swipe at *The Wall*'s director and producer), and his father was played by Alex McAvoy, who had portrayed the wicked schoolmaster in the Parker-Marshall film. Dave's participation was neither asked for, nor received. By that point, the two men's estrangement was such that few in the Pink Floyd circle could easily picture them working together again.

Before *The Final Cut* even reached the shops, both Gilmour and Waters were already ensconced in studios on opposite sides of the English Channel, hard at work on extra-Floyd projects. Pouring his thwarted melodic talents into his new solo album, Dave must have felt like the similarly stifled George Harrison, who in the wake of the Beatles' split had surprised the world with a torrent of suppressed creativity. 'It's very pleasant,' Gilmour said at the time, 'to work without having to argue to get your way (and end up *not* getting your way).'[9] Assisted by most of the other *Final Cut* musicians, meanwhile, Roger plunged headlong into *The Pros and Cons of Hitchhiking* – the song cycle that Gilmour and Mason had had the temerity to reject as unsuitable for Pink Floyd.

As far as Waters was concerned, he could, in any event, manage perfectly well without the Floyd – let alone its meddlesome guitarist. The very name Pink Floyd was an anachronism, and a deceptive one at that; there had been no real group since the days of *Animals* or even *Wish You Were Here*. The three men no longer shared any common ground – musically, philosophically, politically, or personally – and the time had come for Roger Waters to pursue his solo career in name as well as in fact. After all, everyone knew that *he* was Pink Floyd, and they would presumably continue to do so even after he rid himself of that cumbersome alias.

Even for the general public, the writing was already, so to speak, on the wall – in *Rolling Stone*'s 1982 cover story about the film, 'Back in

244

the early seventies, we used to pretend that we were a group . . .' Waters had remarked, 'I started to get very resentful, because I was doing a lot more and yet we were all pretending that *we* were doing it.

'Well, we don't pretend any more. I could work with another drummer and keyboard player very easily, and it's likely that at some point I will.' The future of Pink Floyd, he added, 'depends very much on me'.[10]

David Gilmour, however, saw matters rather differently. Notwithstanding all his differences with Waters – and his refusal to shrink into the role of Roger's unquestioning sideman – he never wanted to see the Pink dinosaur put out to pasture. Dave now insists that he 'always made it absolutely clear to Roger' that he liked being a Floyd and had every intention of remaining one. 'I told him long before he left, "If you go, man, we're carrying on. Make no bones about it, *we would carry on.*" '

Waters just laughed: 'You'll never fucking do it.'

Part Three

COLD COMFORT FOR CHANGE

Chapter 22

Apples and Oranges

The first half of 1984 found the feuding Floyds throwing their full weight behind solo careers. March brought David Gilmour's *About Face* album, and May Roger Waters's *The Pros and Cons of Hitchhiking*, each of which would be showcased in an international tour. And sandwiched between those two releases, albeit attended by far less fanfare, was the reappearance in April of Richard Wright as half of a new recording outfit called Zee.

Wright's collaborator was Dave 'Dee' Harris, formerly of the futurist Birmingham band Fashion. The two were drawn together by a common fascination for the Fairlight – the computerized keyboard wonder that dominates their *Identity* LP with sounds programmed in Rick's home studio, at his Bayswater pied-à-terre, by both Wright and Harris. But it was the latter who claimed the lion's share of the credits (including all the lyrics, lead vocals, and guitars), and Zee's lightweight brand of electrofunk bore little resemblance to anything by Rick's old group. Wright now dismisses *Identity* as 'an experiment that didn't work out'.

The meticulously polished *About Face*, by contrast, marshalled all of Gilmour's musical firepower. To anyone who cared to listen, that familiar-sounding voice and guitar – and the beguiling melodies – made the implicit case that Roger Waters had not, after all, been Pink Floyd's only major contributor. Indeed, such tracks as the almost Gothic 'Until We Sleep' and the mock-symphonic space-out 'Let's Get Metaphysical' sounded far more like vintage Floyd than anything on *The Final Cut*. Midway through the sessions, at Pathé Marconi in Paris, Dave even brought Bob Ezrin in as co-producer.

Other participants included Pino Palladino on fretless bass and Ian Kewley on keyboards (both from the Paul Young Band); Gilmour's 'favourite drummer', Jeff Porcaro of Toto; and his legendary peers Steve Winwood and Pete Townshend, who contributed, respectively, keyboards and lyrics on two songs apiece. Dave traces Townshend's involvement to their encounter some eighteen months earlier at Eel

247

Pie studios, where the Floyd were working on *The Final Cut*: 'He stopped me in the corridor to say how much he had enjoyed my first solo album – I thought that was very nice of him – and also he said that if I ever needed any help with anything, to give him a ring.

'On that second solo album, I was getting a little stuck for words, as is my wont. I told Bob about Pete, and he said, "Go on, call him up, what do you have to lose?" So I called him and said, "Fancy writing a couple of lyrics?" He said, "Sure, love to, send down the tape." He sent back the first run of lyrics the next day; he'd been up all night working on it. That was "Love on the Air".'

Pete went on to write the words for 'All Lovers are Deranged' and a third piece that Dave didn't use because he couldn't relate to the lyrics personally. 'White City Fighting' would become instead a centrepiece for Townshend's subsequent album produced by Chris Thomas – which in turn was to occasion the next chapter of the two guitar heroes' collaboration. Roy Harper, meanwhile, was also given a shot at fashioning lyrics for the same tune. After Gilmour rejected those as well, Harper would record his version, 'Hope', on his own LP, *Whatever Happened to Jugula?*

Dave ended up penning all the other *About Face* lyrics himself: in this area, too, he seemed anxious to prove himself no lightweight. Several songs pondered the encroachment of aging and death; 'Murder', addressed to John Lennon's assassin, vented Gilmour's sorrow and rage over the killing of the ex-Beatle, whom he had never actually met (not even at Abbey Road). And in the best tradition of internecine megaband polemics – Lennon's anti-McCartney diatribe 'How Do You Sleep?'; Keith Richards's Jagger brush-off 'You Don't Move Me Any More – *About Face* also featured a rueful open letter to Waters titled 'You Know I'm Right'.

Dave even belied his apolitical reputation with a tuneful pair of anti-nuke ballads: 'Cruise', a sarcastic commentary on the Reagan Administration's deployment of Pershing-2 'cruise' missiles on British soil; and 'Out of the Blue', whose end-of-the-world message echoed Roger's more graphic 'Two Suns in the Sunset', from the despised *Final Cut*. 'It's not my big priority to try and write songs with a message', Gilmour acknowledges, 'but I see no more reason to shy away from them than sort of head for them. I find that if you steer yourself in that direction, they come out very contrived and preachy. I don't like those by other people, so I try to avoid them myself. But songs like "Cruise" and "Out of the Blue" definitely do have an observation of political reality.'

For all their ambitious scope, however, Dave's lyrics were hardly *About Face*'s strong point; the ever-vigilant Peter Jenner went so far as to place them in 'the bottom drawer of banal rock-writer lyrics'. Highly articulate in conversation, Gilmour had little knack (as he himself fretted to friends at the time) for capturing a striking image or original thought in verse – let alone conveying any of the 'bite' that Roger had given to Dave's Floyd music.

To publicize his album and subsequent tour, Gilmour subjected himself to a decidedly un-Floydlike media blitz, showering interviews upon everyone from specialized music publications to *People* magazine and *The Wall Street Journal*. He presciently courted MTV, furnishing America's groundbreaking all-music channel with an interview and a pair of videos directed by Storm Thorgerson, whose own artistic focus had latterly progressed from graphic design to filmmaking, under the rubric of Greenback Films. MTV duly accorded heavy rotation to *About Face*'s eyebrow-raisingly funked-out single 'Blue Light' (which was even issued in a disco mix, and would be voted worst-ever solo Floyd number by the readers of *Amazing Pudding*). In yet another promotional gambit, the second 45, 'Love on the Air', was released as a limited-edition picture disc shaped like a valve radio. (These two A-sides, as it happens, were the very tracks that featured Winwood.)

But with Waters having so convincingly fostered the impression that he was Pink, few rock critics would grant *About Face* more than the passing indulgence of, say, a solo LP by the Stones' Bill Wyman or the Who's John Entwistle. *Rolling Stone* awarded Gilmour only a squib-like notice (and a middling three stars), wih Kurt Loder concluding: 'Not bad at all, but – except for Pink Floyd cultists – not essential either.'

Hoping to persuade his constituency otherwise, Gilmour launched a fifteen-week, ten-nation tour – the first ever by a lone Floyd – on 31 March in Dublin. For these performances, Dave was obliged to assemble a whole new team of accompanists, including bassist Micky Feat, Gregg Dechert on keyboards, ex-Manfred Mann (and future Firm) drummer Chris Slade, and Jodi Linscott on percussion. The line-up surprisingly also included Raphael Ravenscroft, whose horns had just graced Roger's solo album, and Mick Ralphs, a neighbour of Gilmour's, as second guitarist. Ralphs was the semilegendary former lead guitarist from Mott the Hoople and Bad Company, and his primary role in this company was to pick out discreet harmony leads behind Dave's solos. 'The main reason for him being here,' said Gilmour, 'is that he asked me if he could come.'

The set list consisted of *About Face* in its entirety, about half the *David Gilmour* album and a mere two Pink classics: *The Wall*'s 'Run Like Hell' and 'Comfortably Numb' (with new Roger-less vocal arrangements that would come in most handy when Dave set out to reconstitute a Roger-less Floyd). The show also incorporated a scaled-down complement of strobes, slides, and dry ice – almost a poor man's Pink Floyd. But the main focus now was on Gilmour, his music, and his hard-hitting new band – which, if nothing else, could cook on a good night in a way that the more cerebral Floyd rarely even attempted.

On 30 April both Rick Wright and Nick Mason attended the last of Dave's three sold-out concerts at London's Hammersmith Odeon, and Nick sat in on drums for 'Comfortably Numb'. This triumphant homecoming, which also featured a guest vocal from Roy Harper on 'Short and Sweet', would be broadcast by MTV – whose crew had previously trailed Gilmour across France for a separate tour documentary – as a 'Saturday Night Special' stereo-simulcast by radio stations across the U.S. The two MTV films would also be marketed Stateside on the CBS/Fox videocassette, *David Gilmour*.

The following night, however, only about 200 people turned out for Gilmour's performance at the Odeon in Birmingham, where his new protégés the Dream Academy served as his opening act. 'It was depressing for me,' Dave confessed to Andy Mabbett, 'to go to Birmingham and not sell out one smallish cinema. Similarly round Europe . . . we sold 800 seats in Brussels. It's fine . . . if people don't want it – but I'm not going to keep flogging it.'

The Gilmour roadshow then hit North America, where discouraging ticket sales had forced cancellation of some of the initial Canadian dates. In general, however, the MTV-watching Yanks – for whom Dave added a third Floyd tune, 'Money' – were more responsive than their NATO brethren, enabling the show finally to turn a small profit. The *About Face* tour ended at New York's open-air Pier 84 on 16 July 1984 – as the fates would have it, the very date that Roger Waters launched his tour in Stockholm.

On the face of it, the *Pros and Cons of Hitchhiking* album featured much the same ingredients as that 'Pink Floyd' opus *The Final Cut*. There was Andy Bown on organ, Ray Cooper on percussion, and Raff Ravenscroft on horns. Once again, Michael Kamen not only co-produced, and tickled the ivories, but conducted and arranged the National Philharmonic Orchestra (a service that he also rendered for Dave's 'Let's Get Metaphysical'). Even the Holophonics made a reappearance.

Indeed, the only missing components were Nick Mason – whose place was taken by the same Andy Newmark who had bumped him from *The Final Cut*'s final cut – and David Gilmour. And, in a stunning coup calculated to insure that no one would regret Dave's absence, *Pros and Cons* boasted in his stead the greatest electric guitarist in all of Great Britain, the man whom the Pink Floyd themselves had idolized back in his Cream days – Eric Clapton.

Clapton's participation came about through Carolyne Waters's warm friendship with Eric's wife, Pattie Boyd Harrison Clapton. According to one Clapton intimate, the guitarist impulsively agreed to grace the *Pros and Cons* album and tour at the end of a night-long drinking spree with Roger. Eric's disapproving manager, colleagues, and friends argued that it made no sense, from a musical or a career standpoint, for a major name like Clapton to take a supporting role in some arty theatrical conceit light years removed from his blues roots. But 'Slowhand', who was as stubborn as he was loyal – and who had long romanticized the notion of playing anonymously in another man's band (witness his stint with Delaney and Bonnie after Blind Faith broke up) – insisted on honouring his commitment to Waters.

Roger did not regard the match as so incongruous. The blues, after all, had been his first musical love; in recent years he had built up an impressive collection of old blues sides, rarely listening for pleasure to much else. And on the *Pros and Cons* record he was consciously trying to escape Pink Floyd's lilywhite legacy by incorporating an array of black musical forms and styles. (Whether he had the elusive 'soul' to pull it off convincingly was something else again.)

In the event, Clapton's virtuosity was somewhat constricted by Roger's decision to record the basic tracks on all but the title number before inviting Eric to overdub his guitar and dobro. And with *Pros and Cons* ranking among the wordiest albums in the history of rock and roll, Waters seldom caught his breath long enough for the instrumentalists to do much more than add ornamental touches to his soliloquies.

These consisted of a sequence of dreams within dreams, which are said to befall the sleeping narrator over a period, equal to the length of the album itself, of 42-odd minutes – starting at '4.30 a.m.' (the title of the first song, or dream, which is subtitled 'Apparently They Were

251

Travelling Abroad') and ending with '5.11 a.m. (The Moment of Clarity)'. In the initial dream – so graphically illustrated in the front cover's rear view of a nude bimbo, thumb out to all comers – our freewheeling hero picks up his 'hungry' hitchhiker. By '4.33 a.m.', the young lady is already panting, the narrator reports, '*to feel the power of my engine*'. Come '4.37 a.m.', however, their intimacies are rudely interrupted by the appearance of terrorist Arab castration freaks at the foot of the bed. (Careful with that scimitar, Abdul!)

Our hero and his 'engine', however, remain intact through a series of further nightmares and wet dreams, including a stint on a back-to-nature commune in Wyoming, and a mutually antagonistic encounter with Yoko Ono (*The bitch said something mystical* – '*Herro*').

'Within the context of these dreams,' Waters would later explain, 'the subconscious is weighing up the pros and cons of living with one woman within the framework of a family . . . against the call of the wild, if you like.'[1] In the end, love and matrimony win out: the dreamer is profoundly relieved to discover that he has actually been in his own bed all along, slumbering next to his own dear wife. The last of the album's 370 lines of lyric is '*I couldn't take another moment alone*'.

This extraordinary avalanche of verbiage is marked by an equally astonishing absence of melody. Only towards the end, on the jaunty '5.01 a.m. (The Pros and Cons of Hitch Hiking)' and the soulful '5.06 a.m. (Every Stranger's Eyes)', can one discern the outlines of a recognizable tune.

Even Floyd diehards were at a loss what to make of it all. Was *The Pros and Cons of Hitchhiking* a work of obscure genius too demanding to permit instant appreciation? Or had rampant megalomania eclipsed its maker's ability to distinguish between Great Art and his most private neuroses and puerile doodlings? Or would it all fall into place in live performance? Well, even Lennon had had his *Some Time in New York City*, and Bob Dylan his *Self Portrait* . . .

Some listeners were also distressed by the apparent sexism and misogyny. Feminist groups even organized to rip down *Pros and Cons* posters all over London, on the grounds that the picture of the hitchhiking nymphette amounted to a virtual advertisement for rape.

The reviews were, by and large, no less hostile. Even *Rolling Stone's* Kurt Loder, who had praised *The Final Cut* to the hilt, wrote that *Pros and Cons* reduced 'Waters's customary bile' to 'musical bilge', and that the album would interest only 'postanalytic Pink Floyd fetishists and other highly evolved neurotics . . . I can't imagine that anyone else will sit more than once through this strangely static, faintly hideous record.' After blasting Roger's 'creepy vocal', Loder noted that 'you could count the actual melodies here on Mickey Mouse's fingers' – and suggested that the Floyd's 'most important musical component' was thus revealed to have been, after all, Dave Gilmour ('whose latest solo album assumes new lustre in comparison to this turkey'). The *Rolling Stone* staff underscored Loder's indictment with a rock-bottom rating of one star.

For his touring band, Waters augmented the *Pros and Cons* nucleus of Clapton, Newmark, and Kamen (and backing vocalists Doreen Chanter and Katie Kissoon) with keyboards player Chris Stainton, the ex-King Crimson saxophonist Mel Collins – and Roger's fellow Cambridge High School for Boys alumnus, Tim Renwick. The former Quiver guitarist, who had always regarded Dave as his closest friend in Pink Floyd, says he accepted the job with some 'embarrassment' in light of the friction between Gilmour and Waters.

Tim nonetheless found Roger 'totally charming' during the tour's preliminary stages, when Waters recruited him to help review the Pink Floyd songbook and select which numbers should be featured in the show. (The final choices ran the gamut from 'Set the Controls for the Heart of the Sun' and 'If' to 'Pigs on the Wing' and 'The Gunner's Dream', with three numbers each from *Dark Side*, *Wish You Were Here*, and *The Wall*.) When the actual tour got underway, however, Roger seemed to undergo a 'complete personality change', abruptly metamorphosing from a jovial Jekyll to a haranguing Hyde.

'He's one of these people,' says Renwick, 'who needs to have ultimate control over every single facet of what's going on. I got on with him very well when we were rehearsing, but the moment we hit the road, it was like he was someone else. It was quite demanding working for him.

'There was certainly a lot of tension. I think Roger tends to thrive on it, to create a sort of angst.'

Eric Clapton, of course, was permitted more leeway than the other musicians: 'Being a great improvisor, he would play different stuff every night, play what he felt, and it was great fun playing with him.' Without the easy-going Clapton, says Renwick, 'I suspect things might have got a bit more stringent. He kind of warmed things up a bit.' (In the view of *Rolling Stone* reviewer David Fricke, he also 'nearly stole the show from the special effects team'.)

Eric nonetheless felt increasingly 'stifled' (his word) by the show's rigid choreography, the lack of camaraderie among the players, and

253

the relatively stuffy atmosphere surrounding the tour. After the very first concert, in Stockholm, at a formal celebratory dinner, a hungry Clapton lost patience with the glacially slow service and sent his personal assistant across the road to fetch him a Big Mac and fries. These he devoured with relish while Waters looked on aghast.

Most observers at least found *Pros and Cons* rather more effective in concert than on vinyl, though Fricke still deemed the show 'a petulant echo, a transparent attempt to prove that Roger Waters *was* Pink Floyd'. Following a Pink retrospective augmented by the Floyd's trademark circular screen and many of the original films, Jonathan Park and Mark Fisher's stage set took the form of a giant bedroom, complete with a window and a forty-foot 'working' TV. 'I'm using three 35 mm film projectors behind back progection screens,' Waters explained, 'to create the illusion that we the audience are the hero, in bed in his bedroom, and using that as a basic technique to illustrate the dreams and nightmares that go on.'[2] The films included contributions from Nicolas Roeg, director of *Man Who Fell to Earth*, and animations by Gerald Scarfe in which Roger's lyrical traumas were acted out with comic exaggeration by a sinister Snoopy-esque dog called Reg.

The shows rarely sold out; and even when they did (as at New Jersey's Brendan Byrne Arena), it was because eager scalpers had misjudged the demand – only to be obliged in the end to press their tickets on all comers at half price or less. At the time, Waters professed a philosophical view of the empty seats and frequent cancellations – and the consequences of his own bank account. 'I'm the one who's losing all the money; I'm the one who is underwriting it,' he acknowledged. 'But I have a feeling it was something I *wanted* to do, not *needed* to do . . . I've made a lot of money out of rock and roll. If I lose some doing it, so what.' (By his own estimate, he eventually lost £400,000.)

These remarks, incidentally, were made during a London interview for MTV – Waters having grudgingly accepted that a post-Floyd career would entail flogging his wares in the mass media just like any other rock star. 'If I didn't think it was necessary, I wouldn't be here,' he crisply informed the host of one call-in show. 'I'm not up here for the view.'[3] Hoping to secure airplay for videos promoting his two *Pros and Cons* singles – the title ditty and '5.06 a.m. (Every Stranger's Eves)' – Roger treated an MTV crew to a revealing discussion of his new show, hours before its Earl's Court debut.

But his visitors also wanted a Pink angle, and Waters refused to give them one – responding with a curt 'No' to a question about whether he missed the other Floyds, and snapping, 'This is an area that I don't want to get into,' when the interviewer persisted in asking about *The Wall*. The interview thus ended on a sour note, with the upshot that MTV never aired it – or Roger's vidoes. Over the next few years, Waters, in his turn, would not hesitate to express publicly his low opinion of the fare that MTV *did* broadcast.

In this arena, as in so many others, he provided a study in contrasts with Gilmour, whose early rapport with MTV would be rewarded in spades during the Floyd wars of the late 1980s. The music channel, having since evolved into one of the Rock Biz's most powerful institutions, would give Gilmour's Pink Floyd saturation coverage while virtually freezing Waters out of the picture. The bitter irony was that few 1970s rock-music personages had done more to anticipate – if not precipitate – the 1980s MTV-video revolution than Roger Waters.

'Dave gets more done than Roger,' allows one of the latter's staunchest supporters, 'because he has social grace. Roger has no social grace – everything stays on the surface.' Waters did not – to put it mildly – share Gilmour's effortless knack for making friends and influencing people in the wonderful world of rock and roll.

Public relations aside, later assertions by both Gilmour and Waters concerning their long-term intentions vis-a-vis Pink Floyd are belied to at least some extent by the manner in which they pursued their respective 1984 solo bids. Unlike 1978's *David Gilmour* LP, *About Face* hardly sounds – least of all in its unabashedly 'Floydian' moments – like the work of a man indulging in a temporary departure from his group. Indeed, Gilmour remarked at the time of its release, 'There are three people who are in what is laughingly called the Pink Floyd, and none of us have any plans at the moment to work together on any project.'[4] His tour documentary was even billed *After the Floyd* when it was released on videocassette and included an on-camera reference to Dave, by one of his road crew, as the 'ex-guitarist for Pink Floyd'. Nobody bothered to edit out the 'ex'.

Gilmour, in short, gave his post-Floyd solo career his very best shot; yet even that wasn't enough to boost *About Face* any higher than number thirty-two on the *Billboard* charts, or to help him fill relatively small concert halls. 'I've made this record and done this tour,' he acknowledged, 'to see if it was possible for me to continue without Pink Floyd'.[5] Had the answer proved more resoundingly affirmative, Dave may have felt somewhat less tempted to play his Pink card.

Roger's poor showing, on the other hand, was not entirely a matter of his courageously relinquishing the Floyd mantle only to run up against hostile 'market forces' and a lack of personal name recognition. Faceless as Pink Floyd were, Waters was far and away the band's best-known member; lest anyone miss the connection, the advertising for his performances (unlike Gilmour's) touted the prominent inclusion of 'Old Pink Floyd Stuff'. On top of which, the presence of Eric Clapton alone would normally have been more than enough to guarantee sold out arenas on both sides of the Atlantic.

'I thought,' Waters conceded, 'that out there in Recordland, people did kind of identify me with quite a lot of the work that went into the Floyd . . . [but] the buggers aren't going out and buying the tickets. Which I'm very surprised by.'[6] He could hardly be expected to acknowledge that the underlying reason for much of his audience's disappearance was that *The Pros and Cons of Hitchhiking* (which petered out at number thirty-one on *Billboard*) was, to put it bluntly, such a monumental dud.

In March 1985, after a six-month respite, Roger pressed ahead with a second series of North American dates. This time round the venues, such as New York's Radio City Music Hall, were scaled more realistically; Waters also added 'Another Brick in the Wall' to the programme – something he had previously vowed never to do. Eric Clapton, however, bailed out, taking Tim Renwick with him. (In the end, Renwick would regard the Pros and Cons tour as a 'wonderful break' for having landed him in Eric's own band. Michael Kamen would also collaborate with Clapton, on film and TV scores, and, come 1990, a concerto for guitar and orchestra). Roger replaced the two axemen with singer/songwriter turned guitarist Andy Fairweather-Low (whom Eric himself had recommended on the strength of their stint together on the 1983 ARMS benefit tour inspired by Ronnie Lane) and Jay Stapley.

By this time, the Clapton/Waters relationship had become further complicated by Pattie Clapton's well-publicized friendship with Carolyne Waters's brother Willie Christie. But any ill-will was short-lived; in 1986 Eric and Pattie would even summer together with Roger and Lady Carolyne in the south of France.

There were more lasting strains in Roger's relationship with a record company that refused to support his 1985 return to America, on the grounds that there was no new album to promote. Adding insult to injury, CBS also let it be known that what it really wanted was fresh

Pink Floyd product. True to form, Waters publicly blasted the corporation as 'a machine' with 'no interest in music at all'.

When Nick Mason attended one of Roger's London shows, he not only wasn't invited to play drums on a Floyd oldie, but later let slip that he 'didn't like to hear our music being performed by somebody else. I'd rather we'd done it . . . it made me feel bad to watch it.'[7] Significantly – this was now the autumn of 1985 – Mason also noted that he 'would love to tour again' under the Pink Floyd banner, adding that 'we definitely haven't agreed that it's all over. I think that things have changed because David and myself are interested in revitalizing it, whereas two years ago nobody was . . .' (Mason's frequent racing partner Steve O'Rourke, as it happens, was also more than a bit interested in the idea.)

These tantalizing hints of a Floyd reunion – without Waters, if need be – coincided with the release of a Nick Mason album that, like Wright's, was made in collaboration with a younger musician who tended to dominate the music. While Gilmour and Waters were off failing to conquer the world, Nick and his new partner, Rick Fenn – formerly guitarist with 10cc and Mike Oldfield – had quietly founded a company called Bamboo Music, to produce advertising jingles for the likes of Rothmans cigarettes, Barclays bank, and the HMV record-shop chain. These were so successful that Mason and Fenn decided to try their hand at an album.

Profiles' main impetus, however, was that generous solo-album clause in the Floyd's CBS and EMI contracts. 'They whipped into Britannia Row and did it for peanuts – and did pretty well out of it,' recalls *Profiles* engineer Nick Griffiths. 'But *not* on the basis of actual sales.'

Cementing his alliance with Mason (who is credited as co-composer throughout), David Gilmour gamely sang *Profiles*' nominal single, 'Lie for a Lie'. 'I really like Dave's vocal side,' Nick told Andy Mabbett. 'In a way, on the last [Floyd] albums there hasn't been enough of it – not that this is a substitute . . .' All but one of the other pieces are pleasant synthesized instrumentals that sound as if they had been lifted from the score for a documentary film – which, indeed, some were. Even Griffiths describes *Profiles* as, 'A pretty easygoing album that doesn't do anything at all. Just starts, trundles along, and ends.'

The documentary in question was *Life Could Be a Dream*, director Mike Shackleton's 27-minute profile of . . . Nick Mason. The film opens and closes with scenes of Nick and his Porsche 956 at the 1984

World Endurance Championship Race in Mosport, Canada, where Mason (looking 'every inch the wealthy, middle-aged sportsman', one reporter at the event observed) competed as a member of the Rothmans' Porsche team. During staged flashbacks to his childhood, Nick portrays his own father Bill, driving a 1930 Bentley to a sound-track of the 1954 Crew Cuts hit 'Sh'Boom', newly rerecorded by Mason and Fenn, with 10cc's Eric Stewart on vocals. The drummer is also shown surrounded by model cars in his Highgate study, presenting a selection of archival Pink Floyd photos and home movies. These are capped by the Floyd's 1972 Pompeii performance of 'One of These Days' – under which title a ten-minute edit of the film would be circulated as an in-flight supporting feature. (Mason and Fenn, mean-while, would go on to score the thriller *White of the Eye* directed by Donald Cammell.)

Plugging *Profiles* on a four-day spin around Britain, Nick – who had also recently been appointed 'motoring and exotic transport editor' of *Ritz* magazine – cut a dashing figure as he personally piloted the De Havilland Devon twin-engined executive aeroplane that he jointly owned with David Gilmour. Among the many things they now had in common, the two once and future Floyds had both been taking flying lessons.

'Among players, particularly among British players,' Pete Townshend had declared on MTV's Gilmour documentary, 'he's incredibly highly rated. Adored, I'd say.' For the rest of 1984 and 1985, Dave stepped back from the spotlight to help out on new projects by more than a few of his adoring peers. If some Floyd fans found it surprising that Gilmour should seem so content to play second fiddle to the likes of Townshend and Bryan Ferry, he himself now feels that working with 'some of the great musicians of our time' (and observing how they worked) only strengthened him for the leading role he subsequently assumed.

Rock's biggest event of 1985, the televised transatlantic marathon benefit Live Aid – conceived by Bob Geldof, previously best known around the world as 'Pink' from *The Wall* – featured temporary resurrections of such fractured supergroups as Led Zeppelin and the Who . . . but no Pink Floyd. Though the concerts would inspire Waters to write his most popular solo entry, 'The Tide is Turning (After Live Aid)', the only Floyd represented on stage was Gilmour – in the low-profile role of Bryan Ferry's guitarist.

Dave had recently embellished Ferry's *Boys and Girls* album – a service he would repeat on the lounge lizard's *Bete Noire*. Beyond his ample session fees, Gilmour was rewarded with the devoted friendship of Ferry's keyboards whiz-kid Jon Carin (formerly of the band Industry), whom Dave would soon enlist for a certain project of his own.

In the case of Townshend, Gilmour was initially recruited to play guitar on 'White City Fighting' – the *About Face* reject that Pete had then made a cornerstone of his own *White City* album. 'I was extremely pleased about that,' Dave chuckles, 'because I'm probably the only person who's ever written a song on a Pete Townshend album, apart from Pete.

'I went back to play on that track one day, and he had double-booked by mistake. Simon Phillips was there for something that I wasn't needed on, so Pete found something else for both of us to do. We did a track together, which was "Give Blood". That I was on "Give Blood" as well was an accident.'

White City led in turn to a pair of benefit concerts at London's Brixton Academy in November 1985, where Townshend fronted a motley sixteen-man crew that he dubbed Deep End. In view of Pete's renown as a lead guitarist, Dave's appearance in that role may have discomfited Who aficionados – but not Gilmour himself. 'It's probably every schoolboy guitar player's dream,' he says, 'to play things like "Won't Get Fooled Again" instead of Pete, with Pete singing it. A seriously fun dream.

'He asked me if I would do the shows with him because he wanted to move away from being the guitar hero. He refused point blank to play electric guitar, and people said, "Oh, come on, at least 'Won't Get Fooled Again', strap on a guitar and do it." But he refused, he wanted the whole project to be not "Pete Townshend, guitar hero" but "Pete Townshend, singer, writer, band leader". It was great.' (Pete had also yet to inform the world that his career with the Who had left him partially deaf.)

Gilmour sang two of his own songs – 'Love on the Air' and 'Blue Light' – in the course of Townshend's set of R & B covers, Who hits, and solo favourites. In America the event was preserved for posterity, on both record and videocassette, as *Pete Townshend's Deep End*. (The band would perform a third and final concert the following January, at the Midem festival in Cannes.)

During this period, Dave seemed to be recording with anyone who cared to ask – from the AOR-oriented Supertramp to the

Ezrin-produced 'futurist' band Berlin to the classical guitarist Liona Boyd (whose producer was Michael Kamen). He even lent his talents to a Duran Duran offshoot called Arcadia, featuring Simon LeBon, Roger Taylor, and Nick Rhodes. Also credited on the *So Red the Rose* album – alongside the three teen idols' hairdressers and make-up artists – were the surprising likes of Sting, Herbie Hancock, Roxy Musician Andy Mackay, and Grace Jones. Speaking of whom, Gilmour went so far as to grace *her* album, *Slave to the Rhythm*.

In addition, Dave demonstrated yet again his keen ear for promising new talent, co-producing the Dream Academy's debut album with the trio's principal singer Nick Laird-Clowes, who also shared the songwriting credits with keyboardist Gilbert Gabriel. (The pair's previous band, the Act, had featured lead guitarist Mark Gilmour, whom friends describe as comparably talented but far less driven than his famous brother.) *The Dream Academy* also made use of several *About Face* album and tour veterans, as well as bassist Guy Pratt, who would soon be asked to take the place on the Floyd stage formerly reserved for a certain R. Waters. The cinematic single, 'Life in a Northern Town' – with its opening blast of Floydian wind effects giving way to nostalgically Beatlesque harmonies and layered, almost Spector-like walls of acoustic guitars, cellos, and tympanis – was a deservedly huge hit on both sides of the Atlantic.

The biggest name of all in Gilmour's crowded appointment book was Paul McCartney. Dave (who had first played with Paul in 1979 on Wings' *Back to the Egg*, as part of the all-star 'Rockestra') conjured a soaring Floydian solo for 'No More Lonely Nights', the 1984 hit single from Paul's otherwise catastrophic movie *Give My Regards to Broad Street*. 'He played piano,' Dave recalls, 'did the lead vocal live, cut the whole thing with all the musicians in one three-hour session.' (A third McCartney/Gilmour collaboration – 'We Got Married', would surface in 1989 on the *Flowers in the Dirt* album.)

While Dave was playing with Paul McCartney, Roger agreed to pay tribute to John Lennon on a BBC-TV special commemorating the fifth anniversary of his murder. The programme, called *A Journey in the Life*, showed Waters, joined by Andy Fairweather-Low, in an unprecedented performance of a Lennon Beatles classic. Not only was 'Across the Universe' Roger's first cover in some twenty years, but the visual backdrop, with films of the moon, stars, and comets giving way to psychedelic oil slides, was far more reminiscent of early Pink Floyd than of anything on the Hitchhiking circuit.

This was not, however, to be misconstrued as nostalgia for the group. That very month Waters sent letters to EMI and CBS, officially confirming his departure from Pink Floyd.

Chapter 23

One of These Days

The formal Waters/Floyd split was actually triggered by the tangential matter of Roger's escalating quarrel with Steve O'Rourke over, among other things, contractual commitments for future Pink Floyd product. In June 1985, Waters turned his affairs over to sometime Rolling Stones handler Peter Rudge and terminated (illegally, in Steve's view) his personal management deal with O'Rourke, who was still the manager of the (nonexistent, in Roger's view) Floyd. To get rid of O'Rourke altogether, Waters needed the assent of David Gilmour and Nick Mason. He even offered them, in exchange, the rights to the Pink Floyd name, so convinced was he that they neither could nor would make use of it.

Gilmour and Mason, however, refused to ratify O'Rourke's dismissal. Accordingly, Waters decided to circumvent the issue through the simple means of officially 'leaving' the band or, as his hairsplitting lawyers would later insist, serving 'notice to the record company that he no longer intended to record with Pink Floyd'. He asked EMI and CBS to release him from his contractual obligations as a member of the group. This (in Dave and Nick's view) left the two remaining members with a free hand to confound Roger's scepticism, and reconstitute Pink Floyd without him.

Their secret weapon, meanwhile, was languishing in obscurity in Greece. Richard Wright now divided his time between homes in Rhodes and outside Athens, and a 45-foot yacht called Gala (after his daughter). Since leaving the Floyd, Rick had maintained little ongoing interest in music, the short-lived Zee experiment notwithstanding. 'I was writing little bits and pieces and then leaving them,' he says, 'and I never settled into working hard at something. Half the problem was living in Greece. I met and played with various Greek musicians, which was quite interesting, but didn't do any recordings.'

Yet when he got wind that Dave was contemplating a Roger-less Floyd project, Rick says, 'I realized I had to get back: I was missing it.'

262

Prodded by his new Greek bride, Franka, a fashion designer and former model, Wright approached Gilmour in the summer of 1986 when Dave was on holiday at his own villa in Lindos. 'If you ever need me or want to work with me,' Rick remembers saying, 'I really want to work with you.' Gilmour, recalling Wright's undistinguished performance during the *Wall* sessions, was initially noncommittal.

In the meantime, David Gilmour and Friends had performed a brief set at a benefit for the Colombian Earthquake Relief Fund at London's Royal Albert Hall on 9 February. The 'Friends' included Simon Phillips, Mick Ralphs, Michael Kamen, and Deep End bassist Chucho Merchan, who had suggested the gig in the first place. Dave pointedly opened with his ode to Roger, 'You Know I'm Right', before proceeding to 'Run Like Hell' and 'Comfortably Numb.'

Some Floydophiles in the audience, however, were alarmed by the onetime male model's growing resemblance to their old friend Lulubelle III. Not least of Gilmour's priorities would be to shed a few of those excess pounds before resurfacing in the limelight as the front man of Pink Floyd.

Roger's first project as an officially certified ex-Floyd was a film soundtrack. Right up his Armaggedon alley, *When the Wind Blows* was a heavily ironic feature-length cartoon, based on the book by Raymond Briggs, about a befuddled elderly couple – voices courtesy of John Mills and Peggy Ashcroft – who survive a nuclear attack only to die slowly from the radiation. It is also the sort of thing only a socially-conscious masochist or an author researching a book on Pink Floyd would be likely to want to sit through for nearly an hour and a half.

The opening title song is by David Bowie, who had previously contributed to the film *Snowman* – also written by Briggs and directed by Jimmy Murakimi – and was their original choice to score all of *When the Wind Blows*. But then the Thin White Duke became preoccupied with such celluloid commitments as *Absolute Beginners* and *Labyrinth*, and Waters, who thought Briggs's book was 'very funny and filled a hitherto empty slot in English literature' agreed to take over the job after seeing some early rushes. The Virgin Records soundtrack album additionally features numbers by Genesis, Squeeze, Paul Hardcastle, and the Stranglers' Hugh Cornwell, few of which can be heard in the actual film.

Roger's compositions fill the LP's second side, and include two bona fide songs. Both 'Towers of Faith' (which also failed to survive the movie's final cut) and 'Folded Flags' (heard over the closing credits) are more hard-hitting and focused than anything on *The Pros and Cons of Hitchhiking*, skewering, respectively, the religious rationales for the never-ending strife in the Holy Land, and mindless nationalism and dogma (as personified by a certain 'second-rate actor' who then held high office in Washington DC). ('Towers' also incorporates a swipe at Gilmour, with the repeated phrase '*This is my land*' giving way to '*This is my band*'.) Waters additionally contributed eight snippets of suitably apocalyptic incidental music and *musique concrete*.

When the Wind Blows marked the first occasion Roger billed his accompanists as – wittily enough – 'the Bleeding Heart Band.' Familiar names included guitarist Jay Stapley and saxophonist Mel Collins, plus guest vocalists Paul Carrack (formerly of Squeeze) and Clare 'Great Gig in the Sky' Torry. But Nick Griffiths, who doubled as engineer and co-producer, reports that Waters derived little satisfaction from the finished product: 'Neither Roger nor myself was around when the dub was being done, and they wrecked it. We curse ourselves for it, and now Roger swears he'll never ever again let anyone else make any decision about how his music should be presented.'

When the Wind Blows was, in any case, something of a dry run for Roger's next major project. *Radio K.A.O.S.* found him enlarging upon the theme of nuclear peril (and appropriating the film's recurring phrase 'the powers that be') with a Bleeding Heart Band that now also included Andy Fairweather-Low and the commercially-minded session drummer Graham Broad.

Like *The Wall*, *Radio K.A.O.S.* was simultaneously conceived as a record, a stage show, and a movie (though as of 1990 the nearest thing to the latter has been a short-form video). Dedicated 'to all those who find themselves at the violent end of monetarism', it also has an extraordinarily convoluted (some would say nutty) plot, even by the standard of a Waters concept album, and one that even Roger had to admit was beyond the scope of a single album to convey comprehensibly.

The story's hero – very loosely modelled on Christy Brown, the Irish artist born with cerebral palsy, more recently the subject of the movie *My Left Foot* – is a sort of vegetable savant from an economically depressed mining town in Wales. When his twin brother Benny is jailed for violently protesting against his mine's closure by 'the market forces' Billy is sent to live with an uncle in Los Angeles. Desperately homesick and lonely, he develops an uncanny knack for

264

tuning in to 'Radio Waves' (the title of the first song) without the aid
of a radio. Accessing computers and speech synthesizers, Billy (whom
Waters called 'symbolic of the way it is easy to misjudge people')
finally learns how to speak, and establishes a phone-in relationship
with his favourite rock deejay.

Radio K.A.O.S. takes the form of a dialogue between Billy and a
renegade Jock based on, and played by, Jim Ladd – whose real-life
station, KMET, was coincidentally on the verge of switching to a slick
disco format and ditching its old staff. According to Waters's press
release, 'Billy and Jim share a concern for the increasing domination
of the market forces over everyday life: the station jockey fears the
total depersonalization of radio, while Billy fears that the misuse of
satellite communications, far from bringing people together, has
brought the earth to the edge of destruction.' And Roger further
feared that 'rampant, unrestricted market forces are trampling over
everybody's fucking lives and making this world a horrible place to live
in . . .'[1]

Crippled in all but spirit, Billy then not only perfects his weird
talents 'to the point where he can now control the most powerful
computers in the world', but also contrives to teach the planet a lesson
by staging a mock nuclear attack with four minutes' warning. (The
song 'Four Minutes' lasts, in best *Pros and Cons* style, exactly that.)
The cycle climaxes on what *Sounds*' reviewer called 'a tidal wave of
slurpy sentiment' – with 'The Tide is Turning' and its premise that
Bob Geldof's Live Aid concerts had, if only for one day, '*wrested
technology's sword from the hands of the War Lords*'. Well, at least
K.A.O.S.'s listeners would be left with a more hopeful ending than
The Final Cut's.

'Roger's projection is very personal and intense,' allows Nick
Griffiths. 'I've always felt there needs to be a light part, a balance. The
way *The Wall* keeps bashing you over the head with a sledgehammer,
in the end it hurts.

'That's something I always tried to change, in my own way: "It's a
bit miserable, isn't it? Can't we have a happy ending?" Eventually I did
get my way on *Radio K.A.O.S.*'

Roger has said that the project was originally inspired, with the
working title *Home*, by a pair of encounters incidental to the building
of *The Wall*. The first was in LA, which Waters had derided as a
plastic wasteland until he heard (and then met) Jim Ladd. 'I hadn't
expected to hear anything that anarchic, that funny and clever,' he
recalled. 'It made me realize that my prejudices . . . were all

265

unfounded. Which is a lesson that can't be brought home to one often enough: that you cannot generalize about races, creeds, colours, cultures. In all places there are dull people and bright people, nice people and assholes.'[2]

The second inspiration came in Wales, where Roger had travelled to record the Pontardoulais Male Voice Choir for the remake of 'Bring the Boys Back Home' and was 'struck by their enormous humanity'. Like Ladd, they would be prominently featured on the album they helped inspire.

Radio K.A.O.S. would also seem to owe a debt (however unconscious) to the Who of two decades earlier. Not only does Billy's character resemble Tommy's (both develop extrasensory gifts that compensate for their handicaps), but the album's radio-show format harks back to *The Who Sell Out*. Yet LA's imaginary K.A.O.S. is set a generation and a continent away from the pirate Radio London, and Waters was determined to provide his 'station' with his most hard-edged and contemporary-sounding music to date. To that end, he used a Linn drum machine during the songs' composition, and supplemented Nick Griffiths with the notably high-tech producer Ian Ritchie.

Radio K.A.O.S. was recorded in 'the Billiard Room' of Roger's own house in Barnes, West London, a home studio that Griffiths calls 'on par with anything else in the country'. A year in the making – it would finally surface in June 1987 – K.A.O.S. is undoubtedly a far stronger effort than *Pros and Cons*. Yet there is still something rather cold and barren about it, as if the glut of lyrical ideas and surfeit of technology leave no room for the music to breathe.

Griffiths rates the Bleeding Hearts 'a *hot* band – one of the best in the world'. Yet he acknowledges that 'when I'm working on one of Roger's tracks I often feel what's missing is a really good guitar part. And there's only one guitarist who could ever stand up to Roger. Nowadays he's the benevolent dictator who pays his money, and gets what he wants. The Floyd worked because there was some semblance of democracy.

'I'd love to see the Floyd back together because it's been such a terrible waste. The chemistry between the band was such that the sum of the parts was *far* greater than their individual offerings. Dave and Roger complemented one another so well.'

Gilmour, meanwhile, was bent upon proving that Waters needed him more than he (and Pink Floyd) needed Waters. To this end, he was not averse to recruiting a large cast of talented collaborators for the project that would become *A Momentary Lapse of Reason* – evidence, in some critics' view, of the new Floyd's ersatz character. But Dave (and many of his collaborators) would argue that he was simply more generous than Roger about giving credit where credit was due.

Jon Carin cites the example of an 'intro' and chord progression that he had popped up with during a casual session at Dave's home studio soon after their Live Aid appearance. By the time the synth player was recruited to help out on the new album, the piece had acquired words, a tune, and a title – 'Learning to Fly', Carin, who had forgotten writing the chords in the first place, was pleasantly surprised when he was credited as a co-composer – 'Just shows you what kind of a guy David is.'

'When Dave gets involved with different people and situations,' says Carin, 'it brings out different aspects of his personality. Working with [Roxy Music guitarist] Phil Manzanera on "One Slip" he wrote lyrics that he might not have ordinarily written.' As far as Jon is concerned, the post-Waters Floyd songs, their cluttered bylines notwithstanding, are all '99 per cent Dave'.

Gilmour's co-lyricist on 'Learning to Fly' as well as the heartfelt humanitarian ballad 'On the Turning Away' and the rather more facile 'Dogs of War' was Anthony Moore (whose band Slapp Happy, as it happens, was once managed by Peter Jenner). The lyrics of 'Learning to Fly' were inspired by Dave's own flying lessons or, more specifically, 'by the fact that several mornings Anthony would be there hard at work, and I wouldn't show up. I'd call up and tell someone, and they'd say, "Dave's not coming in today 'cause he's learning to fly." '

That, Gilmour says, was 'the starting point' for 'something a bit wider' – in which learning to fly becomes a metaphor for a man's attempt to take flight spiritually as he stares into the *circling sky, Tongue-tied and twisted, just an earthbound misfit, I.*' For all Roger's subsequent digs at *A Momentary Lapse of Reason*'s lyrics, multiplatinum product in the late 1980s rarely got more poetic than that.

But Gilmour's key partner in the new Floyd – artistically, anyway – was Bob Ezrin, who would be rewarded with a generous cut of the album's royalties. Waters charges that Ezrin had actually agreed to produce *K.A.O.S.*, but was then seduced by the greater financial possibilities of what Roger would call 'the Floyd fraud'. Bob, however, said that he got cold feet at the prospect of contending once more with Roger's 'rigid and intense' attitudes; that Gilmour was much more

267

willing than Waters to accommodate the Ezrin family's needs and schedules; and that in the end it was simply 'far easier for Dave and I to do *our* version of a Floyd record'.[3]

Worried nonetheless that no Floyd record would seem complete without a *concept* and unable to dream one up themselves, Gilmour and Ezrin sought the assistance of such potential conceptualizers as 10cc's Eric Stewart (who had just helped a blocked Paul McCartney pull *Press to Play* out of his hat) and the Liverpool poet Roger McGough (who had once worked with Mike McCartney in the group Scaffold); later they would also flirt with Canadian songwriter Carole Pope. But in the end, according to Ezrin, he and Dave 'decided the atmosphere was the most important thing' and settled for a loose 'motif' inspired by the atmosphere in which they were working.[4]

This was the river Thames, where Dave's turn-of-the-century houseboat, the *Astoria*, which he had converted into a recording studio was moored, sixteen miles outside London. The river, said Bob, eventually 'imposed itself' in all the songs. (At one point, these even included a conciliatory farewell to Waters, titled 'Peace Be with You'. Subsequent events, however, were to rule out its appearance on the album.)

In its early stages, no one could even be sure that the project would remain afloat. Gilmour continued to maintain publicly that the tracks (which featured top sessionman Tony Levin in Roger's stead on bass) might wind up on a solo album, or constitute the beginnings of a brand-new band. But a Pink Floyd album was what his record companies were banking upon, and they were less than knocked out by what they heard of the work-in-progress. Dave was read the riot act at a Thames-side luncheon with Ezrin and Stephen Ralbosky from CBS, who allegedly told him, 'This music doesn't sound a fucking thing like Pink Floyd.'

Gilmour's agreement to revamp the material has been variously attributed to a determination by all concerned to meet the highest possible standard of Floydian excellence (Ezrin's explanation) – or to a mounting conspiracy, extending even into the corporate boardrooms, to fabricate the lucrative Pink Floyd sound (Roger's view). In any case, the new Floyd project would ultimately draw upon fifteen crack session musicians (including Madonna's producer Pat Leonard, who also rewrote 'Yet Another Movie') with a further eighteen players and technicians credited in the album's fine print. Its detractors would seize most of all upon the presence of two well-known outside drummers, Carmine Appice and Jim Keltner – Nick Mason having reportedly told Appice that he was too out of practice to handle all the drumming himself. He did, however, take charge of the sound effects, and, lest we forget, now held the distinction of being the only Pink Floyd member to have remained with the group through every phase of its career.

In all fairness to Gilmour and Co., it is easy now to forget that in 1986 few people in the rock world could imagine the Floyd amounting to much without Waters. 'It was quite an onerous task to try and get together a Floyd album,' says Storm Thorgerson, 'and Dave could get terribly knocked for it. He was putting himself up for heavy grabs. It would have been easier to do one of his solo albums, in fact. So I think he wanted all the help he could get.'

'You can't go back,' Gilmour said at the time. 'You have to find a new way of working, of operating and getting on with it. We didn't make this remotely like we've made any other Floyd record. It was different systems, everything.'⁵ Finally making good on their high-tech reputation, the new Floyd was recorded digitally, with many of the individual parts fed into a MIDI system programmed on an Apple Macintosh computer.

By this time, Dave had also come to appreciate that Rick Wright's presence, if only for appearances' sake, could make the new Floyd seem far more credible to the world at large; the line-up would, after all, then boast just as many members of the original quartet as had the last Pink Floyd album. 'I thought it would make us stronger legally and musically,' Gilmour acknowledged to Karl Dallas. (Note the order of priorities there!)

Accordingly, Wright was summoned to the floating studio: as he remembers it, 'Both sides said, we'll see how it goes.' Since all the material was already in the pipeline, and Gilmour, Carin, and Ezrin had put down most of the keyboard parts (including all the sequencers), there wasn't much in any case left for Rick to do. His contribution would consist of some background reinforcement from his Hammond organ and Fender Rhodes piano, plus a few vocal harmonies. Wright's one solo (in 'On the Turning Away') was ulti-mately dropped from the mix – 'not because they didn't like it,' he says. 'They just thought it didn't fit.' (Ezrin and Carin fared little better with an ambitious orchestral score that they had composed and recorded for the same tune. Gilmour decided that didn't fit either.)

Dave later told a BBC-TV reporter, 'The first day when the three of us got back together . . . it was like putting on a comfortable old pair of shoes.' Setting aside for the moment the extent of Nick and Rick's actual contribution – which Mason acknowledged was dwarfed by Gilmour's, wryly adding that Dave 'also invented the wheel and wrote all the material for the Beatles' – the three longtime Floyds *were* compatible insofar as they were all similarly 'laid back', musically as well as temperamentally. On the old albums, in fact, Gilmour and Mason had tended to play *behind* the bear, in contrast with Waters, whose aggressiveness had always set him apart from the rest of the group. (Note how Roger's tempos picked up after he went solo.)

Nick did join Dave on stage – briefly – in March 1987 at an Amnesty International benefit, *The Secret Policeman's Third Ball*, for an all-star finale of Bob Dylan's 'I Shall Be Released'. But that did not stop Gilmour, who also served as Kate Bush's guitarist, from using the occasion to scout for a Floyd percussionist. Gary Wallis, who played with Nik Kershaw, was vaguely aware of someone 'standing next to me, checking me out over my shoulder. I didn't know who he was, and I just carried on doing the sound check. The next thing I knew, I got a call – "Do you want to go on tour with Pink Floyd?" '

As for Wright, his rehabilitation would not extend to being reinstated as a full Floyd member and partner (partly, he said, on the advice of his own lawyers, who warned that he would then be vulnerable to anti-Floyd lawsuits from Waters; partly, admitted Gilmour, because he and Mason 'didn't particularly want to get in extra partners – we had put up the money and taken all the big risks, and so wanted to take the largest cut'). Instead, Rick was placed on a wage, amounting to $11,000 a week by the time the band hit the road. He was also guaranteed a few 'points' of the new Floyd's recordings and merchandising.

Roger's darkest suspicions were confirmed at an autumn board meeting of Pink Floyd Music Ltd (the clearing-house since 1973 for all Floyd-related financial transactions, with O'Rourke, Waters, Gilmour, Mason, and Wright serving as joint directors and shareholders) where he learned of the opening of a new bank account to pay out and receive money on 'the new Pink Floyd project'. At that, Roger launched the opening shot of the Floyd war that one nameless associate summed up as 'Waters's megalomania versus Gilmour's pent-up frustrations, superheated into a rage for simple vengeance'.[7] On Halloween 1986, Roger initiated High Court proceedings to dissolve the group partnership and thereby terminate the group once and for all.

270

Pink Floyd had, Waters argued, 'become a spent force creatively, and this should be recognized in order to maintain the integrity and reputation of the group name . . . It is only realistic and honest to admit that the group has in practical terms disbanded and should be allowed to retire gracefully from the music scene'. When Roger's lawyers discovered that the partnership's existence had never actually been confirmed in writing – which meant that its dissolution could have little impact on Gilmour and company's plans – they went back to the High Court seeking a 'clarification' to establish that Pink Floyd Music, insofar as it existed for the benefit of the entire band, 'must act in accordance with the unanimous wishes of the group'. Such a ruling would have given Waters the power to veto any further use of the Pink Floyd name.

With these actions, of course, Waters had moved 180 degrees from his earlier offer to let Gilmour and Mason keep the name – which he later said he had made 'for the sake of a quiet life' without full consideration of the ethical issues involved. He was also goaded by O'Rourke's suit against him, initiated four months earlier, demanding £25,000 in back commissions.

Gilmour's team responded with a press release of their own: 'The strength of Pink Floyd always lay in the talents of all four members. Naturally we will miss Roger's artistic input. However, we will continue to work together, as in the past . . . We are surprised Roger thinks the band is "a spent force creatively" as he's had no involvement with the current project. The three of us are very excited by the new material and we would prefer to be judged by the public on the strength of the forthcoming Pink Floyd album.'

Less decorously, Dave told a *Sunday Times* reporter: 'Roger is a dog in the manger and I'm going to fight him . . . No one else has claimed Pink Floyd was entirely them. Anybody who does is extremely arrogant.'

'There's been very few times in Roger's life,' Nick Mason later observed, 'where he's been badly crossed in terms of getting his own way and doing what he wanted, and I think he was flabbergasted by what happened. He really *believed* that we couldn't do it without him. He *believes* he did it all. That's always a problem when you're dealing with people who *believe*.'[8]

Peter Jenner was not alone in detecting a certain irony 'when Roger said he was going to go solo and there was no more Pink Floyd. It seemed to me that *Syd* had left, and they'd continued, and nobody minded about that. It was Syd's band – *he* was the creative driving force – yet they'd gone on calling themselves the Pink Floyd, playing Syd's songs and developing Syd's work, essentially. So if Roger went and the others stayed – well, fine, that's *his* decision.

'In the same way that I'd said "They can't do it without Syd," Roger's now saying, "they can't do it without *me*." It's wonderful, after twenty years of me getting stick from Roger for that, which always came out quite malevolently.'

'The fact of the matter,' says Gilmour, 'is with Roger gone, I'm the only one there to pick up that mantle and bear it. If I don't want to throw away twenty years of my hard work and start again with my solo career, this is what I had to do. Starting with only my solo career would be the nicest thing in some ways; it's very nice to be totally free to do exactly what you want when you want to do it. But people don't know my name. I haven't spent twenty years building up my name, I've spent twenty years building up Pink Floyd's name.'

On 10 November 1986, EMI issued its own statement: 'Pink Floyd is alive, well, and recording in England.'

Chapter 24
Us and Them

The title of the new Pink Floyd album remained a matter of debate almost until the last possible moment, when *Of Promises Broken, Signs of Life,* and *Delusions of Maturity* finally gave way to *A Momentary Lapse of Reason* (a phrase from 'One Slip'), despite David Gilmour's concern that it might be 'too much of a mouthful for a pop record'. It also provided a ready target for Roger Waters's sarcasm – but then so too would have any of the alternatives.

For the icing on his cake, Dave got Storm Thorgerson to conjure a cover, just like in the old days. Though Storm hadn't done one in five years and was initially approached in his 1980s role of film-maker, to create videos to accompany the new material in concert, his surreal vision of hospital beds lined up on a beach would give *A Momentary Lapse of Reason* its final veneer of Floydian authenticity.

Thorgerson's striking image grew out of the phrase *'visions of an empty bed'* (from 'Yet Another Movie') and Gilmour's vague request for 'a bed in a Mediterranean house, with vestiges of relationships that have evaporated, leaving only echoes'. This sparked Storm's suggestion that 'instead of vestiges, we should have lots of beds. I just thought it would be pretty amazing to see 800 beds sitting in line.' His partner Colin Elgie then 'turned my image into a river of beds.' Which might in turn be seen as a sly inversion of 'the bed of a river' – thereby tying the image back into the album's 'river motif'.

'It was absolute hell to do,' says Thorgerson. 'All at once it rained – 800 beds, all out, made up – and then we had to take them back in again. But it works really well – people smile when they see it. 'Cause it's not faked, and people know when they look at the picture that it's real.'

Released in 1987, *A Momentary Lapse of Reason* not only looked like a Floyd album, it sounded more like the classic Floyd of *Wish You Were Here* than anything since then: a return, in the words of *Sounds'* Hugh

Fielder, 'back over the wall to where diamonds are crazy, moons have dark sides, and mothers have atom hearts'. And to many longtime Floyd buffs – not just those casual consumers who couldn't distinguish Roger Waters or Dave Gilmour from Adam – *Momentary Lapse* also sounded surpassingly good, and far more immediately seductive than *Radio K.A.O.S.*

Unlike Roger's album, moreover, it was an instant and massive commercial success, zooming to number three in *Billboard* and eventually selling over three million copies in the U.S. alone. Such statistics reflected more than just the Pink brand name, or even the hoopla of the subsequent Floyd tour; David Bowie, after all, had just sold out arenas across America and yet his latest album had sunk without a trace. *Momentary Lapse*'s popularity, in fact, came as a surprise to most people on the music scene, who had long equated Waters with Pink yet failed to notice that Dave's *About Face* had actually sounded more 'Floydian' than the Floyd's own *Final Cut*, let alone Roger's *Pros and Cons of Hitchhiking*.

Indeed, Gilmour took to presenting *Momentary Lapse* as a restoration of the true Floyd spirit. 'I had a number of problems with the direction of the band in our recent past, before Roger left,' he said. 'I thought the songs were very wordy – and that, because the specific meanings of those words were so important, the music became a mere vehicle for lyrics, and not a very inspiring one . . .

'*The Dark Side of the Moon* and *Wish You Were Here* were so successful not just because of Roger's contributions, but also because there was a better balance between the music and the lyrics than there has been in more recent albums. That's what I'm trying to do with *A Momentary Lapse of Reason* – focus more on the music, restore the balance.'[1]

Then again, one could also find something to admire in the fact that Roger Waters was never much interested in restoring anything. Nor has he ever lacked the courage of his convictions, even if that meant steering Pink Floyd away from what the fans expected, and finally abandoning the group altogether. 'He's continually developing his artistic side – or his obsessions, if you like,' affirms set designer Jonathan Park, who (along with Mark Fisher) refused any part in Gilmour's Floyd revival tour, much preferring the post-Pink challenge of *K.A.O.S.* The dispute between the restless Waters and his relatively complacent ex-colleagues was, as much as anything else, over the question of whether it was desirable – or possible – to recreate the glories of their common past.

274

Lapse of Reason's arrival hot on the heels of *Radio K.A.O.S.*, with competing tours to match, triggered a sharp escalation of hostilities as both camps pressed their cases in the media. Thus was Pink Floyd's inscrutable anonymity shattered once and for all in the crossfire of attacks and counterattacks.

'You'd almost forget this was a rock and roll band,' marvels David Fricke, who wove both sides of the vindictive feud into a *Rolling Stone* cover story. 'It was more like Martin Luther and the true meaning of the Cross.' It also made for riveting copy: the 'Floyd issue' became *Rolling Stone*'s biggest seller of 1987.

Lapse of Reason was a 'forgery', Waters told Fricke; 'If one of us was going to be called Pink Floyd, it's me.' His ex-colleagues were only in it for the money, he charged on Britain's Radio Clyde; 'I personally think it's despicable. Don't get me wrong – I've loved Pink Floyd. I feel very, very passionately hurt by what's going on now. I think it should have been allowed gracefully to remain what it was, which was a serious rock band, trying to do good work until it fell apart. And when it fell apart, it should have been left, as far as I'm concerned. But the lure of the dollar is a very powerful lure.'

According to Dave, 'Roger sent letters out to every promoter in North America saying he would sue them if they put our tickets on sale, and put an injunction on them to prevent them – seal the bank accounts and all that stuff . . .

'We spent a lot of money fighting him. We had to have a team of lawyers in every city ready and briefed in case it was suddenly in front of a judge and we had to get someone there in twenty minutes. It never happened, but we had to be prepared for it.'[2]

Gilmour and Mason's reprisals often took the form of offhand wisecracks. When, for instance, a reporter happened to ask Nick his worst nightmare, he offered 'Roger back in Pink Floyd!' And Dave, after stressing that the outwardly sombre Floyd always did have a sense of humour, added: 'I mean, Roger laughed at least once a year.'

In making their case to journalists, it hardly hurt that Gilmour and Mason (by whom Waters felt particularly betrayed) were inherently more affable and accommodating than their opponent. The favourable press coverage, in turn, played some part in their emergence as the clear victors in the battle for the hearts and minds – and pockets – of the Pink Floyd constituency. At which point they could well afford to be relatively temperate in their criticisms of Waters.

Roger did have his advocates, notably the broadcaster and former *Rolling Stone* editor Timothy White, who wrote a sharply pro-Waters

275

exposé for *Penthouse*. 'In terms of this Floyd controversy,' he ventures, 'I view Roger Waters as a personality tangled up in hurt and his own sadly conflicted sense of propriety; like many very sensitive people, Roger doesn't always know how to fight effectively. By contrast, I perceive in Gilmour the wire-pulling flair of an efficient and spiteful field marshall; therein his strength in the current fray.'

Their fight almost literally descended to the sewer with a report in the *Sun* that Waters had 'paid an artist to make 150 toilet rolls with Gilmour's face on every sheet'. While Rupert Murdoch's scandal rag was not the most reliable source of news, the story did underscore just how nasty – and how public – the Floyd war had become.

'If one's kids behaved like that, fought in public like we have,' Nick Mason quips, 'I'd be very, very cross with them. There would be no pocket money for a week.' He contends that Waters 'wanted the band to finish, and he could have finished it by staying in it. His big mistake was to leave. Because by leaving, suddenly it regenerated itself.

'Roger said it was creatively dead. Quite right, it was. But by leaving it, the ashes suddenly picked up. Dave had been incredibly repressed by Roger, particularly over the last years of Roger wanting to do more and more. There was a whole bunch of stuff waiting to get out, which I don't think Dave even realized.

'Particularly at our advanced age in the music business, when you suddenly really have to fight for something – and you've actually got someone fighting against you – it doesn't half generate a bit of drive. We could have taken five years to make another album, but Roger looking over the gunsights at us made it happen in ten months. The same with the tour. There was absolutely no "maybe we should, maybe we shouldn't". It was "let's do it, *now*, who do we need, how will we do it". It was galvanizing.

'I think most bands work best when they're just that little bit hungry, when they want to prove themselves. That's why young bands are always so much hotter. The group spirit is there. Everyone wants to get on with it, do it together. It all turns sour later when they're worrying about who did what, and who's really the leader of the band, and can they buy another house in the south of France.'

Gilmour and Mason did agree to let Waters have sole jurisdiction over everything relating to *The Wall* show. Ultimately, however, Roger would be forced to concede 'that the only case that the law is interested in me bringing is one saying, "Well, if you go on calling yourself Pink Floyd I demand that you pay me 20 or 25 per cent of the

276

cake." I'm not interested in the cake! So I don't think there's very much that I can do.'[3]

While wrapping up work on their album, Gilmour and Mason spent five months devising the staging of the new Floyd show with lighting designer Marc Brickman, production director (and longtime Britannia Row boss) Robbie Williams, and set designer Paul Staples. The cost of mounting the tour ran to over $3 million – much of which Dave and Nick had to raise out of their own pockets. Even Steve O'Rourke was not yet sufficiently convinced to invest any of his own cash.

Gilmour says that he and Mason 'typed up lists of titles from the first record onward right through. Every title, we'd tick against them reasons for doing them or not doing them. Like if I sang or co-wrote it, Rick co-wrote it, whatever. Or if we had a great piece of film to go with it. Or if it was a great song.' His lead vocals, he notes, were originally featured on all but three of the final choices: 'Shine on You Crazy Diamond', 'Another Brick in the Wall (Part 2)', and 'Run Like Hell'.

The original plan had been to perform *The Dark Side of the Moon* in its entirety on selected dates, but, Mason says, it 'wasn't satisfactory when you're moving from city to city to do that because it's not a broad enough view of our library of work. People would have been disappointed to miss out on stuff from *Wish You Were Here* and *The Wall*, and it didn't feel right to switch back. But I still like it as an idea for the future.'

In the end, nothing at all was chosen from *The Final Cut* (no surprise there), or *Animals* – though 'Sheep' came close, and the famous forty-foot pig, at least, would put in an appearance. (Albeit with a sex change – Dave and Nick having conspired to circumvent Roger's copyright on the original pig concept by equipping 'her' with a Brobdingnagian pair of balls.) The pre-*Dark Side* years were represented only by 'One of These Days' and the concerts' short-lived opener, 'Echoes' – though the band did make 'Arnold Layne' a staple of their afternoon sound checks.

'There's something about a lot of the earlier material,' says Mason, 'that's just a bit *too* early, that feels dated – perhaps lyrically.' Even when they performed the ecstatically received 'Echoes', he notes, 'Dave didn't really feel comfortable singing about albatrosses and sunshine. It was just a bit too sort of . . .' The droll drummer chuckles and rolls his eyes.

277

'I love "Astronomy Dominé". The trouble is, you're right back into the I Ching and interstellar exploration. I think that's something Dave would have some problem with as he approaches dignified middle age, shrieking out this information to the audience. It's easier to talk about how hard life is and how depressed one gets.'

That, of course, had long been Roger's specialty. Gilmour insists that the bad blood between him and Waters never affected his appreciation for, and identification with, his rival's lyrics: 'Why should I suddenly feel strange about singing a lyric I didn't feel strange about singing for ten years? They are very good lyrics, that I agree with and can feel for myself. I'd have been proud to write some of those lyrics.

'Even the songs that Roger supposedly wrote by himself,' he adds, 'it's never the full story. You can never say exactly what happened when that record was made. The whole ending part of "Another Brick in the Wall (Part 2)", he didn't write the guitar solo or the chords in that section. He didn't make up the drum parts, the rhythm. I'm not going to abandon something I've worked really hard on, or feel I had something major to do with, just because it says Roger wrote it. Life is too short.'

For instrumental support, Gilmour tapped his old friend Tim Renwick on second guitar; Jon Carin on keyboards; Scott Page (who had also graced *Momentary Lapse*) on saxophone; Guy Pratt on bass; and Gary Wallis on percussion, plus back-up singers Margaret Taylor and Rachel Fury. 'Dave has an incredible character judgement,' says Carin. 'He picks people not because they're technical musicians but because they have a certain gift that he responds to. We all know how to play, but the big priority is that we can tune in to a certain mood or atmosphere. I think that's what Pink Floyd has always been about.

'If it had been anyone else – even Led Zeppelin – I wouldn't have done it because I was so adamant about doing my own album. But I liked David so much – and the Floyd's music – that I said, I'll just do one leg. Next thing I knew, I was a 78-year-old man, *still* playing with the Floyd!'

Such talk cuts little ice with Timothy White. 'It's as if Paul McCartney had elected to continue the Beatles with perhaps Ringo plus a revolving cast of characters,' he charges. 'In other words, say, after the Beatles broke up and while John Lennon was still living, McCartney decided that his solo career with Wings wasn't successful enough and decided to hire Ringo and call it the Beatles. *That*, to me, is what the new so-called Pink Floyd is like.

278

'The current musical infantry under the Floyd banner raises the question of what constitutes a genuine *band*. Tim Renwick plays guitar, Guy Pratt plays bass, Jon Carin plays synthesizers – yet this band is still supposed to be Pink Floyd.

'All concerned are in my opinion coasting largely on the past, cashing in for all it's worth, and sharing few organic creative goals that I can honestly discern. I think it's time the public began asking itself what separates the integrity of a band's performances in concert and in the control room from a Disney-world special effects display with a cast of dozens.'

Then again, the revived Who and Rolling Stones would stage 1989 stadium extravaganzas with similarly augmented personnel. Beyond the fact that neither Keith Moon nor Brian Jones was still alive to bitch about it, the more pertinent question here may be the one Roger Waters had posed, years earlier, in *The Wall* (particularly 'In the Flesh'): whether or not such megatours are inherently so dehumanizing that, to much of the audience, it scarcely matters who is (or isn't) onstage.

Under a cloak of secrecy, the new Floyd rehearsed their show for four weeks at Toronto's Pearson International Airport, in a suitably spacious Canadian Airlines hangar whose 'bonded' status freed the band from paying the usual customs duty on sound equipment. The Floyd did whet the fans' appetites with televised hints that something spectacular was in the works. 'No half measures,' Dave promised. 'If you're going to do it big, make it *big*.' Added Mason: 'There's no point at our advanced age of doing an average show. I mean, then why bother?'

On 15 August, Waters hit town with his *Radio K.A.O.S.* tour, which he had launched in Providence, Rhode Island only three days before. Unamused by the coincidence, Roger ordered that no one from the rival Floyd camp be allowed in. That night, Toronto's Kingswood Music Theatre was patrolled by members of his crew who had once worked with Pink Floyd, and could thus recognize any former colleagues who might have thrown in their lot with Gilmour's faction. Scott Page, however, managed to slip through the dragnet because nobody knew what the new Floyd's sax player looked like.

'It was a good show,' he allows. 'It had a lot of concept, and Roger was surrounded with all kinds of great guys.' Namely, Andy Fairweather-Low, Jay Stapley, Mel Collins, Paul Carrack (who

279

actually sang such former Gilmour showcases as 'Money'), and Graham Broad. The report Page brought back to Pearson Airport was nonetheless tinged with relief: 'It didn't *sound* like Pink Floyd at all. All the tunes that they did sounded like *funk* tunes. The magic was not happening.'

Less biased observers often felt it *was* happening, albeit in a thoroughly post-Pink way. *Rolling Stone*'s Fricke hailed the 'art-bop thrills' of Roger's 'Armageddon radio play' as 'a significant personal victory' in the Floyd wars. Like the album, the show took the format of a 'Radio K.A.O.S.' broadcast, complete with spoofy 'commercials' and compered by deejay Jim Ladd – who would pointedly sign off on old Floyd tunes with the phrase 'words and music by Roger Waters'. There was even a telephone in the audience, enabling fans to 'call in', Billy-style, with questions and requests. (And Waters, whose late-1980s image incorporated tailored silk suits and street-cool shades, was certainly looking a lot sharper than his ex-mates.)

From the perspective of set designer Jonathan Park, '*Pros and Cons* was a breakaway from the Floyd; Roger was finding his feet and I'm not sure the show was completely successful. But for *K.A.O.S.* he had everything in focus – the music, the artistic side, his obsessions.' Yet like the *Pros and Cons* tour – and unlike the Floyd competition – the *K.A.O.S.* cavalcade was unaccompanied by any stampede to the box office. 'I'm competing against myself and I'm losing,' Waters acknowledged. He nevertheless professed himself satisfied that 'the connections one makes in quality make up for the ones you make in quantity'.[4]

If Roger's attitude towards his ex-colleagues had yet to mellow – he let one 'caller' know that he now kept Gilmour in mind when singing the first section of the venomous 'Pigs' (much as Margaret Thatcher had displaced Mary Whitehouse in the second) – Waters had at least grown far more tolerant of his fans. (Except for one who was refused an autograph when Roger saw that the proferred copy of *The Wall* had already been signed by Dave, Nick, and Rick.) 'I actually find myself going down and sort of touching the people in the front row, and weird things like that . . .' he confessed. 'I am past the stage now in my career where I expect the audience to cop what's going on, even slightly.'[5]

Roger even appeared to be enjoying himself on stage. The rock and roll fascist routine on 'In the Flesh', for instance, was belied by the broad grin on his face when he sang, '*He don't look right to me, get him up against the wall!*' The 'queers' and 'coons' thus singled out for the firing squad seemed, in turn, positively to revel in the spotlight. *The Wall* had indeed been turned inside out, all that angst and alienation having in the fullness of time ripened into nostalgic camp.

Waters was so pleased with both *Radio K.A.O.S.* and his Bleeding Heart Band that he lost no time in putting down tracks – both in his Billiard Room, and at Nassau's Compass Point Studios between legs of his tour – chronicling the further adventures of Billy and Jim. The title, another jab at his ex-band, was *Amused to Death*. 'Radio K.A.O.S. was hopefully universal in its pained concern.' Roger told Timothy White, 'but my new album's themes involve anguish in my own backyard.'[6]

Gerald Scarfe, who had had no part in the computerized graphics of the *K.A.O.S.* album and tour, weighed in with an *Amused to Death* cover depicting three familiar-looking gentlemen drowning in a giant martini glass. But word of an early 1989 release would prove premature; Waters proceeded to break with his record companies (reportedly over the presence on their roster of a band called Pink Floyd), and his album was indefinitely shelved.

Roger's former colleagues, meanwhile, cleaned up big. Progressing from arenas to stadiums and domes, the 1987 Pink Floyd World Tour (launched in Ottawa on 9 September) was extended through 1988, and then, by popular demand, well into 1989. And much as Waters might disparage the shows as 'all gravy and no meat' and harass the players with legalistic gambits including a writ demanding $35,295 in copyright fees for his original pig concept, the band's ex-leader increasingly seemed less a threat than a nuisance to the new Pink Floyd.

In New York, the Floyd followed one of their arena concerts with an unannounced 3 a.m. performance in the cellar of the far-East Village nightspot, The World. The band's customary set list was scrapped in favour of 'Been Down So Long It Looks Like Up to Me', 'Respect', 'Born Under a Bad Sign', 'I Heard It Through the Grapevine', 'Kansas City', and 'Living for the City' (plus some untitled blues jams). Other stops on the neverending tour were in for similar surprises. 'It keeps us out of a rut,' explained the man who had once fronted an R and B cover band called Jokers Wild, 'and gives us a chance to enjoy ourselves.'

In Atlanta, Gilmour added to the line-up a third female singer, Durga McBroom, without even auditioning her beforehand, on the strength of her photograph and the Nile Rogers album cited in her resumee. It was Dave's whim, the black singer explains, to bring 'a bit of colour' to a full-length Floyd concert film. In the end, most of the 1987 Atlanta footage was scrapped,* but Durga stayed, eventually bringing yet more colour to the picture when her sister Lorelei replaced Margaret Taylor.

In Tokyo, the Floyd were obliged to drop 'On the Run' from their performance because their electronic tour de force exceeded the legally permissable levels of power usage. In its place they showcased the three girls on another *Dark Side of the Moon* favourite: 'The Great Gig in the Sky', which Clare Torry had been singing on the *K.A.O.S.* tour. Despite Jim Ladd's 'words and music by Roger Waters' slogan, this was one Floyd classic that had been composed solely by Rick Wright; it would remain a staple of all his band's subsequent performances.

In London, the Floyd marked their homecoming with an outdoor concert on the longest day of 1988 – whose midsummer night's sunshine rendered their lights and films invisible during the first half. (They could hardly move the Wembley Stadium show back an hour; the London underground still stops running at midnight.) Former associates like Joe Boyd (now a leading film producer) and Peter Jenner (still managing up-and-coming bands) felt nonetheless touched that the band had gone to the trouble of mailing them unsolicited tickets.

In Berlin, a Floyd performance by the western side of that wall triggered riots in the eastern side from fans clamouring to get close enough to hear the music. Nobody could yet imagine that in little over a year Berlin's Wall, too, would collapse as utterly as Pink's after his 'Trial'.

In Moscow, where leading indigenous bands like the Araks had long modelled themselves after the Floyd, Dave, Nick, Rick and friends packed the 30,000-capacity Olympic Stadium for five nights in far and away the greatest and most euphorically received rock music spectacle ever staged back in the USSR.

In Venice, 200,000 fans overwhelmed St Mark's Square for a free Pink Floyd concert performed on a floating stage in the Grand Canal. The transformation of these venerable landmarks into a Floydian stage set, in what was variously described as 'the most spectacular concert in

---

* The Atlanta concerts did yield videoclips for 'Dogs of War' and 'On the Turning Away', plus live B-sides of the latter and 'Run Like Hell'.

282

the history of rock' or 'the rape of Venice', was televised all over Europe and much of Asia to a further audience estimated at nearly one hundred million. Despite cash payments of $2 million to the city by Pink Floyd and the Italian government network RAI, and the Floyd's attempt to tone down their amplification from its customary 100 decibels to 60, there was a subsequent storm of protest (largely over the city's failure to provide public toilets, first aid, and sleeping accommodation). Mayor Antonio Casellati and the entire city council resigned: thereby demonstrating that rock and roll can, after all – however inadvertently – bring down a government.

But the Pink Floyd member who might once most have appreciated that had already been banished to a Floydian footnote. Earlier in 1989, the new Floyd had at last released their full-length concert video, re-shot at New York's Nassau Coliseum, and titled *Delicate Sound of Thunder* after the live album, with its suitably outlandish Thorgerson cover depicting the companion Pink Floyd spirits of 'sound' and 'light'. At the film's very end, by which time most viewers will have already hit the rewind button, an acknowledgement (of sorts) finally scrolls across the screen: ORIGINAL PIG CONCEPT BY R. WATERS.

Yet if the remaining Floyds, the Rock Biz, and the world at large had written off Roger Waters, all were in for a stunning surprise. Not that a man so renowned both for his cleverness and for his competitiveness should have been expected to resign himself to permanent eclipse by his former subordinates. But who would have thought that Waters would reclaim the world's spotlight with a *tour de force* that not only lived up to its billing as 'the largest musical production ever', but ranked as a global cultural and political event right up there with Woodstock and Live Aid?

The resurrection of *The Wall* in Berlin on 21 July 1990 came about through an extraordinarily fortuitous convergence of circumstances. The first was Roger's introduction to the 72-year-old British war hero Leonard Cheshire; the most decorated Royal Air Force bomber ever, Group Captain Cheshire had flown more than one hundred sorties over Nazi-occupied Europe, including several to Berlin. He went on to serve as Britain's official observer when the Americans dropped the A-bomb on Nagasaki, effectively ending World War II.

That searing experience helped transform the great warrior into a great humanitarian; on his return to England he founded the first of 265 Cheshire Homes for the disabled. Forty-four years later, in September 1989, he launched his crowning philanthropy, the Memorial Fund for Disaster Relief, with the aim of raising £500 million – £5 in memory of each life lost in all the wars of the twentieth century – to be held in trust for the victims of any future disasters. Hoping to publicize the fund on a grand scale, Cheshire then enlisted Live Aid promoter Mike Worwood – who put him on to Roger Waters.

They established an instant rapport, with Waters finding Cheshire 'extremely impressive', perhaps the only 'true Christian' he had ever known. 'We might seem an unlikely partnership,' allowed Cheshire, 'but there is a connection between us because of Roger's father being killed at Anzio.'[7] Waters agreed in principle to stage a benefit performance of *The Wall*, setting aside his longstanding vow never to resurrect his magnum opus unless and until the Berlin Wall came down (i.e., until hell froze over).

A few weeks later, miraculously, the Berlin Wall did indeed crumble – providing Cheshire and Waters with a godsend of a locale for their benefit, and *The Wall* with more than a few new layers of symbolic significance. Characteristically, Roger cautioned that he was 'in no sense going to Berlin to celebrate what I consider to be a victory of capitalism over socialism . . . I'm going there to celebrate the victory of the individual. . . .'[8]

Yet the resurrection of his *Wall* at Potzdamer Platz – for twenty-nine years a no man's land and killing field separating East from West – was to occasion an ecstatic exorcism not only of the Cold War, but the World War that had preceded it. For Potzdamer Platz was also the site of the infamous bunker where Adolf Hitler, the man who had launched World War II from Berlin (and whose numberless victims had, apropos of *The Wall*, included Roger's own father), died by his own hand on 30 April 1945.

Recasting his autobiographical psychodrama in the manner of the periodic all-star performances of *Tommy*, Waters recruited an unlikely two-dozen of his legendary peers, spanning four decades of rock history – from Joni Mitchell (*Goodbye Blue Sky*) and Van Morrison and the Band (*Comfortably Numb*) through Cyndi Lauper (*Another Brick in the Wall (Part 2)*) and Sinead O'Connor (*Mother*). 'The Trial' alone would be enhanced by five cameo star turns: Tim Curry as the prosecuting lawyer, Thomas Dolby as the teacher, Ute Lamper as the wife, Marianne Faithfull as the mother, and Albert Finney as the judge.

But Roger didn't stop there. With the prestige and influence of Leonard Cheshire at his service, he was able to bring on board an East German symphony orchestra and choir and the 100-piece Marching Band of the Combined Soviet Forces – ideologically balanced with a pair of helicopters from the U.S. 7th Airborne to grace the intro of 'Another Brick in the Wall (Part 2)'. In keeping with the event's grandiose proportions, the new Wall itself measured 550 feet wide and eighty-two feet high. Gerald Scarfe's creepy inflatables were likewise recast to scale – 'the largest puppets ever made'.

With a projected live audience of 200,000 – and tens of millions more watching on TV – and with production costs soaring past $8 million (to be more than recouped through video rights and sales, and an album magnificently co-produced by Nick Griffiths) – Waters was obliged to wriggle out of *The Wall*'s original premise as a statement *against* massive rock concerts. *Over the top* was the order of the day.

Among the few rock icons who did not receive invitations were 'Mr Gilmour' and 'Mr Mason', as Roger now called them ('Mr Wright' was never even mentioned); 'philosophically, politically, physically, and musically,' Waters said, 'we no longer share a point of view. I have no more respect for them.'[9] The Cold War between the superpowers might be over, but the feuding Floyds, it seemed, were as far as ever from settling their differences.

Not that the other Floyds' absence was much remarked during the ecstatic festivities of 21 July. The fans had enough to keep them entranced, what with searchlights buzzing the sky; fireworks exploding overhead; the Soviet Army band oompahing along to 'Bring the Boys Back Home' with the song's title emblazoned upon the Wall in letters six storeys high; and even a new, diabolically improved pig glowering over the Wall while Roger, bedecked in full military regalia, mocked the shade of the Führer with his goose-stepping 'In the Flesh' and 'Run Like Hell'. It was enough to get 200,000 Berliners bellowing along with the final chorus '*Tear down the Wall!*' – art echoing life in one of rock history's finest hours.

Surveying the rubble of his Wall – 2,500 'bricks' all told – Waters allowed that perhaps he wasn't, after all, finished with his magnum opus. 'I can feel a sneaking feeling building up inside me,' he told a reporter from MTV (which was once again eating out of his hand), 'that after all this work it would be a shame if we didn't perform it somewhere else . . .' For Roger Waters, as for the global body politic, the tide – to paraphrase the show's stirring finale – was indeed turning.

285

Epilogue
Wish You Were Here

'This is definitely the biggest thing ever to hit Columbus,' declares one of the 240 clean-cut Ohio State University students whose good grades qualified them for the coveted position of Pink Floyd usher. For the first time ever, rockophobic college authorities have permitted the staging of a concert at their 66-year-old football stadium, and all tickets were snapped up within hours of going on sale on campus. Though the original plan was merely to give OSU's nearly 100,000 students first crack at Ohio Stadium's 63,016 seats, any townies wishing to see the show were left with no choice but to pay scalpers upwards of $40.

Throughout the past twenty-four hours, local stations have been regaling the state capital virtually nonstop with The *Dark Side of the Moon, Wish You Were Here,* and *The Wall.* As the band's minibus with its police escort proceeds through the sprawling campus, groups of jocks – some wearing nothing but electric pink shorts – interrupt their volleyball to cheer and to shake their fists in approval at the smoked windows. On a campus that supported President Reagan's reelection by 72 per cent to 28 per cent, dormitory windows are now festooned with bouquets of pink balloons and announcements of 'post-Pink' parties; and at least one campus bar attempts to lure customers with the promise of pink beer. (At the tour's previous university stop, some students went so far as to repaint their dorms pink.)

In the eye of this storm of Pinkmania are three soft-spoken English gentlemen whose greying hair, unprepossessing appearance and total lack of airs or pretentions would appear the absolute antithesis of anyone's idea of rock superstars. Seemingly oblivious to the antics of their all-American devotees. David Gilmour and Nick Mason talk sport with their debonair manager, Steve O'Rourke, while Rick Wright, quiet as ever, nurses his everpresent cigarette.

A lively rock and roll spirit is far more apparent in the trans-atlantic, multi-ethnic troupe of five supplementary musicians and

287

three back-up singers, who provide a running commentary on the pandemonium swirling all around them. Saxophonist Scott Page even captures it all on videotape. A boisterous and irreverent bunch, some of them were barely out of their playpens when underground London celebrated its Summer of Love to the soundtrack of the Pink Floyd's *The Piper at the Gates of Dawn*. The new Floyd bassist, Guy Pratt, was a teenage Floyd fan not so very long ago, 'going mad in the front rows' during his heroes' Earls Court performances of *The Wall*.

Following a string of open-air concerts in the 'Sun Belt' during which rain was so pervasive that the band had begun calling it the Pink Flood tour, the weather is at last gloriously cooperative. Behind the stadium, thousands of ticketless fans camp out on the playing fields, hoping at least to hear the show. The sole discordant note is provided by 'Christian' picketers brandishing the signs WORSHIP GOD NOT PINK FLOYD SINNERS and REPENT PINK FLOYD IDOLATORS, and chanting slogans linking rock and roll to such ungodly pursuits as homosexuality and drugtaking.

'Have you ever noticed,' observed Guy Pratt, the bassist with the pop star good looks, 'that these anally-retentive bigots are almost invariably ugly?'

'They must act like that because they could never get laid,' cracks Scott Page.

'This is the side of America that really scares me,' says Pratt. 'I can't even watch television when I'm in this country.' The gaunt Rick Wright merely shrugs with the world-weary manner of one who has seen it all many times before.

After the sound check, as the Ohio State hordes begin flooding into their seats, David Gilmour takes a casual tour of inspection of the vast stadium. 'Gilmour is the most aware person ever,' remarks Page. 'He won't say much, and half the time you wonder if he notices what's going on. But he sees *everything*, every little detail to do with the lights, whatever.'

At first it simply doesn't occur to any of the fans that this stocky 42-year-old wandering the aisles could possibly be the leader of the fabled act they have all come to witness. When he is finally recognized, however, Dave signs a few autographs with an air of cheerful resignation.

'He's a very casual guy,' notes second guitarist and longtime friend Tim Renwick. 'Someone like that could get so big-headed, if he wanted to, probably with good justification. But he wanders around, he knows all the crew, and he makes it his business to keep an eye on stuff. Anyone involved in the whole crew could go up to Dave and talk to him about something. He's basically one of the lads – very serious about what he's doing, but able to be low key. He can't really be bothered by bodyguards and all that business.

'He despises all the bullshit showbiz razzmatazz side of things, and has decided not to get trapped in that star syndrome which tends to cut you off from everyone else. I admire him very much for being able to deal with his success like this.'

(Gilmour is, in fact, discreetly watched by one hulking armed guard; in the post-Lennon era, even the relatively anonymous Floyd guitarist has received his share of death threats.)

To see the band's three elder statesmen backstage, whiling away the moments before their show – stuffing their faces at the lavish buffet; reminiscing about Syd Barrett's cats; chuckling at the mordant wise-cracks supplied by New Yorker Howie Hoffman in his paid capacity of 'Ambiance Co-ordinator'; even (in the case of Mason) curling up with a well-thumbed paperback – you might not suppose that these were the stars of the biggest tour in rock history. Biggest, at least, by the measure of its custom-built stage, production effects, and quadrophonic PA system (which fill 56 trucks); the personnel involved (over 100); the time spent on the road (nearly a year now); and the ground covered (approaching 150 shows on three continents, with yet a fourth over the horizon). Not to mention the sizes of the venues and the numbers of tickets sold.

Just after the sun goes down, the Floyd's trademark 32-foot circular screen, now ringed with computer-controlled Vari-Lites, begins to swirl oranges and greens, and the first siren strains of the epic Syd Barrett tribute 'Shine on You Crazy Diamond' resound through the billowing dry ice. Despite the music's languid tempo, the audience seems transfixed to a degree almost unheard-of at a late-1980s rock concert, and drowns each familiar lick in tumultuous applause. 'There is something incredible,' Renwick says later, 'about looking out at 70,000 people and there's no movement, really intense – not like your normal heavy metal gig where everyone's milling around and falling over and throwing up.'

A *Momentary Lapse of Reason*, which occupies the rest of the show's first half, is enhanced by a sequence of Storm Thorgerson films featuring the handsome young actor Langley Iddens. ('Is *he* in Pink Floyd?' a teenage girl in the audience asks eagerly.) After punting down Cambridge's River Cam to appropriately aquatic sound effects from the quadrophonic PA, Iddens trades his boat for

289

a plane that soars out of the screen and across the stadium during 'Learning to Fly'.

From the privileged vantage point of the lighting booth, one wonders how much of any stadium-rock show can possibly register with those numberless anonymous specks a quarter of a mile away from the stage; but at least the Floyd do take their venues' scale very much into account. 'The idea is always to pull the last kid in the last seat of the stadium into the show,' says lighting director Marc Brickman. 'That's also why the stage is so high and wide.' 'The psychology of the quad,' Guy Pratt enthuses after the show, 'is so wonderful because if you're at the back, you've still got stuff going on behind you. You're *inside* the event.'

All the while, computer-operated light banks and four mobile robotic 'Floyd 'droids' cast ever-shifting shapes and colours over the stage. Jets of brilliant laser light shoot over the audience, coalescing into a shining green sea of laser waves for 'Terminal Frost'.

But it is in the second half that the fans get what they really came to hear and see. On 'One of these Days (I'm Going to Cut You Into Little Pieces)' the famous forty-foot inflatable anatomically corrected pig, searchlight eyes glowering, lurches over the cheering crowd whose fervour, if possible, only intensifies when the sounds of alarm bells and ticking clocks announce 'Time', the first of five selections from *The Dark Side of the Moon*. During 'One the Run' Iddens reappears on screen, strapped to a hospital bed, in a revisionist reference to the *Lapse of Reason* album cover; when the piece ends, a giant inflatable bed crashed into the stage in flames.

So it goes through 'Welcome to the Machine', 'Us and Them', and 'Money', each illustrated with vintage mindbending Floyd film footage. And as always, the entire stadium, with no incitement from Gilmour, sings along with him throughout the acoustic 'Wish You Were Here'. The set climaxes with 'Comfortably Numb' (the hands-down favourite of everyone involved in the tour) wherein Brickman inundates the high base of the stage with white smoke – to simulate that moment in the Floyd's famous 1980 concerts when Dave played his big solo atop the Wall – and the largest mirrorball in history splits open to flower into dazzling petals.

For the final encore, 'Run Like Hell', Brickman and his team, unleashing what he calls 'Warp Factor Number 10', pull out all the stops with the special effects; and even the near-full moon is briefly dimmed by the fireworks display that lights up the Columbus skies.

By the time Pink Floyd hit their next city, the tour, heretofore distinguished by its near-military precision and efficiency, has taken such a farcical turn that the band is now calling it Spinal Tap. Nick Mason's passport and computer have mysteriously vanished from his Columbus hotel room; then after the Floyd's private jet lands at the Pittsburgh airport, Rick Wright and the auxiliary musicians and singers are obliged to broil on the tarmac for two hours because someone forgot to arrange for ground transportation. 'This would never happen if Steve were here,' sighs Wright. O'Rourke, along with Gilmour and Mason, have taken the day off to attend the Indiannapolis 500. 'They received us like royalty there,' car-freak Nick reports later. 'On a scale of enjoyment from one to ten, I'd rate the day at least a fifteen.'

Not so for the rest of the musicians. The Floyd's Pittsburgh hotel is hosting, of all things, a convention of blind bowlers; and most of the guests appear to be equipped with metal canes or seeing-eye dogs. In attending to their special needs, the hotel staff has neglected to get the Floyd entourage's rooms ready in time for their arrival.

The following afternoon the chauffeur loses his way during the short drive to Three Rivers Stadium, then ends up driving the band to the stage door full-speed in reverse. It's almost enough to make Dave Gilmour, jolted out of a discussion of a tennis tournament, lose his legendary cool. 'Fucking dickhead,' he curses the oblivious driver. Even the fans' zeal seems to have got slightly out of hand: among such customary Floyd totems as silkscreen banners depicting characters from *The Wall* against the album cover's white brick backdrop, a real pig's head, decked out in sunglasses, leers atop a blood-stained pole.

To cap it all off, the power blows during 'Sorrow', occasioning an unplanned ten-minute intermission. 'That song was getting a bit boring, anyway,' Gilmour drily announces when the sound and lights are restored. 'Let's try another one.' From there on in, the performance proceeds to its usual spectacular form, and 51,101 mostly-young Pittsburghers respond with rapturous ovations.

The day's mishaps have hardly dented the musicians' morale. Amid their tireless clowning, the younger ones repeatedly describe this tour as the greatest experience of their lives, and voice a boundless admiration for and fascination with the man who now runs Pink Floyd. 'David's so consistently fantastic – a real professional,' rhapsodizes synth maestro Jon Carin. 'I've learned more from this than from anything I've ever done.'

'Dave encourages you to play your own thing within his structure,' says percussionist Gary Wallis. 'That's why he employed you, for what *you* do. Some bands, when you fuck up they snarl and give you the bad eye, whereas Dave just laughs. By doing that, you want to correct yourself a lot more.

'The reason we all started to play when we were kids was not for money, but for sheer musical enjoyment. This is definitely like being in your first band again.'

'He's a real thrill seeker,' the voluble Scott Page confides of his deceptively avuncular boss. 'Here we are out on a big giant tour, and the guy is out jetskiing, cableskiing, hang gliding, flying 757s – he wants to be able to do *everything*.

'Every night when we hang with the crew or in the hotel rooms, the conversation *always* comes back to Gilmour. He really affects everybody, in a strange way.'

The saxophonist, who confesses to having heard only one Pink Floyd song ('Another Brick in the Wall') before joining the expanded line-up, now counts himself 'their biggest fan. To me, Gilmour is the *master* of melody. He can kill you with two little notes, every night he's immaculate. Every night the hair stands up on my arm when he plays "Comfortably Numb". Every night I hear him do his thing and my eyes are watering.

'This is the easiest gig I've ever had, as far as there's no pressure. One night we're on the bandstand, and all the synthesizers go down. You'd think Gilmour would be freaking – but he's *laughing*. There's no tension, the guy's not worried about it at all. Big deal. And that kind of low pressure makes it really easy to work.

'Dave's such a positive-thinking guy. So's Nick Mason. It took a while for some of us to realize that Nick brings something that you just can't buy, a style and feel that's a big part of the Pink Floyd magic. Rick, too.'

As to the fourth member of the classic Pink Floyd line-up, everyone, from Gilmour on down, acknowledges that, were it not for Roger Waters, they would never be here. Nobody, however, wishes he were here. Tim Renwick remembers how, on the *Pros and Cons* tour, Waters used to get 'very very obsessive about things. Dave is almost the exact opposite, very very relaxed. He leaves a lot of things up to you, whereas Roger would have very fixed ideas: "You are going to do *this*!" This tour has been much more fun, much more sense of camaraderie, a real group.'

'Roger was just so intense,' says Scott Page. 'You hear the stories of the different camps at the gigs, and the special dressing rooms, and certain people not being able to be around, and getting thrown out – whereas with Dave and Nick it's just real comfortable. Everyone says right now is the happiest time; Gilmour is having the time of his life.

'Poor Roger, I think he's paying reverse dues for all his years of putting the thumb on people, making everybody miserable. Now he has to see the thing go on without him, that he thought couldn't go on. The biggest Pink Floyd tour ever – the biggest tour in the world.'

'This is the happiest tour that I've ever been on,' declares Rick Wright, 'in terms of friendship, and being with the other musicians. After *The Wall*, where the ego trips made life really unbearable, this tour is the opposite. You can tell in the way we play, the way the music is sounding onstage. Nick and Dave are playing better than ever before, partly because of the good feelings we have for each other backstage. This year has gone so fast, and I know when we finish I'm going to miss it.'

As we talk in the hotel lobby, two teenage boys interrupt to ask if we knew which floor Pink Floyd are staying on, saying they've been dreaming for years of getting one of their autographs. When Rick deadpans that he was unaware the Floyd were even at that hotel, the boys glumly wander off.

'There are two advantages to our anonymity, to our never having sold ourselves with our faces,' Wright observes. 'One is that you can walk around the street with no problem. The other advantage, which we're now finding out, is that since nobody looks on us as rock stars we can go out at forty-five and play our music as long as we want, because people have never come to see *us* like they'd go to see Mick Jagger or Rod Stewart. There'll come a time when people won't accept Mick Jagger as a sixty-year-old man prancing around. But I can see now Pink Floyd playing into their seventies. Because a Pink Floyd show is not the individuals, it's the music and the lights.'

Whereupon the two autograph hounds resurface, having finally gleaned the secret of Rick's identity – only to discover that they've left their pens at home. One attempts to stem the embarrassment with, 'What do you think of Roger Waters?'

'He's a very clever man,' Wright replies. And then he takes it upon himself to borrow paper and pen from the front desk so that the boys might have their Pink Floyd autograph.

In Cambridge, tucked away in a cul-de-sac in his semi-detached home, the man who named the Pink Floyd follows a quiet, solitary existence.

Among his everyday hobbies and pastimes, only the unfinished canvases –
painted in a style that is, to say the least, abstract – give any indication that
this is an individual of any exceptional sensibility. The rest of Roger Barrett's
time is whiled away tending his beloved garden and his coin collection;
watching TV and reading (everything from Shakespeare to the daily newspapers to books on home improvement and mathematics); and endlessly
redecorating his cozy Shangri-La. He has not touched a guitar in years, and
the only music he ever listens to is jazz and the classics – never pop or rock
and roll.

This portly, balding, middle-aged man is not entirely unaware of that
other life he led as 'Syd', or of the ongoing fascination others have with his
extinguished alter ego's work and legacy. But any lingering memories are
rarely accompanied by any trace of pleasure or satisfaction – with the
exception, however perverse, of his trip to America, which he is tickled pink
as an old sailor to have visited. As for the rest: it was a difficult and
demanding life that he would never again wish upon anyone, least of all
himself.

Yet Syd's Floyd records continue to bring in more than enough to
subsidize Roger Barrett's modest pleasures and needs; he rarely buys
anything, and money in the bank means nothing to him. Occasionally,
moreover, he does think about his old friends Dave, Rick, Nick and Rog.

Any Syd freaks so presumptuous as to track him down, however, are
likely to find their faces on the receiving end of a slammed door. But though
he seldom ventures beyond the parameters of his English garden, the man
who was once Syd is settled and reasonably content – and almost determi-
nedly ordinary as he works through his simple daily routines.

Sometimes, he even dreams that he will soon be well enough to hold down
a nine to five London office job, and commute every day into the big city.

Selected Discography
with Peak Chart Positions

Pink Floyd   UK singles
Arnold Layne; Candy and a Currant Bun (1967; Columbia DB 8156) **#20***
See Emily Play; The Scarecrow (1967; Columbia DB 8214) **#6**
Apples and Oranges; Paintbox (1967; Columbia DB 8310)
It Would Be So Nice; Julia Dream (1968; Columbia DB 8410)
Point Me at the Sky; Careful with That Axe, Eugene (1968; Columbia DB 8511)
Another Brick in the Wall (Part 2); One of My Turns (1979; Harvest HAR 5194) **#1**
Money (remake); Let There Be More Light (1981; Harvest HAR 5217)
When the Tigers Broke Free; Bring the Boys Back Home (1982; Harvest HAR 5222)
Not Now John; The Hero's Return (Parts 1 & 2) (1983; Harvest HAR 5224)
Learning to Fly; One Slip (1987; EMI EM 26)
On the Turning Away; Run Like Hell (live) (1987; EMI EM 34)

Pink Floyd   LPs
The Piper at the Gates of Dawn: Astronomy Domine; *Lucifer Sam; Matilda Mother; Flaming; *Pow R. Toc H.; Take Up Thy Stethoscope and Walk; Interstellar Overdrive; The Gnome; Chapter 24; Scarecrow; Bike* (1967; Columbia SX/SXC 6157 [U.K.]. The U.S. edition – Tower T/ST 5903 – omitted [*] and added See Emily Play) **#131**
Tonite Lets All Make Love in London (soundtrack album): Interstellar Overdrive (three truncated excerpts) (1968; Instant INLP 002 [U.K.]) (rereleased with unedited 'Interstellar Overdrive' and bonus Floyd track 'Nick's Boogie', 1990 – See For Miles SEE CD 258)
A Saucerful of Secrets: Let There Be More Light; Remember a Day; Set the Controls for the Heart of the Sun; Corporal Clegg; A Saucerful of Secrets;

See Saw; Jugband Blues (1968; SX/XCS 6258 [U.K.], Tower T/ST 5131 [U.S.])

More: Cirrus Minor; The Nile Song; Crying Song; Up the Khyber; Green Is the Colour; Cymbaline; Party Sequence; Main Theme; Ibiza Bar; More Blues; Quicksilver; A Spanish Piece; Dramatic Theme (1969; Columbia SCX 6346 [U.K.], Tower ST 5169 [U.S.]) **#153**

Ummagumma: Astronomy Domine (live); Careful with That Axe, Eugene (live); Set the Controls for the Heart of the Sun (live); A Saucerful of Secrets (live); Sysyphus; Grantchester Meadows; Several Species of Small Furry Animals Gathered Together in a Cave and Grooving with a Pict; The Narrow Way; The Grand Vizier's Garden Party (1969; Harvest SHDW $^1/_2$ [U.K.], STBB 388 [U.S.]) **#74**

Zabriskie Point (soundtrack album, featuring various artists) Heart Beat, Pig Meat; Crumbling Land; Come In Number 51, Your Time is Up (1970; MGM 2315 002 [U.K.]; SE-4468ST [U.S.])

The Best of Pink Floyd: Chapter 24; Matilda Mother; Arnold Layne; Candy and a Currant Bun; Scarecrow; Apples and Oranges; It Would Be So Nice; Paintbox; Julia Dream; See Emily Play (1970; Columbia 5C054-04299 [Holland]; rereleased throughout Continental Europe in 1974 as **Masters of Rock Vol. 1,** Harvest C054-04299)

Atom Heart Mother: Atom Heart Mother: If; Summer '68; Fat Old Sun; Alan's Psychedelic Breakfast (1970; Harvest SHVL 781 [U.K.]; SKAO 382 [U.S.]) **#55**

Relics: Arnold Layne; Interstellar Overdrive; See Emily Play; Remember a Day; Paintbox; Julia Dream; Careful with That Axe, Eugene; Cirrus Minor; The Nile Song; Biding My Time; Bike (1971; EMI Starline SRS 5071 [U.K.]; Harvest SW 759 [U.S.]) **#152**

Meddle: One of These Days; A Pillow of Winds; Fearless; San Tropez; Seamus; Echoes (Harvest SHVL 795 [U.K.]; SMAS 832 [U.S.]) **#70**

Obscured by Clouds: Obscured by Clouds; When You're In; Burning Bridges; The Gold It's in the . . .; Wot's . . . Uh the Deal; Mudmen; Childhood's End; Free Four; Stay; Absolutely Curtains (1972; Harvest SHSP 4020 [U.K]); ST 11078 [U.S.]) **#46**

The Dark Side of the Moon: Speak to Me; Breathe in the Air; On the Run; Time (+ Breathe Reprise); The Great Gig in the Sky; Money; Us and Them; Any Colour You Like; Brain Damage; Eclipse (1973; Harvest SHVL 804 [U.K.]); SMAS 11163 [U.S.]) **#1**

A Nice Pair: (rerelease of **Piper** and **Saucerful,** with the former substituting the live **Ummagumma** version of 'Astronomy Domine' for the studio original in North American editions): (1974; Harvest SHDW 403 [U.K.]; SABB [U.S.]) **#36**

Wish You Were Here: Shine On You Crazy Diamond (Parts 1–5)); Welcome to the Machine; Have a Cigar; Wish You Were Here; Shine on You Crazy Diamond (Parts 6–9) (1975; Harvest SHVL 814 [U.K.]; Columbia PC 33453 [U.S.]) **#1**

Animals: Pigs on the Wing (Part 1); Dogs; Pigs (Three Different Ones); Sheep; Pigs on the Wing (Part 2) (1977; Harvest SHVL 815 [U.K.]; Columbia JC 34474 [U.S.]) **#3**

The Wall: In the Flesh?; The Thin Ice; Another Brick in the Wall (Part 1); The Happiest Days of Our Lives; Another Brick in the Wall (Part 2); Mother; Goodbye Blue Sky; Empty Spaces; Young Lust; One of My Turns; Don't Leave Me Now; Another Brick in the Wall (Part 3); Goodbye Cruel World; Hey You; Is There Anybody Out There? Nobody Home; Vera; Bring the Boys Back Home; Comfortably Numb; The Show Must Go On; In the Flesh; Run Like Hell; Waiting for the Worms; Stop; The Trial; Outside the Wall (1979; Harvest SHDW 411 [U.K.]; Columbia PC2 36183 [U.S.]) **#1**

A Collection of Great Dance Songs: One of These Days; Money (remake); Sheep; Shine On You Crazy Diamond (edited); Wish You Were Here; Another Brick in the Wall (Part 2) (1981; Harvest SHVL 822 [U.K.]; Columbia TC 37680 [U.S.]) **#31**

The Final Cut: The Post War Dream; Your Possible Pasts; One of the Few; The Hero's Return; The Gunners Dream; Paranoid Eyes; Get Your Filthy Hands Off My Desert; The Fletcher Memorial Home; Southampton Dock; The Final Cut; Not Now John; Two Suns in the Sunset (1983; Harvest SHPF 1983 [U.K.] Columbia QC 38243 [U.S.]) **#6**

Works: One of These Days; Arnold Layne; Fearless; Brain Damage; Eclipse; Set the Controls for the Heart of the Sun; See Emily Play; Several Species of Furry Animals Gathered Together in a Cave and Grooving with a Pict; Free Four; Embryo (1983; Capitol 11276 [U.S.]) **#68**

A Momentary Lapse of Reason: Signs of Life; Learning to Fly; The Dogs of War; One Slip; On the Turning Away; Yet Another Movie (+ Round and Round); A New Machine (Part 1); Terminal Frost; A New Machine (Part 2); Sorrow (1987; EMI CDP 7 480682 [U.K.]; Columbia CK 40599 [U.S.]) **#3**

Delicate Sound of Thunder (live): Shine On You Crazy Diamond; Learning to Fly; Yet Another Movie (+ Round and Round); Sorrow; The Dogs of War; On the Turning Away; One of These Days; Time; Wish You Were Here; Us and Them [on CD, cassette only]; Money; Another Brick in the Wall (Part 2); Comfortably Numb; Run Like Hell (1988; EMI CDS 7914 802 [U.K.]; Columbia C2K 44484 [U.S.]) **#9**

Knebworth: The Album (live double album from the all-star June 30, 1990 concert): Comfortably Numb; Run Like Hell (1990; Polydor 843 921 [U.K.]; 847 042-2 [U.S.]) **#92**

Solo LPs

Syd Barrett

The Madcap Laughs: Terrapin; No Good Trying; Love You; No Man's Land; Dark Globe; Here I Go; Octopus; Golden Hair; Long Gone; She Took a

Long Cold Look; Feel; If It's in You; Late Night (1970; Harvest SHVL 765 [U.K.])

Barrett: Baby Lemonade; Love Song; Dominoes; Is It Obvious; Rats; Maisie; Gigolo Aunt; Waving My Arms in the Air; Wined and Dined; Wolfpack; Effervescing Elephant (1970; Harvest SHSP 4007 [U.K.])

Syd Barrett (reissue of **Madcap** and **Barrett,** constituting those LPs' first appearance in the U.S.); (1974; Harvest SHDW [U.K.]; SAAB 11314 [U.S.]) #163

The Peel Sessions (live): Terrapin; Gigolo Aunt; Baby Lemonade; Effervescing Elephant; Two of a Kind (1988; Strange Fruit SFPSCD043 [U.K.])

Opel: Opel; Clowns & Jugglers; Rats; Golden Hair; Dolly Rocker; Word Song; Wined and Dined; Swan Lee (Silas Lang); Birdie Hop; Let's Split; Lanky (Part 1); Wouldn't You Miss me (Dark Globe); Milky Way; Golden Hair (instr.) (1988; Harvest CDP 7912062 [U.K.]; Capitol CS 91206 [U.S.])

David Gilmour

David Gilmour: Mihalis; There's No Way Out of Here; Cry from the Street; So Far Away; Short and Sweet; Raise My Rent; No Way; Deafinitely; I Can't Breathe Anymore (1978; Harvest SHVL 817 [U.K.]; Columbia JC 35388 [U.S.]) #29

About Face: Until We Sleep; Murder; Love on the Air; Blue Light; Out of the Blue; All Lovers Are Deranged; You Know I'm Right; Cruise; Let's Get Metaphysical; Near the End (1984; Harvest SHSP 2400791 [U.K.]; Columbia FC 39296 [U.S.]) #32

Nick Mason

Nick Mason's Fictitious Sports: Can't Get My Motor to Start; I Was Wrong; Siam; Hot River; Boo to You Too; Do Ya?; Wervin'; I Am a Mineralist (1981; Harvest SHSP 4116 [U.K.]; Columbia FC 37307 [U.S.])

Profiles *(with Rick Fenn):* Malta; Lie for a Lie; Rhoda; Profiles (Parts 1 & 2); Israel; And the Address; Mumbo Jumbo; Zip Code; Black Ice; At the End of the Day; Profiles (Part 3) (1985; Harvest MAF 1 [U.K.]; Columbia CK 40142 [U.S.])

Roger Waters

Music from 'The Body' *(with Ron Geesin):* Our Song; Sea Shell and Stone; Red Stuff Writhe; A Gentle Breeze Blew Through Life; Lick Your Partners; Bridge Passage for Three Plastic Teeth; Chain of Life; The Womb Bit; Embryo Thought; March Past of the Embryos. More than Seven Dwarfs in Penis-Land; Dance of the Red Corpuscles; Body Transport; Hand Dance – Full Evening Dress; Breathe; Old Folks Ascension; Bed-Time – Dream-Time; Piddle in Perspex; Embryonic Womb-Walk; Mrs Throat

Goes Walking; Sea Shell and Soft Stone; Give Birth to a Smile (1970; Harvest SHSP 4008 [U.K.])

The Pros and Cons of Hitchhiking: 4:30am (Apparently They Were Travelling Abroad); 4.33am (Running Shoes); 4.37am (Arabs with Knives and West German Skies); 4.39am (For the First Time Today [Part 2]); 4.41am (Sexual Revolution); 4.47am (The Remains of Our Love); 4.50am (Go Fishing); 4.56am (For the First Time Today [Part 1]); 4.5am (Dunroamin, Duncarin, Dunlivin); 5.01am (The Pros and Cons of Hitchhiking); 5.06am (Every Stranger's Eyes); 5.11am (The Moment of Clarity (1984; Harvest SHVL 2401051 [U.K.]; Columbia FC 39290 [U.S.]) **#31**

When the Wind Blows (soundtrack album featuring various artists, with the second half consisting of Roger Waters compositions): The Russian Missile; Towers of Faith; Hilda's Dream; The American Bomber; The Anderson Shelter; The British Submarine; The Attack; The Fallout; Hilda's Hair; Folded Flags (1986; Virgin CDV 2406 [U.K.])

Radio K.A.O.S.: Radio Waves; Who Needs Information; Me or Him; The Powers That Be; Sunset Strip; Home; Four Minutes; The Tide Is Turning (After Live Aid) (1987; Harvest CDP 7 468652 [U.K.]; Columbia CK 40795 [U.S.]) **#50**

The Wall Live in Berlin: In the Flesh (with Scorpions); The Thin Ice (w/Ute Lemper); Another Brick in the Wall (Part 1); The Happiest Days of Our Lives; Another Brick in the Wall (Part 2, w/Cyndi Lauper); Mother (w/Sinead O'Connor and the Band); Goodbye Blue Sky (w/Joni Mitchell; Empty Spaces (w/Bryan Adams); Young Lust (w/Bryan Adams); Oh My God – What a Fabulous Room (w/Jerry Hall); One of My Turns; Don't Leave Me Now; Another Brick in the Wall (Part 3); Goodbye Cruel World; Hey You (w/Paul Carrack); Is There Anybody Out There? (w/Rundfunk Orchestra & Choir); Nobody Home; Vera (w/Rundfunk Orchestra & Choir); Bring the Boys Back Home (w/Rundfunk Orchestra & Choir and the Military Orchestra of the Soviet Army); Comfortably Numb (w/Van Morrison and the Band); In the Flesh; Run Like Hell; Waiting for the Worms; Stop (4 previous selections w/Rundfunk Orchestra & Choir and the Military Orchestra of the Soviet Army); The Trial (w/Tim Curry, Thomas Dolby, Ute Lemper, Marianne Faithfull, Albert Finney, and the Rundfunk Orchestra & Choir); The Tide is Turning (w/'The Company') (1990; Mercury 846 611-2 [U.K.]; 846 611-2 [U.S.]) **#56**

Richard Wright

Wet Dream: Mediterranean C; Against the Odds; Cat Cruise; Summer Elegy; Waves; Holiday; Mad Yannis Dance; Drop in from the Top; Pink's Song; Funky Deux (1978; Harvest SHVL 818 [U.K.]; Columbia JC 35559 [U.S.])

Zee – Identity *(with Dave Harris):* Confusion; Voices; Private Person; Strange Rhythm; Cuts Like a Diamond; By Touching; How Do You Do It; Seems We Were Dreaming (1984; Harvest SHSP 2401011 [U.K.])

Floyd's All-Time best-sellers . . .
1. *Dark Side of the Moon* (total world sales: approx. 25 million)
2. *The Wall* (approx. 17 million)
3. *Wish You Were Here* (approx. 10 million)
4. *Animals* (approx. 6 million)
5. *A Momentary Lapse of Reason* (approx. 6 million)

. . . And the fans' choice*
BEST FLOYD ALBUM:
1. *Wish You Were Here*
2. *Dark Side of the Moon*
3. *The Wall*
4. *Animals*
5. *The Piper at the Gates of Dawn*

WORST FLOYD ALBUM: *The Final Cut*

BEST FLOYD SONG:
1. 'Comfortably Numb'
2. 'Shine on You Crazy Diamond
3. 'Echoes'
4. 'Wish You Were Here'
5. 'Time'

WORST FLOYD SONG:
'Dogs of War'

BEST FLOYD SLEEVE: *Animals*
BEST SOLO ALBUM: *Radio K.A.O.S.* (Waters)
WORST SOLO ALBUM: *The Pros and Cons of Hitchhiking* (Waters)
BEST SOLO SONG: 'The Tide Is Turning' (Waters)
WORST SOLO SONG: 'Blue Light' (Gilmour)

* from *The Amazing Pudding*'s 1989 readers', poll

Note:
Serial numbers given here correspond to the original vinyl LP releases for all albums released before 1985, and the CD versions thereafter. LP chart positions are for the U.S. only. All chart positions are drawn from *Billboard* magazine.

Sources

Note: All other substantial quotes, unless otherwise identified in the text, are drawn from personal interviews with the author.

Prologue

1 Connor McNight interview with Roger Waters and Nick Mason, *ZigZag* magazine, July 1973.
2 *Melody Maker*, 19 May 1973.

Chapter 1

1 *Days in the Life: Voices from the English Underground 1961–1971*, edited by Jonathon Green (London: Heinemann, 1988), pp. 32–33.
2 Connor McNight interview with Waters and Mason, *ZigZag*, July 1973.

Chapter 2

1 Tommy Vance interview with Roger Waters, BBC Radio One, broadcast 30 November 1979.
2 'Treading Waters', by Scott Cohen, *Spin*, September 1987.
3 'Over the Wall with Pink Floyd', by Richard Hogan, *Circus*, August 1982.
4 Connor McNight interview with Waters and Mason, *ZigZag*, July 1973.
5 'Architectural Abdabs', by Barbara Walters, *The Regent Street Poly Magazine*, Autumn 1965.
6,7 *Voxpop: Profiles of the Pop Process*, by Michael Wale (London: Harrap, 1972).

Chapter 3

1 *Days in the Life: Voices from the English Underground, 1961–1971*, edited by Jonathon Green (London: Heinemann, 1988), p. 110.
2 *The British Invasion*, by Nicholas Schaffner (New York: McGraw-Hill, 1982), p. 142.
3,4 *Pink Floyd: A Visual Documentary* by Miles, (London: Omnibus Press, 1980, unnumbered pages.
5 *Days in the Life*, p. 120.
6 *Pink Floyd: A Visual Documentary*.
7 'Making the Rounds of Way-Out London', by Kenneth Rexroth. *The San Francisco Examiner*, 4 December 1966.
8 *Pink Floyd: A Visual Documentary*.

Chapter 4

1 *International Times*, No. 29.
2 *It Was Twenty Years Ago Today*, by Derek Taylor (New York: Fireside, 1987), p. 177.
3 *Days in the Life: Voices from the English Underground 1961–1971*, edited by Jonathon Green (London: Heinemann, 1988), p. 139.
4 *Melody Maker*, 14 January 1967.

Chapter 5

1 *Days in the Life: Voices from the English Underground 1961–1971*, edited by Jonathon Green (London: Heinemann, 1988), pp. 105–6.
2 *Pink Floyd*, by Rick Sanders (London: Futura Books, 1975), p. 25.
3,4 *The British Invasion*, by Nicholas Schaffner (New York: McGraw-Hill, 1982), p. 142.
5 'The Pink Floyd Story': six-part series presented by Nicky Horne; broadcast Capital Radio (London) 17 December 1976–21 January 1977.
6 'Treading Waters' by Scott Cohen, *Spin*, September 1987.

Chapter 6

1 *Pink Floyd: A Visual Documentary*, by Miles (London: Omnibus Press, 1980), unnumbered pages.
2 *Days in the Life: Voices from the English Underground 1961–1971*, edited by Jonathon Green (London: Heinemann, 1988), p. 165.
3,4 *Pink Floyd: A Visual Documentary*.

5   'The Pink Floyd Story,': six-part series presented by Nicky Horne; broadcast Capital Radio (London) 17 December 1976–21 January 1977.
6   *Days in the Life*, p. 113.
7   *The British Invasion*, by Nicholas Schaffner (New York: McGraw-Hill, 1982), p. 143.
8   Capital Radio, 'The Pink Floyd Story'.
9,10   Miles interview with Joe Boyd (on tape), 1976.
11   *Days in the Life*, p. 203.

Chapter 7

1   *Days in the Life: Voices from the English Underground 1961–1971*, edited by Jonathon Green (London: Heinemann, 1988), p. 142.
2   *Days in the Life*, p. 166.
3   Connor McNight interview with Waters and Mason, *ZigZag*, July 1973.
4   Capital Radio, 'The Pink Floyd Story'.
5   *Disc and Music Echo*, 29 July 1967.
6   *New Musical Express*, 19 August 1967.
7   *New Musical Express*, 12 August 1967.
8   *Melody Maker*, 12 August 1967.

Chapter 8

1   'The Pink Floyd Story,' six-part series presented by Nicky Horne; broadcast Capital Radio (London) 17 December 1976–21 January 1977.
2   *Days in the Life: Voices from the English Underground 1961–1971*, edited by Jonathon Green (London: Heinemann, 1988), p. 168.
3   'Syd Barrett Careening through Life', by Kris DiLorenzo, *The Trouser Press*, February 1978.
4   'Innerview '80': Jim Ladd interview with Waters, broadcast 1980.

Chapter 9

1,2   Connor McNight interview with Waters and Mason, *ZigZag*, July 1973.
3   *The British Invasion*, by Nicholas Schaffner (New York: McGraw-Hill, 1982),p. 154.
4   *Pink Floyd: A Visual Documentary*, by Miles, (London: Omnibus Press, 1980), unnumbered pages.
5   *Fab(ulous)*, January 1968.
6   *ZigZag*, July 1973.
7   Syd Barrett feature by Nick Kent, *New Musical Express*, 13 April 1974.

8   *Opel* (Syd Barrett fanzine), No. 8.
9   'Behind Pink Floyd's Wall,' by Mick Brown and Kurt Loder, *Rolling Stone*, 16 September 1982.

Chapter 10

1   *Days in the Life: Voices from the English Underground 1961–1971*, edited by Jonathon Green (London: Heinemann, 1988), p. 167.
2,3 'Syd Barrett Careening through Life,' by Kris DiLorenzo, *The Trouser Press*, February 1978.
4   *Syd Barrett: The Making of the Madcap Laughs*, by Malcolm Jones (Middlesex, U.K.: Orange Sunshine (Pill) Press, 1986), p. 6.
5   *The Trouser Press*, February 1978.
6   *Pink Floyd: A Visual Documentary* (Miles).
7   *The Trouser Press*, February 1978.
8   Michael Wale interview with Rick Wright, broadcast October 1974, BBC Radio One, 'Rockspeak'.
9   *The Trouser Press*, February 1978.
10 *Days in the Life*, p. 167.
11 *New Musical Express*, 2 October 1982.

Chapter 11

1   Jonathon Green's *Days in the Life* interviews with Jenner and Marsh (unedited transcripts).
2   Chris Salewicz interview with Waters, *Q* magazine, August 1987.
3   Green interview with Jenner.
4   'The Pink Floyd Story,': six-part series presented by Nicky Horne; broadcast Capital Radio (London) 17 December 1976–21 January 1977.
5   *Pink Floyd: The Early Years* (New York: Wise Publications, 1978), p. 7.
6   *The Amazing Pudding* (Pink Floyd fanzine), No. 14.
7,8 Connor McNight interview with Waters and Mason, *ZigZag*, July 1973.
9   David Fricke interview with David Gilmour, *Musician*, December 1982.
10 Capital Radio, 'The Pink Floyd Story'.
11 Parke Puterbaugh 1984 interview with Gilmour (unedited transcript).
12 *Rolling Stone*, 26 November 1970.
13 *Clowns and Jugglers* (Syd Barrett fanzine).
14 *The Work of Hipgnosis: 'Walk Away Renee,'* text by Storm Thorgerson, (Limpsfield, Surrey, U.K.: Paper Tiger), 1978, p. 87.
15 *ZigZag*, July 1973.
16 Capital Radio, 'The Pink Floyd Story'.
17 *ZigZag*, July 1973.

18   *Musician*, December 1982.
19   *ZigZag*, July 1973.
20   Q, August 1987.

Chapter 12

1   *Top Pops & Music Now*, 15 September 1969.
2   New York University radio interview, September 1970.
3   Parke Puterbaugh 1984 interview with Gilmour.
4   'Treading Waters' by Scott Cohen, *Spin*, September 1987.
5,6   Connor McNight interview with Waters and Mason, *ZigZag*, July 1973.

Chapter 13

1   Capital Radio, 'The Pink Floyd Story'.
2   'Rock Over London': radio interview with Waters, 15 March 1985.
3   New York University radio interview, September 1970.
4   Connor McNight interview with Waters and Mason, *ZigZag*, July 1973.
5   *Rock on the Road*, edited by Mick Gold (London: Futura, 1976), p. 151.
6   *ZigZag*, July 1973.

Chapter 14

1   *Melody Maker*, 7 March 1970.
2   Chris Salewicz interview with Waters, Q, August 1987.
3   Connor McNight interview with Waters and Mason, *ZigZag*, July 1973.
4   Mary Turner interview with Waters, broadcast Westwood One 'Off the Record', 11 March 1985.
5   David Fricke interview with David Gilmour, *Musician*, December 1982.
6   'Rhapsody in Pink', by Lenny Kaye, *High Times*, February 1988.
7   'The Pink Floyd Story', six-part series presented by Nicky Horne; broadcast Capital Radio (London) 17 December 1976–21 January 1977.

Chapter 15

1   *Voxpop: Profiles of the Pop Process*, by Michael Wale (London: Harrap, 1972).
2   'The Pink Floyd Story,' six-part series presented by Nicky Horne; broadcast Capital Radio (London) 17 December 1976–21 January 1977.

3   'Pink Floyd: Looking Like Hell' by Derek Jewell, *The Sunday Times*, 20 February 1972.
4   'The Pringle Show', broadcast Montreal Radio, December 1978.
5   *Melody Maker*, 19 May 1973.
6   Aired on Capital Radio, 'The Pink Floyd Story'.
7   Connor McNight interview with Waters and Mason, *ZigZag*, July 1973.
8   *Sounds*.
9   *Melody Maker*, 19 May 1973.
10 David Fricke interview with David Gilmour, *Musician*, December 1982.
11 Capital Radio, 'The Pink Floyd Story'.
12 Chris Salewicz interview with Waters, *Q*, August 1987.
13 'Treading Waters', by Scott Cohen, *Spin*, September 1987.

Chapter 16

1   'The Pink Floyd Story': six-part series presented by Nicky Horne; broadcast Capital Radio (London) 17 December 1976–21 January 1977.
2   BBC Radio One, 'Rockspeak', October 1974.
3   *Pink Floyd: A Visual Documentary* (Miles).
4   Capital Radio, 'The Pink Floyd Story'.
5   BBC Radio One, 'Rockspeak', broadcast October 1974.
6   Philippe Constantin interview with Waters (originally published in French in *Rock et Folk*). *Street Life*, 24 January 1976.
7   Tom Stock interview with Gilmour, *Beat Instrumental*, July 1978.
8   *Street Life*, 24 January 1976.
9   *People* magazine, 12 March 1984.
10 'Floyd Juggernaut . . . the Road to 1984?' by Nick Kent and Pete Erskine. *New Musical Express*, 24 November 1974.
11 'Dirty Hair Denied', by Pete Erskine. *New Musical Express*, 11 January 1975.

Chapter 17

1   *Street Life*, 24 January 1976.
2   *Bricks in the Wall*, by Karl Dallas (London: Baton Press, 1987).
3   'The Pink Floyd Story', six-part series presented by Nicky Horne; broadcast Capital Radio (London), 17 December 1976–21 January 1977.
4   *Street Life*, 24 January 1976.
5,6 Capital Radio, 'The Pink Floyd Story'.
7   *Street Life*, 24 January 1976.
8,9 Capital Radio, 'The Pink Floyd Story'.

306

10   *Bricks in the Wall*, p. 112.
11,12,13   *The Work of Hipgnosis: 'Walk Away Renee,'* text by Storm Thorgerson, (Limpsfield, Surrey, U.K.: Paper Tiger), 1978, p. 148.

Chapter 18

1   *'The Boy Looked at Johnny': The Obituary of Rock and Roll,* by Julie Burchill and Tony Parsons (London: Pluto Press, 1978), p. 32.
2   Andy Kershaw interview with Rat Scabies, BBC Radio One, broadcast 6 December 1986.
3   'The Pink Floyd Story', six-part series presented by Nicky Horne; broadcast Capital Radio (London) 17 December 1976–21 January 1977.
4   'Pink Floyd – The Inside Story', by David Fricke, *Rolling Stone,* 19 November 1987.
5   *New Musical Express,* 12 February 1977.
6   Chris Salewicz interview with Waters, Q, August 1987.
7   'Welcome to the Machine' by Karl Dallas, *Melody Maker,* 26 March 1977.
8   *Sounds,* 26 March 1977.
9   'From Pink to Black Despair', by Derek Jewell, *The Sunday Times* (London), 20 March 1977.
10   'The Song Remains the Same', by Michael Oldfield, *Melody Maker,* 26 March 1977.
11   Tommy Vance interview with Waters, BBC Radio One broadcoast 30 November 1979.
12   Timothy White memo to the author.
13   'Behind Pink Floyd's Wall', by Mick Brown and Kurt Loder., *Rolling Stone,* 16 September 1982.

Chapter 19

1   Interview with Gilmour for 'Caio 2001' (Italian radio), 13 August 1978.
2   'The Invisible Touch', by David Sinclair, Q, August 1988.
3   Montreal Radio, 'The Pringle Show', broadcast December 1978.
4   *Brain Damage,* February 1988: Glenn Povey and Richard Ashton interview with Gilmour.
5   *Juke* magazine, 9 November 1985.
6   'Spotlight on Pink Floyd', broadcast FM-104 (Brisbane, Australia) 2 February 1988.
7   'Behind Pink Floyd,' Wall', by Mick Brown and Kurt Loder, *Rolling Stone,* 16 September 1982.
8,9,10   'Innerview '80': Jim Ladd interview with Waters, broadcast 1980.
11   *Bricks in the Wall,* by Karl Dallas (London: Baton Press, 1987), p. 141.
12   *Melody Maker,* 2 August 1980: 'Up Against the Wall', by Michael Watts.

13   David Fricke interview with David Gilmour, *Musician*, December 1982.
14   'Gaze into the Rock Void with Roger Waters and his Pink Floyd', by Richard Hogan, *Circus*, 15 April 1980.
15   *Melody Maker*, 2 August 1980.
16   *Musician*, December 1982.
17   Tommy Vance interview with Waters, BBC Radio One, 30 November 1979.
18   'Up Against the Wall of Secrecy with Pink Floyd', by Richard Hogan, *Circus*, 4 March 1980.
19,20   *Musician*, December 1982.
21,22   'Pink Floyd – The Inside Story', by David Fricke, *Rolling Stone*, 19 November 1987.
23   *Musician*, December 1982.
24   *Rolling Stone*, 19 November 1987.
25   *Bricks in the Wall*, p. 60–61.
26   Pink Floyd feature by Timothy White, *Penthouse*, September 1988.
27   *The Toronto Star* reprinted in *The Amazing Pudding #27*.
28   *Rolling Stone*, 7 February 1980.
29   *Melody Maker*, 9 August 1980.
30   *Melody Maker*, 1 December 1979.

Chapter 20

1   BBC-2 'Arena' documentary, 'Scarfe on Scarfe': broadcast 12 December 1986.
2   *Scarfe by Scarfe*, by Gerald Scarfe (London: Hamish Hamilton, 1986), unnumbered pages.
3   *New Musical Express*, 18 November 1978.
4   *Bricks in the Wall*, by Karl Dalls (London: Baton Press, 1987), p. 139.
5   Chris Salewicz interview with Waters, *Q*, August 1987.
6   *Bricks in the Wall*, p. 139.
7   *Q*, August 1987.
8   *Bricks in the Wall*, p. 123–124.
9   *Is That It?*, by Bob Geldof, Weidenfeld & Nicolson (New York), 1987, p. 178–179.
10   Richard Ashton interview with Alan Parker, *Phoenix* (University of Kent) magazine, Spring 1984.
11   *Bricks in the Wall*, p. 124.
12   A.B. Foster interview with Parker. BBC Radio One, 'Saturday Live', 1984.
13   'Behind Pink Floyd's Wall', by Mick Brown and Kurt Loder. *Rolling Stone*, 16 September 1982.
14   *Is That It?* p. 188.
15,16   *Is That It?* p. 191.
17,18   *Bricks in the Wall*, p. 127.
19   *Rolling Stone*, 16 September 1982.